Jetpack Compose by Tutorials

Second Edition

By Denis Buketa & Prateek Prasad

Jetpack Compose by Tutorials

Denis Buketa & Prateek Prasad

ISBN: 978-1-950325-83-2

Table of Contents

Book License

By purchasing *Jetpack Compose by Tutorials*, you have the following license:

- You are allowed to use and/or modify the source code in *Jetpack Compose by Tutorials* in as many apps as you want, with no attribution required.
- You are allowed to use and/or modify all art, images and designs that are included in *Jetpack Compose by Tutorials* in as many apps as you want, but must include this attribution line somewhere inside your app: "Artwork/images/designs: from *Jetpack Compose by Tutorials*, available at www.kodeco.com".
- The source code included in *Jetpack Compose by Tutorials* is for your personal use only. You are NOT allowed to distribute or sell the source code in *Jetpack Compose by Tutorials* without prior authorization.
- This book is for your personal use only. You are NOT allowed to reproduce or transmit any part of this book by any means, electronic or mechanical, including photocopying, recording, etc. without previous authorization. You may not sell digital versions of this book or distribute them to friends, coworkers or students without prior authorization. They need to purchase their own copies.

All materials provided with this book are provided on an "as is" basis, without warranty of any kind, express or implied, including but not limited to the warranties of merchantability, fitness for a particular purpose and noninfringement. In no event shall the authors or copyright holders be liable for any claim, damages or other liability, whether in an action of contract, tort or otherwise, arising from, out of or in connection with the software or the use or other dealings in the software.

All trademarks and registered trademarks appearing in this guide are the properties of their respective owners.

Before You Begin

This section tells you a few things you need to know before you get started, such as what hardware and software you'll need, where to find the project files for this book, and more.

What You Need

To follow along with this book, you'll need the following:

- **Kotlin 1.7**: Since Jetpack Compose relies on a special Kotlin compiler, you need Kotlin 1.7 both to write the code and for the compiler to process special Jetpack Compose annotations.
- **Android Studio Dolphin**: Jetpack Compose is available publicly for use and doesn't require any special versions of Android Studio. The minimum version of Android Studio the book supports is Android Studio Dolphin.
- **Android 5.1+**: The `minimumSdkVersion` for the projects targets API 21, so you need a device or an emulator running API 21 or higher. Note for running UI Tests we recommend a device running at least Android 10.
- **Jetpack Compose 1.2.1 or greater**: The projects for this are built using v1.2.1 of Jetpack Compose. You are free to use later versions, however we recommend sticking to the version used by the book to avoid any migration or compatability issues when following along.

Book Source Code & Forums

Where to Download the Materials for This Book

The materials for this book can be cloned or downloaded from the GitHub book materials repository:

- https://github.com/kodecocodes/jet-materials/tree/editions/2.0

Forums

We've also set up an official forum for the book at https://forums.kodeco.com/c/books/jetpack-compose-by-tutorials. This is a great place to ask questions about the book or to submit any errors you may find.

"To my family and friends. Thank you for supporting me and being patient as I worked on this book. I've told you "no" so many times when you called me to hang out, but you never made me feel guilty about it. Many thanks to the team at Kodeco (http://www.kodeco.com/), my co-author, the editors and everyone involved in this book. You've been a great support and I've enjoyed working with you."

— Denis Buketa

"Dedicated to my wonderful partner Rimil. Thank you for your patience, and your unconditional love and belief in me. This one's for you!"

— Prateek Prasad

About the Authors

Denis Buketa is an author of this book. Denis is an experienced professional based in Zagreb, Croatia with a decade of experience in the tech industry. After working as an Android developer, he has transitioned into an engineering management role where he is passionate about leadership, management, mentoring, and business development. In his personal time, Denis enjoys expanding his knowledge through audiobooks and podcasts, relaxing by playing video games, and working out.

Prateek Prasad is an author of this book. He's a senior engineer and a product designer. He specializes in building mobile apps and has been doing so ever since high school. He also mentors beginners in the tech industry on MentorCruise and OpenClassrooms. In his free time, he likes playing music or nerding out about outer space.

About the Editors

Antonio Roa-Valverde is a tech editor of this book. He's a software engineer specialized in Android development. He's interested in innovation and shaping new products with potential impact on people. Google Developer Group co-organizer in Innsbruck and Munich. You can find him close to the mountains, either hiking, riding the mountain-bike or catching some curvy roads by motorcycle.

Prajwal Belagavi is a tech editor of this book. He's a Software Engineer with a passion for mobile development based in Bangalore. He likes to explore new domains in the field of Computer Science and to contribute to open source projects. In his spare time, you can find him playing badminton or watching food vlogs or flying his drone trying to reach sky high!

Darryl Bayliss is the final pass editor for this book. Darryl is a software engineer with a soft spot for mobile development, based in London. He has a passion for helping small businesses that do good for people and the planet, as well as educating people on becoming better engineers. Away from the computer, you can find him reading books, involved in some fantastical game involving dragons or playing his new favourite pastime Chess.

Acknowledgments

Content Development

We would like to thank **Tino Balint** for his contributions as an author to the previous edition of this book.

Introduction

If you've been an Android developer the past couple of years, you probably thought that the UI toolkit you use every day is not that easy to grasp. This is because over the years, as Android developed and grew as a platform, the tools for building user interfaces became more powerful and the design system became more beautiful.

Sadly, with all those changes and with newer versions of Android, the process of building interfaces became **more complex**. Additionally, it became increasingly harder to write code that supports all Android versions, as many new APIs and features aren't fully backwards compatible. That means that building components from the standard toolkit doesn't guarantee that those components will work on older versions of the operating system.

Moreover, the number of programming and markup languages you need to learn is overwhelming. Not only do you find Android apps written in Kotlin or Java, but you also have to learn Groovy for your build scripts and XML for your UI development.

This **further increases the complexity** of learning Android development, and it makes it harder to follow the code. You have to read through multiple different files, just to learn how a single feature of the project works. If only there was a tool that uses Kotlin, has a clear syntax and lets you develop UI without much sweat...

Well, look no more! **Jetpack Compose** is the one UI toolkit to rule them all. It's a fresh look at building user interfaces, providing:

- A Kotlin-powered API.
- Declarative ways to build the UI so it reacts to state changes.
- A powerful and composable set of components that you can combine, style and animate.

In this book, you'll learn how to build a powerful app using Jetpack Compose, how to style your apps using Material Design, special animations and state transitions, how to use modifiers and much more! This book will serve you as a central point that holds all the information you need to dive deep into Jetpack Compose, then apply it to your personal and production level projects.

How to Read This Book

The book is aimed at Android developers who aren't familiar with Jetpack Compose and developers who know a little about the toolkit, but haven't had the chance to use it.

If you're **completely new to Jetpack Compose**, we recommend reading it one chapter at a time, in the **order of sections and chapters** shown in the table of contents.

If you're **familiar with the fundamentals** of Jetpack Compose, you can skip to "Section II: Composing User Interfaces" instead. There, you'll continue learning about custom UI components, state management and best practices for styling your UI.

If you're **already using Jetpack Compose** in your projects but want to know about more complex topics and interoperability with legacy UI toolkits, jump to "Section III: Building Complex Apps With Jetpack Compose". You'll build complex use cases on a real-world project and learn about animations and the Compose lifecycle.

At whatever level of knowledge you are, it's useful to check out the book structure and its contents. This book is split into three main sections.

Section I: Getting Started With Jetpack Compose

Android UI Toolkit is **over 10 years old now**! Over the years, it has received numerous updates in terms of functionality, types of UI elements it provides and optimizations. But because of the way the UI team initially developed the toolkit, it also **grew in complexity and the amount of code** for even the simplest of components.

Finally, in 2020, a miracle happened: **Jetpack Compose**. The new UI toolkit was announced and started being seriously developed by Google. Jetpack Compose is a new and fresh toolkit, **built completely in Kotlin**, that offers a clean and **declarative** way to develop custom components and beautiful interfaces.

In this section, you'll learn all about:

- The fundamental components Jetpack Compose provides.
- How to build common user interface components such as containers, navigation controls and lists.

In these four chapters, you'll dive deep into the API and learn so much about this wonderful new UI toolkit.

Section II: Composing User Interfaces

When working on apps and user interfaces, it's not only important to know what each piece of the interface should be, but also how all these pieces **come together** to build a beautiful and fully-functional design that'll wow your users.

Now that you've amassed quite a lot of knowledge about the basics of Jetpack Compose and its fundamental UI elements, you're ready to dive deeper into building custom Compose elements, **managing their state** in a performant way and **styling them** using modifiers and built-in Material Design features.

Over the next four chapters, you'll learn how to:

- Attach `LiveData` structures to your state management.
- Rely on different styling modifiers.
- Combine these topics to create a powerful UI!

Section III: Building Complex Apps With Jetpack Compose

Now that you've built your app's basic UI, it's time to take it to another level. In this section, you'll apply custom, complex designs that help you stand out from thousands of similar apps! This usually involves building **complex custom components** and applying **animations** to represent state changes when your users interact with the UI.

Over the next five chapters, you'll dive deeper into the Jetpack Compose API to learn how to:

- Connect Compose UI to legacy Android code.
- React to Compose UI lifecycles.
- Animate different state changes and user interactions.

In the process, you'll build an awesome app that represents a real-world project and you'll apply some best practices to improve the **user experience**.

Section IV: UI Testing & Accessibility

Once you've mastered creating a complex App with Jetpack Compose, it's good to know how to prove the UI you create works as expected. Enter **UI Testing**, which Compose allows you to do seamless with its own API specially created for writing UI Tests. Don't forget about **Accessibility** too, an important concept that allows your app to hook into system features to make it easier for users with disabilities or those struggling with a range of inhibitary issues.

In these two chapters. You'll dive into the API for both concepts and learn how easy is it to use them.

Section IV: Glances & Keeping Upto Date With Jetpack Compose

In this final section, you'll take a look at where else Jetpack Compose is being used. For instance, the world of **Widgets** is being replaced with a new solution called **Glances**. There are also other places where Compose is appearing, such as **WearOS**, multiplatform development and more!

These final two chapters will look at each, helping you to appreciate the impact Jetpack Compose is having on Android development and beyond!

Section VI: Appendices

In this supplementary section, you can find appendices to accompany the book. For this edition there is just one appendix, a handy comparision between Widget objects and Composables so you can pick up quickly what the equivalent UI component is.

We hope you're ready to jump in and enjoy getting to know the power of Jetpack Compose!

Section I: Getting Started With Jetpack Compose

Android UI Toolkit is **over 10 years old now**! Over the years, it has received numerous updates in terms of functionality, types of UI elements it provides and optimizations. However, because of the way the UI team initially developed the toolkit, it also **grew in complexity and the amount of code** for even the simplest of components.

Finally, in 2020, a miracle happened: **Jetpack Compose**. The new UI toolkit was announced and started being seriously developed by Google. Jetpack Compose is a new and fresh toolkit, **built completely in Kotlin**, that offers a clean and **declarative** way to develop custom components and beautiful interfaces.

In this section, you'll learn all about:

- The fundamental components Jetpack Compose provides.
- How to build common user interface components such as containers, navigation controls and lists.

In the following four chapters, you'll dive deep into the API and learn so much about this wonderful new UI toolkit.

Chapter 1: Developing UI in Android

By Prateek Prasad

The **user interface (UI)** is the embodiment of your mobile app. You could say it's an ever-evolving relationship between a user and the system they interact with. When you look at the big picture, it's easy to understand why UI design is so important: It's one of the most common reason products succeed or fail.

In this chapter, you'll learn the **design concepts** behind the existing **Android UI toolkit**. You'll review the basics of showing the layout on screen, how to make **custom views**, and the **technical principles** behind it. You'll learn the reasons behind these concepts, their drawbacks, and their influence on **Jetpack Compose**. Or Compose, for short.

After that, you'll learn about Compose — the awesome new UI toolkit for Android, which is making all the Android kids super hyped! :]

You'll see how Compose approaches each of the concepts of the current Android UI toolkit, how it improves upon them, and why it's the next evolutionary step in Android development.

Unwrapping the Android UI Toolkit

In Android, you build your UI as a tree-based hierarchy of **layouts** and **widgets**. In code, layouts are represented by `ViewGroup` objects. They are **containers** controlling the **position and behavior of their children** on the screen.

On the other hand, widgets are represented by `View` objects. They display individual UI components like buttons and text boxes.

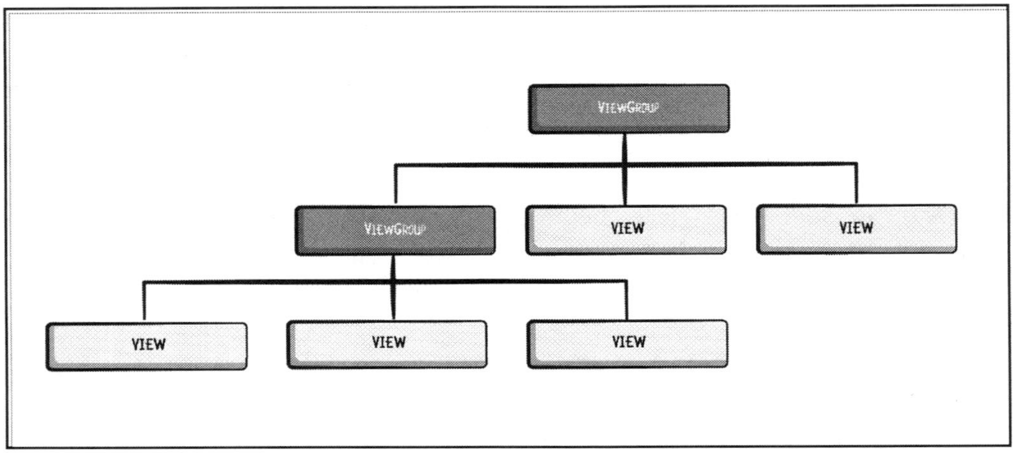

View Hierarchy

As you can see in the image, you define each screen in Android as a tree of `ViewGroup` and `View` objects. `ViewGroups` can contain other `ViewGroups` and `Views`. If you're familiar with computer science structures, you'll recognize `ViewGroups` are like **nodes** of the **tree structure**, where each `View` is a **leaf**.

The most important thing to notice here is your `View` objects are responsible for the look of your UI. So it makes sense to begin by looking at how you implement and use the `View` class.

View

As mentioned before, a `View` in the **Android UI toolkit**, represents the *basic building block* for UI components. It occupies a rectangular area on the screen where it **draws** the specific UI component, like a button or a text field.

Users Interact with the UI

But user interfaces aren't designed to be static — at least, most of them aren't. Your users want to interact with the UI by clicking, dragging or typing into it.

Fortunately, `Views` also support this type of interaction and events. Specialized `Views` often expose a specific set of **event listeners** that you use to manage interactive events.

As you know, *with great power comes great responsibility*, and the Android `View` component is definitely powerful. Every UI component you've ever used is a direct or indirect subclass of `View`.

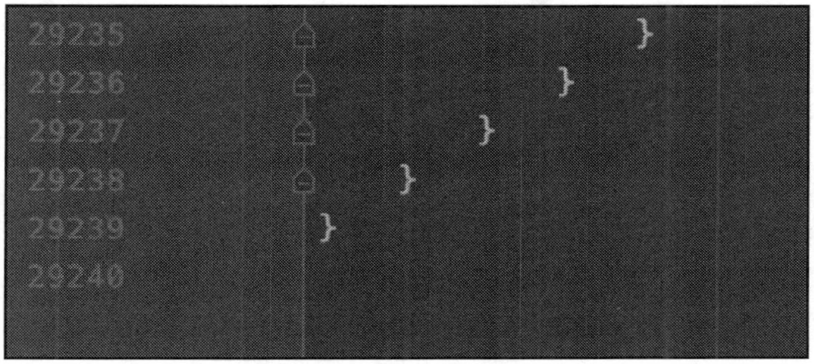

Lines of Code in View.java

As Android grew as a platform, `View` got bigger and bigger. In the current API, the **View.java** file has *over 29,000 lines of code*. Don't believe it? Open it and check it by yourself! :]

This means the current Android UI toolkit *scales poorly* and is increasingly harder to maintain.

Imagine yourself fixing a specific bug in the `View` class file. Every small change you make in the base `View` will reflect in who knows how many ways on the entire Android UI toolkit! You could be fixing one small bug, but at the same time creating dozens or hundreds of others!

`View` is *beyond the point of refactoring*, yet the only way for the current Android UI toolkit to evolve is to make this class even bigger. And this issue is amplified when building **custom** Views.

Implementing Custom Views

Despite the functionality provided by `View` and the other custom widgets the current API offers, there are cases where you need to create custom views to solve specific problems.

Given how the entire UI toolkit is built on top of the `View`, you'd think it would be very easy to build something custom, that extends the `View` as its parent?

Think again! If you want to build even the simplest of custom `Views`, you have to go through all of these steps:

```
class MyWidget : View {

  // 1 - Overriding constructors
  ...

  // 2 - Inflating layout
  ...

  // 3 - Parsing attributes
  ...

  // 4 - Getters
  ...

  // 5 - Setters
  ...

  // 6 - Measuring and Layout
  ...
```

```
    // 7 - Handling touch events
    ...
}
```

The first thing to do is create a class extending from `View`. Writing custom views to solve a particular problem is hard. You need to:

1. Override the `View` constructors. Yes, there are multiple, each with its own use case!
2. To inflate the specific layout, you have to define it as an **XML resource**.
3. To customize your `View` from XML, you have to create special XML attributes and add them to the **attrs.xml** file.
4. To modify your custom widget, you have to add the necessary **properties** and their respective **getters and setters** to the class.
5. You have to think about **styles** and how your `View` behaves in different display modes, such as **light and dark** theme.
6. If you need **custom measurements** or layouts, you have to override the specific callbacks.
7. Do you need to handle touch events? Then you need **extra code to add touch & gesture support**!

There are a lot of things to think about when writing custom views. And as a developer, you want a clean and easy API you can easily expand with your custom implementation. Unfortunately, the current Android UI toolkit is anything but easy.

ViewGroup

After implementing your custom view, you need to add it to your UI. But before you do, you have to choose the correct `ViewGroup` for your container. That might not be such an easy decision, you'll probably end up with more than one. When creating a layout for your screen, you have to choose which `ViewGroup` to use as your root view.

There are many different types of `ViewGroups` in Android. Some common implementations are `LinearLayout`, `RelativeLayout` and `FrameLayout`. Each of these expose a different set of parameters you can use to arrange their children:

- **LinearLayout**: Use this when you want to organize children in a row or column.
- **RelativeLayout**: Enables you to specify the location of child objects relative to each other or to the parent.
- **FrameLayout**: One of the simplest containers, it lets you stack widgets, vertically on top of one another. It is usually used to host a single widget or a `Fragment`.

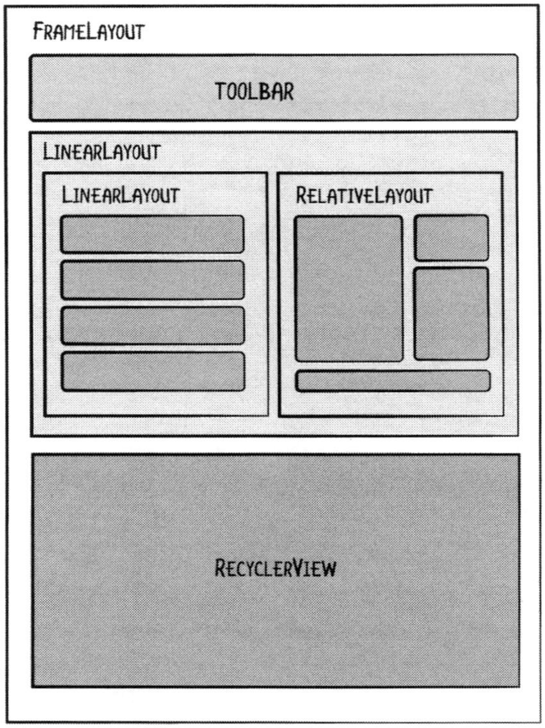

Nested ViewGroups

However, UIs are not always so simple that you can use just one `ViewGroup` in your layouts. When building more complicated UIs, you often define different areas of the screen and use the specific `ViewGroup` best matching your use case.

That leads to a lot of **nested** `ViewGroups`, making your code hard to read and maintain. Most importantly, it **decreases the performance** of your app.

Recently, the Android UI toolkit received a new `ViewGroup`, to address this issue — `ConstraintLayout`. It allows the creation of large and complex layouts with a flat view hierarchy. In short, you use it to create complex **constraints** between views so you don't have to nest layouts. Each constraint describes if a `View` is constrained to the start, end, top or bottom of another `View`.

This doesn't quite solve the problem of nested layouts. There are times when you can get better performance by combining simpler `ViewGroups` rather than using `ConstraintLayout`.

You could argue that sometimes in complex UIs, it's easier to understand how the layout is organized when you have some level of nesting. Ironic, right? :]

It's not easy to pick a `ViewGroup` when building your UIs. Usually, it becomes easier as you gain experience, but new developers still have a hard time when they start playing with Android.

Displaying Views

Imagine you've successfully created your layout. You picked the right `Views`. You created a custom `View` to solve a specific problem. You used the correct `ViewGroups` to organize your `Views`. Now, you want to display your beautiful layout.

But there are *still many more steps* you need to take to achieve this behavior!

If you're experienced with the Android UI toolkit, you know usually your UI is defined in XML files. Android provides an XML schema for including `ViewGroup` and `View` classes. Your layout might look like this:

```
<?xml version="1.0" encoding="utf-8"?>
<FrameLayout
  xmlns:android="http://schemas.android.com/apk/res/android"
  android:layout_width="match_parent"
  android:layout_height="match_parent">

  <TextView
    android:layout_width="wrap_content"
    android:layout_height="wrap_content"
    android:text="Hello World"
    android:layout_gravity="center"/>

</FrameLayout>
```

This *simple* layout displays a text saying "Hello World".

All this work *still isn't enough* to display your UI. To render that layout on the screen, you need to connect it with your `Activity` or `Fragment`. If you're working with an `Activity`, you'd do:

```
class MyActivity : AppCompatActivity() {

  override fun onCreate(savedInstanceState: Bundle?) {
    super.onCreate(savedInstanceState)
    setContentView(R.layout.activity_layout)
  }
}
```

Using `setContentView(ViewResource)`, the `Activity` takes care of creating a window where you place your UI. This is the simplest way to display UI elements in Android.

`Fragments`, on the other hand, represent a piece of behavior or a portion of the UI within an `Activity`. You can combine multiple `Fragments` in a single `Activity` to build a multi-pane UI, and you can also reuse a `Fragment` in multiple activities. Think of a `Fragment` as a modular section of an `Activity`.

```
class MyFragment : Fragment() {

  override fun onCreateView(
    inflater: LayoutInflater,
    container: ViewGroup?,
    savedInstanceState: Bundle?
  ): View {
      return inflater.inflate(R.layout.layout, container, false)
  }
}
```

To provide a layout for a fragment, you must implement `onCreateView()`. The Android system calls it when it's time for the fragment to draw its UI.

Your implementation of this method must return a `View` that's the root of your `Fragment`'s layout. To return a layout from `onCreateView()`, you **inflate** it from a layout resource you define in XML.

To help you, `onCreateView()` provides a `LayoutInflater` — a component that reads the XML definition, and builds Kotlin and Java objects using the attributes and properties you define, such as the `View` **width**, **height**, **color**, **constraints** and custom attributes.

This process is called **layout inflation**, as layouts are similar to balloons — you need to inflate them to take shape and do some work! :]

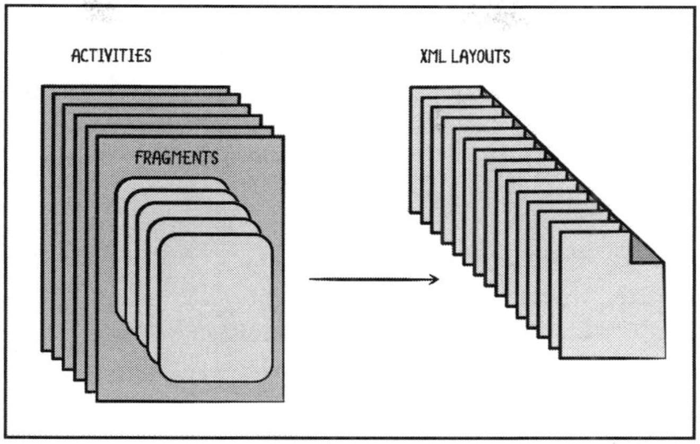

Non-scalable Layout System

Imagine that you you need a screen with an `Activity` and a `Fragment` inside it. To create the screen, you need the following files: **MyActivity.kt**, **my_activity.xml**, **MyFragment.kt**, **my_fragment.xml**, extra attributes defined in **attrs.xml** and special styling defined in **styles.xml**.

For such a **simple screen**, you have to write **too much code**.

As you see, the current Android UI Toolkit scales *very poorly*. Modern applications usually have numerous features each with its own XML layout, attributes, styles, Kotlin or Java code and much more.

The volume of files makes it difficult to organize those files in the resource folder. And if you decide to define list or page items for **dynamic UI components**, things get **even more complicated**.

Separating Concerns

It's hard enough to get from a simple layout definition to displaying your UI on the screen. If you want to see your UI in action, you have to connect it to your business logic.

It's good practice to separate your business logic from your UI logic. This concept is known as **separation of concerns (SoC)**. It's a design principle in computer science that says you should separate a program into distinct sections, with each section addressing a distinct **concern**.

A concern is a set of information affecting the code of a computer program. It can be as general as the details of the hardware that runs an app or as specific as the name of the class to instantiate.

SoC includes two main concepts: **coupling** and **cohesion**. You can think of your app as a group of modules. **Each module contains many units**. In general, you want to reduce coupling as much as possible and increase cohesion. But what do these terms mean?

Coupling & Cohesion

Dependencies between different modules represent **coupling**. Parts of one module can influence another. If you make a change to the code in one module, depending on the coupling, you'll have to change other modules as well.

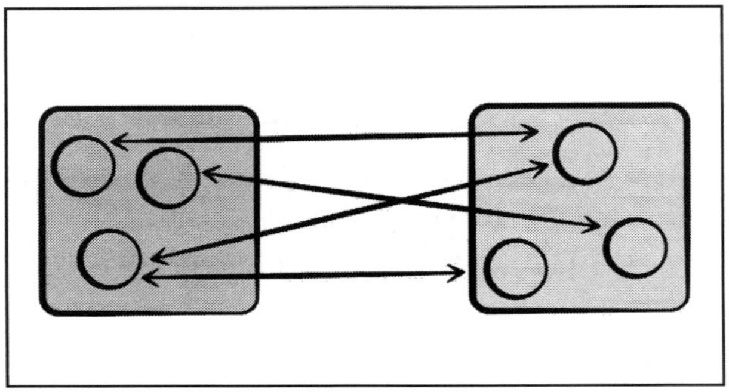

Coupling

On the other hand, cohesion describes how the units inside of a given module are related to one another.

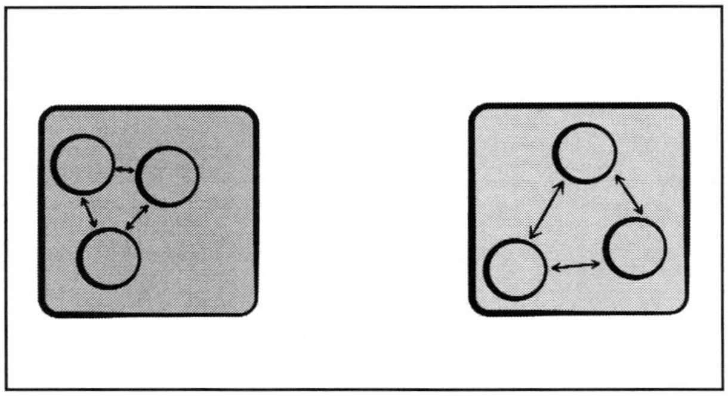

Cohesion

So, the goal is to group as much related code as possible. This makes your code maintainable over time and scalable as your app grows. More importantly, the impact of any change you make is isolated to its own module.

With this in mind, think about how you usually organize code when implementing the Android UI. Note that you have two modules that depend on each other.

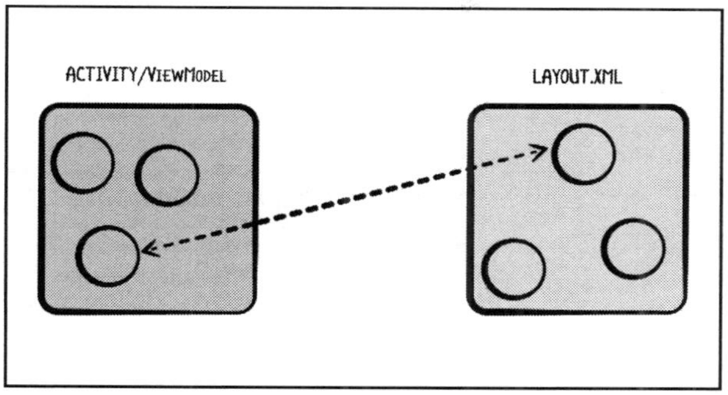

Modules when Implementing Android UI

Why did you define these modules like this? Well, each of these modules are written in distinctly different languages, and the differences between them cause the framework to force this kind of design.

Your `ViewModel` and layout can be closely related and, therefore, coupled but you don't have a choice of drawing the line of separation, because you write them in different languages, with different semantical properties.

In other words, these units **should be cohesive, but they can't be because of the language difference**. They rely on each other in order to work, but the **dependency is implicit**.

This is because of the language difference and the fact you can't directly communicate to the XML file. You have to inflate it into a Kotlin or Java object, and communicate with that.

For this reason, as your `ViewModel` and your layout grow, they become very difficult to maintain.

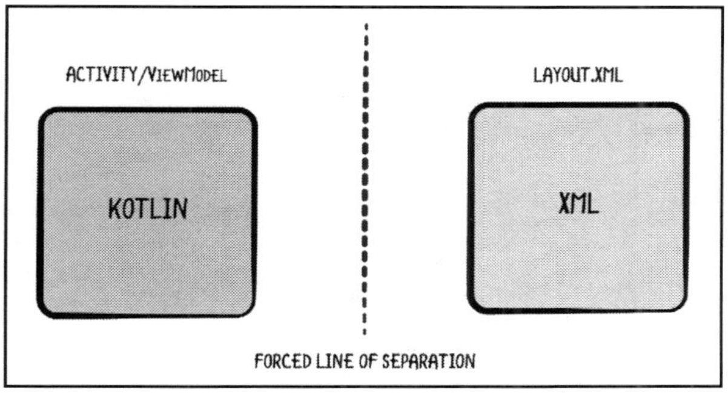

Forced Line of Separation of Concerns

Imperative Thinking

Whenever the user performs a specific action in your UI, you have to capture that event, update the **View state** and the UI to represent the newly given state. You do this over and over throughout the lifecycle of your app.

If you want something to animate when your state changes, you need to define how your view changes between different states. This programming style is known as **imperative programming**.

Being imperative means you are commanding or telling the program to do what you want or show the `Views` you need. It uses statements in the form of functions to change a program's state. Imperative programming focuses on describing the steps for *how* a program should operate.

Traditionally, in Android, you use the imperative style to build and manage your UIs. You define the layout in **XML** and mutate it later using functions in **Java/Kotlin**.

Imagine a UI for a calendar event. The required properties are a title, an event owner and a link to an online meeting. Other optional properties are a guest list and a room name. If there are more than five guests, the app should collapse the guest list.

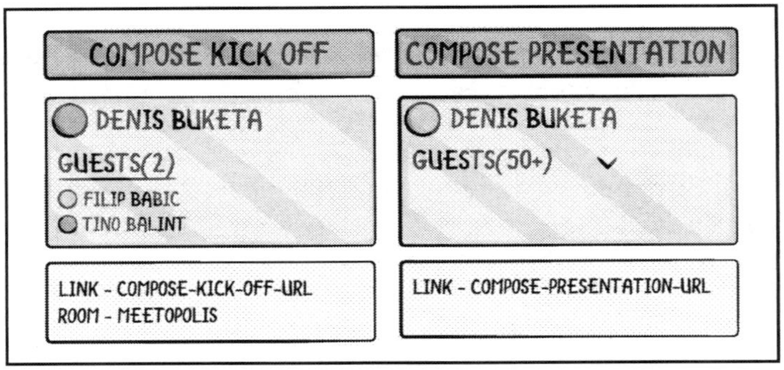

Calendar Event

With imperative thinking, you might use the following code to render the event card:

```
fun renderEventCard(event: Event) {
  // Handle event title
  setTitle(event.title)

  // Handle event owner
  setOwner(event.owner)

  // Handle event call link
  setCallLink(event.callLink)
```

```
    // Handle guest list visibility
    if (event.guests.size > 0 && !hasGuestList()) {
      addGuestList()
    } else if (event.guests.size == 0 && hasGuestList()) {
      removeGuestList()
    }

    // Handle case with more than 5 guests
    if (event.guests.size > 5 && !isGuestListCollapsed()) {
      collapseGuestList()
    } else if (event.guests.size > 0 && isGuestListCollapsed()) {
      expandGuestList()
    }

    // Handle guest count badge
    if (event.guests.size <= 50) {
      setGuestCountText("$count")
    } else {
      setGuestCountText("50+")
    }

    // Handle Event Room
    if (event.isRoomSelected && !isRoomAdded()) {
      addRoom()
    } else if (!event.isRoomSelected && isRoomAdded()) {
      removeRoom()
    }
  }
```

The function is just a showcase of how many different states you would need to handle for the given case of a calendar event.

After setting the basic properties like the title, owner and call link, you have to handle four different `if` statements for various states the card might have — like showing the collapsible guest list, guest count or meeting room.

When building the UI for this use case, you need to think about the following:

- Which UI you'd like to display for any given data.
- How to respond to events.
- How your UI changes over time.

Just by the number of `if` checks, there are sixteen different states for your calendar card.

This seemed like a simple use case, but it's actually *very complex*, and lots of bugs can creep in as you develop it. Imagine a more complex example, where you also need to handle the animations between states.

Handling how the UI changes over time is the hardest part of building a UI. But if you can generalize the behavior, you can try to simplify it! :]

Inheritance

One way to make your life easier when it comes to updating your UI is to extract parts of your UI to custom view classes.

If you have components you often reuse throughout your app, just create a custom view and keep all that code in one place.

You already saw making a custom view is hard, but it's useful in situations like this. There's a well-known principle describing how to organize your code that way — **composition over inheritance**.

This is a principle in object-oriented programming (OOP) that says that classes should achieve polymorphic behavior and code reuse by their composition — that is, by containing instances of other classes that implement the desired functionality — rather than inheriting from a base or parent class.

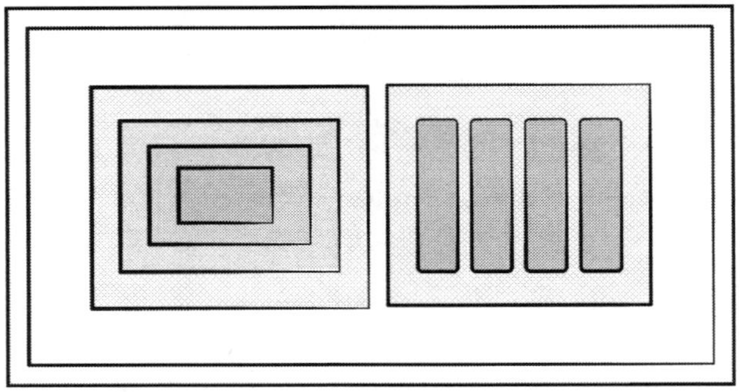

Inheritance vs Composition

In the current Android UI toolkit, inheritance plays a huge role — and that causes problems. For example, `Button` is one of the most-used widgets in every Android app. When you look at `Button`'s class hierarchy, you'll see something like this:

```
java.lang.Object
  ↳ android.view.View
      ↳ android.widget.TextView
          ↳ android.widget.Button
```

Button's Class Hierarchy

It seems to make sense, as `Buttons` display text. The issue is `TextViews` do a lot of things. For instance, you can make a button selectable.

Selectable Button

What about `ImageButton`? Can you guess what class `ImageButton` extends? Well, take a look at its class hierarchy:

```
java.lang.Object
  ↳ android.view.View
      ↳ android.widget.ImageView
          ↳ android.widget.ImageButton
```

ImageButton's Class Hierarchy

As you see, you have two buttons sharing the same logic except one uses an image, while the other uses text for its content. Yet, they extend different classes.

Now, imagine you need a button with an image *and* text. Which class should you extend? The answer isn't simple.

Inheritance not only introduces a lot of unnecessary logic, it limits the classes you can inherit from. In Kotlin and Java, **you can only inherit from one parent**, there is no multiple inheritance.

Data Flow

There's one more thing to look at in the current Android UI toolkit, to do with state and the data flow between the UI and the business logic. When talking about state, it's important to consider three main questions:

- What is the source of truth?
- Who owns the state?
- Who updates the state?

It's not simple to answer these questions in Android development, which is why you have so many different architectural patterns.

You have Model-View-Controller (MVC), Model-View-ViewModel (MVVM), Model-View-Presenter (MVP), Model-View-Intent (MVI) and many more. These patterns help define and reason about your app's data flow and state management.

Take the `Spinner` component, for example.

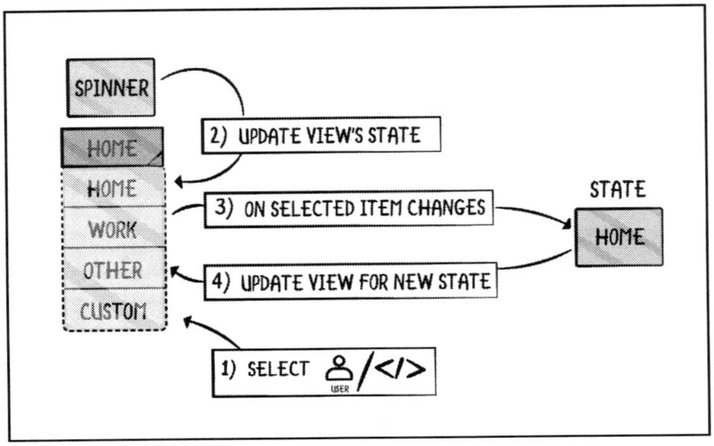

Spinner and State Management

`Spinner` offers a listener called `onSelectedItemChanged` telling you when a user changed the value — but it happens after the value changes. It's hard to build your UI to be a representation of your model if your UI also owns and manages their internal state.

In this example, `Spinner` will update its state and notify you about the state change. Your model will update the state and, if you have the logic to update the `Spinner` when your state changes, you'll update the `Spinner` once more for that change.

But you cannot reliably know if you are the one changing the `Spinner` state, or if the event came from the user. The onus to keep the `Spinner`'s internal state and the model's state in sync is on you, which introduces a lot of unnecessary complexity and room for errors.

You've been reading about a lot of complexity and issues the current UI toolkit provides, so if some of those hit you hard, you'll be glad to hear that there *is* hope! :]

Introduction to Jetpack Compose

In the previous sections, you went through some important concepts and issues regarding the original Android UI toolkit. Now, it's time to say hello to **Jetpack Compose**!

Jetpack Compose is Android's modern toolkit for building native UI. When you learned about how difficult building a UI in Android with the original Android UI toolkit is, you started with the basic, familiar building blocks, `View` and `ViewGroup`. So it makes sense to kick off this introduction with the basic building blocks of Jetpack Compose — **composable functions**.

Composables

Like all great tutorials, this one will start with the "Hello World!" example! :]

```
@Composable
fun GreetingWorld() {

}
```

You can break this code into two parts: First, it's a function and second, that function has an annotation called `@Composable`.

That's pretty much all you need to create a new widget. Ready for the big surprise? In Compose's world, you call these widgets **composables**.

You'll notice that you don't have to extend any class (looking at you, `View`) or override constructors or other functions. All you need to care about is that you write a function and use this new fancy annotation.

Get ready because you'll see that one *a lot*!

In this example, you want to show a message to the user that says "Hello World!". To do that, you can do the following:

```
@Composable
fun GreetingWorld() {
  Text(text = "Hello world!")
}
```

In Compose, calling a function that displays something on the screen is known as **emitting the UI**. So, to emit your message, you need to call a `Text` function.

`Text` is also a composable function and it's one of the default composable functions making up Jetpack Compose. One thing to notice is composable functions can only be invoked from other composable functions — if you try to remove `@Composable`, you'll get an error stopping you from using `Text()`.

But what if you want to pass in a specific message or name, or another kind of parameter to the composable? Well, you can do this:

```
@Composable
fun Greeting(name: String) {
  Text(text = "Hello $name!")
}
```

Since composables are functions, you can pass data to them as function parameters. In your example, you add a property `name` to `Greeting()` and use that data when invoking `Text()`.

The simplest way to think about composables is to understand they're functions that take your data and transform it into your UI. Another way to put it — in Compose, **the UI is a function of the data (state).**

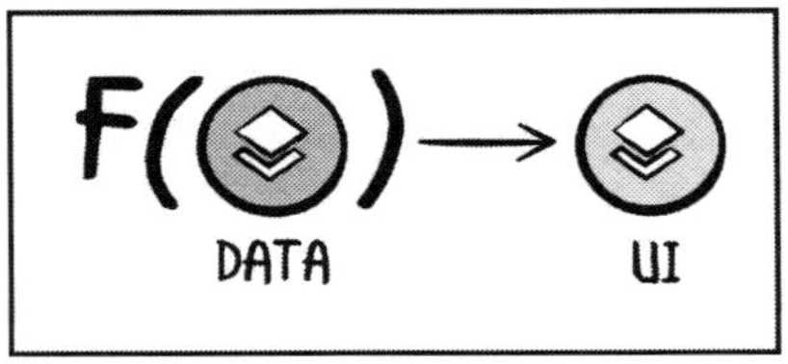

UI as a Function of Data

You've probably heard how functional programming, and having pure functions is all the rage. By using Compose you can be a part of the cool group of kids! :]

Jokes aside, this functional paradigm makes it simpler to write and refactor the code. It also makes it easier to visualize it.

Displaying Composables

When it comes to displaying composables, you still use activities or fragments as a starting point. To display the `Greeting` composable you just saw, you do the following:

```
class MainActivity : AppCompatActivity() {

  override fun onCreate(savedInstanceState: Bundle?) {
    super.onCreate(savedInstanceState)
```

```
        setContent {
          Greeting("World")
        }
    }
}

@Composable
fun Greeting(name: String) {
  Text (text = "Hello $name!")
}
```

You connect composables with your activities using a **content block**. `setContent()` defines the `Activity`'s layout. Instead of defining the layout content with an XML file, you just call composable functions.

The magic behind Jetpack Compose is how it transforms these composable functions into the app's UI elements. Chapter 2, "Learning Jetpack Compose Fundamentals", will explore this in more detail!

Using Kotlin

Jetpack Compose allows you to write your UI using Kotlin, the amazing language that is so much better than rusty old XML. Not just that — Jetpack Compose is built entirely in Kotlin!

Let's see how using Kotlin features and programming practices that follow OOP can solve the difficulties you read about earlier.

Separation of Concerns

You've seen how having different languages to build your business logic and your UI leads to forced separation of concerns. With Jetpack Compose, that line disappears.

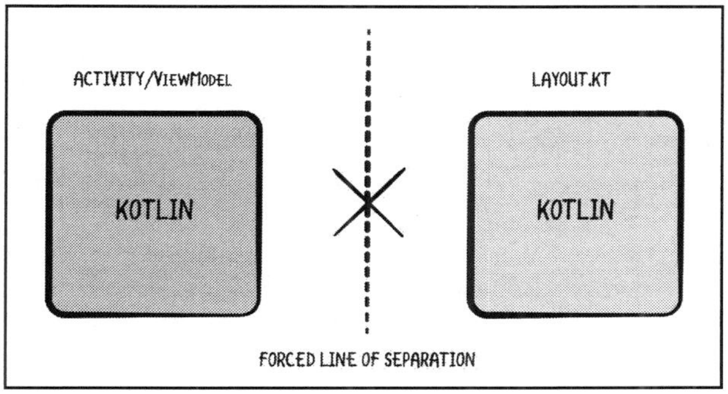

Control of the Line of Separation of Concerns

By using Kotlin to write your UI, you take responsibility for drawing the line of separation. You can do whatever makes the most sense in your situation. You don't have to conform to the forced limitations of the operating system.

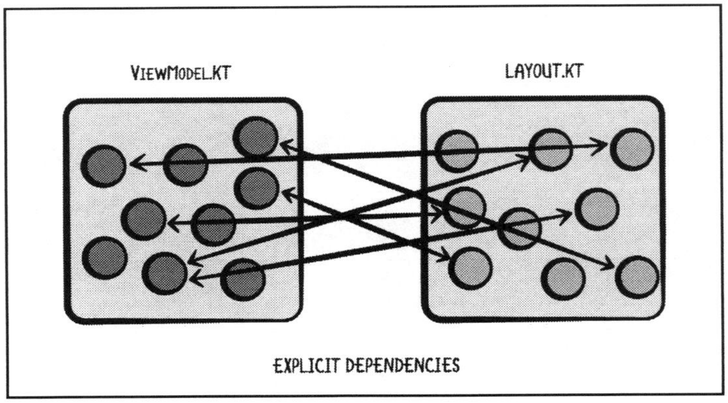

Explicit Dependencies

That means many of the implicit dependencies you had between your layout and business logic now become explicit.

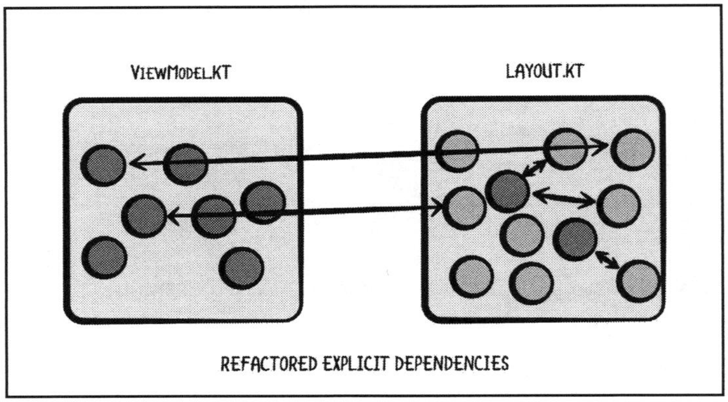

Refactoring Explicit Dependencies

Having your UI and business logic written in the same language allows you to refactor those dependencies to reduce the coupling and increase cohesion in your code.

A framework shouldn't separate your concerns for you. This doesn't mean that you should mix your logic and UI. But by writing everything in Kotlin, you can apply all the good practices to define where you want to draw the line between the two.

Declarative Thinking

You've read about how the design of the original Android UI toolkit requires you to write imperative code. Whatever architecture you use, you'll find yourself writing the code that describes *how* your UI changes over time.

In Jetpack Compose, you'll have to shift how you think about UI in terms of **declarative programming**.

Declarative programming is a programming paradigm where you don't focus on describing *how* a program should operate, but *what* the program should accomplish. For example, you need to describe how your UI **should show a hidden** `Button`, rather than **how it should hide** a `Button`.

Remember that example with the event card? You can write that same logic declaratively using Jetpack Compose.

```
@Composable
fun EventCard(event: Event) {
  Title(event.title)
  Owner(event.owner)
  Call(event.callLink)

  if (event.guests.size > 0) {
    Guests(collapsed = event.guests.size > 5) {
      if (event.guests.size > 50) {
        Badge(text="50+")
      } else {
        Badge(text="$count")
      }
    }
  }

  if (event.isRoomSelected) {
    Room(event.room)
  }
}
```

Note how you described *what* should happen without saying anything about *how* it should happen. The app will add the guest list and the room name only if they exist. The list collapses when there are more than five guests.

This representation is purely based on the state of the **event** model. Making it much easier to understand what exactly is going on.

Remember those concerns about syncing your UI and your model state? You no longer need to worry how your UI changes over time. By using this declarative approach, you describe how the UI should look, while the framework controls how you get from one state to the other.

Additionally, the composable function is a function definition, but it describes all possible states of your UI in one place.

Composition

In the example with `Buttons` and `ImageButtons`, you saw how inheritance can lead to specific problems. Jetpack Compose allows you to address those problems by favoring **composition over inheritance**. By examining the same example, you'll see how to approach that problem.

To make a button widget, you do something like this:

```
@Composable
fun TextButton(text: String) {
  Box(modifier = Modifier.clickable(onClick = { ... })) {
    Text(text = text)
  }
}
```

Note how, in this example, you have a `Box`, which is a composable letting you **stack multiple composables, vertically on top of one another**. It's also using `Modifier.clickable()`, to make the composable clickable. For now, you don't need to worry about modifiers.

You'll learn about the `Box` component in later chapters. And in Chapter 6, "Using Compose Modifiers" you'll learn about modifiers in greater detail. For now, just know that `Box()` allows you to wrap your `Text()` and you use a `Modifier` to make it clickable.

Now, what if you need a button with an image, as in the previous example? You do something like this:

```
@Composable
fun ImageButton() {
  Box(modifier = Modifier.clickable(onClick = { ... })) {
    Icon(painterResource(id = R.drawable.vector),
contentDescription = "")
  }
}
```

Here, you use `Icon()` instead of `Text()`. The next chapter covers this in more detail. For now, it's enough to say this composable allows you to display vectors or static images.

To wrap up the example, if you need a button with text and an image, you can do this:

```
@Composable
fun TextImageButton(text: String) {
   Box(modifier = Modifier.clickable(onClick = { ... })) {
      Row(verticalAlignment = Alignment.CenterVertically) {
         Icon(painterResource(id = R.drawable.vector),
contentDescription = "")
         Text(text = text)
      }
   }
}
```

Here, you combined *(i.e composed)* the `Icon` and the `Text` composables in one `Row`. A `Row` is similar to a horizontal `LinearLayout`, where items will be positioned one next to the other, horizontally. By doing so, you successfully created a button with an image and text. So easy! :]

Since Compose is based on functions and there is no inheritance involved by design, there is no need to override functionality you do not need.

And that's it. With Compose, there's no need to do anything **extra**, you simply add the composables you need. You build your widgets from other widgets that you've already created or that Jetpack Compose offers you.

Encapsulation

In the **Data Flow** section, you saw how the data flows between the UI and your business logic. You saw in the old Android UI toolkit, views also manage their own internal state and they expose callbacks that you use to capture the change in their internal state.

Compose is designed in a way where your UI is a representation of your data. Meaning your UI components — in this case, composables — aren't responsible for *managing* state. They *represent* your state.

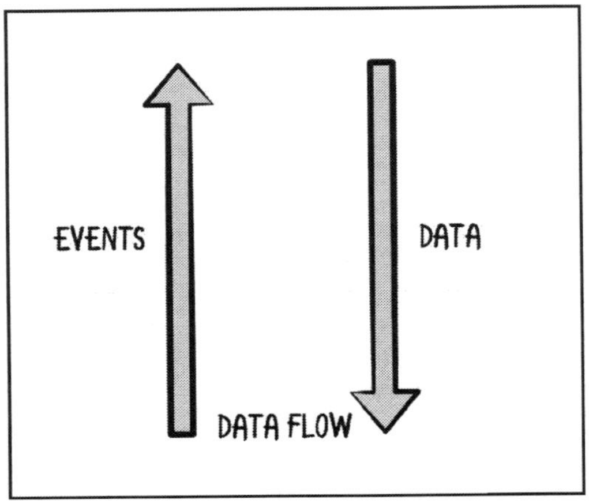

Data Flow

Kotlin allows you to pass down data in the form of function parameters, but you can also pass the callbacks to propagate the events to mutate the state up. This is how you implement the public APIs of your composable functions.

Imagine you want a list of posts that the user can click. You could create a `Post` composable like this:

```
@Composable
fun Post(post: PostData, onClickAction: () -> Unit) {
  Box(modifier = Modifier.clickable(onClick = onClickAction)) {
    Row {
      Icon(bitmap = post.image, contentDescription = "")
      Text(text = post.title)
    }
  }
}
```

You pass the `PostData` down to the function to render a specific `Post` and you also pass a callback to receive the click event when the user clicks the `Post`.

You should strive to have **Unidirectional data flow**, which means data should flow down to your UI (your composables), and events should flow from your UI to your `ViewModels`.

Recomposition

Recomposition is one of the most important concepts in Jetpack Compose. It's the mechanism used by compose to update the UI based on state changes. Recomposition allows any composable function to be **re-invoked** at any time to re-render the component based on new data.

Understanding recomposition is useful when updating your UI with new state. Whenever state changes, Compose will **re-invoke** all the composables that depend on that state and update your UI.

Chapter 2, "Learning Jetpack Compose Fundamentals" will go into more detail about the recomposition step. For now, just be aware that this concept means you don't have to manually update your UI when the state changes, as you had to do with the old Android UI toolkit.

Imagine you have a list of posts like this:

```
@Composable
fun Posts(livePosts: LiveData<List<Post>>) {
  val posts by livePosts.observeAsState(initial = emptyList())

  if (posts.isNotEmpty()) {
    PostList(posts)
  } else {
    MessageForEmptyPosts()
  }
}
```

If the number of posts isn't zero, you show a list of posts. If the number of posts is zero, you show a message.

Here, you see how you can use `LiveData` and observe it as a state. You'll learn more about this in Chapter 7, "Managing State in Compose".

The idea behind this is you observe the `Posts`' state. Whenever the `livePosts` data changes, Compose re-invokes `Posts()` and **re-evaluates** the logic inside.

If there are no posts, Compose calls `MessageForEmptyPosts()` and your app shows a message for the user. If there are posts, Compose calls `PostList(posts)` and your app shows the list of posts.

All of this happens automagically!

Jetpack Compose's Tech Stack

By now, you have a better idea of how Compose tries to solve the problems of the old Android UI toolkit. You've seen examples of what's possible with Jetpack Compose, but how is it all wired under the hood?

Two parts categorize the different components that make up Jetpack Compose: the **development host** and the **device host**.

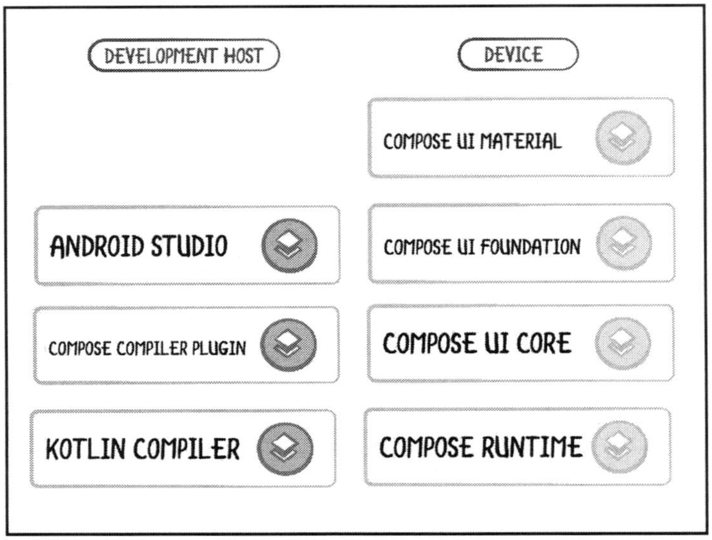

Jetpack Compose Tech Stack

Development Host

The development host contains all the tools to help you write your code.

At the bottom, you have a **Kotlin compiler**. Jetpack Compose is written in Kotlin and uses a lot of Kotlin features, which makes it so flexible and easy to use. You've seen how Compose uses trailing lambdas to make the code more readable and intuitive.

On top of that, you have a **Compose Compiler Plugin**. Even though you use `@Composable` as an annotation, Compose doesn't use the annotation processor. This plugin works at the type system level and also at the code generation level to change the types of your composable functions.

If you're not familiar with **annotation processors**, or APTs, they are a special system within the build process that analyze specific annotations and generate code based on them.

This is a great thing because you can use the generated code instead of writing it yourself, but sometimes it's terrible as it **greatly increases the build time** for your project. But because Compose doesn't use APTs, it doesn't slow down your builds!

On top of that, you have **Android Studio**, which includes Compose-specific tools, simplifying the work you do with Compose.

Device Host

The second part of this tech stack is your **device**; that is, the environment that runs your Compose code.

At the bottom, there's a **Compose Runtime**. At its core, the Compose logic doesn't know anything about Android or UIs. It only knows how to work with tree structures to emit specific items. That makes it even more interesting because you could use Compose to emit things other than UIs.

On top of that lies **Compose UI Core**. It handles input management, measurement, drawing, layout etc.

These two layers support the widgets the next layer provides — **Compose UI foundation**. It contains basic building blocks like `Text`, `Row`, `Column` and default interactions.

Finally, there's **Compose UI Material**, an implementation of the Material Design system. It provides Material components out of the box, making it easy to use Material Design in your app.

Key Points

- **View.java**'s size makes the old Android UI toolkit hard to maintain and scale.
- Creating custom views is hard and requires too much code.
- Unlike **imperative programming**, **declarative programming** simplifies code and makes it easier to understand.
- In the old Android UI toolkit, it's not clear what the source of truth is, who owns it and who updates it.
- In Jetpack Compose, you use **composables** to build your UI.
- Composables are just functions annotated with `@Composable`.
- Jetpack Compose is written in Kotlin and allows you to use all the Kotlin features.
- In Jetpack Compose, your UI is a **function of data**.
- You use `setContent { }` as the entry point to display your composables.
- In Compose you control where to draw the line of separation of concerns between your business logic and UI.
- Jetpack Compose favors **composition over inheritance**.
- In Jetpack Compose, you use function parameters to pass down the data and callbacks to propagate events up. This is called **Unidirectional data flow**
- Jetpack Compose uses **recomposition** to **re-invoke** composables when the state changes.
- Jetpack Compose doesn't use the annotation processor, but rather a **Compose Compiler Plugin** that changes the type of composable functions.

Where to Go From Here?

That was a *really brief* comparison of the original Android UI toolkit and Jetpack Compose! :]

By now, you should have a sense of the potential of Jetpack Compose.

Keep the excitement up for the following chapters, where you'll get your hands dirty while learning about some of the existing composables you can use to build your UI.

In the first section of the book, you'll cover the fundamentals, learn how to use layout and how to create lists — one of the most important UI components! See you there!

Chapter 2: Learning Jetpack Compose Fundamentals

By Tino Balint

In this chapter, you'll cover the basics of Jetpack Compose. You'll learn how to write **composable functions**, the building blocks used to create beautiful UI with Jetpack Compose. You'll see how to implement the most common composable functions such as text, image or button elements. For each composable function, you'll discover how it's used and what its properties are. Finally, you'll implement those composable functions yourself and test them inside the app!

Before you start writing code, however, you need to know how an element shown on the screen becomes a composable function.

Composable Functions

In the first chapter, you learned how using XML to build UI differs from using Jetpack Compose. The biggest issues with the former approach are:

- The UI isn't scalable.
- It's hard to make custom views.
- State ownership is often scattered between multiple owners.

All of these issues find their root cause in the way the Android `View` builds its state and draws itself and its subclasses. To avoid those issues, you need to start fresh and use a different basic building block. In Jetpack Compose, this building block is called a **composable function.**

To make a composable function, you do this:

```
@Composable
fun MyComposableFunction() {
  // TODO
}
```

You first annotate a function with **@Composable** — a special **annotation class**. Any function annotated this way is also called a **composable function**, as you can *compose* it within other composable functions.

Annotation classes simplify the code by attaching metadata to it. **Javac,** the java compiler, uses an **annotation processor** tool to scan and process annotations at compile time.

This creates new source files with the added metadata. In short, by using annotations, you can add behavior to classes and generate useful code, without writing a lot of boilerplate.

This specific annotation changes the type of that function or expression to a `Composable`, meaning that :

- Only other composable functions can call it
- The composable can only be invoked from a compose scope

Much like coroutines.

The source code for the `Composable` annotation class looks like this:

```
@MustBeDocumented
@Retention(AnnotationRetention.BINARY)
@Target(
    AnnotationTarget.FUNCTION,
    AnnotationTarget.TYPE,
    AnnotationTarget.TYPE_PARAMETER,
    AnnotationTarget.PROPERTY_GETTER
)
annotation class Composable
```

You can see the Composable annotation class has three annotations of its own:

1. **@MustBeDocumented**: Indicates that the annotation is a part of the public API and should be included in the generated documentation.

2. **@Retention**: Tells the compiler how long the annotation should *live*. By using `AnnotationRetention.BINARY`, the processor will store the code in a binary file during compilation.

3. **@Target**: Describes the contexts where the type applies. `@Composable` can be applied to types, parameters, functions and properties.

In the previous chapter, you learned that to start building the UI, you need to call `setContent()`. That's the Compose way to bind the UI to an Activity or Fragment, similar to how `setContentView()` works.

But it doesn't work with `Views` or XML resources, instead it works with composable functions!

Setting the Content

The signature for `setContent()` looks like this:

```
fun ComponentActivity.setContent(
    parent: CompositionContext? = null,
    content: @Composable () -> Unit
) { ... }
```

You can see `setContent()` is an extension function of `ComponentActivity`. Extension functions add additional functionality to a class without changing its source code. That means you can use `setContent()` on any `ComponentActivity` or its subclasses, like `AppCompatActivity`.

Calling `setContent()` sets the given composable function named `content` as the root view, to which you can add any number of elements. You'll call the rest of your composable functions from within this container.

Notice how `content` is also annotated with `@Composable`. Because of the aforementioned `@Target`, you can apply it to function parameters, as well.

This specific use case marks the lambda function you pass in as a composable function, allowing you to call other composable functions and access things like **resources** and the **context** of Jetpack Compose.

Another parameter inside `setContent()` is the `CompositionContext`, which is a reference to the parent composition. `CompositionContext` is used to coordinate scheduling of composition updates in a composition tree. It ensures that invalidations and data flow logically through the parent and child composition.

The parent of the root composition is a `Recomposer` which determines the thread where **recomposition** happens — one of the most important features of Jetpack Compose.

In simple terms, recomposition is an event that asks the app to **re-draw** the current UI with new values. Recomposition happens every time a value such as state changes.

You'll learn more about managing states and how recomposition works in Chapter 7, "Managing State in Compose".

Now you've gone over the basics of Jetpack Compose, you can dive into composable functions! :]

Basic Composable Functions

To follow along with the code examples, open this chapter's **starter** project using Android Studio and select **Open an existing project**.

Next, navigate to **02-learning-jetpack-compose-fundamentals/projects** and select the **starter** folder as the project root. Once the project opens, let it build and sync and you'll be ready to go!

The starter project consists of three packages and **MainActivity.kt**.

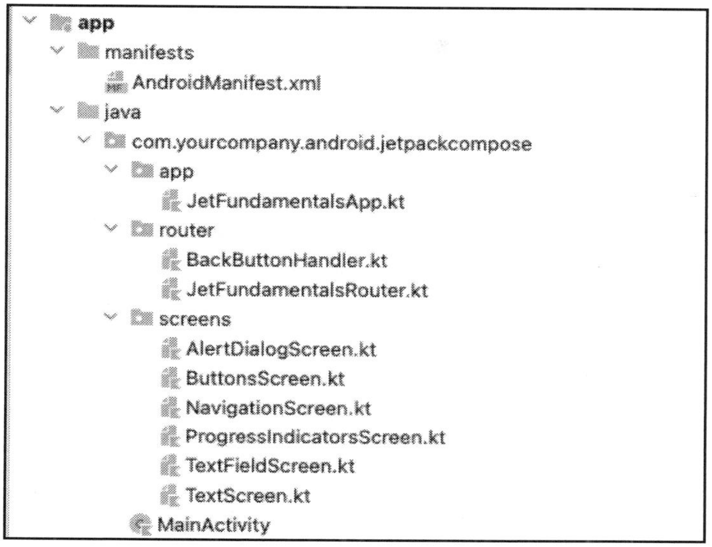

Project Packages

Here's what you should know about the contents:

- **app**: Has only one composable function, which acts as a root layout in your app. You won't need to change it since it only contains the app navigation, which is already set up for you!
- **router**: Has two helper classes to handle navigation between screens and the **Back** button. You won't need to change anything here, either.
- **screens**: Consists of multiple composable functions for different screens. You'll implement these in this chapter, except for **NavigationScreen.kt**, which contains a layout for navigation that's already made for you.
- **MainActivity.kt**: Contains the `setContent()` call, setting the first composable function and acting as a root UI component.

Once you're familiar with the file organization, build and run the app. You'll see a screen with basic navigation, as shown below.

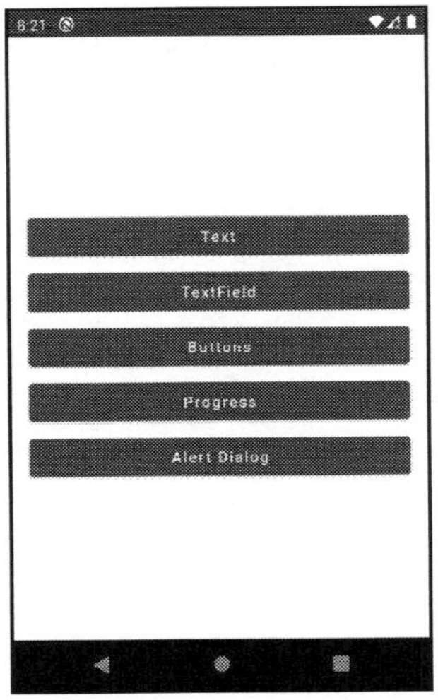

Navigation Screen

The screen contains five buttons, each leading to an empty screen when you click on it. By pressing **Back**, you return to the main screen.

Your goal is to implement a composable function for each of the empty screens. So get to it! :]

Text

When you think about the UI, one of the first things that come to mind is a basic text element, or `TextView`. In Jetpack Compose, the composable function most similar to a `TextView` is called **Text**. Let's see it in action.

Open **TextScreen.kt** and you'll see two composable functions: `TextScreen()` and `MyText()`:

```
@Composable
fun TextScreen() {
  Column(
    modifier = Modifier.fillMaxSize(), // 1
    horizontalAlignment = Alignment.CenterHorizontally, // 2
    verticalArrangement = Arrangement.Center // 3
  ) {
    MyText()
```

```
    }

    BackButtonHandler {
      JetFundamentalsRouter.navigateTo(Screen.Navigation)
    }
  }

  @Composable
  fun MyText() {
    //TODO add your code here
  }
```

TextScreen is already complete. It's a composable function using a Column component to list out items in a vertical order. In that sense, a Column is just like a vertical LinearLayout!

It also uses **modifiers** and two Column properties to style the Column, then align it and its children. Here's more about the properties you're using:

1. By using **modifiers**, you can style each Compose element in multiple different ways. You can change its alignment, size, background, shape and much more. In this case, by using Modifier.fillMaxSize(), you're telling the Column to **match** its parent's width and height.
2. By using horizontalAlignment, you're telling the Column to center its children horizontally.
3. Using verticalArrangement, you tell the Column to vertically centre its children.

You'll learn more about **modifiers** in Chapter 6, "Using Compose Modifiers"! Right now, what's important is how to add text elements to your composable functions. Also ignore the BackButtonHandler(), as it's a special composable built to handle back clicks, and you don't need to change it!

Now, change MyText()'s code to the following:

```
@Composable
fun MyText() {
 Text(text = )
}
```

You'll see a variety of choices to import the Text, but make sure to pick the one that comes from **androidx.compose.material**. You'll also get a prompt to provide a text to display. Add the following code as the text parameter:

```
stringResource(id = R.string.jetpack_compose)
```

Compose has an easy-to-use way to import strings, drawables, and other **resources** into your UI elements. Normally, to get a string from resources, you call `getString()` on a given `Context`. Since you're working with composable functions, you need a composable function that allows you to do that.

Fortunately, there are many composable functions allowing you to retrieve different types of resources. In this case, you use `stringResource()`, which takes the ID of a string resource you want to load.

Build and run the app. Then on the main screen, click the **Text** button. You should see the following screen:

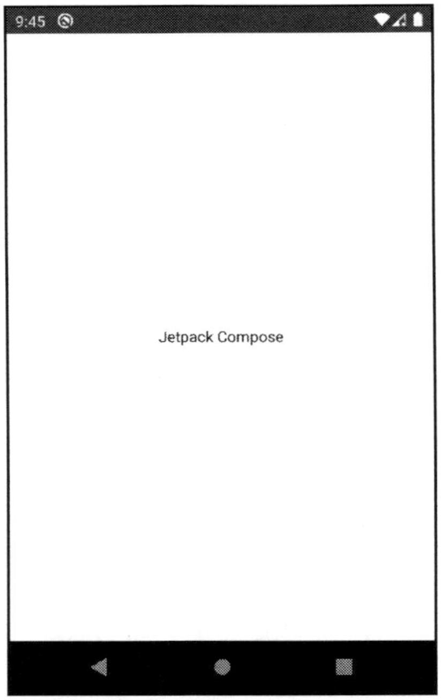

Non-Styled Text

Awesome! There's now a simple text in the middle of the screen that reads **Jetpack Compose**. :]

Now you've implemented the basic `Text()`, it's best to see what other functionality `Text()` provides. Take a moment to check out what `Text()` has to offer by inspecting the source code:

```
@Composable
fun Text(
    text: String,
```

```
    modifier: Modifier = Modifier,
    color: Color = Color.Unspecified,
    fontSize: TextUnit = TextUnit.Unspecified,
    fontStyle: FontStyle? = null,
    fontWeight: FontWeight? = null,
    fontFamily: FontFamily? = null,
    letterSpacing: TextUnit = TextUnit.Unspecified,
    textDecoration: TextDecoration? = null,
    textAlign: TextAlign? = null,
    lineHeight: TextUnit = TextUnit.Unspecified,
    overflow: TextOverflow = TextOverflow.Clip,
    softWrap: Boolean = true,
    maxLines: Int = Int.MAX_VALUE,
    onTextLayout: (TextLayoutResult) -> Unit = {},
    style: TextStyle = LocalTextStyle.current
)
```

It offers a wide range of parameters for different style treatments. The first, `text`, lets you set the text to display and is the **only required parameter**.

The second, `modifier`, is more complex and offers many different features. In the previous example, you saw how `Column()` used modifiers to fill the parent size. Modifiers allow you to customize the look and feel of your composables. You'll learn more about modifiers in Chapter 6, "Using Compose Modifiers".

For now, take a moment to explore some of the parameters the `Text()` element exposes. Below is a short list of the most common ones:

- **color**: Lets you set the text color.
- **fontSize**: Changes the font size. You measure it in **scalable pixels (sp)**.
- **fontStyle**: Lets you choose between normal and italic font.
- **fontWeight**: Sets the weight of the text to **Bold**, **Black**, **Thin** and similar types.
- **textAlign**: Sets the horizontal alignment of the text.
- **overflow**: Determines how the app handles overflow, using either **Clip** or **Ellipsis**.
- **maxLines**: Sets the maximum number of lines.
- **style**: Lets you build a specific style and reuse it, rather than explicitly setting all the other parameters. The current app theme defines the default style, making it easier to support different **themes**.

There are many more parameters, but these are the most important and commonly-used ones.

If you want to know more about `Text()` , use **Command-Click** on Mac or **Control-Click** on Windows or Linux to click on the `Text` function call, and preview the source code and documentation.

Now you've displayed text in your UI, it's time to style it to make it look nicer! :]

Styling Your Text

In this section you'll display the text in *italics* with **bold** weight. You'll also change the **color** to use the primary color of the app and change the **text size** to 30 sp.

Change `MyText()`'s code to the following:

```
@Composable
fun MyText() {
  Text(text = stringResource(id = R.string.jetpack_compose),
       fontStyle = FontStyle.Italic, // 1
       color = colorResource(id = R.color.colorPrimary), // 2
       fontSize = 30.sp, // 3
       fontWeight = FontWeight.Bold // 4
  )
}
```

There are a few things happening here:

1. Using `fontStyle`, you make the text *italicized* by using `FontStyle.Italic`.
2. Passing in a `color`, you change the color of the text. Also notice how `colorResource()` lets you easily fetch a color from your resources.
3. The `fontSize` parameter lets you pass in the size in **scalable pixels**. Notice the `.sp` property call. Compose has a way to transform `Integer` values into `dp` and `sp` by calling respective properties! These are extension properties, so make sure to add the `.` operator.
4. Finally, `fontWeight` makes the text **bold**.

Now build and run the project and open the Text screen to see the new version of your styled text:

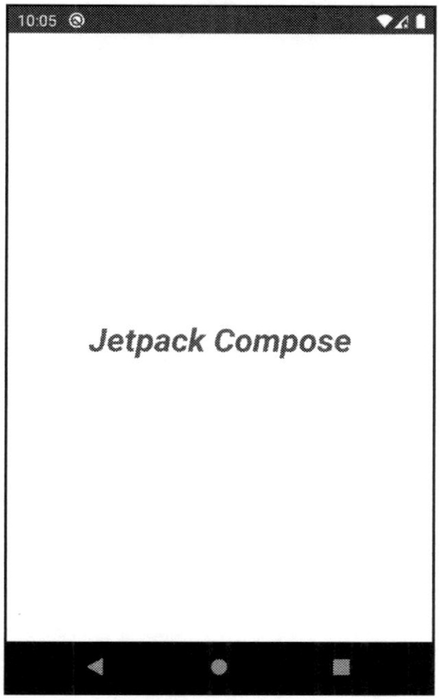

Styled Text

You've applied all the styles and the text looks much nicer! Feel free to experiment with other parameters and change the text to your own liking.

Upto now, you've had to build and run your app every time you made a change in the `Text` before you could see the result. This makes building complex UI a tedious process because running and building the app for each change takes time. You'll now learn how to avoid that and make your life easier!

Previewing Changes

When you work with XML, there's an option to split the screen so you can see both the code and a preview of your UI. You'll be happy to know Compose offers a similar option!

To use it, you need to annotate your composable function with **@Preview**, like so:

```
@Composable
@Preview
fun MyText() {
  Text(...)
}
```

This allows the Compose compiler to analyze the composable function and generate a preview of it within Android Studio. Now, select the **Split** option on the top-right side of Android Studio. You'll see a preview like this:

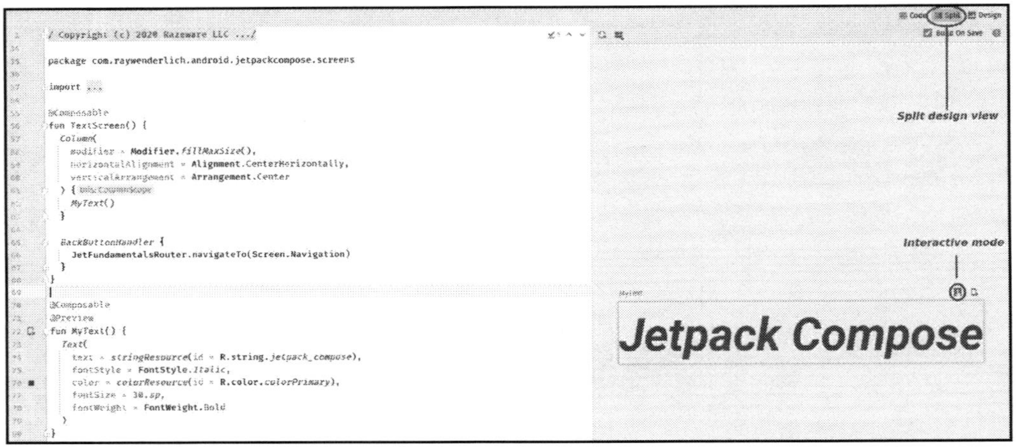

Preview

You can also click the small icon above the preview to enter interactive mode. This lets you perform actions and see how the state changes. You don't need that for the current screen, but it helps when building interactive UI components that require user input.

One thing to keep in mind is that if you're using preview, your functions need to either:

- Have no parameters
- Have default arguments for all parameters
- Provide a `@PreviewParameter` as well as a special factory that provides the parameters you want to draw on the UI

You just added your very first composable to the screen, awesome job! But showing static text is a bit dull! Next, you'll see how to implement an input field, so users can write something in the app!

TextField

In the legacy Android UI toolkit, you'd use an `EditText` to show input fields to the user. The composable counterpart for an `EditText` is called a `TextField`.

Open **TextFieldScreen.kt** and you'll see two composable functions:

```
@Composable
fun TextFieldScreen() {
  Column(
      modifier = Modifier.fillMaxSize(),
      horizontalAlignment = Alignment.CenterHorizontally,
      verticalArrangement = Arrangement.Center
  ) {
    MyTextField()
  }

  BackButtonHandler {
    JetFundamentalsRouter.navigateTo(Screen.Navigation)
  }
}

@Composable
fun MyTextField() {
  //TODO add your code here
}
```

You'll make your first `TextField` inside `MyTextField()`, similar to what you did in the previous example. Change the code in `MyTextField()` like so:

```
@Composable
fun MyTextField() {
  val textValue = remember { mutableStateOf("") }

  TextField(
    value = textValue.value,
    onValueChange = {
      textValue.value = it
    },
    label = {}
  )
}
```

Make sure you import the `TextField` package from **androidx.compose.material** and the `remember()` and `mutableStateOf()` packages from **androidx.compose.runtime**.

That seems like a lot of code for a simple input field, but it will make sense in a minute!

A `TextField` should allow the user to input text, and the entered text must not disappear or change if the `TextField` recomposes. For your `TextField` to work properly, you must provide a value that **doesn't change during recomposition** — in other words, a **state** value. Using `mutableStateOf()`, you wrap an empty `String` into a state holder, which you'll use to store and display the text within the input field.

You also wrapped the state into `remember()`, which is Compose's way of telling the recomposer that the value should be persisted through recomposition. If you didn't use `remember()` here, every time you changed the state, it would be **lost and set to the default** value — an empty string.

Next, you connected the value of the `textValue` holder to the `TextField`, and within the `onValueChange` callback, you changed the internal value of the state holder.

What's going to happen now is every time the user taps on a key on their keyboard, the internal state will change. This will trigger recomposition and re-drawing the `TextField` with new text. That's all going to happen really fast, and you won't be able to notice a difference!

Build and run the app to see your changes. Click the **TextField** button from the navigation and you'll see a screen like this:

Non-Styled Text Field

It's a screen with an empty `TextField`. When you click on that text, a keyboard opens and you can write normally, as you'd expect.

Improving the TextField

If you take a closer look at the screen, you'll see the current `TextField` is very basic. It's missing a **hint** and some expected default styling, like a border.

To add the hint and the border, you'll use a special type of `TextField` called `OutlinedTextField`. But before you do that, explore the signature of the `TextField` so you know how you can style the component.

Take a look at the `TextField` signature, and you'll see something like this:

```
@Composable
fun TextField(
    value: TextFieldValue,
    onValueChange: (String) -> Unit,
    label: @Composable () -> Unit,
    keyboardOptions: KeyboardOptions = KeyboardOptions.Default,
    keyboardActions: KeyboardActions = KeyboardActions(),
    ...
)
```

Like the `Text` composable function, `TextField` has many parameters to change its style. Since some of the parameters are the same, this section will only explain the most important new ones.

- **value**: The current text displayed inside the `TextField`. Note that it's of type `TextFieldValue` and not `String`.
- **onValueChange**: A callback that triggers every time the user types something new. The callback provides a new `TextFieldValue` so you can update the displayed text.
- **label**: The label that's displayed inside the container. When the user focuses on the text, the label will animate above the writing cursor and stay there.
- **keyboardOptions**: Sets the keyboard options such as `KeyboardType` and `ImeAction`. Some available `KeyboardTypes` are: **Email**, **Password** and **Number** while important `ImeActions` are: **Go**, **Search**, **Previous**, **Next** and **Done**.
- **keyboardActions**: Allows the developer to set callbacks for keyboard `ImeActions`.

There are many more parameters, but these are some of the core features you'll use in most apps.

Feel free to explore these parameters and play around with them. When you're ready, move onto the `OutlinedTextField` component, a **material design** inspired input field! :]

Adding an Email Field With OutlinedTextField

Your next step is to create an email input, one of the most common text fields. Replace the code of `MyTextField` with the following:

```
@Composable
fun MyTextField() {
  val textValue = remember { mutableStateOf("") }

  val primaryColor = colorResource(id = R.color.colorPrimary)

  OutlinedTextField(
    label = { Text(text = stringResource(id =
R.string.email)) },
    colors = TextFieldDefaults.outlinedTextFieldColors(
        focusedBorderColor = primaryColor,
        focusedLabelColor = primaryColor,
        cursorColor = primaryColor
    ),
    keyboardOptions = KeyboardOptions.Default.copy(keyboardType
= KeyboardType.Email),
    value = textValue.value,
    onValueChange = {
      textValue.value = it
    },
  )
}
```

An `OutlinedTextField` is a styled `TextField`, it uses a special internal function to draw and animate a border around the field and a description text. This composable is most similar to the `TextInputLayout` XML widget that ships with the material library.

To add a **hint**, or a **label** as it's known in Compose, you use the `label` property and pass in another composable function. This is the beauty of Compose — whenever you need some functionality, you can use other composable functions to fill that need. In this case, you need to display a text that gives the user a hint about what the input data should be by using a `Text()`.

The second parameter you added is `colors`. It changes the colors for different parts of the `TextField`. In this case, you use the primary color from resources to change the border and label colors in focused state and cursor color.

The last change is to change the `keyboardType` to `KeyboardType.Email`. To do this you use the `KeyboardOptions.Default` instance of `KeyboardOptions` and make a new copy of the object with the desired `keyboardType`. This will open a keyboard that makes it easier to write email domains when `TextField` is in focus.
Build and run your app to test your new email input. The **TextField** screen will look like this:

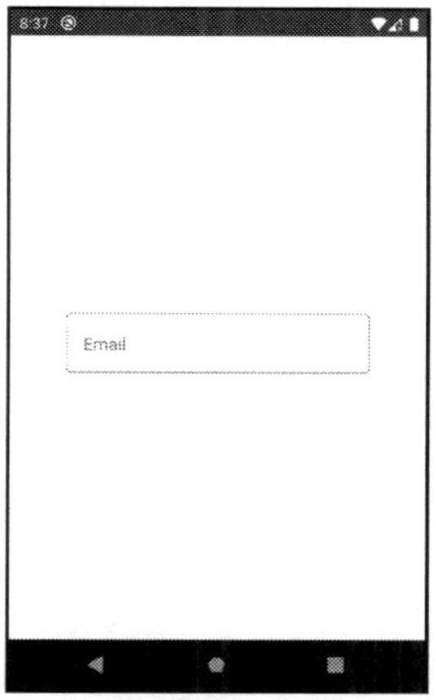

Styled TextField

The text field has a border and a hint that reads: **Email**. Click it to gain focus.

Focused TextField

The hint **animates** to the top of the border and your text field comes to life in green. Next, you'll learn how to add a **button** and how to handle click events.

Buttons

With what you've learned so far, you know how to read text from a screen and how to display it. The last thing you need to make a basic form is a **button**.

There are many types of buttons in the Android world, but all of them have one thing in common, they can be clicked. Next, you'll see how to implement one, and how to handle the click actions!

Open **ButtonsScreen.kt** and look at the code:

```
@Composable
fun ExploreButtonsScreen() {
  Column(
    modifier = Modifier.fillMaxSize(),
    horizontalAlignment = Alignment.CenterHorizontally,
    verticalArrangement = Arrangement.Center
  ) {

    MyButton()
    MyRadioGroup()
    MyFloatingActionButton()

    BackButtonHandler {
      JetFundamentalsRouter.navigateTo(Screen.Navigation)
    }
  }
}

@Composable
fun MyButton() {
  //TODO add your code here
}

@Composable
fun MyRadioGroup() {
  //TODO add your code here
}

@Composable
fun MyFloatingActionButton() {
  //TODO add your code here
}
```

You can see there are four composable functions in the file. `ExploreButtonsScreen()` centers and displays the main layout. You'll use the three empty functions to practice working with the different types of buttons.

Building a Login Button

First, you'll make the basic button you'd expect to see while logging in. Start by adding the following code to `MyButton()`:

```
@Composable
fun MyButton() {
  Button(
    onClick = {},
    colors = ButtonDefaults.buttonColors(backgroundColor =
colorResource(id = R.color.colorPrimary)),
    border = BorderStroke(
      1.dp,
      color = colorResource(id = R.color.colorPrimaryDark)
    )
  ) {
    Text(
      text = stringResource(id = R.string.button_text),
      color = Color.White
    )
  }
}
```

In the code above, you aren't performing any actions when the user clicks the button. However, you are using an **empty lambda expression** as `onClick` to keep it enabled.

To change the background color of the button, you use the `ButtonDefaults` instance and call `buttonColors` method on it with the desired background color as a parameter. This method also allows you to change `disabledBackgroundColor`, `contentColor` and `disabledContentColor` if needed.

You also use a `BorderStroke` to set the background color and add a border with a width of **1 dp** and a dark primary color. Each `BorderStroke` has to define a color and its width. You can add them to many components, such as buttons, cards and much more.

Finally, you add a `Text()` as the content of the button, as you learned previously, and set the text color to `Color.White`. The `Color` component is another part of the Compose framework that defines commonly used colors like `White`, `Black`, `Gray` and so on.

Now, build and run the app and open the **Buttons** screen.

Button

This is how a button with a border looks in Jetpack Compose. It's a simple component following Material Design. You haven't added any specific actions within the `onClick` handler, but you get the idea! You can set it up to call any functions you want to execute, any time the user taps the button.

Exploring Button

Now, look at the signature of a `Button` composable function to see what it can do:

```
@Composable
fun Button(
    onClick: () -> Unit,
    enabled: Boolean = true,
    elevation: Dp = 2.dp,
    shape: Shape = MaterialTheme.shapes.small,
    border: BorderStroke? = null,
    content: @Composable RowScope.() -> Unit,
    ...
)
```

Below is a list of the the most important parameters to get a better understanding:

- **onClick**: The most common property you'll use with buttons, this calls a function when the user clicks the button. If you don't provide `onClick`, the button will be disabled.
- **enabled**: Allows you to control when a button is clickable.
- **elevation**: Sets the elevation of a button. The default elevation is **2 dp**.
- **shape**: Defines the button's shape and shadow. With `MaterialTheme.shapes`, you can choose a shape's size: **small**, **medium** or **large**. Or you can specify a custom shape as well.
- **border**: Draws a border around your button.
- **content**: A composable function that displays the content inside the button, usually text.

Again, there are many more parameters, but for the sake of simplicity, only the most important ones are listed.

Now that you know what's possible with `Button`, you can create as many buttons, along with their borders and background colors, as you need!

Next, you'll make a radio button or, more specifically, a group of radio buttons.

RadioButton

The composable function you use to make radio buttons is named **RadioButton**. A radio button is a small, circular button the user can select. They're usually used for multiple choice forms or filters, where you can only choose one option at a time.

For example, you might have one radio button to opt in to receiving a newsletter and another to opt out, and only one of the two choices can be selected at the same time. This type of component is called a **radio group**.

At this time, Jetpack Compose doesn't have an implementation for a radio group so you'll have to make a custom group yourself! Don't worry though, you will get a sense of how easy it is to fill some of the API's gaps yourself.

Change the code in `MyRadioGroup` to the following:

```
@Composable
fun MyRadioGroup() {
  val radioButtons = listOf(0, 1, 2) // 1
```

```
  val selectedButton = remember
{ mutableStateOf(radioButtons.first()) } // 2

  Column {
    radioButtons.forEach { index -> // 3
      val isSelected = index == selectedButton.value
      val colors = RadioButtonDefaults.colors( // 4
        selectedColor = colorResource(id =
R.color.colorPrimary),
        unselectedColor = colorResource(id =
R.color.colorPrimaryDark),
        disabledColor = Color.LightGray
      )

      RadioButton( // 5
        colors = colors,
        selected = isSelected,
        onClick = { selectedButton.value = index } // 6
      )
    }
  }
}
```

There's a lot going on in the snippet above so here's a breakdown to make it easier to understand:

1. You create a list of three different options with values ranging from `0` to 2. These options are indices representing each radio button.
2. You create a `selectedButton` state that remembers which button is selected. It also selects the first button by default.
3. Using a `forEach` loop, you add a button to your `Column` in each iteration of the loop.
4. You can change the color of a `RadioButton` using the `RadioButtonDefaults.colors()`. You pass in a color for each of the different states `RadioButton` can appear in.
5. At the end of each loop iteration, you build a `RadioButton` and set both the `onClick` handler and its color when it's selected.
6. Every time a user taps the button, you'll change which button is selected in the state. This triggers a **recomposition** and your UI will update!

Now, build and run your app to try your new creation.

Radio Button

You now see three radio buttons on the screen. The first is selected by default. When you select another radio button, you can see the animation that switches between the buttons.

Exploring RadioButton

To learn more about `RadioButton`, look at its signature:

```
@Composable
fun RadioButton(
    selected: Boolean,
    onClick: () -> Unit,
    modifier: Modifier = Modifier,
    enabled: Boolean = true,
    interactionState: InteractionState = remember
{ InteractionState() },
    colors: RadioButtonColors = RadioButtonDefaults.colors()
)
```

There are fewer parameters than usual, here are the most important ones:

- **selected**: Toggles the current state of the button between selected and not selected.
- **interactionState**: Allows you to define interactions such as drag gestures and touches.
- **colors**: The color combination for the `RadioButton`. Use the `RadioButtonDefaults` instance to call `colors()` on it to change the default color for different states. The available colors for different states are `selectedColor`, `unselectedColor` and `disabledColor`.

You're almost done with this overview of commonly used UI components. There's one more type of buttons for you to complete — `FloatingActionButtons`!

FloatingActionButton

Floating action buttons are named that way because they have a higher elevation that places them above all content. They're used to place the primary action of your app within easy reach for your users.

For your next step, you'll create a simple floating action button using an icon. Start by changing the code in the `MyFloatingActionButton` to the following:

```
@Composable
fun MyFloatingActionButton() {
  FloatingActionButton(
      onClick = {},
      backgroundColor = colorResource(id =
R.color.colorPrimary),
      contentColor = Color.White,
      content = {
        Icon(Icons.Filled.Favorite, contentDescription = "Test
FAB")
      }
  )
}
```

Here, you add an **empty lambda expression** to keep the button enabled. Next, you set the **background and content color**. Finally, you set the **icon** by using `Icon()` and the predefined, filled, `Favorite` icon and a test `contentDescription` for accessibility.

The `Icons` object contains predefined and commonly used icons in the Android world in their vector form. Similar to what the `Color` object does for colors. You can choose between `Filled`, `Default`, and `Outlined` style treatment for these default icons.

Exploring FloatingActionButton

To learn more about the `FloatingActionButton`, check out its signature:

```
@Composable
fun FloatingActionButton(
    onClick: () -> Unit,
    modifier: Modifier = Modifier,
    shape: Shape =
MaterialTheme.shapes.small.copy(CornerSize(percent = 50)),
    backgroundColor: Color = MaterialTheme.colors.secondary,
    contentColor: Color = contentColorFor(backgroundColor),
    elevation: FloatingActionButtonElevation =
FloatingActionButtonDefaults.elevation(),
    content: @Composable () -> Unit
)
```

You're already familiar with most, if not all of the, parameters. The important thing to remember here is a `FloatingActionButton` has an elevation, is clickable and you add content to it by using another composable function. In most cases, you'll want to use an `Icon()` for the content. The signature of an `Icon()` is very simple:

```
@Composable
fun Icon(
   imageVector: ImageVector,
   contentDescription: String?,
   modifier: Modifier = Modifier,
   tint: Color = LocalContentColor.current.copy(alpha =
LocalContentAlpha.current)
)
```

`Icon`'s main feature is it allows you to set a vector of the `ImageVector` type, which serves as an icon. There are multiple implementations of `Icon`, which allow you to provide different types of assets, such as `ImageBitmap` and `Painter`!

Now you've finished the `FloatingActionButton`, build and run the app to see the result.

Action Button

Your floating action button appears with a **favorite** icon in the shape of a heart. When you click it, it produces a **ripple** effect. You can also notice it has a small shadow underneath it, because of its elevation.

The buttons look awesome, and you've learned a lot about them! Nice job! :]

More Buttons to Use

Here's a brief overview of the other types of buttons in Jetpack Compose:

- **IconButton**: Similar to a floating action button but without the floating part — it has no elevation. It's commonly used for navigation.
- **OutlinedButton**: Similar to an `OutlinedTextField`, this offers additional functionality like borders.

- **IconToggleButton**: Has two states for icons that you can toggle on and off.
- **TextButton**: Most commonly found in cards and dialogs, use this button for less pronounced actions.

After learning about all those buttons, you're ready to move on and discover new elements.

Progress Bars

When you perform long operations like fetching data from a server or a database, it's good practice to show a progress bar. The progress bar reduces the feeling of waiting too long by displaying an **animation**, and it gives the user a sense something is happening.

When you only want the user to know that work is taking place, spinning animated progress bars are a good choice.

In cases where you want to track progress and show the user how close they are to finishing the work, you want a progress bar that fills with a color as the progress occurs. This is very common when downloading or uploading files!

Jetpack Compose offers solutions to handle both cases. Open **ProgressIndicatorScreen.kt** and notice there's only one composable function in this file:

```
@Composable
fun ProgressIndicatorScreen() {

  Column(
      modifier = Modifier.fillMaxSize(),
      horizontalAlignment = Alignment.CenterHorizontally,
      verticalArrangement = Arrangement.Center
  ) {
    //TODO add your code here
  }

  BackButtonHandler {
    JetFundamentalsRouter.navigateTo(Screen.Navigation)
  }
}
```

That's because it's so easy to display progress bars with Jetpack Compose that you don't need additional custom composable functions.

Try it out by adding one circular and one linear progress bar inside `Column()` like so:

```
Column(
   modifier = Modifier.fillMaxSize(),
   horizontalAlignment = Alignment.CenterHorizontally,
   verticalArrangement = Arrangement.Center
) {
  CircularProgressIndicator(
      color = colorResource(id = R.color.colorPrimary),
      strokeWidth = 5.dp
  )
  LinearProgressIndicator(progress = 0.5f)
}
```

The column should stay as-is — it's only there to position the elements inside it, and to center them.

You're building both types of progress indicators here. First, you build the `CircularProgressIndicator`, defining an indicator `color` and a `strokeWidth`. These properties serve as styling. You don't have to define the animation yourself, it's already pre-baked into the component!

Then, you build the `LinearProgressIndicator`, and you set its progress to be 50%. Usually, you'd update this progress as your operations are computed within the system, but for the sake of simplicity, you'll make it static for this exercise.

Exploring the Progress Indicators

Since these are really simple components to implement, they also have very simple definitions. Open the `CircularProgressIndicator` signature, and you'll see the following:

```
@Composable
fun CircularProgressIndicator(
   progress: Float,
   modifier: Modifier = Modifier,
   color: Color = MaterialTheme.colors.primary,
   strokeWidth: Dp = ProgressIndicatorDefaults.StrokeWidth
)
```

This function offers a small range of styling. The most important parameter is the progress, which ranges from `0.0` to `1.0` — the number determines the filled ratio of the progress bar. If you don't set the progress, the progress bar will run an infinite spinning animation.

The other styling options change the color and the stroke width. The default stroke width is **4 dp**.

On the other hand, the `LinearProgressIndicator` signaturelooks like this:

```
@Composable
fun LinearProgressIndicator(
  /*@FloatRange(from = 0.0, to = 1.0)*/
  progress: Float,
  modifier: Modifier = Modifier,
  color: Color = MaterialTheme.colors.primary,
  backgroundColor: Color = color.copy(alpha =
IndicatorBackgroundOpacity)
)
```

The options are almost the same, except it doesn't offer the ability to change the stroke width. Though you usually use a linear progress bar to indicate **static** progress, you can also use it with an infinite animation by not setting the `progress` parameter. The animation will then go from left to right until the operation completes.

Now you've explored these progress bars, build and run the app, then open the **Progress** screen from the navigation menu:

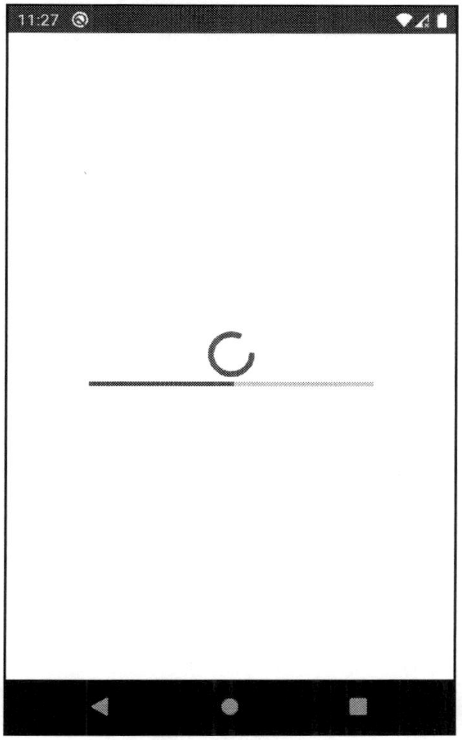

Progress Bars

You can see two progress bars on the screen. The circular one is always spinning in animation while the linear one stays static at the halfway point.

This example shows how simple Jetpack Compose makes it to implement the most common features you use while making apps!

Now, it's time to learn about a more complex element, where you'll have to handle states and actions.

AlertDialog

The next composable function you'll implement is an `AlertDialog`. Dialogs are used to alert the user about an action, or to request confirmation. For example, you can use a dialog to confirm whether the user wants to delete an item, request they rate the app and so on. They are very common in apps, and are used across all operating systems — not just Android!

The most important part of working with a dialog is to handle the state that determines when to show or dismiss that dialog. You'll start by adding an alert dialog that has only one button: **Confirm**. The dialog will close when the user clicks the button or clicks outside the dialog.

To implement this behavior, open **AlertDialogScreen.kt** and change code inside `MyAlertDialog` to the following:

```
@Composable
fun MyAlertDialog() {
  val shouldShowDialog = remember { mutableStateOf(true) } // 1

  if (shouldShowDialog.value) { // 2
    AlertDialog( // 3
      onDismissRequest = { // 4
        shouldShowDialog.value = false
        JetFundamentalsRouter.navigateTo(Screen.Navigation)
      },
      // 5
      title = { Text(text = stringResource(id =
R.string.alert_dialog_title)) },
      text = { Text(text = stringResource(id =
R.string.alert_dialog_text)) },
      confirmButton = { // 6
        Button(
          colors = ButtonDefaults.buttonColors(backgroundColor =
colorResource(id = R.color.colorPrimary)),
          onClick = {
            shouldShowDialog.value = false
```

```
                JetFundamentalsRouter.navigateTo(Screen.Navigation)
              }
            ) {
              Text(
                text = stringResource(id = R.string.confirm),
                color = Color.White
              )
            }
          }
        )
      }
    }
```

That is a lot of code you had to add, but it's mostly using components you've previously encountered. Let's go through it step-by-step:

1. You add a state representing whether to show the dialog or not, and sets the initial state to `true`.

2. Using an `if` statement, you add logic to display the `AlertDialog` only if the state value is `true`. Because Compose renders the UI by calling functions, if the value is `false`, it won't call the function — and in turn, it won't display the dialog!

3. Using `AlertDialog()`, you create your dialog, which has a `title`, a `text` message, a **dismiss request handler**, and a `confirmButton()`.

4. In `onDismissRequest`, you change the state of the dialog to dismiss it, then tell `Navigation` to return to the main navigation screen. `JetFundamentalsRouter` is a pre-baked class used for navigation. You need to call `navigateTo` and add the screen you want to go to as a parameter.

5. You set the `title` and `text` as two `Text()`s and use the provided `stringResources()` to fill it.

6. Finally, you add a `Button()` as the `confirmButton`. Clicking the button dismisses the dialog and navigates to the main navigation screen, just like in `onDismissRequest()`. You add a `Text()` to display the text inside the button with a white color and a predefined string resource.

Now you've prepared the dialog, build and run the app. On the navigation menu, select the **Alert Dialog** screen.

Alert Dialog

Upon opening the screen, an alert dialog automatically appears. It has a basic title and the text you set. Clicking outside the dialog or inside the confirm button dismisses the dialog and returns you to the previous screen.

Implementing the alert dialog might have looked complicated due to the code size, but most of the code only dealt with styling the alert and handling click events.

Dialogs are easy to create in Jetpack Compose, but keep in mind that you have to handle the state, which requires more effort when you want to reuse dialogs on multiple screens.

Exploring AlertDialog

It's important to note that the `AlertDialog` composable you used comes from the `androidx.compose.material` package, meaning, it is built using the Material Design specs. There are several types of dialogs but the most common type is the `AlertDialog` you used, so open its signature to see what it can do:

```
@Composable
fun AlertDialog(
  onDismissRequest: () -> Unit,
  confirmButton: @Composable () -> Unit,
```

```
    modifier: Modifier = Modifier,
    dismissButton: @Composable (() -> Unit)? = null,
    title: @Composable (() -> Unit)? = null,
    text: @Composable (() -> Unit)? = null,
    shape: Shape = MaterialTheme.shapes.medium,
    backgroundColor: Color = MaterialTheme.colors.surface,
    contentColor: Color = contentColorFor(backgroundColor),
    properties: DialogProperties = DialogProperties()
)
```

There are new parameters to go through here:

- **onDismissRequest**: Executes when a user clicks outside the dialog or presses the **Back** button.
- **confirmButton**: A button that confirms a proposed action. It's usually a `TextButton`.
- **dismissButton**: This button dismisses an action. It's also usually a `TextButton`.
- **title**: Sets the title text with a composable function.
- **text**: Sets the text inside the dialog with a composable function.
- **contentColor**: The color used by elements within the `AlertDialog`.
- **properties**: Platform-specific properties for further customization.

Throughout this chapter you saw how simple and straightforward Compose APIs are but most importantly how you can mix and match different Composables, slot them together and build larger, more complex pieces of UI.

This is the power of this new framework, it abstracts away the unnecessary complexity and lets you focus on the important bits. Over the course of the next few chapters you will learn how to harness this capability even further to build more complex screens and UIs.

For now, great job going through all of these fundamental components and learning so much about Jetpack Compose! :]

Key Points

- Create composable functions with `@Composable` annotation.
- Use `setContent()` inside an `Activity` as the root of your composable functions.
- Use `remember()` to preserve the values of your state through **recompositon**.
- Preview your composable functions by adding `@Preview`.
- `Text()` displays a simple text.
- `TextField()` allows you to retrieve input from a user. For more styling options, use `OutlinedTextField()`.
- Use `Button()` as the primary element of your app that handles click events.
- Use `RadioButton()` as an element that the user can select. To make a group of radio buttons, you have to write the logic yourself.
- Use `FloatingActionButton()` when you need a button that displays above other elements.
- `CircularProgressIndicator()` and `LinearProgressIndicator()` allow you to either track progress or show a loading animation.
- `AlertDialog()` is simple to use but requires state handling to work correctly.
- **Review all the parameters** that composable functions have to offer to better understand what they can do.
- Use `Icons` and `Color` objects to access a list of predefined icons and colors prepared by the Jetpack Compose framework.

Where to Go From Here?

In this chapter, you learned how to create composable functions and how they work under the hood. You wrote some basic functions that represent UI elements, that almost all apps use.

If you want to learn more about different Material Design-based components, check out the official reference guide: https://developer.android.com/reference/kotlin/androidx/compose/material/package-summary on the Android developer documentation website.

In the next chapter, you'll learn how to use containers such as `Column`, `Row`, `Box`, and how to group and position different elements to create a more complex user interface!

Chapter 3: Building Layout Groups in Compose

By Tino Balint

In this chapter, you'll learn about layouts in Jetpack Compose. Each layout has a specific usecase, and you'll learn how to pick the right one for the UI you want to build. Finally, you'll group composable functions inside different kinds of layouts to make a more complex UI.

In the previous chapter, you focused on displaying the elements onscreen; this time, you'll focus on positioning those elements.

As always, it's best to start with the basics. Read on to discover what the Jetpack Compose replacements for the basic layouts in Android are.

Using Basic Layouts in Jetpack Compose

In the previous chapter, you learned how to write basic composable functions. The next step is to build a more complex UI by positioning those elements in a specific way—arranging them.

When working with XML, you achieve that by using a layout, a class that extends `ViewGroup`. `ViewGroup` can hold zero or more views and is responsible for measuring all of its children and positioning them on the screen according to different rules.

In Jetpack Compose, the replacement for `ViewGroup` is called **Layout**. Look at the source code to understand how `Layout()` works:

```
@Composable inline fun Layout(
  content: @Composable () -> Unit,
  modifier: Modifier = Modifier,
  measurePolicy: MeasurePolicy
)
```

There are two important parameters here:

1. **content**: A composable function that holds children of the `Layout`.
2. **measurePolicy**: Responsible for defining measuring and layout behavior.

Measuring and positioning the elements is a complex job. That's why Jetpack Compose offers predefined layout types that handle this for you.

Every implementation of these predefined layouts has its own logic for positioning the children. With this in mind, there are layouts that order items vertically or horizontally, layouts that build complex UI with navigation drawers and simpler layouts, which stack children vertically. All of those layouts use `measurePolicy` to position items in different ways, so you don't have to do it yourself!

When thinking about basic layouts, the first thing that might come to mind is a `LinearLayout`. Your next step is to learn about `LinearLayout`'s composable counterpart.

Linear Layouts

To follow the code in this chapter, make sure to open this chapter's **starter** project, within the chapter materials.

A `LinearLayout` characteristically positions its children in a linear flow. This flow is called an **orientation** and can be horizontal or vertical. In Jetpack Compose, there are two different composable functions that replace `LinearLayout`, one for each orientation. You'll start with the horizontal version—a **Row**.

Using Rows

Open **RowScreen.kt** and look inside. You'll see an empty composable function, `MyRow()`, where you'll write your code. You'll add a `Row`, a `LinearLayout` counterpart, when it comes to horizontal layouts.

Start by replacing `MyRow()` with the following code:

```
@Composable
fun MyRow() {
  Row(verticalAlignment = Alignment.CenterVertically,
    horizontalArrangement = Arrangement.SpaceEvenly,
    modifier = Modifier.fillMaxSize()) {

    THREE_ELEMENT_LIST.forEach { textResId ->
      Text(
        text = stringResource(id = textResId),
        fontSize = 18.sp
      )
    }
  }
}
```

Here, you added a `Row()` with several different parameters.

You used `Alignment.CenterVertically` to center the children vertically, `Arrangement.SpaceEvenly` for each child to have an equal amount of space in between and `Modifier.fillMaxSize()` to make the layout fill the entire screen.

That final step is important because otherwise, a `Row` would take up only the space it needs to draw its children, since none of its children have weight defined. Without filling the screen size, the arrangement and alignment wouldn't matter and all items would be placed at the top-left of the screen, one after another. You'll learn more about weights in a moment.

Inside the `Row()`, you placed three `Texts` using a predefined list that holds string resources. You also increased their font size for readability.

Build and run, then tap on the **Row** button from the navigation menu and take a look at the screen:

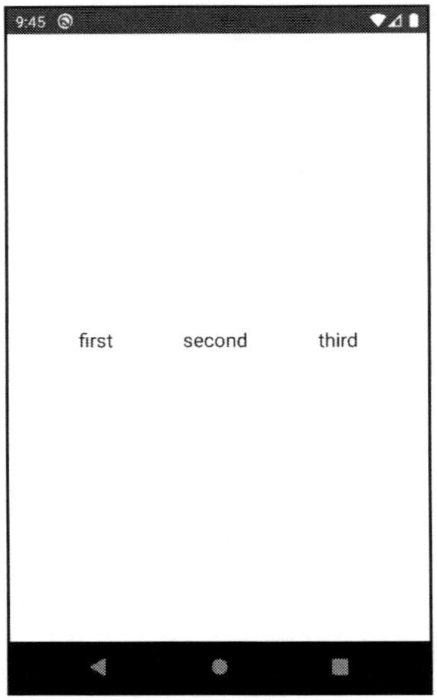

Row

You can see three text fields that are centered vertically and arranged so there's equal spacing on all sides.

> **Note**: This is a good time to experiment with different arrangements and observe their result.

Now that you know how to position elements horizontally inside a row, it's time to explore the `Row()` signature, to see what else you can do.

Exploring Rows

Open the `Row()` signature, to look at what you can do with it:

```
@Composable
inline fun Row(
```

```
    modifier: Modifier = Modifier,
    horizontalArrangement: Arrangement.Horizontal =
Arrangement.Start,
    verticalAlignment: Alignment.Vertical = Alignment.Top,
    content: @Composable RowScope.() -> Unit
)
```

As you see, there are two new parameters for you to work with: `horizontalArrangement` and `verticalAlignment`.

You use arrangements to position children relative to one another. The possible horizontal arrangements are:

- **SpaceBetween**: The `Row()` places each child with an equal amount of space, without calculating in spacing before the first child, or after the last child.
- **SpaceEvenly**: Similar to `SpaceBetween`, the `Row()` places the children with an equal amount of space, but this time it includes starting or ending spacing.
- **SpaceAround**: The `Row()` places children just like with `SpaceEvenly`, but reduces the space between consecutive children by half.
- **Center**, **Start**, **End**: The `Row()` places children at the center, start or end without space between them.

Using `Alignment` you position the children in a specific way within the parent. Specifically, `verticalAlignment` aligns the children vertically in three different ways:

- **Top**: Aligns the children to the top of the parent.
- **CenterVertically**: Aligns the children in the center of the parent, vertically.
- **Bottom**: Aligns the children to the bottom of the parent.

The final way to position children inside a `Row` is by using **weights**. To add weights, you need to use a special way to access the `weight()` modifier from Compose. In the above example with three `Text` elements, you could use it like so:

```
@Composable
fun RowScope.MyRow() { // This composable is called from inside
the Row
   Text(
     modifier = Modifier.weight(1 / 3f), // here
     ...
   )
}
```

You can set the `weight` of a composable by using a `modifier` parameter. The `weight` can only be set inside a `RowScope` which is a scope for the children of a `Row()`. If you're writing code directly inside the `Row()`, you can use `Modifier.weight()` without extra code.

If you need to make a custom composable that you use inside a `Row`, your composable needs to be an extension function of the `RowScope` like in the example above. Note that in this case, you won't be able to use the composable outside of a `Row()`.

Within `weight()` you define how big of a fraction of the parent the child will take up. In this case, you gave each child a third of the parent! :]

If a child doesn't have a weight, the `Row` will calculate its width using the preferred width first, e.g. using the `size()` modifier. It will then calculate the sizes of the children with weights, proportionally to their weight, based on the remaining available space.

This means if there is an element taking up `200dp` in width, and you use weights, the weighted children will take up the screen width, minus the `200dp` that's already taken. If none of the children have weight, the `Row()` will be as small as possible to fit all its children without spacing.

`Rows` represent *horizontal* arrangement of items, and such is its name. Following this logic, a vertical arrangement of items is called a **Column**. Let's see how to use it!

Using Columns

The Compose counterpart for a vertically-oriented `LinearLayout` is a `Column`.

Open **ColumnScreen.kt** and you'll see a similar situation as before—an empty `MyColumn()`, which you'll implement.

Fill in the function, so it looks like this:

```
@Composable
fun MyColumn() {
  Column(
    horizontalAlignment = Alignment.CenterHorizontally,
    verticalArrangement = Arrangement.SpaceEvenly,
    modifier = Modifier.fillMaxSize()
  ) {

    THREE_ELEMENT_LIST.forEach { textResId ->
      Text(
        text = stringResource(id = textResId),
```

```
            fontSize = 22.sp
          )
        }
      }
    }
```

The `Column()` implementation is the same as the `Row()`, except you swapped the arrangements and alignments from horizontal to vertical. This is because the items are already placed vertically in a `Column`, and you need to define how they **behave horizontally** and how to **space them vertically**. With `Rows`, the situation is the opposite—items are placed horizontally, and the `Row` needs to know how they **behave vertically** and how to **space them horizontally**.

Build and run and select the **Column** button from the navigation menu.

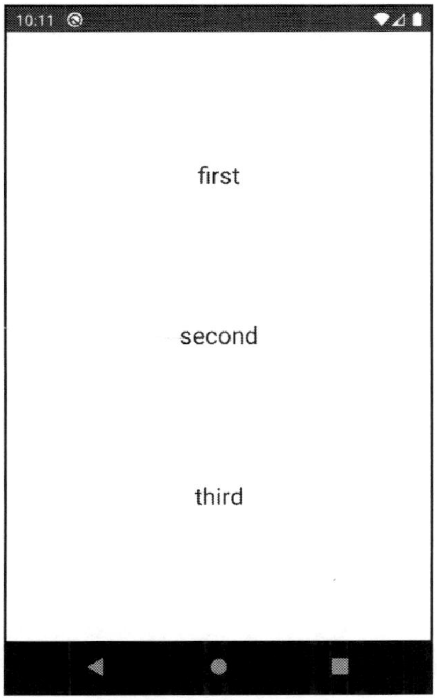

Column

This time, you see that the items are arranged vertically instead of horizontally, with the same spacing.

Now, you've seen how `Column` and `Row` are similar to `LinearLayouts`. They're more powerful, however, because you can arrange the children in several different ways—which the `LinearLayout` doesn't allow.

Exploring Columns

Now you've learned how to use `Columns`, check how they differ from a `Row`, by opening the `Column()` signature:

```
@Composable
inline fun Column(
  modifier: Modifier = Modifier,
  verticalArrangement: Arrangement.Vertical = Arrangement.Top,
  horizontalAlignment: Alignment.Horizontal = Alignment.Start,
  content: @Composable ColumnScope.() -> Unit
)
```

As you learned before, the parameters are almost the same, but take a closer look and you'll see that the layout swaps the arrangements and alignments. This means you can do all the same things inside the `Column` as in a `Row`, but with different orientations.

Next, you'll learn about a composable counterpart for a `FrameLayout`, called a **Box**.

Using Boxes

The composable counterpart for a `FrameLayout` is called a `Box`. Just like `FrameLayout`, it's used to display children relative to their parent's edges, and allows you to stack children. This is useful when you have elements that need to be displayed in those specific places or when you want to display elements that overlap, such as dialogs.

Now, open **BoxScreen.kt** and you'll find the usual empty function,`MyBox()`. Add the following code to complete it:

```
@Composable
fun MyBox(
  modifier: Modifier = Modifier,
  contentModifier: Modifier = Modifier
) {
  Box(modifier = modifier.fillMaxSize()) {
    Text(
      text = stringResource(id = R.string.first),
      fontSize = 22.sp,
      modifier = contentModifier.align(Alignment.TopStart)
    )

    Text(
      text = stringResource(id = R.string.second),
```

```
      fontSize = 22.sp,
      modifier = contentModifier.align(Alignment.Center)
    )

    Text(
      text = stringResource(id = R.string.third),
      fontSize = 22.sp,
      modifier = contentModifier.align(Alignment.BottomEnd)
    )
  }
}
```

This time, the function has two parameters—a `modifier` and a `contentModifier`, with default arguments of `Modifier`, the empty modifier implementation. This way, you can pass in custom modifiers that will change how the parent `Box` or each piece of content behaves. After which each element can chain more modifier function calls, to apply additional customization.

This is a good practice, as you can pass in a custom modifier that applies padding or styling to the parent `modifier`, and then reuse custom styles throughout your app, while the end component adds a bit more customization, based on the component. You can do the same for content based modifiers.

Here, the `Box()` has three text fields, as in previous examples, and uses the`align` modifier to position those text fields in three different places.

Build and run, then select the **Box** option from the navigation menu to see the result:

Box

The text fields appear diagonally across the screen, with the first one at the top-left corner, the second one in the center and the last one at the bottom-right corner.

Using a `Box` is really useful in specific situations, and they make positioning elements incredibly easy.

Exploring Boxes

When you have multiple children inside a `Box`, they're rendered in the same order as you placed them inside the `Box`. Here's the implementation:

```
@Composable
fun Box(
  modifier: Modifier = Modifier,
  contentAlignment: Alignment = Alignment.TopStart,
  propagateMinConstraints: Boolean = false,
  content: @Composable BoxScope.() -> Unit
)
```

`contentAlignment` allows you to set the default `Alignment` to its children. If you want to have different `Alignments` between each child, you need to set `Alignment` by using `Modifier.align()` on a child.

`propagateMinConstraints` defines if the minimal constraints should be passed and used for the content too. By default, the constraints of the `Box()` won't be taken into account when measuring the children.

You can set the `Alignment` to any edge of the screen as well as in relation to the center, using any of the following types of alignment:

- **TopStart**
- **TopCenter**
- **TopEnd**
- **CenterStart**
- **Center**

- **CenterEnd**
- **BottomStart**
- **BottomCenter**
- **BottomEnd**

Where each of the alignments refers to which part of the screen the `Box` will attach an item to.

Next, you'll learn about one of the first layouts introduced in Jetpack Compose: the **Surface**.

Using Surfaces

`Surface` is a new layout that serves as a central metaphor in **Material Design**. What's unique about `Surface` is it can only hold one child at a time, but it provides many style treatments for the content of its children, such as the elevation, border and more.

It's time to see the `Surface` in action. Open **SurfaceScreen.kt** and look at the contents:

```
@Composable
fun SurfaceScreen(modifier: Modifier = Modifier) {

  Box(modifier = modifier.fillMaxSize()) {
    MySurface(modifier = modifier.align(Alignment.Center))
  }

  BackButtonHandler {
    JetFundamentalsRouter.navigateTo(Screen.Navigation)
  }
}

@Composable
fun MySurface(modifier: Modifier) {
  //TODO write your code here
}
```

To show all that the `Surface` can do, the example is set inside a full-screen `Box()` and an `Alignment.Center`. All that's left is to implement the empty `MySurface()`. To do this, add the following code to finish it:

```
@Composable
fun MySurface(modifier: Modifier) {
  Surface(
      modifier = modifier.size(100.dp), // 1
      color = Color.LightGray, // 2
      contentColor = colorResource(id =
R.color.colorPrimary), // 2
      elevation = 1.dp, // 3
      border = BorderStroke(1.dp, Color.Black) // 4
  ) {
    MyColumn() // 5
  }
}
```

There are many small steps in this code, so go over them one by one:

1. You first set the size of the surface to `100dp` in both height and width using `Modifier.size()`.
2. Then you set the color of the surface to `Color.LightGray` and the color of its content to `colorPrimary`. The surface will be gray, and `Surface` will set the `contentColor` to all the elements it applies to—such as `Text` elements.
3. You add an elevation of `1dp` to raise the `Surface` above other elements.
4. You also add a black border to outline the `Surface`.
5. Finally, you set the child to the `Surface` to be the `MyColumn()` you defined earlier.

This is a perfect example of the power of Jetpack Compose. You can **reuse** each of the screens and composable functions you implemented before. This time, you reused `MyColumn()`, with three vertical `Text` elements.

Build and run and select **Surface** from the navigation menu.

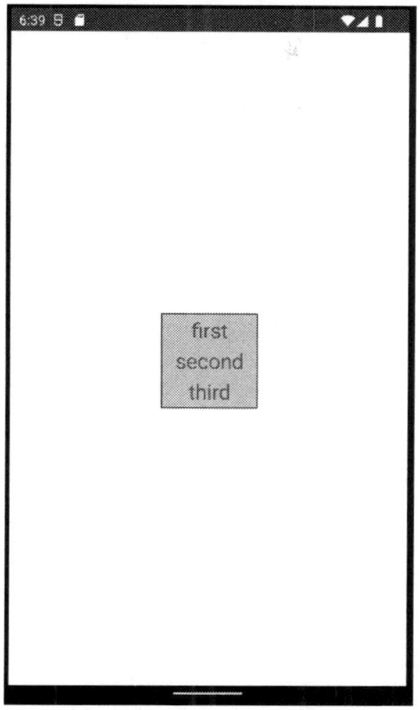

Surface

At the center of the screen is the `Surface` in a light gray color with a black border. Within it is the previously-implemented custom `Column`.

Previously, all the `Text` elements used the default, black color, but using `contentColor` you changed the text color of `Column`'s children to use a green color.

If you're reading the grayscale version of the book, you might not notice the color change as easily, so make sure to build and run the app and preview the changes directly on your phone!

Now let's see what else the `Surface()` allows you to do.

Exploring Surfaces

To see what else a `Surface()` has to offer, open its signature:

```
@Composable
fun Surface(
    modifier: Modifier = Modifier,
    shape: Shape = RectangleShape,
    color: Color = MaterialTheme.colors.surface,
    contentColor: Color = contentColorFor(color),
    border: BorderStroke? = null,
    elevation: Dp = 0.dp,
    content: @Composable () -> Unit
)
```

These parameters define `Surface`'s purpose. There are five purposes in total:

- **Shape**: Clips the children with the defined `shape`.
- **Color**: Fills the shape with a `color` you define.
- **Border**: Draws borders, if they're set.
- **Elevation**: Sets the elevation and draws an appropriate shadow.
- **Content**: Sets the default color for its content with the defined `contentColor`.

The most common way to use a `Surface` is as the root layout of your components. Since it can hold only one child, that child is usually another layout that positions the rest of the elements. The `Surface()` doesn't handle positioning—its child does.

> **Note**: There's a popular custom `Surface` implementation called `Card`. A `Card` has exactly the same five purposes and can only hold one child. The only difference between the `Card` and a `Surface` are its default parameters. A `Card` has a predefined elevation and uses a material theme shape with rounded corners.

Now that you've learned all the basic layouts available in Jetpack Compose, your next step is to learn about a more advanced layout that lets you create a fully-functional UI. That element is called a **Scaffold**.

Scaffold

The `Scaffold` is a new layout that Jetpack Compose introduced. You use it to implement a visual layout following the standard **Material Design** structure you are all familiar with by now. It combines several different material components to construct an entire screen. Because the `Scaffold()` offers multiple ways to build your UI, it's best to jump into the code, and play around with it!

Using Scaffold

Open **ScaffoldScreen.kt** and look inside. You'll see three empty composable functions:

```
@Composable
fun MyScaffold() {
  //todo write your code here
}

@Composable
fun MyTopAppBar(scaffoldState: ScaffoldState) {
  //todo write your code here
}

@Composable
fun MyBottomAppBar() {
  //todo write your code here
}
```

You'll use these empty functions to implement your own `Scaffold` and to add top and bottom app bars.

Start by entering the following code inside `MyScaffold()`. It should look like so:

```
@Composable
fun MyScaffold() {
  val scaffoldState: ScaffoldState = rememberScaffoldState()
  val scope: CoroutineScope = rememberCoroutineScope()

  Scaffold(
      scaffoldState = scaffoldState,
      contentColor = colorResource(id = R.color.colorPrimary),
      content = { MyRow() },
      topBar = { MyTopAppBar(scaffoldState = scaffoldState,
scope = scope) },
      bottomBar = { MyBottomAppBar() },
      drawerContent = { MyColumn() }
  )
}
```

First, you create the scaffold state by calling `rememberScaffoldState()`, then you assign it to the `Scaffold()`. You set `contentColor` to the primary color of the app and `content` to `MyRow()`, which you previously implemented.

Then you create a `scope`, using `rememberCoroutineScope()`. You need to use coroutines to trigger certain `Scaffold()` behavior, such as opening and closing the drawers.

Next, you set the top and bottom bar content to the composables you haven't implemented yet. Here you pass the `scaffoldState` and the scope that'll be used by coroutines.

Finally, you set `MyColumn()` as your drawer. There's a lot going on here, but you'll see how it connects together in a moment.

Make sure to update the `MyTopAppBar` signature to the following:

```
@Composable
fun MyTopAppBar(scaffoldState: ScaffoldState, scope:
CoroutineScope) {}
```

Build and run, then click the **Scaffold** option from the navigation menu.

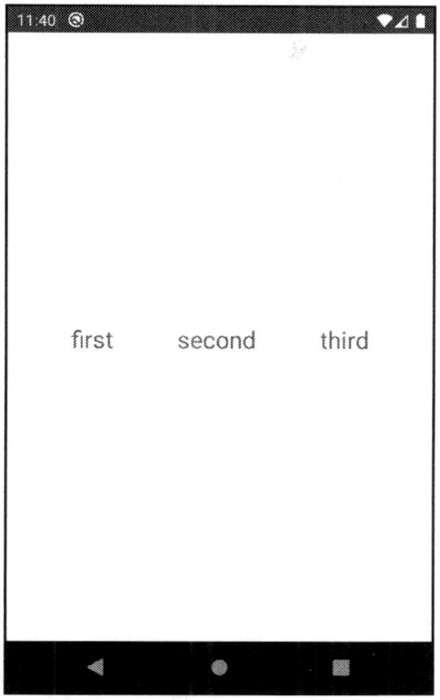

Scaffold

You can see the `MyRow()` with the three `Text` elements on the screen, but the top and bottom app bars aren't showing. That's not surprising since you haven't implemented them yet. :]

Additionally, you can open the navigation drawer by swiping from the left to the right side of the screen, to show the `MyColumn` from before.

Now let's finish the screen by implementing the top and bottom bars.

Completing the Screen

To complete the screen, implement the two remaining composables. Add the following code to complete `MyTopAppBar()`:

```
@Composable
fun MyTopAppBar(scaffoldState: ScaffoldState, scope:
CoroutineScope) {
  val drawerState = scaffoldState.drawerState

  TopAppBar(
```

```
    navigationIcon = {
      IconButton(
        content = {
          Icon(
            Icons.Default.Menu,
            tint = Color.White,
            contentDescription = stringResource(R.string.menu)
          )
        },
        onClick = {
          scope.launch { if (drawerState.isClosed)
drawerState.open() else drawerState.close() }
        }
      )
    },
    title = { Text(text = stringResource(id =
R.string.app_name), color = Color.White) },
    backgroundColor = colorResource(id = R.color.colorPrimary)
  )
}
```

First, you create a new value called `drawerState`, using the `scaffoldState`. You'll use this to access the `Scaffold`'s drawer.

Then, you add an existing predefined implementation of the `TopAppBar()`. You add an `IconButton()` with the `Menu` icon and `White` content color as the `navigationIcon`.

For the click action of the `IconButton()`, you initiate opening the drawer by changing the `drawerState` inside the `scaffoldState`.

To change the `drawerState`, you must do it from a coroutine or another suspend function. In this case you launch a coroutine by using the `scope` passed from the parent composable. This will open the drawer whenever you click the menu icon.

The `navigationIcon` is a predefined parameter you can use to define the first element in the `TopAppBar`, which usually represents a **Home** or **Back** button.

Then you define the `title`, represented by a simple `Text` element that shows the app name. Showing a title in the top bar is common pattern for most Android apps.

The `TopAppbar` is a pretty straightforward component that lets you define an `elevation`, a `backgroundColor`, `title` and `navigationIcon` separately, or combined in a single `content` function, and special `actions` that define another composable function for menu actions. Play around with other parameters to see how they style the `TopAppBar`.

Now, implement the `MyBottomAppBar()`:

```
@Composable
fun MyBottomAppBar() {
  BottomAppBar(
    content = {},
    backgroundColor = colorResource(id = R.color.colorPrimary))
}
```

For `MyBottomAppBar()`, you add an existing implementation of the bottom app bar with empty content. You also define `colorPrimary` as the background color.

Build and run again and check the changes to the screen:

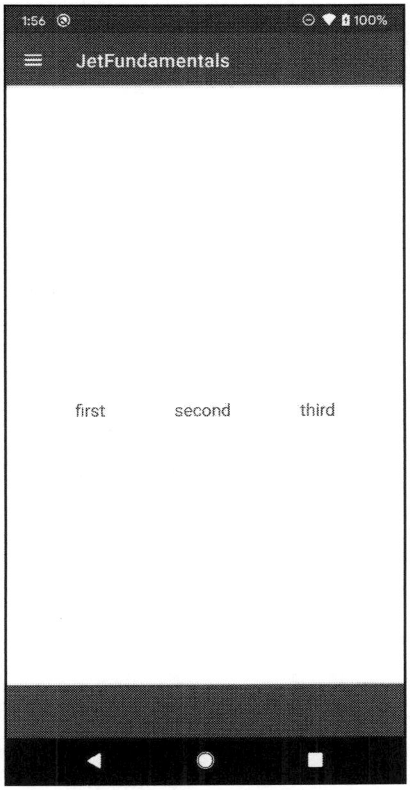

Scaffold With App Bars

The screen now shows top and bottom bars as well. The top bar contains the Menu icon, which opens the drawer when the user clicks it.

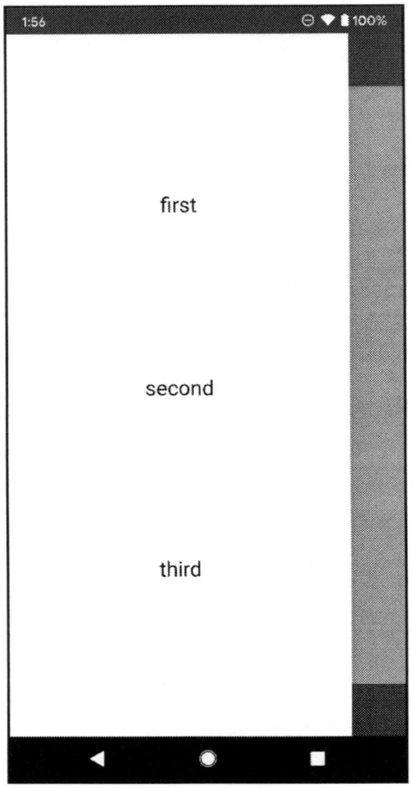

Drawer

The drawer shows the three text fields from `MyColumn()`. To dismiss the drawer, just click anywhere on the screen, outside of the drawer, or swipe the drawer left.

You've now learned how to group your composables inside layouts, to position them and to give them common properties. You can achieve this by using either multiple basic layouts or one of the advanced layouts.

Aside from `Scaffold`, advanced layouts also include a `ConstraintLayout`. `ConstraintLayout` lets you position children by defining constraints between them, just like the version you find in XML.

You'll dive deep and learn more about `ConstraintLayout` in Chapter 9, "Using ConstraintSets in Composables". But before all that, let's explore the `Scaffold()` signature.

Exploring Scaffold

To learn more about all the parameters the `Scaffold()` lets you use, open its signature:

```
@Composable
fun Scaffold(
    modifier: Modifier = Modifier,
    scaffoldState: ScaffoldState = rememberScaffoldState(),
    topBar: @Composable () -> Unit = {},
    bottomBar: @Composable () -> Unit = {},
    snackbarHost: @Composable (SnackbarHostState) -> Unit =
{ SnackbarHost(it) },
    floatingActionButton: @Composable () -> Unit = {},
    floatingActionButtonPosition: FabPosition = FabPosition.End,
    isFloatingActionButtonDocked: Boolean = false,
    drawerContent: @Composable (ColumnScope.() -> Unit)? = null,
    drawerGesturesEnabled: Boolean = true,
    drawerShape: Shape = MaterialTheme.shapes.large,
    drawerElevation: Dp = DrawerDefaults.Elevation,
    drawerBackgroundColor: Color = MaterialTheme.colors.surface,
    drawerContentColor: Color =
contentColorFor(drawerBackgroundColor),
    drawerScrimColor: Color = DrawerDefaults.scrimColor,
    backgroundColor: Color = MaterialTheme.colors.background,
    contentColor: Color = contentColorFor(backgroundColor),
    content: @Composable (PaddingValues) -> Unit
)
```

You can see that it has lots of features and components. This breakdown will give you a clear picture of what each of them do, and how to use them:

- **scaffoldState**: The state of the layout. Unlike the basic layouts, `Scaffold` requires custom handling of its state. This is important because it can hold several different components that can change its visibility or content. A common example of handling state is changing whether a drawer displays or not.
- **topBar**: A composable that renders the top app bar. While you could create a custom composable, Jetpack Compose offers you a predefined composable to save you from reinventing the wheel.
- **bottomBar**: This composable renders the bottom app bar. As with the previous parameter, you can choose whether to use a custom composable or the predefined `BottomAppBar`.
- **snackbarHost**: As the name implies, this component hosts a `SnackBar`. It handles the state that determines when `SnackBar`s should be shown.

- **floatingActionButton**: Lets you set a composable for the main `FloatingActionButton` on the screen. The default `FloatingActionButton` is recommended for consistency with Material Design specs.
- **drawerContent**: Use this composable for drawers that require a custom implementation.
- **content**: A composable shown inside `Scaffold`. This is where you put the main content of the screen.

There are also many other parameters which are less important, but you can explore them if you want to play around with your `Scaffold`.

Now you can move onto building more components in Compose and complex UI, with the knowledge you gained in the first few chapters! :]

Key Points

- Use `Layouts` to group and position your elements on the screen.
- `Row` lets you position elements horizontally on the screen.
- `Column` lets you position elements vertically on the screen.
- Use vertical or horizontal `Arrangement` to change the position of elements inside the `Row` or `Column`.
- Use **weights** to change the **proportion** of the screen your elements will use.
- `Box` allows you to vertically stack the elements on top of each other.
- Within `Row`, `Column`, `Box`, or other functions, you gain access to hidden modifiers from the `RowScope`, `ColumnScope`, `BoxScope` and other scope types, respectively.
- If you want to build components that should only be used within `Row`, `Box` or other grouping composables, you can make them an extension function to the appropriate `RowScope`, `BoxScope` or other scopes, respectively.
- Making an extension function composable to any `Scope` gives you access to the `Scope`'s modifiers in the function.
- Group multiple basic layouts to create a more complex screen.

- Use `Surface` to clip the elements inside it with an option to add the border and elevation.
- `Surface` can hold only one child.
- Add another layout inside `Surface` to position the elements.
- `Card` is a just a `Surface` with default parameters.
- `Scaffold` lets you build out a conventional material design screen by using individual composable functions.
- Use `ScaffoldState` to handle states for the components inside the scaffold.
- Use `DrawerState` to handle the drawer state, within a `Scaffold()`.
- `rememberScaffoldState()` will remember the state of the scaffold and preserve it during the recomposition.
- `rememberCoroutineScope()` lets you create a composable-bound `CoroutineScope` to launch coroutines and perform actions like closing or opening drawers.

Where to Go From Here?

You now know how to use multiple predefined composables to implement different features. You've also learned how to group and position them inside layouts to make a complete screen.

Next, you'll learn about different ways of making lists, how to make adapters and how to get the same result as when you use a `RecyclerView`. Finally, you'll learn how to implement custom grids.

See you in the next chapter!

Chapter 4: Building Lists With Jetpack Compose

By Prateek Prasad

In previous chapters, you learned about different elements in Compose and how to group and position them inside layouts to build complex UIs. Using that knowledge, you can create most screens you can think of.

However, you've not learned how to build one of the most common UI components mobile apps use. What happens when you have to display more elements than you can fit on the screen? In that case, while the elements are all composed, the limited screen size prevents you from seeing all of them. There are even situations where you want to dynamically add new elements on the screen and still be able to see them all, like a social media feed for instance.

The solution to this problem is allowing your content to scroll, either vertically or horizontally. The traditional way of achieving this in XML is to use `ScrollView`, which allows you to scroll content vertically. For horizontal scrolling, you use `HorizontalScrollView`. Both of them can have only one child view inside them, so to add multiple elements, you need to use a single layout that wraps those elements.

Jetpack Compose gives you a new way to achieve the same result — using scrollable and lazily composed containers.

In this chapter, you'll learn how to make lists and grids in Jetpack Compose. You'll learn how to show content that scrolls vertically or horizontally and how to build an alternative for the traditional `RecyclerView` using composable functions.

Using Vertical Scrolling Modifiers

As you know by now, `Column` is the replacement for `LinearLayout` in the vertical orientation. In Jetpack Compose, you can use the same `Column` composable with an additional modifier that enables scrolling! Let's see how to implement a simple scrolling `Column`.

To follow along with the code examples, open Android Studio and select **Open an Existing Project**. Then, navigate to **04-building-lists-with-jetpack-compose/projects** and select the **starter** folder.

Once the project builds, you'll see the following structure:

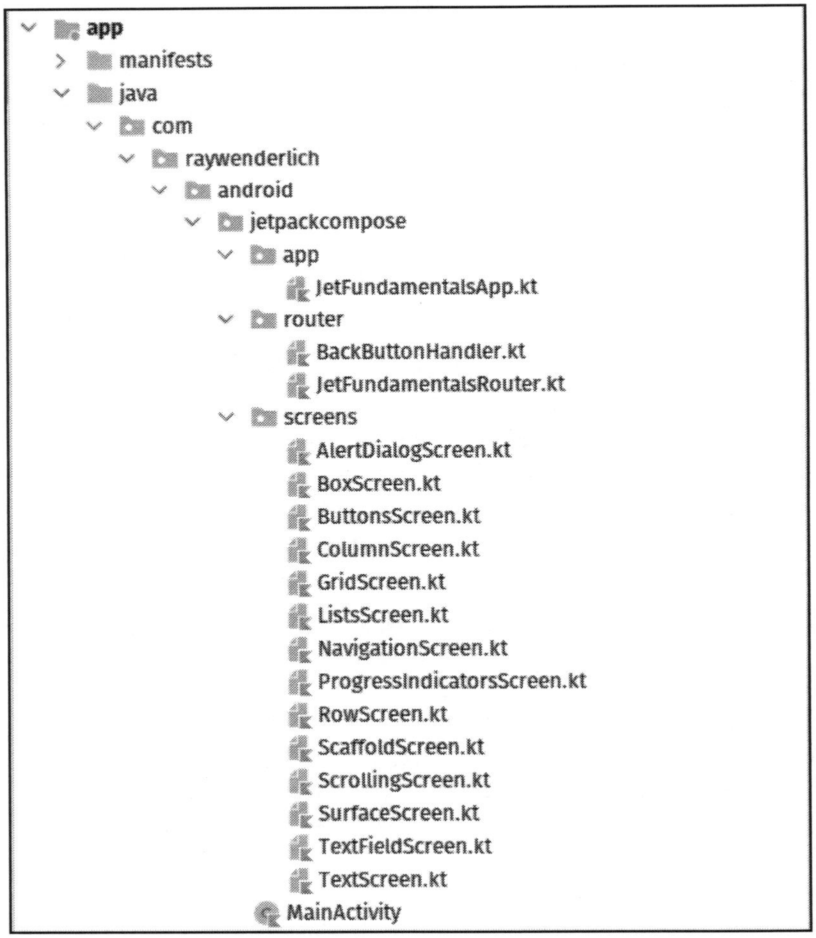

Project Structure

You'll start off by building a vertically scrollable `Column` after which you'll explore its horizontal counterpart. To do that, open **ScrollingScreen.kt** and you'll see two composable functions — `ScrollingScreen()` and `MyScrollingScreen()`:

```
@Composable
fun ScrollingScreen() {
  MyScrollingScreen()

  BackButtonHandler {
    JetFundamentalsRouter.navigateTo(Screen.Navigation)
  }
}

@Composable
fun MyScrollingScreen() {
  //TODO add your code here
}

@Composable
fun BookImage(@DrawableRes imageResId: Int, @StringRes
contentDescriptionResId: Int){
  Image(
    bitmap = ImageBitmap.imageResource(imageResId),
    contentDescription =
stringResource(contentDescriptionResId),
    contentScale = ContentScale.FillBounds,
    modifier = Modifier.size(476.dp, 616.dp)
  )
}
```

As in the previous chapters, `ScrollingScreen()` is already set up to handle the back navigation, so you only need to implement `MyScrollingScreen()`. There is also a `BookImage` composable which is predefined. It creates an image of a book in a specific size with the image and content description passed as a parameter.

Change the code of `MyScrollingScreen()` to the following, and include the required imports with the help of Android Studio:

```
@Composable
fun MyScrollingScreen(modifier: Modifier = Modifier) {
  Column(modifier =
modifier.verticalScroll(rememberScrollState())) {
    BookImage(R.drawable.advanced_architecture_android,
R.string.advanced_architecture_android)
    BookImage(R.drawable.kotlin_aprentice,
R.string.kotlin_apprentice)
    BookImage(R.drawable.kotlin_coroutines,
R.string.kotlin_coroutines)
  }
}
```

Here, you added three existing `BookImage` composables to the `Column`. You used existing drawable and string resources for the parameters. To make the `Column` scrollable, you called `verticalScroll()` , and passed in `rememberScrollState()`. This creates a scroll state based on the scroll orientation and persists the scroll position so it isn't lost after recomposition.

What happens here is that you'll show a `Column`, a vertical list of items. But if the items no longer fit the screen, it will be scrollable and you'll be able to go through each item individually.

Build and run the app, then select **Scrolling** from the navigation menu. You'll see the three images, one below the other — but unfortunately, they don't fit on the screen together. Luckily, you made the screen scrollable! :]

Scroll down to see the images that aren't displayed yet.

Scrolling Column

Using a scrollable `Column` is very easy, but there is much more you can do with it. Let's explore how it works.

Exploring the Scrollable Modifier

Look at its source code to see what a `verticalScroll` can do and how it works when you use it:

```
fun Modifier.verticalScroll(
  state: ScrollState,
  enabled: Boolean = true,
  flingBehavior: FlingBehavior? = null,
  reverseScrolling: Boolean = false
)
```

First, look at the function parameters. You are already familiar with some of them, but there are a few important new ones:

- `scrollState` is the current state of the scroll. It determines the offset from the top and can also start or stop **smooth scrolling** and **fling animations**.
- `enabled` enables or disables scrolling. If it's disabled, you can still programmatically scroll to a specific position using the `state` property. But the user can't use scrolling gestures.
- `flingBehavior` is used to perform a fling animation with a given velocity.
- `reverseScrolling` allows you to reverse the direction of the scroll. In other words, setting it to `true` lets you scroll up. Note that its default value is `false`.

It's important to understand that `verticalScroll()` is a **modifier**. This means that you can make your custom composables scrollable as well, by applying it to their modifiers, if that suits your use case.

You applied vertical scrolling to a `Column`. If you want to apply **horizontal scrolling**, you use a **Row** instead.

Using Horizontal Scrolling Modifiers

Vertical scrolling now works on your screen — but in some cases you need a horizontal scroll, instead.

Just as you had to use a different component for horizontal scrolling called `HorizontalScrollView`, Jetpack Compose offers its own composable called `Row`, but you need to set the modifier . To achieve horizontal scroll, you need to apply `horizontalScroll()`, which works the same as `verticalScroll()` but in a different direction.

Let's implement a scrollable `Row`. Inside `MyScrollingScreen()`, replace the `Column` with a `Row`and `verticalScroll` with a `horizontalScroll`:

```
@Composable
fun MyScrollingScreen(modifier: Modifier = Modifier) {
  Row(modifier =
modifier.horizontalScroll(rememberScrollState())) { // here
    ...
  }
}
```

You don't have to do anything else! The scrollable `Row` is almost identical to the scrollable `Column` in terms of the default behavior. It sets up the horizontal scroll automatically, using `horizontalScroll()`.

Build and run the app and then select **Scrolling** again in the navigation menu. You'll still see the same three images, but now, the scroll works horizontally. And you accomplished this by changing just one line of code!

Scrolling Row

Scrollable columns and rows are great when you have static content, like in the previous examples. However, they aren't a good idea for data collections that are dynamic. That's because scrollable composables compose and render all the elements inside eagerly, which can be a heavy operation when you have a large number of elements to display.

In such cases, as you know from the traditional View system, you'd use a `RecyclerView` to optimize the loading and rendering of the visible elements on the screen. But how does Jetpack Compose deal with this issue? Let's find out! :]

Lists in Compose

To display a large collection of elements in Android, you used the `RecyclerView`. The only elements `RecyclerView` renders are the ones visible on the screen. Only after the user begins to scroll does it render the new elements and display them on screen. It then recycles the elements that go off the screen into a pool of **view holders**.

When you scroll back to see the previous elements, it re-renders them from the pool. Thanks to this behavior, re-rendering is so quick that it's almost as if the elements were never removed from the screen in the first place. This optimization mechanism gives `RecyclerView` its name.

Loading data only when it's needed is called **lazy loading** and Jetpack Compose doubles down on this method to handle lists. The main two components you use for lazy lists in Compose are the `LazyColumn` and `LazyRow`.

Introducing LazyColumn & LazyRow

`LazyColumn` and `LazyRow` are used for vertical and horizontal scenarios, respectively.

`RecyclerView` uses a `LayoutManager` to set its orientation, but Jetpack Compose doesn't have `LayoutManagers`. Instead, you use two different composable functions to change the orientation. The composables work in almost the same way as `RecyclerView`, but without needing to recycle.

When you use `LazyColumn` or `LazyRow`, the framework composes only the elements that can be shown on the screen. When you scroll, new elements are composed and the old ones are disposed off. When you scroll back, the old elements are recomposed. Jetpack Compose doesn't need a recycled `ViewHolder` pool because its recomposition handles caching more efficiently.

Let's implement both vertical and horizontal lists to categorize the books you showed earlier.

Creating Lists With LazyColumn & LazyRow

There are many awesome books in our kodeco.com library and in different categories. It's best to show them all categorized, so you can easily pick and choose your favorites.

To do this, you'll build a screen with a vertical list, where each composable item inside the list is another horizontal list. You'll split the vertical list into book categories and each book category will have a horizontal list of books that belong there. Look at the image below to get a better understanding:

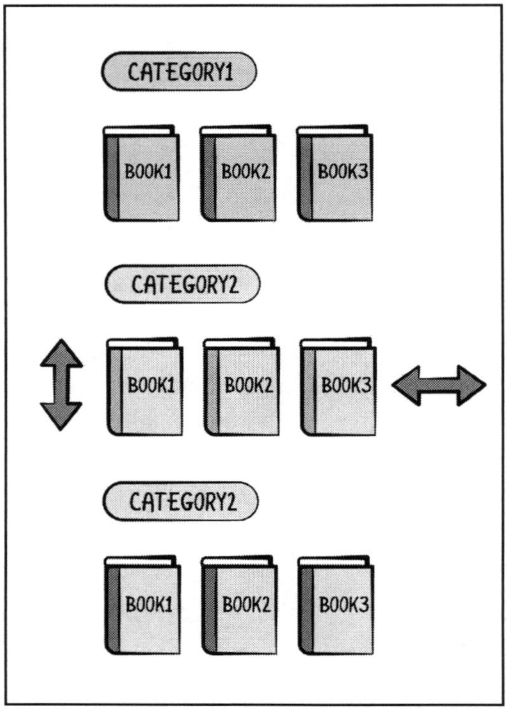

Book Categories

You can see the list of book categories scrolls vertically, while the categories themselves contain books thatscroll horizontally. Your task is to duplicate that implementation, except with a dynamic number of categories and books. That way, as write more books, you can just add them to the list!

Now, open **ListsScreen.kt**. This file contains a predefined property named `items` with a list of book categories. That's the data you'll display on the screen. At the bottom of the file, you'll find the following composable functions:

```
@Composable
fun ListScreen() {
  MyList()
  BackButtonHandler {
    JetFundamentalsRouter.navigateTo(Screen.Navigation)
  }
}

@Composable
fun MyList() {
  //TODO add your code here
}

@Composable
fun ListItem(bookCategory: BookCategory, modifier: Modifier =
Modifier) {
  //TODO add your code here
}
```

`ListsScreen()` is a provided composable that handles the navigation for you, so you don't need to worry about it. Your task is to implement `MyList()` and the `ListItem()`.

Add the following code inside `MyList()` and include the required imports from the `androidx.compose.material` package for `Text` composable and `androidx.compose.foundation` for other composables:

```
@Composable
fun MyList() {
  LazyColumn {
    items(items) { item -> ListItem(item) }
  }
}
```

Here, you added a LazyColumn() and set the items parameter with the items property containing your data. items is a list of objects of the BookCategory type. Each BookCategory contains a String with the category name and a list of images showing the books that should appear in that category.

Within the trailing lambda, for each item parameter inside the list of items, you create a new ListItem component. This lambda represents the function to transform each of the objects within items to composable elements.

This way you can call any number of composable functions to represent your items and you can add special rendering logic depending on the item type, its position and more!

Next, you'll implement ListItem(). Replace ListItem() with the following code and, once again, don't forget to include the required imports with the help of Android Studio:

```
@Composable
fun ListItem(bookCategory: BookCategory, modifier: Modifier =
Modifier) {
  Column(modifier = Modifier.padding(8.dp)) {
    Text(
      text = stringResource(bookCategory.categoryResourceId),
      fontSize = 22.sp,
      fontWeight = FontWeight.Bold,
      color = colorResource(id = R.color.colorPrimary)
    )
    Spacer(modifier = modifier.height(8.dp))

    // TODO
  }
}
```

This looks like a lot of code, but what it does is quite straightforward. First, you added a Column() as the parent layout of the composable so you can align its children vertically. The Column() uses a padding modifier to add some space near the borders.

The top child of Column() is a Text(). You need this to display the title of the category, which is passed as the text argument. Note how you styled the text by changing the font size, weight and color.

The next element is a `Spacer`, which adds some space between the category name and the rest of the content. This will let you show the category name on top of the horizontal list of books.

Now add the following code underneath the `Spacer`, to add the horizontal list of books:

```
LazyRow {
  items(bookCategory.bookImageResources) { items ->
    BookImage(items)
  }
}
```

Similar to how you built a vertical list with `LazyColumn`, using a `LazyRow` you create a horizontal list. It receives the list of book images as a parameter and a lambda that builds `BookImage`s. Also add the `BookImage()` in a separate function:

```
@Composable
fun BookImage(imageResource: Int) {
  Image(
    modifier = Modifier.size(170.dp, 200.dp),
    painter = painterResource(id = imageResource),
    contentScale = ContentScale.Fit,
    contentDescription = stringResource(R.string.book_image)
  )
}
```

A `BookImage` is a wrapper for an `Image` composable. `Image()` displays the book image for each element in the list. You used a `size` modifier to set a static size of `170dp` width and `200dp` height.

Since the list you passed as an argument to `LazyRow()` contains resource IDs instead of the actual images, you need to use `painterResource()` to retrieve the correct asset. Finally, by using `ContentScale.Fit`, you make the image adapt to the size you specified earlier and set the content description with the provided string.

Now, build and run the app. Once the main screen loads, click the **List** button in the navigation menu. Your app will show the following screen:

List

As you see, the books are sorted by category. You can scroll vertically to browse book categories and horizontally to browse books in each category.

By the way, if you're interested in any of the books you see, you can find them in our book library! :]

Compared to the verbose implementation of a `RecyclerView`, lists in Jetpack Compose are easy to use and understand. Their signature requires only a few parameters to make them work and its extremely flexible with how you want to customize them. Let's dive a bit deeper into their implementation.

Exploring Lists

Now you understand the difference and how to implement specific lists, take a look at the signature for `LazyColumn` and `LazyRow`:

```
@Composable
fun LazyColumn(
```

```
    modifier: Modifier = Modifier,
    state: LazyListState = rememberLazyListState(),
    contentPadding: PaddingValues = PaddingValues(0.dp),
    reverseLayout: Boolean = false,
    verticalArrangement: Arrangement.Vertical =
        if (!reverseLayout) Arrangement.Top else
Arrangement.Bottom,
    horizontalAlignment: Alignment.Horizontal = Alignment.Start,
    flingBehavior: FlingBehavior =
ScrollableDefaults.flingBehavior(),
    userScrollEnabled: Boolean = true,
    content: LazyListScope.() -> Unit
)

@Composable
fun LazyRow(
    modifier: Modifier = Modifier,
    state: LazyListState = rememberLazyListState(),
    contentPadding: PaddingValues = PaddingValues(0.dp),
    reverseLayout: Boolean = false,
    horizontalArrangement: Arrangement.Horizontal =
        if (!reverseLayout) Arrangement.Start else
Arrangement.End,
    verticalAlignment: Alignment.Vertical = Alignment.Top,
    flingBehavior: FlingBehavior =
ScrollableDefaults.flingBehavior(),
    userScrollEnabled: Boolean = true,
    content: LazyListScope.() -> Unit
)
```

The most important parameter to notice here is `content` which represents the content inside the list. This content is of a `LazyListScope` type and not your usual `Composable` type.

Take a look at the `LazyListScope` interface to learn why is it so important.

```
interface LazyListScope {

    fun item(key: Any? = null,contentType: Any? = null,content:
@Composable LazyItemScope.() -> Unit)

    fun items(
        count: Int,
        key: ((index: Int) -> Any)? = null,
        contentType: (index: Int) -> Any? = { null },
        itemContent: @Composable LazyItemScope.(index: Int) ->
Unit
    )

    @ExperimentalFoundationApi
    fun stickyHeader(key: Any? = null, contentType: Any? = null,
```

```
content: @Composable LazyItemScope.() -> Unit)
}
```

The interface provides a set of functions which help you when building lists:

- `items()` allows you to set a list of item data you would like to use in each of your list items. Once you set the data, you also need to provide an `itemContent` which is a composable used for displaying every item in your list.
- `item()` allows you to add a new composable item to your list. Note that you can use different composable types every time.
- `stickyHeader()` allows you to set the header composable that will remain visible on the top of the list, even after you scroll down to see new items. Note that this function is annotated with `@ExperimentalFoundationApi` which means that it's still in experimental stage and might change or be removed in the future.

Unlike the `RecyclerView`, lists in Jetpack Compose don't require an adapter, view holder layout managers and an RecyclerView element in your XML files just to make it work. Using one of the two very simple functions, you can either show a horizontal or a vertical list that is performant and customizable!

There are also extension functions like `itemsIndexed`, which has same features as `items()` but also provides you with an index for each of your items.

That's all for the theory. So far you've implemented simple lists and a list of horizontal lists for your books. The last thing you need to learn how to do is build **grids**.

Grids in Compose

When working with a `RecyclerView`, you can use different types of `LayoutManagers` to place your elements on the screen in different ways. To make grids, for example, you use a `GridLayoutManager` and then set the number of columns inside the grid.

Implementing grids in Jetpack Compose is far simpler than that. The grid you'll implement resembles what you saw in the last list example. This time, however, the elements won't scroll horizontally but will be fixed in place, instead.

To better visualize the problem, look at the following image:

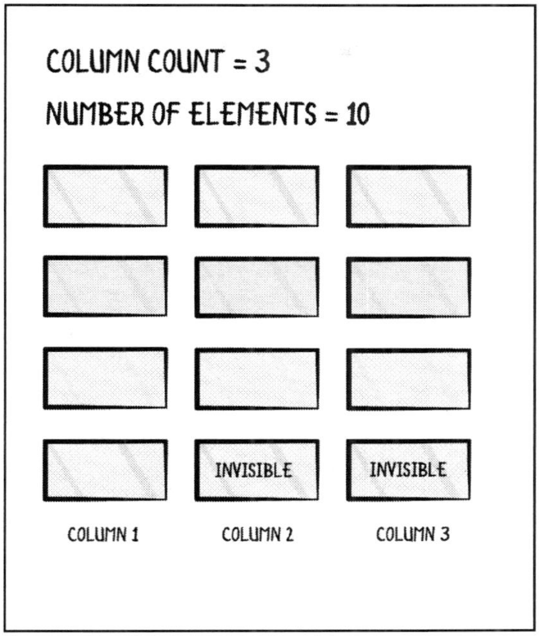

Grid Calculation

As you see, your grid contains ten elements distributed across three columns. The last row shows only one element in the first column, because that's the last element in your dataset. There are two more elements next to it, but they're marked as invisible for demonstrational purposes.

Implementing a Grid

Open **GridScreen.kt** and take a moment to look inside. You'll find the usual function to handle the navigation and a list containing the icons that you'll use as the grid's content. At the bottom of the file, you'll find the following composable functions that you need to implement:

```
@Composable
fun GridScreen() {
  //TODO add your code here

  BackButtonHandler {
    JetFundamentalsRouter.navigateTo(Screen.Navigation)
  }
}
```

```
@Composable
fun GridIcon(iconResource: ImageVector) {
  //TODO add your code here
}
```

Replace the `GridScreen` code with the following.

```
@Composable
fun GridScreen() {
  LazyVerticalGrid( //1
    modifier = Modifier.fillMaxSize(), //2
    columns = GridCells.Fixed(3), //3
    content = {
      items(items.size) { index -> //4
        GridIcon(items[index]) //5
      }
    }
  )

  BackButtonHandler {
    JetFundamentalsRouter.navigateTo(Screen.Navigation)
  }
}
```

Here's a breakdown of the code you just replaced:

1. You added a `LazyVerticalGrid` as the container for your grid.
2. You used the `fillMaxSize` modifier to ensure the grid takes up all the available space in the screen.
3. You set the number of columns that the grid should have to 3, using the `GridCells.Fixed()` property.
4. You passed in the size of your data set into the `items()`.
5. For each item in the list, you called the `GridIcon` composable, passing in the icon as a parameter.

Note: There are two types of `GridCells`:

• **Fixed** sets the fixed amount of cells on the screen.

• **Adaptive** adds as many rows or columns as possible to fit the screen with the provided `minSize` as the minimum size parameter.

The `content` lambda here works the same as with `LazyRow` or `LazyColumn`. You provide the collection of data and a composable which is used for every grid cell. `LazyVerticalGrid` then calculates and positions your composable in a grid depending on the `cells` parameter.

You will now implement the `GridIcon` composable to render your grid.

Implementing GridIcon

Each `GridItem()` will show the icon you passed in. Replace the `GridIcon` with the following code to achieve such behavior:

```
@Composable
fun GridIcon(iconResource: ImageVector) {
  Icon(
    imageVector = iconResource, //1
    tint = colorResource(R.color.colorPrimary), //2
    contentDescription = stringResource(R.string.grid_icon), //3
    modifier = Modifier //4
      .size(80.dp)
      .padding(20.dp)
  )
}
```

Here's a breakdown of the code block:

1. You set the `imageVector` of the `Icon` to the parameter passed to the composable.
2. You set the `tint` of the icon to `colorPrimary` using the `colorResource` composable.
3. You set the `contentDescription` of the icon for accessibility.
4. You set the size of the icon to **80dp** and the padding around the icon to **20dp**.

Build and run the app, then click the **Grid** button in the navigation menu. You'll see the following screen:

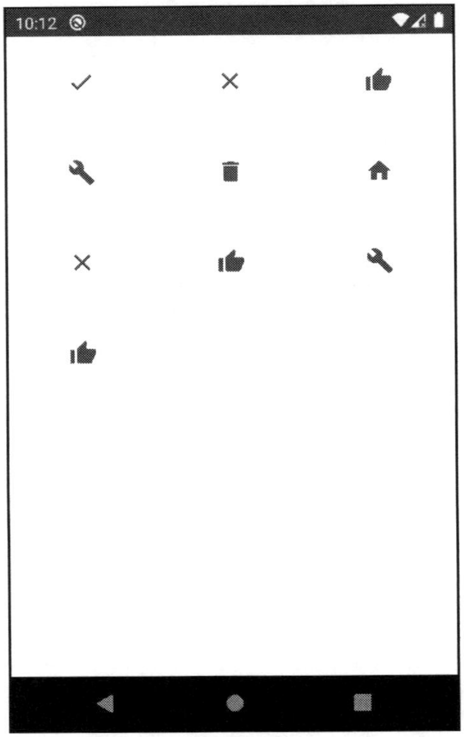

Grid With Three Columns

Awesome! You have a grid of icons on the screen, placed in three columns. You can increase the number of icons inside the `items` list to make the grid scrollable. To experiment with different column counts, increase the size of the list to the desired value and see the result. Keep in mind that you're limited to the number of columns that fit the screen.

Congratulations! You've learned a lot about how to lay out large numbers of elements in Jetpack Compose.

Key Points

- Use `Column` with the `verticalScroll` modifier to make the content vertically if it doesn't fit the screen.
- Use `Row` with the `horizontalScroll` modifier to make the content scroll horizontally if it doesn't fit the screen.
- You can make your own composables scrollable by adding the `verticalScroll` or `horizontalScroll` modifiers.
- Use scroll modifiers only for a fixed amount of content.
- For dynamic and larger amounts of content, use the lazy counterparts of `Row`, `Column` and `Grid` instead.
- The composable alternatives to `RecyclerView` are called `LazyColumn` and `LazyRow` for the vertical and horizontal scenarios, respectively.
- You can group lists inside each other to make content scrollable in both directions.
- To make grids, use a `LazyVerticalGrid`.
- You can use `LazyRow` and `LazyColumn` components if you want to manually add items to the list, allowing you to build headers and footers. Learn more about them here: https://developer.android.com/reference/kotlin/androidx/compose/foundation/lazy/package-summary#lazycolumn.

Where to Go From Here?

In this chapter, you learned how to make scrollable content, scrollable lists for dynamically created elements and custom grids.

You're ready to implement this UI functionality in your own apps. This wrapped up the entire first section! In the next section and the next chapter, you'll learn how to build more complex custom composables using all the knowledge you've gained so far.

See you there! :]

Section II: Composing User Interfaces

When working on apps and user interfaces, it's not only important to know what each piece of the interface should be, but also how all these pieces **come together** to build a beautiful and fully-functional design that'll wow your users.

Now that you've learnt the basics of Jetpack Compose and its fundamental UI elements, you're ready to dive deeper into building custom Compose elements, **managing their state** in a performant way and **styling them** using modifiers and built-in Material Design features.

Over the next four chapters, you'll learn how to:

- Attach `LiveData` structures to your state management.
- Rely on different styling modifiers.
- Combine these topics to create a powerful UI!

You'll build on the knowledge from the previous section of the book by learning new parts of the Jetpack Compose toolkit.

Chapter 5: Combining Composables

By Denis Buketa

Great job on completing the first section of this book! Now you know the basic pillars of Compose, you have everything you need to tackle the challenges of the second section.

The goal of the second section is to show you Jetpack Compose in action. Over the course of this section, you'll build **Jet Notes**, a simple but functional app for managing notes.

Each chapter in this section will explain certain concepts you'll apply to gradually build the different parts of the app. **Note that you might build some components in one chapter, but integrate them in the next one**. Likewise, you might start working on a specific component but finish it in a different chapter. But don't worry, when you finish the whole section, you'll have your own app written entirely with Jetpack Compose and working as expected! :]

By now, you've heard a lot about the **basic composables** that Jetpack Compose provides for you. In this chapter:

- You'll learn how to **think** about UI design when building it with Jetpack Compose.
- You'll see how you can **combine** basic composables to create **complex UI**.
- You'll create two components with different **complexity** for **Jet Notes**.

Let's first explore the features you'll build for your app.

Application Features

Before you start writing code, have a look at the app concept and its features:

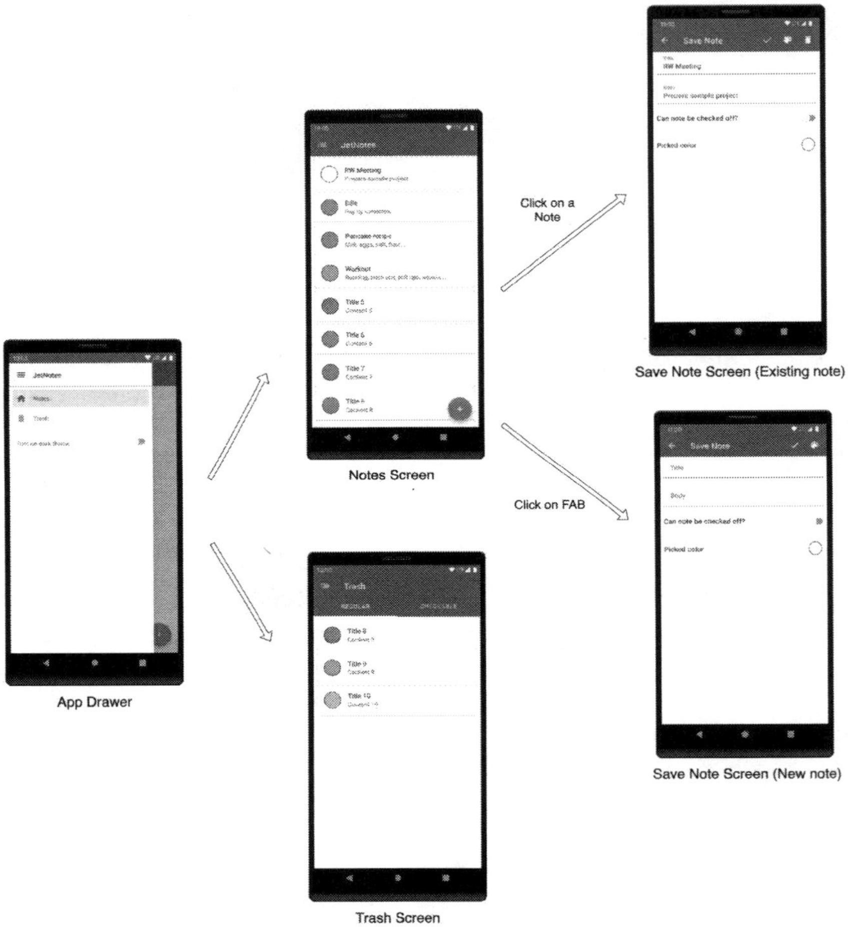

Application Overview

Don't worry about the details on each screen. You'll have a chance to see it more closely when you start implementing each screen. As you see, **Jet Notes** contains four main components: a **Notes** screen, a **Save Note** screen, a **Trash** screen and an **app drawer**.

The **Notes** screen displays the list of created notes. From here, the user can open an existing note, create a new one or open the app drawer.

The **Save Note** screen has two modes: an **edit** mode and a **create a new note** mode. When the user clicks on a note in the **Notes** screen, the **Save Note** screen will open in edit mode. The user can then edit the note or simply move it to the **Trash** screen by clicking a trash icon on the app bar.

To create a new note, the user taps on the Floating Action Button (FAB) available in the **Notes** screen. That opens the **Save Note** screen in the mode for creating a new note.

There are two types of notes: **regular** notes and **checkable** notes. Checkable notes are notes the user can mark — or check — as **done**. The user can make any note checkable by using a `switch` component in the **Save Note** screen. In the **Notes** screen, checkable notes have a checkbox to mark the note as done.

Tapping the navigation icon on the app bar or swiping from the left border of the screen opens the **app drawer**. The app drawer switches between the **Notes** and the **Trash** screens. Using the drawer, a user can also change the app's theme from light to dark.

In the **Trash** screen, the user can switch between regular and checkable notes using two tabs. The user can select notes and restore them or delete them permanently.

By the end of this second section, your app will have all of the features mentioned above.

Now you've familiarized yourself with the app and its features, it's time to start coding! :]

Project Overview

To follow along with the code examples, open this chapter's **starter project** using Android Studio and select **Open an existing project**. Navigate to **05-combining-composables/projects** and select the **starter** folder as the project root.

Once the project opens, let it build and sync and you'll be ready to go!

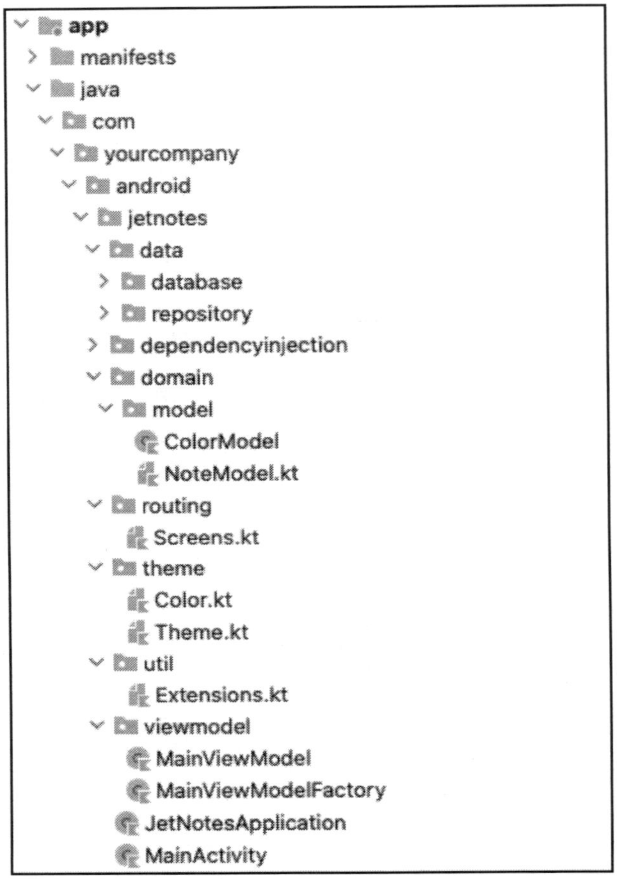

Project Structure

Here are the packages already set up for you and what they contain:

- **data**: Contains the code related to the database storing the notes. It lets you add, remove and update notes.
- **dependencyinjection**: Has one class responsible for creating and providing the dependencies you'll need.
- **domain**: Contains two domain models named `NoteModel` and `ColorModel`, they represent **notes** and **colors**, respectively.
- **routing**: Contains app's screens.

- **theme**: Contains color definitions and a composable function that lets you change the app's theme.
- **util**: Provides an extension method for creating `Color` instances from `String` color hex definitions.
- **viewmodel**: Contains the `ViewModel` you'll need to implement to manage notes.
- **JetNotesApplication.kt**: An `Application` that initializes the dependency injector.
- **MainActivity.kt**: Contains the `setContent()` call, which sets the first composable function and behaves as the root UI component.

Once you're familiar with the file organization, build and run the app. You'll see an empty screen with no content, as shown below:

Empty Starter Project — App State

Skip ahead to the **final project** and you'll see that you'll build components in this chapter, but you won't fully finish them or integrate them into **Jet Notes** yet. However, you can use the **final project** as a reference to track your progress while you build the composables. In the next chapters, you'll iterate upon them and improve the app.

Thinking in Compose

Before you start coding, look at the **Notes** screen design once more and try to **think in Compose**. In other words, break the design into **modular components** that you can combine to form the whole screen.

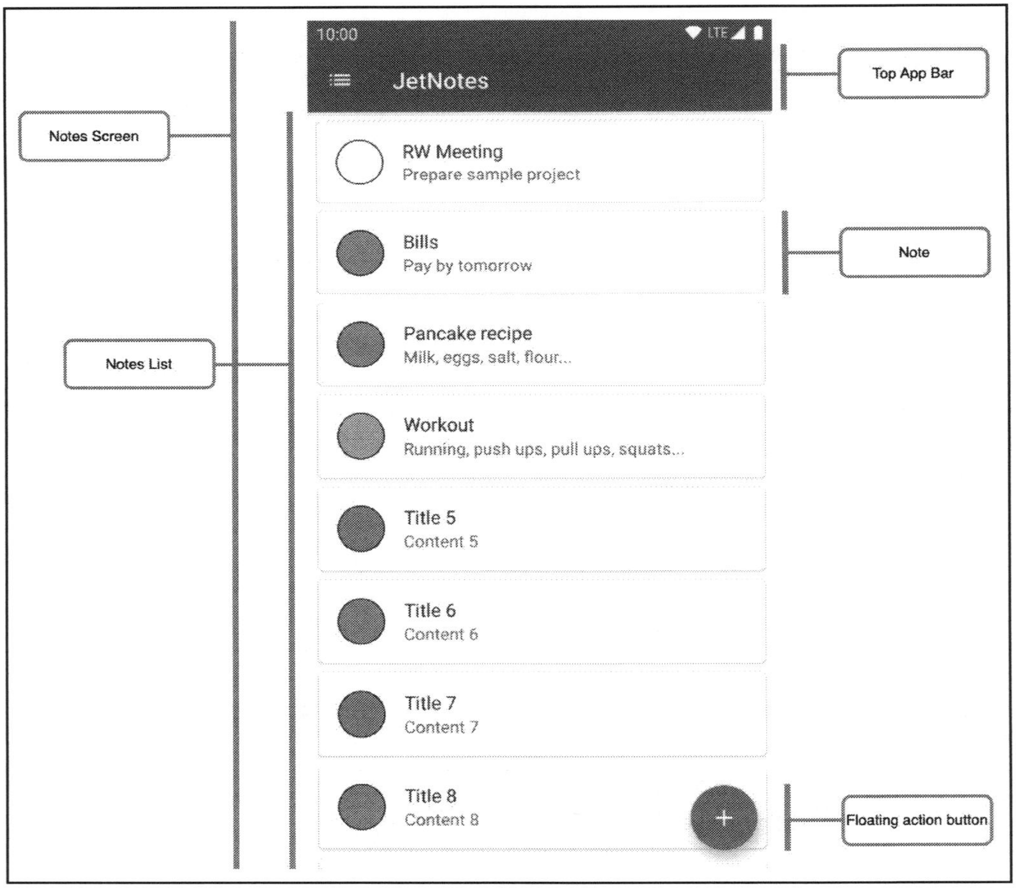

Notes Screen — Components

For example, you can break the **Notes** screen into the following components:

- **Notes Screen**: This component represents the whole **Notes** screen.
- **Top App Bar**: Responsible for displaying the top app bar, which holds the navigation action and the title.
- **Notes List**: Renders the list of created notes.
- **Floating Action Button**: Opens the **Save Note** screen so the user can create a new note.
- **Note**: Represents an individual note.
- **App Drawer**: Contains the drawer that displays when the user swipes from the side or taps on the navigation icon.

In Compose, these components are all represented by **composable functions**. As a developer, you get to decide how deep you want to break down a specific design into its components.

It's also important to consider how you'll use each component. For example, look at the design of the **Notes** and the **Trash** screens. Both screens use the same **Note** component, so creating a reusable **Note** composable makes sense.

This is a great example of **thinking in Compose**.

Bottom-up Approach

When building your apps with Jetpack Compose, it's smart to start with smaller composables and build your way up through the design. You call this way of working a **bottom-up** approach.

This is smart because building your app from the smallest components lets you decouple and reuse your code from the very start. By the time you reach the highest-level components, such as the **Notes & Trash Screens**, you'll have built all the fundamental components, so you can easily reuse them in those two screens. This saves time and helps with stability, by reducing the amount of code you need to write!

Now, look at the **Notes** screen again and consider which component is a good candidate to start with.

If you follow the **bottom-up** approach and choose the most fundamental components, you need to start with the **Note** composable. After building the **Note**, you'll be able to use it all over the app.

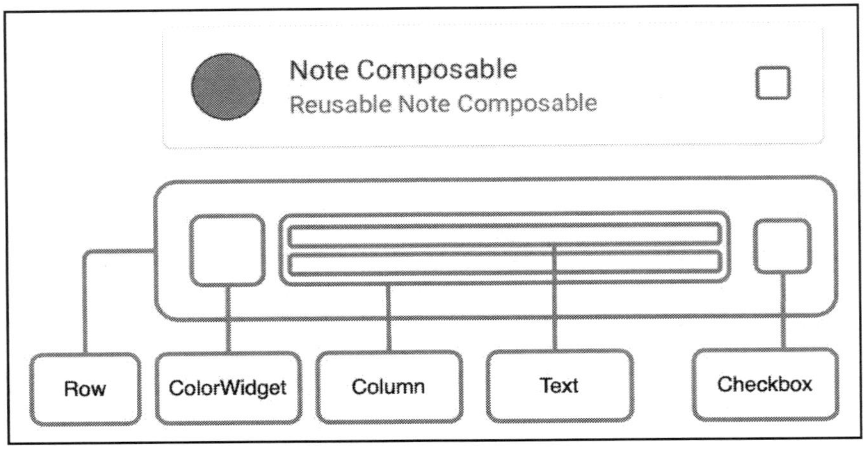

Note Component

When you try to break down the **Note** component, you'll notice that you can build it with the **basic composables** you learned about in the previous section. The color widget, the note's description and the checkbox are organized in a `Row`. The note's title and its description are organized in a `Column`.

Now you have an idea about how to break down your composable, it's time to start coding! :]

Creating the Note Composable

Use Android Studio to create a new package called **ui.components**. Then, in that package, create a new Kotlin file named **Note.kt**. Finally, add the following code to **Note.kt**:

```
import androidx.compose.runtime.Composable
import androidx.compose.ui.tooling.preview.Preview

@Composable
fun Note() {

}

@Preview
@Composable
```

```
private fun NotePreview() {
  Note()
}
```

In this code, you simply created a composable function to represent your note. You also added a `NotePreview()` to preview the composable you're building in Android Studio.

For this to work, make sure you've selected the **Split** option at the top-right corner in Android Studio. This option allows you to preview your composables in the Design panel, while still being able to modify the code.

Build your project now. At this stage, you still won't see anything in the Preview panel because haven't added any composables that emit your UI. Let's do that next!

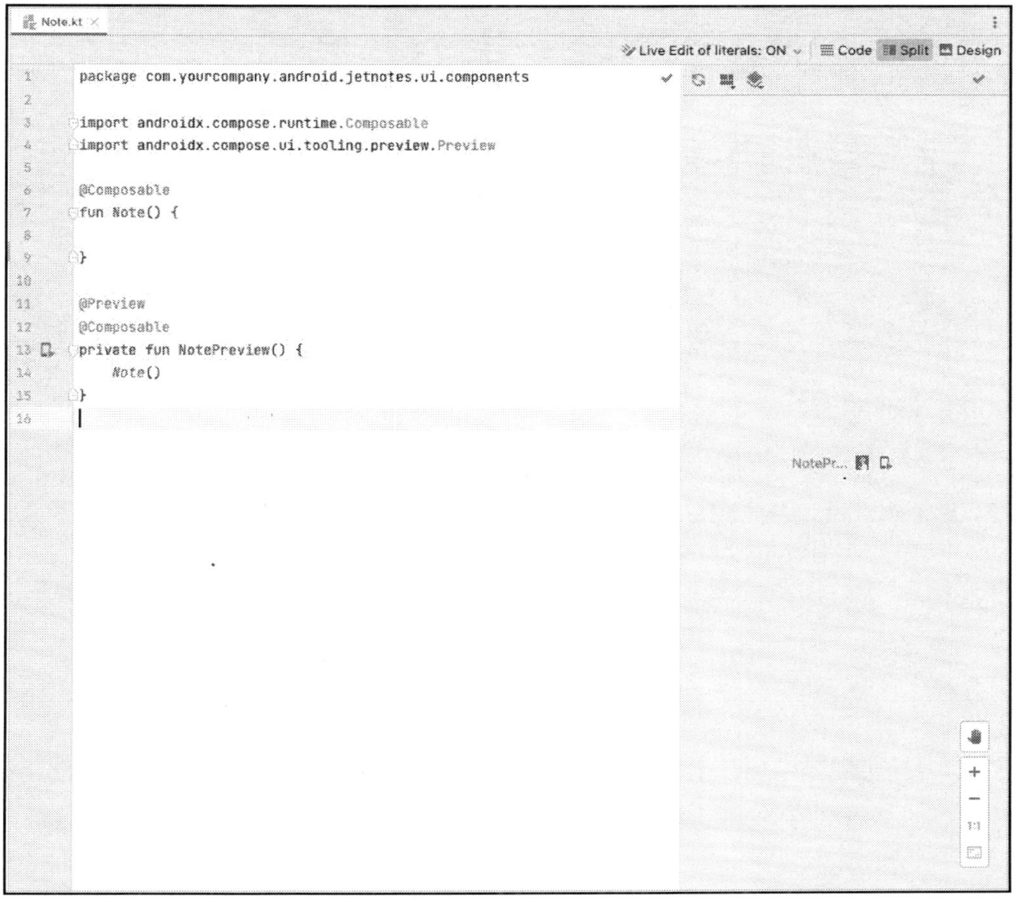

Android Studio - Preview

Emitting the Note's Content

Now you've built the `Note` composable, your next step is to add the code to emit the note's content. Add the following code to `Note()`'s body:

```
Box(
  modifier = Modifier
    .size(40.dp)
    .background(green)
)
Text(text = "Title", maxLines = 1)
Text(text = "Content", maxLines = 1)
Checkbox(
  checked = false,
  onCheckedChange = { },
  modifier = Modifier.padding(start = 8.dp)
)
```

For this to work, add the following imports to **Note.kt**:

```
import androidx.compose.foundation.background
import androidx.compose.foundation.layout.Box
import androidx.compose.foundation.layout.padding
import androidx.compose.foundation.layout.size
import androidx.compose.material.Checkbox
import androidx.compose.material.Text
import androidx.compose.ui.Modifier
import androidx.compose.ui.unit.dp
import com.yourcompany.android.jetnotes.theme.green
```

You've just added composables to represent the color widget, title, content and checkbox. Don't bother with the color widget for now — you won't style it in this chapter. That widget relies heavily on **modifiers**, which you'll learn about in Chapter 6, "Using Compose Modifiers". At this point, if you see modifiers in code, don't spend too much time thinking about them. Just know they make the UI look a bit nicer. :]

Build your project and you should see something like this in your preview:

Note Composable — Preview

By adding these composables, you've managed to accomplish something: The note's components now appear in the Preview panel. However, as you can see, they're stacked on top of each other. Remember that when you add composable functions, you're **describing the hierarchy** of the elements to render on the screen.

Previously, you read how, at its core, Compose only knows how to work with trees to emit specific items. So, you can represent the hierarchy you're describing with composable functions by a tree where the nodes are composables.

The four composables inside `Note()` will produce the following tree with four nodes:

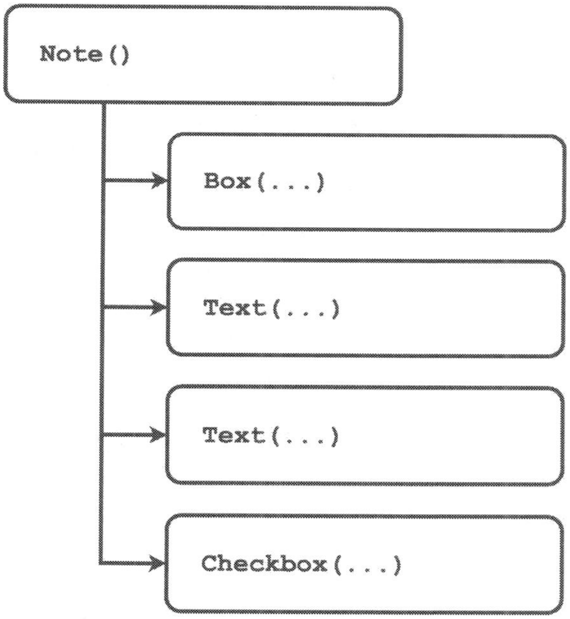

Note Composable - Tree Hierarchy

This is exactly what describing Jetpack Compose as a **declarative** toolkit means. The body of the function *describes* how the UI will look. In this case, the UI will contain four elements. Since no layout policy is described here, the composables will stack upon one other. This is exactly what the preview panel displayed.

It's not, however, what you want. For your next step, you'll add **layout structure** to your composable. Start by replacing the `Note()` body with the following code:

```
Row(modifier = Modifier.fillMaxWidth()) {
  Box(
    modifier = Modifier
      .size(40.dp)
```

```
      .background(green)
  )
  Column(modifier = Modifier.weight(1f)) {
    Text(text = "Title", maxLines = 1)
    Text(text = "Content", maxLines = 1)
  }
  Checkbox(
    checked = false,
    onCheckedChange = { },
    modifier = Modifier.padding(start = 8.dp)
  )
}
```

Add the necessary imports as well:

```
import androidx.compose.foundation.layout.Column
import androidx.compose.foundation.layout.Row
import androidx.compose.foundation.layout.fillMaxWidth
```

In the previous code, you organized the title and content in a column. You then aligned the resulting column in a row, along with the `Box()` and `Checkbox()` composables.

Build your project again or refresh the Preview panel, and you'll see something like this:

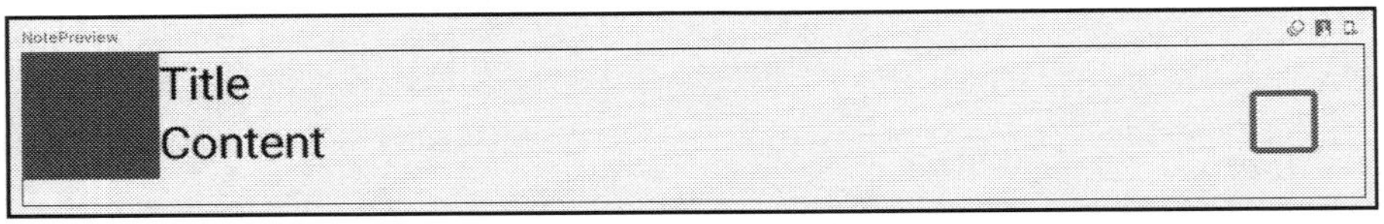

At this point, your `Note()` doesn't look quite like it did in the initial design. To make them match, you need modifiers. But hey, no worries! You'll continue working on it in Chapter 6, "Using Compose Modifiers".

Right now, you'll focus on building the remaining complex composables that make up your app.

Building the App Drawer Composable

The next thing you'll do is a little more complex. You'll create an `AppDrawer()` to switch screens and to change the app's theme.

Once again, before you start coding, look at the design and try to break it into smaller components.

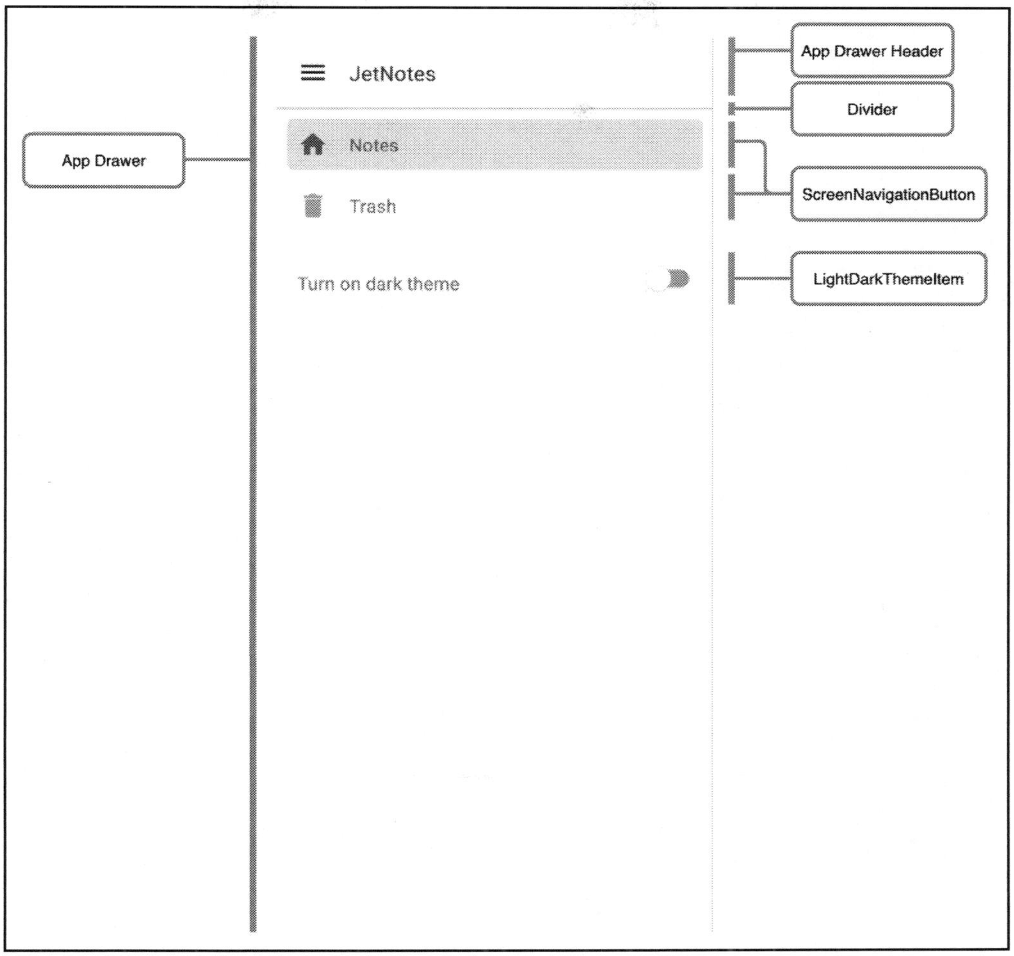

App Drawer — Components

As shown in the figure, you can split this UI component into the following composables:

- **AppDrawer**: Your root composable for the drawer.
- **AppDrawerHeader**: Contains a header with a drawer icon and the app's title.
- **ScreenNavigationButton**: Represents a button the user can tap to switch between screens.
- **LightDarkThemeItem**: Lets the user change between light and dark themes.

Let's build these components!

Adding a Header to the Drawer

Once again, you'll take the **bottom-up** approach to building the `AppDrawer()`. You'll implement smaller components first, then combine them. In **ui.components**, create a new file named **AppDrawer.kt**. Then, add the following code to it:

```
@Composable
private fun AppDrawerHeader() {
  Row(modifier = Modifier.fillMaxWidth()) {
    Image(
      imageVector = Icons.Filled.Menu,
      contentDescription = "Drawer Header Icon",
      colorFilter = ColorFilter
        .tint(MaterialTheme.colors.onSurface),
      modifier = Modifier.padding(16.dp)
    )
    Text(
      text = "JetNotes",
      modifier = Modifier
        .align(alignment = Alignment.CenterVertically)
    )
  }
}

@Preview
@Composable
fun AppDrawerHeaderPreview() {
  JetNotesTheme {
    AppDrawerHeader()
  }
}
```

For this to work, add the following imports as well:

```
import androidx.compose.foundation.Image
import androidx.compose.foundation.layout.Row
import androidx.compose.foundation.layout.fillMaxWidth
import androidx.compose.foundation.layout.padding
import androidx.compose.material.MaterialTheme
import androidx.compose.material.Text
import androidx.compose.material.icons.Icons
import androidx.compose.material.icons.filled.Menu
import androidx.compose.runtime.Composable
import androidx.compose.ui.Alignment
import androidx.compose.ui.Modifier
import androidx.compose.ui.graphics.ColorFilter
import androidx.compose.ui.tooling.preview.Preview
import androidx.compose.ui.unit.dp
import com.yourcompany.android.jetnotes.theme.JetNotesTheme
```

With this code, you've created a composable for the app drawer header. It's a relatively simple composable, where you use an `Image()` and a `Text()` and organize them in a `Row()`.

You also added modifiers to add padding and alignment to these components. Again, don't bother yourself with modifiers as much. You'll learn more about them in the next chapter.

For the `Image()`, you used a `colorFilter` to set its color. Specifically, you used `MaterialTheme.colors.onSurface` for the tint. The `MaterialTheme.colors` palette is drawn from the system and the root composable functions you use. If you check out the code in `AppDrawerHeaderPreview()` you'll see the following:

```
@Preview
@Composable
fun AppDrawerHeaderPreview() {
  JetNotesTheme {
    AppDrawerHeader()
  }
}
```

The root composable is `JetNotesTheme()` in your case. This is a predefined composable function in the **Theme.kt** file. As you use that for the root component, it passed down all its defined colors to the rest of the components, effectively styling them all in the same way. However, that theme doesn't specify the `onSurface` color yet, so the default value is `Color.Black`.

For now, that's all you need to know about theming. You'll learn more in Chapter 8, "Applying Material Design to Compose". You could also preview your composable without it, though, if it's confusing.

Build your project and you'll see the following result in your preview panel:

AppDrawerHeader Composable — Preview

Creating the Navigation Button Composable

Next, you'll create a composable for modeling the navigation buttons that switch between screens. To do so, add the following code to **AppDrawer.kt**:

```
@Composable
private fun ScreenNavigationButton(
  icon: ImageVector,
  label: String,
  isSelected: Boolean,
  onClick: () -> Unit
) {
  val colors = MaterialTheme.colors

  // Define alphas for the image for two different states
  // of the button: selected/unselected
  val imageAlpha = if (isSelected) {
    1f
  } else {
    0.6f
  }

  // Define color for the text for two different states
  // of the button: selected/unselected
  val textColor = if (isSelected) {
    colors.primary
  } else {
    colors.onSurface.copy(alpha = 0.6f)
  }

  // Define color for the background for two different states
  // of the button: selected/unselected
  val backgroundColor = if (isSelected) {
    colors.primary.copy(alpha = 0.12f)
  } else {
    colors.surface
  }
}
```

Add the following import as well:

```
import androidx.compose.ui.graphics.vector.ImageVector
```

In the design, the **Screen Navigation** button has an icon and a label. Here, you've added two parameters to your composable to allow that: `icon` and `label`.

You've also given the button two states: **selected** and **unselected**. To track which state the button is in, you added the parameter `isSelected`.

Each state renders differently. The code you added to the body of the function prepares colors for both states. Notice that you used `primary`, `onSurface` and `surface` colors; these colors are defined in your `JetNotesTheme()` from **Theme.kt**. As mentioned previously, if some of these colors aren't specified when you create a color palette for the theme, the default values are used.

Also notice that you've added the `onClick` parameter. Since your button is clickable, it's a good practice to expose that behavior through a lambda function so that the parent composable can take responsibility for it. You'll learn more about how to handle clicks and other events in Chapter 7, "Managing State in Compose".

Next, add the following code to the bottom of `ScreenNavigationButton()`:

```
Surface( // 1
  modifier = Modifier
    .fillMaxWidth()
    .padding(start = 8.dp, end = 8.dp, top = 8.dp),
  color = backgroundColor,
  shape = MaterialTheme.shapes.small
) {
  Row( // 2
    horizontalArrangement = Arrangement.Start,
    verticalAlignment = Alignment.CenterVertically,
    modifier = Modifier
      .clickable(onClick = onClick)
      .fillMaxWidth()
      .padding(4.dp)
  ) {
    Image(
      imageVector = icon,
      contentDescription = "Screen Navigation Button",
      colorFilter = ColorFilter.tint(textColor),
      alpha = imageAlpha
    )
    Spacer(Modifier.width(16.dp)) // 3
    Text(
      text = label,
      style = MaterialTheme.typography.body2,
      color = textColor,
      modifier = Modifier.fillMaxWidth()
    )
  }
}
```

Add the following imports as well:

```
import androidx.compose.foundation.layout.Arrangement
import androidx.compose.material.Surface
import androidx.compose.foundation.clickable
```

```
import androidx.compose.foundation.layout.Spacer
import androidx.compose.foundation.layout.width
```

There's quite a bit of code here, but here's a breakdown:

1. You use `Surface()` to provide the background color and shape for your button.
2. Inside `Surface()`, you use a `Row()` to align the icon and label for the button.
3. Finally, you used `Spacer()` to add some space between the icon and the label.

Now, you need to create a preview function to visualize your button in the Preview panel. In the same file, add the following function:

```
@Preview
@Composable
fun ScreenNavigationButtonPreview() {
  JetNotesTheme {
    ScreenNavigationButton(
      icon = Icons.Filled.Home,
      label = "Notes",
      isSelected = true,
      onClick = { }
    )
  }
}
```

Don't forget to import the `Home` icon:

```
import androidx.compose.material.icons.filled.Home
```

As you see, `ScreenNavigationButtonPreview()` just calls your `ScreenNavigationButton()`, passing in the parameters it needs. Apart from the icon and label for the button, note how you define its state as **selected** using `isSelected = true`. In addition, note how `onClick()` just uses an empty lambda as its argument, since you don't need this behavior for the preview.

Build your project and you should see the following result:

ScreenNavigationButton Composable — Preview

Great! Now, your drawer button is done and you're ready to move on to the next task.

Adding a Theme Switcher

The theme switcher is a toggle button that lets the user change the app's theme from light to dark.

Add the following code to the end of **AppDrawer.kt**:

```
@Composable
private fun LightDarkThemeItem() {
  Row(
    Modifier
      .padding(8.dp)
  ) {
    Text(
      text = "Turn on dark theme",
      style = MaterialTheme.typography.body2,
      color = MaterialTheme.colors.onSurface.copy(alpha = 0.6f),
      modifier = Modifier
        .weight(1f)
        .padding(start = 8.dp, top = 8.dp, end = 8.dp, bottom =
8.dp)
        .align(alignment = Alignment.CenterVertically)
    )
    Switch(
      checked = JetNotesThemeSettings.isDarkThemeEnabled,
      onCheckedChange =
{ JetNotesThemeSettings.isDarkThemeEnabled = it },
      modifier = Modifier
        .padding(start = 8.dp, end = 8.dp)
        .align(alignment = Alignment.CenterVertically)
    )
  }
}

@Preview
@Composable
fun LightDarkThemeItemPreview() {
  JetNotesTheme {
    LightDarkThemeItem()
  }
}
```

Also include the following imports, to avoid Android Studio's complaints:

```
import androidx.compose.material.Switch
import
com.yourcompany.android.jetnotes.theme.JetNotesThemeSettings
```

The code you added is quite straightforward. For this composable, you used a `Row()` to align the content horizontally. The content is a `Text()` and a `Switch()`, the interesting part is what the `Switch()` does.

Look at this composable and you'll observe that the `checked` and `onCheckedChange` parameters rely on `JetNotesThemeSettings.isDarkThemeEnabled` to handle the state. There are a few new concepts here, but you'll learn more about them in Chapter 7, "Managing State in Compose". For now, don't worry about them. Just consider this mechanism allows you to change the app's theme internally.

Build the project and, in the preview, you'll see the following:

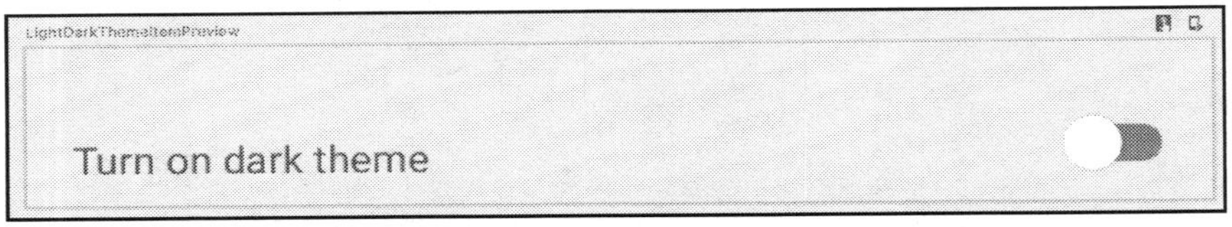

LightDarkThemeItem Composable — Preview

Well done! With this, you've completed all the necessary components for the app drawer.

Wrapping up the App Drawer

In the previous sections, you created the different building blocks you need to build the drawer. Now, you need to put them all together. To do so, add the following code to **AppDrawer.kt**:

```
@Composable
fun AppDrawer(
  currentScreen: Screen,
  onScreenSelected: (Screen) -> Unit
) {
  Column(modifier = Modifier.fillMaxSize()) {
    AppDrawerHeader()

    Divider(color = MaterialTheme.colors.onSurface.copy(alpha =
.2f))

    ScreenNavigationButton(
      icon = Icons.Filled.Home,
      label = "Notes",
      isSelected = currentScreen == Screen.Notes,
      onClick = {
        onScreenSelected.invoke(Screen.Notes)
      }
    )
```

```
      ScreenNavigationButton(
        icon = Icons.Filled.Delete,
        label = "Trash",
        isSelected = currentScreen == Screen.Trash,
        onClick = {
          onScreenSelected.invoke(Screen.Trash)
        }
      )
      LightDarkThemeItem()
    }
  }
```

Add the following imports as well:

```
import androidx.compose.material.icons.filled.Delete
import com.yourcompany.android.jetnotes.routing.Screen
import androidx.compose.material.Divider
import androidx.compose.foundation.layout.Column
import androidx.compose.foundation.layout.fillMaxSize
```

There's not much new in this code, you've just used the composables you created earlier. The important step you've taken here is you've organized those composables into a `Column()` to give your drawer a proper layout.

In the design, you can see there's a line between the drawer's header and buttons. To add the line, you used a `Divider()`. Then, for the color, you created a new object with the `onSurface` color, but with a different `alpha` property.

Check `AppDrawer`'s parameters: `currentScreen` and `onScreenSelected`. With `currentScreen`, you control which screen navigation button is selected. For example, if you want to select the **Notes** button, you'd call the `AppDrawer` composable with `Screen.Notes` as an argument.

Remember how you exposed the click event in the `ScreenNavigationButton()`? Here, you use a similar technique to expose the select screen event with the `onScreenSelected` parameter. By doing that, you let the parent composable react to the event.

Notice how this composable passes the lambda argument to `onClick()` of each navigation button. This is used to notify the system that you selected a new screen.

Finally, add the following code to the bottom of **AppDrawer.kt**:

```
@Preview
@Composable
fun AppDrawerPreview() {
  JetNotesTheme {
```

```
        AppDrawer(Screen.Notes, {})
    }
}
```

Here, you passed `Screen.Notes` as the `currentScreen`. By doing that, you selected the **Notes** button.

Since you're calling the `AppDrawer()` within a composable marked with `@Preview`, you don't need to specify any actions for when a screen is selected. Therefore, you just passed an empty function as an argument.

Build your project once more and you'll see your completed drawer in your preview:

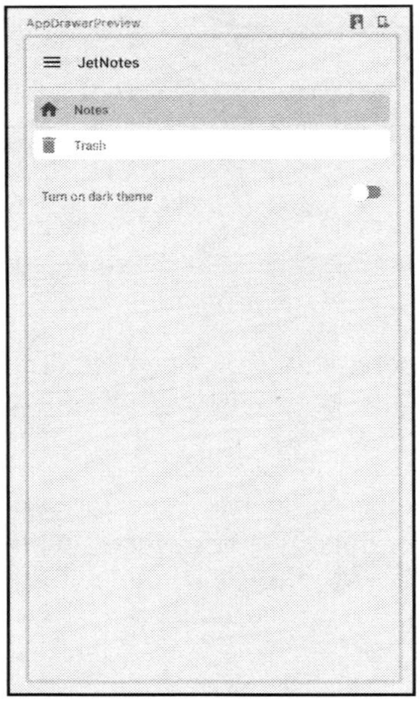

LightDarkThemeItem Composable — Preview

You already saw how calling composable functions results in a tree. Whenever you call the `AppDrawer()`, Compose will generate a tree where each node is a composable used to create it.

Right now, this tree contains only the **UI elements**. Later, you'll see there are other types of nodes as well. When you compare the `AppDrawer()` and the `Note()`, you'll see the first one is more complex. However, if you pay attention, you'll notice both are composed of pretty much the same **basic composables**.

That's the beauty of Jetpack Compose. It's so easy to create complex composables from the most basic ones.

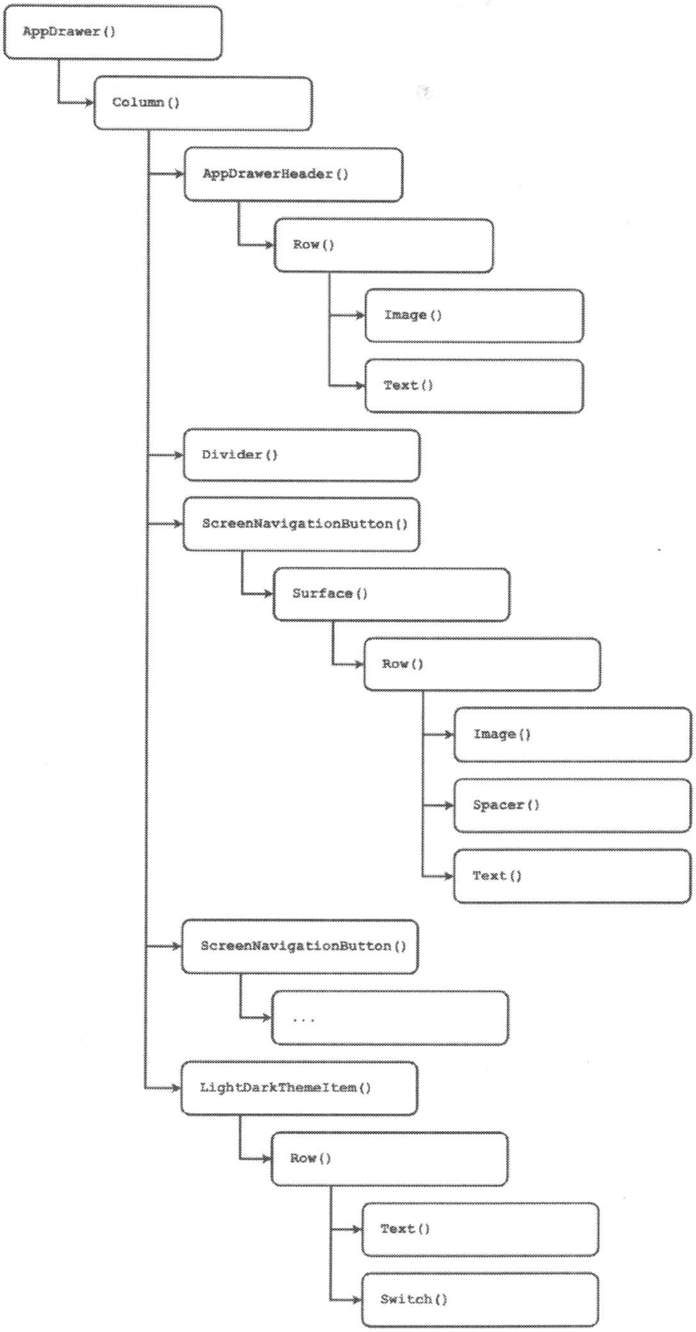

AppDrawer Composable — Compose Tree

Putting all the Pieces Together

After all this work, it would be a shame not to see the different composables you built working together in your app. So your final step will be to put the puzzle pieces together.

Go to **MainActivity.kt** and add the following code inside the `setContent()`:

```
JetNotesTheme {
  val coroutineScope = rememberCoroutineScope()
  val scaffoldState: ScaffoldState = rememberScaffoldState()

  Scaffold(
    scaffoldState = scaffoldState,
    drawerContent = {
      AppDrawer(
        currentScreen = Screen.Notes,
        onScreenSelected = { screen ->
          /* TODO */
          coroutineScope.launch {
            scaffoldState.drawerState.close()
          }
        }
      )
    },
    content = {
      Note()
    }
  )
}
```

Add the following imports as well, to avoid compilation errors:

```
import androidx.compose.material.Scaffold
import androidx.compose.material.ScaffoldState
import androidx.compose.material.rememberScaffoldState
import androidx.compose.runtime.rememberCoroutineScope
import com.yourcompany.android.jetnotes.routing.Screen
import com.yourcompany.android.jetnotes.theme.JetNotesTheme
import com.yourcompany.android.jetnotes.ui.components.AppDrawer
import com.yourcompany.android.jetnotes.ui.components.Note
import kotlinx.coroutines.launch
```

Don't worry if you don't understand some of the concepts or composables in this code. Just note the use of your `AppDrawer()` and `Note()`. The other code is here to allow you to easily integrate these composables.

You'll learn more about the `Scaffold()` and theming in Chapter 8, "Applying Material Design to Compose". You'll also get more context about the `ScaffoldState` in Chapter 7, "Managing State in Compose".

Build and run the app. You'll see the **Note** composable on the screen, as shown below. To see your app drawer in action, pull the left edge of the screen toward the right.

Right now, the app isn't that impressive, but don't worry. You'll make it look like the expected design throughout the following chapters.

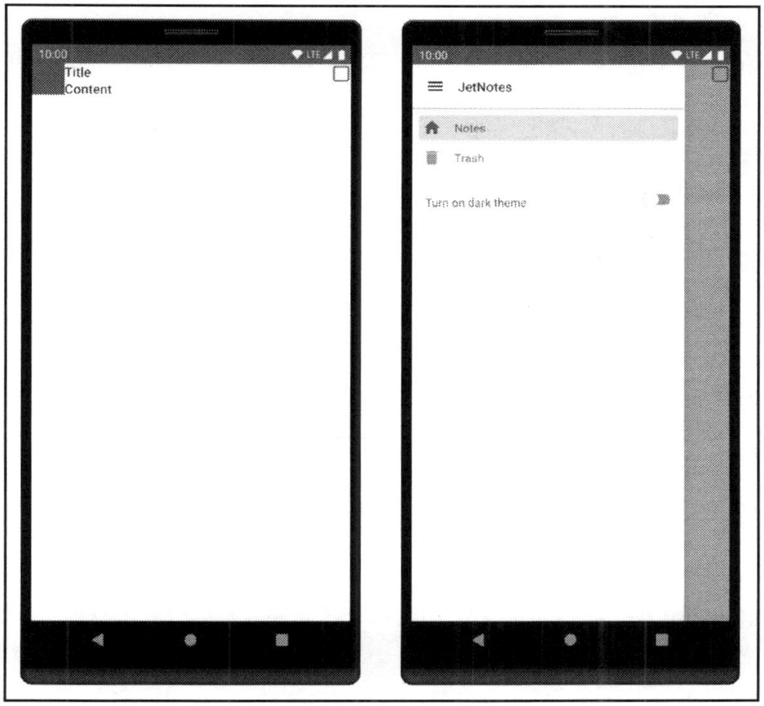

Note Composable and App Drawer Composable

You can find the final code for this chapter in **05-combining-composables/projects/final**.

Key Points

- Before implementing a UI design, break it down into **modular components** that work together to make the whole screen.
- When implementing a specific UI design, use a **bottom-up** approach. Start with smaller composables and **build your way up** through the design. This will let you decouple and reuse code from the very start.
- Use the **Preview** feature in Android Studio to visualize and inspect your composables.
- Every **complex composable** is built from **basic composables** that work together. It's a small puzzle of simple elements.
- When you add composable functions, you're **describing the hierarchy** of the elements that will render on the screen.
- Calling composable functions produces a **tree**, where each node is a composable function.

Where to Go From Here?

Congratulations on finishing the chapter! I hope it was a nice ride for you! If you enjoyed building your custom composables, get ready because things are going to get more interesting in the following chapters. :]

In this chapter, you learned how you can use basic composables to create complex ones. You also saw how you should think about your UI design and what approach to take when implementing it.

In the next chapter, you'll learn **how to style** your composables using **modifiers**. You'll also continue adding more composables to improve **Jet Notes**.

Chapter 6: Using Compose Modifiers

By Denis Buketa

A beautiful UI is essential for every app. It doesn't just look nice, it also makes your app *more fun* to use. In the previous chapter, you learned how to create complex composables using basic ones. You also started working on the `Note` and `AppDrawer` composables. Now, you'll learn how to make your composables look as beautiful as they are in your ideal design.

In this chapter, you'll:

- Learn **how to style** your composables using **modifiers**.
- Style `Note` to make it look like it should in the final design.
- Add more composables to **Jet Notes**.

From this point on, every composable you complete will be as beautiful as in your design, by adding those modifiers you've been hearing about for the past few chapters. :]

Modifiers

Modifiers tell a UI element how to **lay out**, **display** or **behave** within its parent layout. You can also say they **decorate** or **add behavior** to UI elements.

In the previous chapter, you started working on `Note()`.

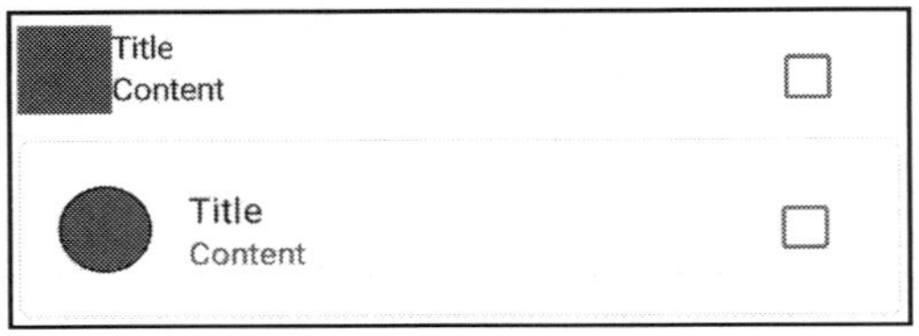

Note composable - current and final state

In the figure above, you can compare where you left off (above) with how it'll look like by the end of this chapter (below).

To follow along with the code examples, open this chapter's **starter project** in Android Studio and select **Open an existing project**.

Next, navigate to **06-using-compose-modifiers/projects** and select the **starter** folder as the project root. Once the project opens, let it build and sync and you're ready to go!

Note if you skip ahead to the **final project**, you'll be able to see the completed `Note()` and some other composables you'll implement during this chapter.

Whatever you choose, we'll start off by building the `NoteColor` widget.

Adding NoteColor

The first thing you'll improve in your `Note()` is the `NoteColor`. In the **ui.components** package, create a new Kotlin file named **NoteColor.kt**, then add the following code to it:

```
@Composable
fun NoteColor() {
  Box(
    modifier = Modifier
      .size(40.dp)
      .background(Color.Red)
  )
}

@Preview
```

```
@Composable
fun NoteColorPreview() {
  NoteColor()
}
```

To make this work, add the following imports:

```
import androidx.compose.foundation.background
import androidx.compose.foundation.layout.Box
import androidx.compose.foundation.layout.size
import androidx.compose.runtime.Composable
import androidx.compose.ui.Modifier
import androidx.compose.ui.graphics.Color
import androidx.compose.ui.tooling.preview.Preview
import androidx.compose.ui.unit.dp
```

Look at the code now and you can see you created a `Box` and passed a modifier to it. In this example, you used two modifier functions: `Modifier.size()` and `Modifier.background()`.

`Modifier.size()` declares the size of the content. You pass the value in **density-independent pixels (dp)** and set the element width and height to the same value.

`Modifier.background()` draws a **shape** with a solid color behind the content. In this case, you passed `Color.Red`.

As you can see, you can easily **chain** several modifiers, one after the other, to **combine** them. In this example, you started the **modifier chain** with `Modifier`, which represents an empty modifier object.

Finally, you used `NoteColorPreview()` to preview your composable in the preview panel.

Build your project and check the preview. You'll see something like this:

NoteColor — Preview

Congratulations, you just created a very simple composable that is `40dp` in size and has a red background. Let's see if we can make it even nicer!

Chaining Modifiers

Now you have the basic `NoteColor()`, but you still have to add a couple of modifiers to make it match the design.

The next thing you'll do is to make your composable's content round. In the previous example, you saw how to chain multiple modifiers. Here, you'll apply the same principle and change the code so it includes one additional modifier:

```
@Composable
fun NoteColor() {
  Box(
    modifier = Modifier
      .size(40.dp)
      .background(Color.Red)
      .clip(CircleShape) // Add the new clip modifier here
  )
}
```

Don't forget to include these imports as well:

```
import androidx.compose.foundation.shape.CircleShape
import androidx.compose.ui.draw.clip
```

Now, build your project and check the preview. You'll see something like this:

NoteColor - Preview

Surprised? Don't blame yourself if you tried to refresh the preview panel, expecting a different result. :]

The **order of modifiers** in the chain matters. Each modifier not only **prepares** the composable for the next modifier in the chain, but it also **modifies** the composable at the same time.

With this in mind, try to break down the code you wrote. With `Modifier.size()`, you defined the width and the height of the composable.

After that, you have `Modifier.background(Color.Red)`. Since UI elements are represented by rectangular blocks, you end up with a red square.

Then you added `Modifier.clip()`, which clips the content to a specific shape. Since the two modifiers before already modified the composable, your composable didn't change. The content remained the same.

To make this clearer, try adding another `Modifier.background` composable to the chain:

```
@Composable
fun NoteColor() {
  Box(
    modifier = Modifier
      .size(40.dp)
      .background(Color.Red)
      .clip(CircleShape)
      .background(Color.Yellow) // Add the new background
modifier here
  )
}
```

Build the project and check the preview. You'll see something like this:

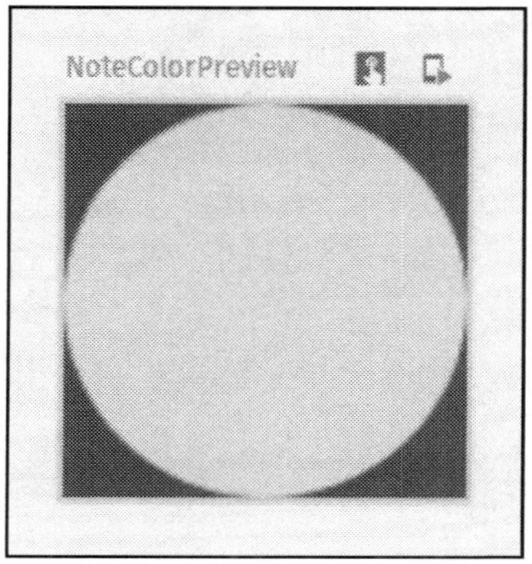

NoteColor - Preview

Now, you can visualize the effect that `Modifier.clip()` has on your composable. It clipped the **future content** into a circle shape, so when you applied the `Modifier.background(Color.Yellow)`, you ended up with a yellow circle in the red square.

Taking this behavior into consideration, you can now continue working on `NoteColor()` to make it look like the design. Reorder the modifiers to get a circular shape with a specific color:

```
@Composable
fun NoteColor() {
  Box(
    modifier = Modifier
      .size(40.dp)
      .clip(CircleShape)
      .background(Color.Red)
  )
}
```

Here, you moved `Modifier.clip()` to come before the point where you specify the composable background. With that, you clipped the content of your composable to a circle whose width and height are set to the value you specify with `Modifier.size()`.

Build the project and check the preview:

NoteColor - Preview

Excellent! You just created a composable that emits a colored circle of the size you specified.

Rounding out the NoteColor

There are a few more things you need to add before wrapping up this composable. One thing that's missing is the border. To add that, update the code in `NoteColor()` like so:

```
@Composable
fun NoteColor() {
  Box(
    modifier = Modifier
      .size(40.dp)
      .clip(CircleShape)
      .background(Color.Red)
      .border( // new code
        BorderStroke(
          2.dp,
          SolidColor(Color.Black)
        ),
        CircleShape
      )
  )
}
```

To make Android Studio happy, add the following imports as well:

```
import androidx.compose.foundation.BorderStroke
import androidx.compose.foundation.border
import androidx.compose.ui.graphics.SolidColor
```

Here, you added `Modifier.border()`, which gives you a border with the appearance you specified using the `border` and `shape`. For the `border`, you passed `BorderStroke()`, which defined the width of the border and its color. For the `shape`, you used the same shape as you did when clipping the content.

Build the project and you'll see something like this in the preview panel:

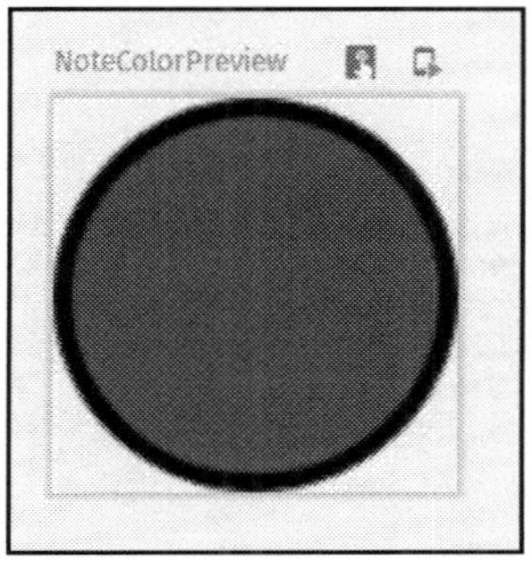

NoteColor - Preview

Adding Some Padding

If you check the design you'll notice that there should be some padding around `NoteColor()`. To fix that, update the code like this:

```
@Composable
fun NoteColor() {
  Box(
    modifier = Modifier
      .padding(4.dp) // Add the padding modifier here
      .size(40.dp)
      .clip(CircleShape)
      .background(Color.Red)
      .border(
        BorderStroke(
          2.dp,
          SolidColor(Color.Black)
        ),
        CircleShape
      )
  )
}
```

Don't forget to add the necessary import:

```
import androidx.compose.foundation.layout.padding
```

`Modifier.padding()` applies additional space to each edge around the content. In the code above, you used `4.dp`. Note that when you don't specify which edge to pad, the padding will be applied to all of them. You can also specify to which edge you want to apply the padding with the following **named arguments**: `start`, `top`, `end` and `bottom`.

It's important to pay attention to the order in the chain where you added the modifier. You want your circle to be the size you specify with the `Modifier.size`. You also want your padding to be applied around that circle. So, the best place to put `Modifier.padding` is just before `Modifier.size`.

By doing that, you'll first apply the padding to your composable, then you'll **reserve** the space of the specified size for your content.

Build the project and check the preview. It will now look like this:

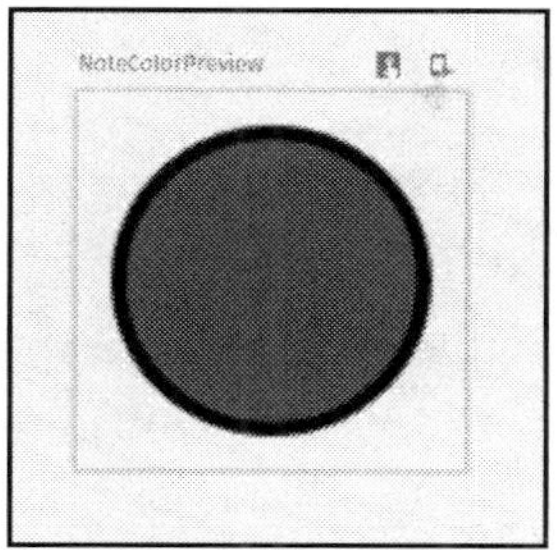

NoteColor - Preview

Improving NoteColor’s Usability

Regarding `NoteColor()`, you have all the necessary code to fulfill the design. However, a substantial improvement to making the composable reusable is to allow users to specify different arguments.

Right now, you’ve hard-coded the values for the size, background color, padding and border width, but your users should be able to change them.

To implement this, just expose those values as parameters by replacing `NoteColor()` with the following code:

```
@Composable
fun NoteColor(
  color: Color,
  size: Dp,
  padding: Dp = 0.dp,
  border: Dp
) {
  Box(
    modifier = Modifier
      .padding(padding)
      .size(size)
      .clip(CircleShape)
      .background(color)
      .border(
        BorderStroke(
          border,
          SolidColor(Color.Black)
        ),
        CircleShape
      )
  )
}
```

Don't forget this import:

```
import androidx.compose.ui.unit.Dp
```

Here, you changed the signature of `NoteColor()` to accept a `color`, `size`, `padding` and `border`. You then replaced the hard-coded values with the new parameters.

Now, you need to adapt `NoteColorPreview()` and specify the right parameters. Replace `NoteColorPreview()` with the following code:

```
@Preview
@Composable
fun NoteColorPreview() {
  NoteColor(
    color = Color.Red,
    size = 40.dp,
    padding = 4.dp,
    border = 2.dp
  )
}
```

Here, you've used the same values as before, so your preview should remain the same.

Build the project to make sure everything works as expected.

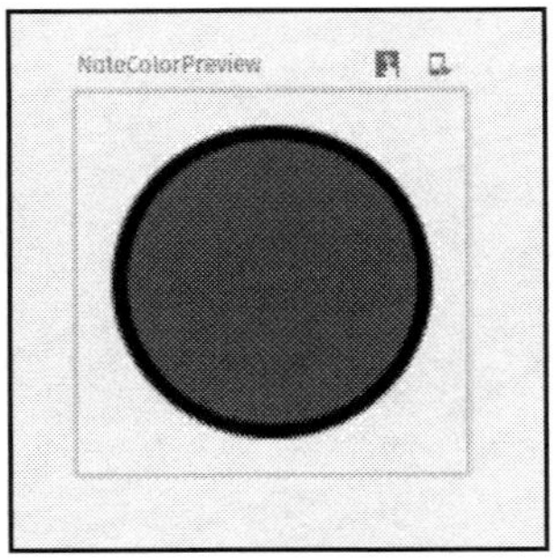

NoteColor — Preview

The next step is to add your new component to the `Note`.

Adding NoteColor to Note

Great work on completing `NoteColor()`! You can now use it in your `Note` to make it match the design.

In **Note.kt**, replace the `Note()` implementation with the following code:

```
@Composable
fun Note() {
  Row(modifier = Modifier.fillMaxWidth()) {
    NoteColor( // NoteColor instead of Box
      color = green,
      size = 40.dp,
      padding = 4.dp,
      border = 1.dp
    )
    Column(modifier = Modifier.weight(1f)) {
      Text(text = "Title", maxLines = 1)
      Text(text = "Content", maxLines = 1)
    }
    Checkbox(
      checked = false,
      onCheckedChange = { },
      modifier = Modifier.padding(start = 8.dp)
    )
  }
}
```

In the code above, you removed the `Box` you used as a placeholder, then added your beautiful `NoteColor`.

Build the project now and you'll see something like this in the preview panel:

Note Composable — Preview With NoteColor

While you're here, check out the modifiers you added in the previous chapter, when you were working on `Note`.

For `Row()`, you used `Modifier.fillMaxWidth()`. This modifier allows you to specify the fraction of the available width the composable should use. By default, the fraction is `1f`. So in this case, you specified the `Row` should take the maximum available width.

For `Column()`, you used `Modifier.weight()`. If you're familiar with the weight property in XML layouts, then you already know what it does. With `weight`, you size the element's width proportional to its weight relative to other weighted sibling elements.

Check the definition of this modifier. It's defined in RowScope, which means you can use it on elements in a Row. In this case, you used it to make the Column take the available width between NoteColor and Checkbox.

Adding a Background to Note

Look at Note's design and notice it has a white background, its corners are rounded and there's a small shadow around it. Luckily, you can easily use modifiers to add those features!

Update Note() code to add the necessary modifiers to Row(), as shown below:

```
@Composable
fun Note() {
  val backgroundShape: Shape = RoundedCornerShape(4.dp)
  Row(
    modifier = Modifier
      .padding(8.dp)
      .shadow(1.dp, backgroundShape)
      .fillMaxWidth()
      .heightIn(min = 64.dp)
      .background(Color.White, backgroundShape)
  ) {
    ...
  }
}
```

As usual, don't forget to add the necessary imports:

```
import androidx.compose.foundation.shape.RoundedCornerShape
import androidx.compose.ui.draw.shadow
import androidx.compose.ui.graphics.Color
import androidx.compose.ui.graphics.Shape
import androidx.compose.foundation.layout.heightIn
```

With this code, you introduced four modifiers, two of which are completely new to you:

- **Modifier.padding**: Adds some space between the note and screen edges.
- **Modifier.shadow**: Creates DrawLayerModifier, which draws the shadow. The elevation defines the visual depth of a physical object. Furthermore, the physical object has a shape. In this case, you defined that the elevation should be 1.dp and, for the shape, you used RoundedCornerShape() to define that the corners should be rounded with a radius of 4dp.

- **Modifier.background**: This is a simple one. As you already learned, it draws a shape with a solid color behind the content.
- **Modifier.heightIn**: Constrains the height of the content between `min` and `max` values. In this case, you don't need a `max` value, but you do need a `min` because you want your composable to be at least `64dp` in height.

Now, build your project and run the app to check how `Note` looks.

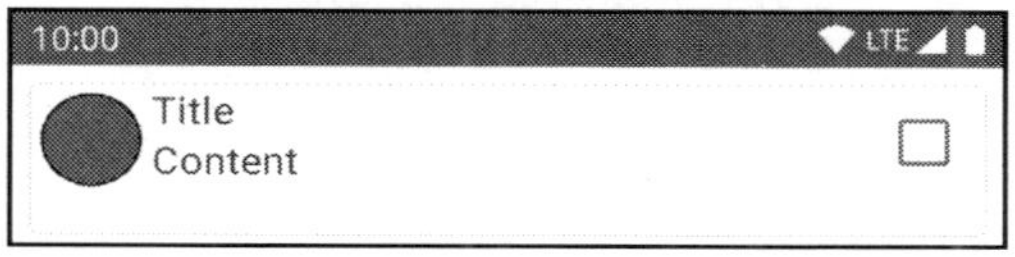

Note Composable With Background

Great! You've successfully added a background to your note. Pay attention to the corners: They're rounded now, and there's a shadow around the note. Also, see how the height of the note matches what you specified.

At this point, however, you've probably noticed that the overall composable looks awkward. That's because its content isn't centered. Fixing the alignment will be your next task.

Centering Text & Checkbox Composables

You're getting closer and closer to completing your `Note()`. It now has the correct shape and the right elements, but they aren't positioned properly yet.

Your first step is to fix the position of the `Text` and `Checkbox`. To do this, update the code for `Column` and `Checkbox` in `Note()` so it looks like this:

```
Column(
  modifier = Modifier
    .weight(1f)
    .align(Alignment.CenterVertically)
) {
  Text(text = "Title", maxLines = 1)
  Text(text = "Content", maxLines = 1)
}
Checkbox(
  checked = false,
  onCheckedChange = { },
  modifier = Modifier
    .padding(16.dp)
    .align(Alignment.CenterVertically)
)
```

For this to work, add this import:

```
import androidx.compose.ui.Alignment
```

The key to aligning your composables in this code is `Modifier.align(alignment: Alignment.CenterVertically)`. This modifier allows you to align elements vertically within the `Row`, so they are centered.

Just like `Modifier.weight()`, this modifier is defined in a `RowScope`. That means you can only use it in a `Row`. Notice you also added `Modifier.padding()` to `CheckBox()` to make it look nicer. This doesn't affect the composable alignment, but it's a good practice to pay attention to the details.

Build and run the app and your note will look like this:

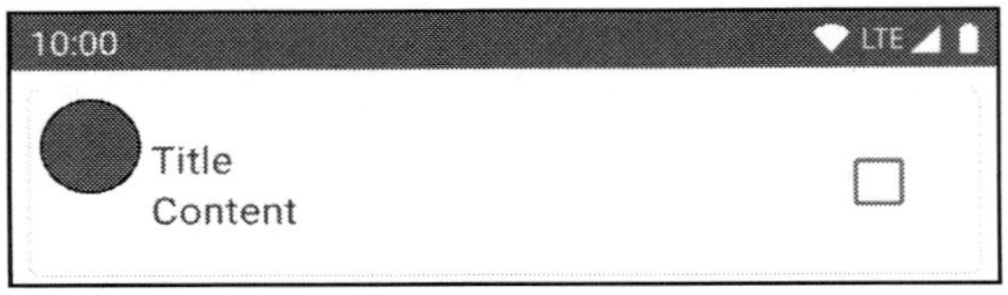

Note Composable Centered Text

Now, both the text and the checkbox are nicely centered in the note.

Centering NoteColor

When you look at `NoteColor`, you realize you can't apply a modifier to it like you did for the `Column` and `Checkbox`. The `NoteColor` doesn't expose a modifier as its parameter. It's time to fix that!

In **NoteColor.kt**, update `NoteColor()` so it looks like this:

```
@Composable
fun NoteColor(
  modifier: Modifier = Modifier, // 1
  color: Color,
  size: Dp,
  padding: Dp = 0.dp,
  border: Dp
) {
  Box(
    modifier = modifier // 2
      .padding(padding)
      .size(size)
      .clip(CircleShape)
```

```
        .background(color)
        .border(
          BorderStroke(
            border,
            SolidColor(Color.Black)
          ),
          CircleShape
        )
    )
}
```

There are two things to notice here:

1. You added a **modifier** as a **parameter** to your custom composable and you initialized it with an empty `Modifier`.

2. You used that modifier as the first in your chain of modifiers in `Box()`. Remember that, earlier, you used an empty `Modifier` here instead.

> **Note**: Take the time to digest the difference between using `modifier` vs `Modifier`. Only one single character separates the two, but the meaning is completely different. Understanding this can help you avoid quite a few bugs in the future.

What you just did is considered a good practice when creating custom composables with Jetpack Compose. It's always useful to **expose the modifier as a parameter** and to allow users of that composable to add other modifiers, as needed.

Now, go back to **Note.kt** and align the `NoteColor` as well:

```
NoteColor(
  modifier = Modifier.align(Alignment.CenterVertically),
  color = green,
  size = 40.dp,
  padding = 4.dp,
  border = 1.dp
)
```

As you see, you can now apply the same logic as you did for the `Text` and `Checkbox`, so you add `Modifier.align()` to `NoteColor`.

Build and run the app.

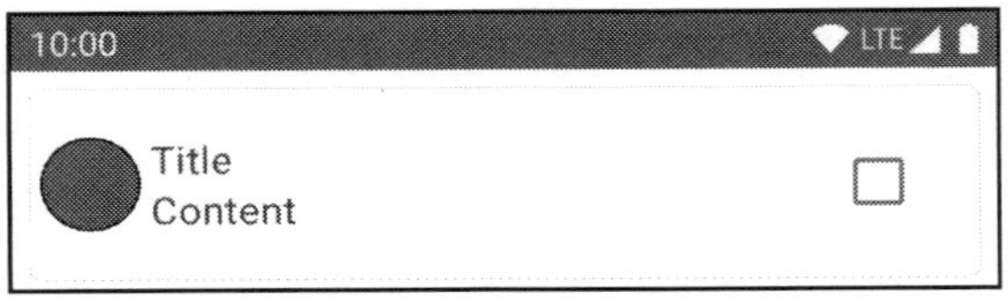

Note Composable Centered

Nice! Every component is now nicely centered in the note. However, the `NoteColor` and the `Text` are a bit cramped on the left side of the note. You'll work on that next.

Taking Advantage of the Modifier Parameter

As mentioned before, when working on custom composables it's a good practice to think about how someone might use that composable.

For `NoteColor` you exposed the `color`, `size`, `padding`, `border` and `modifier` to make it more **flexible**. However, you have to be careful *not* to overdo it. Having a lot of parameters can introduce more complexities than you need.

By exposing the modifier as a parameter, you suddenly allow a lot of customization for your composable. That means you might be able to remove some parameters because the behavior they provided can be taken over by the modifier.

For `NoteColor`, notice that you're passing the padding as a parameter. That was useful when you didn't have the modifier as a parameter, but now, you don't need it. You'll do something about that next. :]

Open **NoteColor.kt** and update the code to look like this:

```
@Composable
fun NoteColor(
  modifier: Modifier = Modifier,
  color: Color,
  size: Dp,
  border: Dp
) {
  Box(
    modifier = modifier
      .size(size)
      .clip(CircleShape)
      .background(color)
```

```
        .border(
          BorderStroke(
            border,
            SolidColor(Color.Black)
          ),
          CircleShape
        )
    )
}

@Preview
@Composable
fun NoteColorPreview() {
  NoteColor(
    color = Color.Red,
    size = 40.dp,
    border = 2.dp
  )
}
```

In the code above, you removed `padding` from the composable's parameters. You also removed `Modifier.padding()` from the chain of modifiers for the `Box`. You also updated `NoteColorPreview` so it doesn't include padding in the parameters.

Now, you'll get the padding by calling the composable through the `modifier`.

Applying the Padding

In **Note.kt**, update `NoteColor` like this:

```
NoteColor(
  modifier = Modifier
    .align(Alignment.CenterVertically)
    .padding(start = 16.dp, end = 16.dp), // here
  color = green,
  size = 40.dp,
  border = 1.dp
)
```

To add horizontal padding to `NoteColor`, you added `Modifier.padding()` to the `Modifier` that you pass as one of its parameters.

Build and run the app, and you'll see the following result:

Note Composable With Modifiers

Great job, your note almost matches the design now!

However, the devil is in the details, and there's one thing still missing: the text style. Right now, both the title and the content have the same text style. You'll work on this next.

Styling Title & Content

Look at the note design once again and you'll see that the title and content have specific text styles. The content text is smaller and has a different color. You won't use modifiers in this case, but it's as good a place as any to wrap up the UI of your `Note`.

In **Note.kt**, edit the code for `Column()` so it looks like this:

```
Column(
  modifier = Modifier
    .weight(1f)
    .align(Alignment.CenterVertically)
) {
  Text(
    text = "Title",
    color = Color.Black,
    maxLines = 1,
    style = TextStyle(
      fontWeight = FontWeight.Normal,
      fontSize = 16.sp,
      letterSpacing = 0.15.sp
    )
  )
  Text(
    text = "Content",
    color = Color.Black.copy(alpha = 0.75f),
    maxLines = 1,
    style = TextStyle(
      fontWeight = FontWeight.Normal,
      fontSize = 14.sp,
```

```
        letterSpacing = 0.25.sp
      )
    )
  }
```

To avoid complaints from Android Studio, add these imports:

```
import androidx.compose.ui.text.TextStyle
import androidx.compose.ui.text.font.FontWeight
import androidx.compose.ui.unit.sp
```

Here, you used the `style` and `color` in your `Texts` to apply **Material Design** to your note.

`TextStyle()` is a styling configuration for the `Text`. It exposes different parameters like `fontWeight`, `fontSize`, `letterSpacing` and more that let you style the text.

In Chapter 8, "Applying Material Design to Compose", you'll see how you can use Material components provided in Jetpack Compose to easily accomplish the same result. But for now, it's good to notice that you can accomplish the same thing using basic components.

Build and run the app. The note now looks like this:

Note Composable

Well done! Your note composable is now as beautiful as it is in the design. :]

Now that you've completed the `Note`, it would be nice to add some new composables to **Jet Notes**.

Adding the Color Composable

No, you're not experiencing *deja vu*. This will be a different composable from the previous `NoteColor`. :] Since you've completed `NoteColor`, it makes sense to add a composable relying on it to build extra functionality.

So now, you'll start working on a color picker composable, like the one shown below:

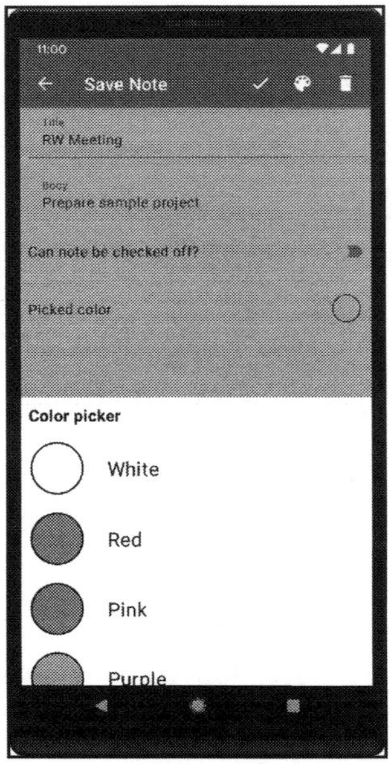

Color Picker

The color picker allows the user to color code their notes by assigning specific colors to them. The user can open the color picker by clicking on the color palette icon in the app bar or by pulling from the bottom edge of the screen.

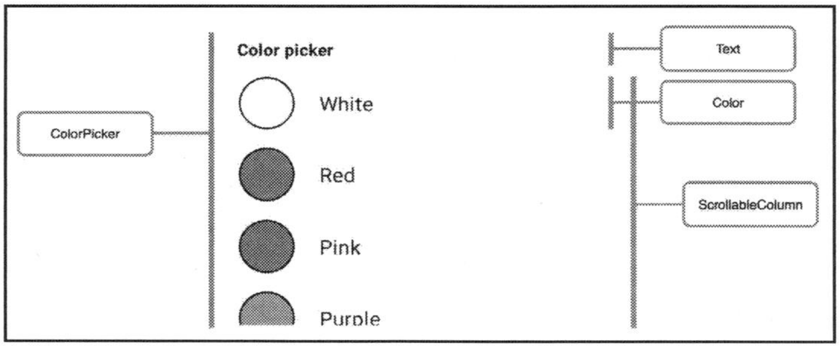

Color Picker — Components

You can break this composable down into smaller ones, as shown in the figure above. By following the **bottom-up** approach, you'll work on `ColorItem` first.

You'll use this composable in the **Save Note** screen.

Creating the ColorItem

Start by creating a new package called **screens** in the **ui** package. Then, in this package, create a new Kotlin file named **SaveNoteScreen.kt**. Finally, add the following code to **SaveNoteScreen.kt**:

```
@Composable
fun ColorItem(
  color: ColorModel,
  onColorSelect: (ColorModel) -> Unit
) {
  Row(
    modifier = Modifier
      .fillMaxWidth()
      .clickable(
        onClick = {
          onColorSelect(color)
        }
      )
  ) {
    NoteColor(
      modifier = Modifier.padding(10.dp),
      color = Color.fromHex(color.hex),
      size = 80.dp,
      border = 2.dp
    )
    Text(
      text = color.name,
      fontSize = 22.sp,
      modifier = Modifier
        .padding(horizontal = 16.dp)
        .align(Alignment.CenterVertically)
    )
  }
}
```

For this to work, you need to add the necessary imports:

```
import androidx.compose.material.Text
import androidx.compose.foundation.clickable
import androidx.compose.foundation.layout.Row
import androidx.compose.foundation.layout.fillMaxWidth
import androidx.compose.foundation.layout.padding
import androidx.compose.runtime.Composable
import androidx.compose.ui.Alignment
import androidx.compose.ui.Modifier
import androidx.compose.ui.unit.dp
import androidx.compose.ui.unit.sp
import com.yourcompany.android.jetnotes.domain.model.ColorModel
import com.yourcompany.android.jetnotes.ui.components.NoteColor
```

```
import com.yourcompany.android.jetnotes.util.fromHex
import androidx.compose.ui.graphics.Color
```

OK, it's time to break down the code. In the design, two components work together to make the `ColorItem` composable: `NoteColor` and `Text`. They're aligned next to each other, so you use a `Row` to position them.

There's one new modifier here you haven't used so far: `Modifier.clickable()` in `Row`. With that modifier, you made the whole `ColorItem` clickable. As mentioned before, it's a good practice to expose click events to parent composables.

To accomplish that, you passed the `onColorSelect(color)` call for the `onClick`. `onColorSelect` is of type `(ColorModel) -> Unit`, which is known as a function type. This specific function type says that the function that will be passed to it should take `ColorModel` as an argument.

To execute it, you used the default call operator: `onColorSelect(color)`, using the function name. This means when the user clicks on a note, the function passed for the `onColorSelect` parameter will execute.

`ColorItem` has two parameters:

- A `color` parameter of type `ColorModel`, which represents a model class for the color.
- The `onColorSelect` parameter of type `(ColorModel) -> Unit`. This is a lambda that takes `ColorModel` as an argument. That way, you allow the parent composable to know which color the user selected.

Previewing the ColorItem

Finally, add the following preview function to the bottom of **SaveNoteScreen.kt** so you can preview your `ColorItem`:

```
@Preview
@Composable
fun ColorItemPreview() {
  ColorItem(ColorModel.DEFAULT) {}
}
```

Don't forget to add the `Preview` import:

```
import androidx.compose.ui.tooling.preview.Preview
```

Here, you just invoked `Color` with the default color defined in **ColorModel.kt**. For `onColorSelect`, you passed an empty lambda since you don't need it for the preview to work. Thanks to Kotlin, you're able to pass the second argument as a trailing lambda.

Now, build the project. In the preview panel, you'll see this:

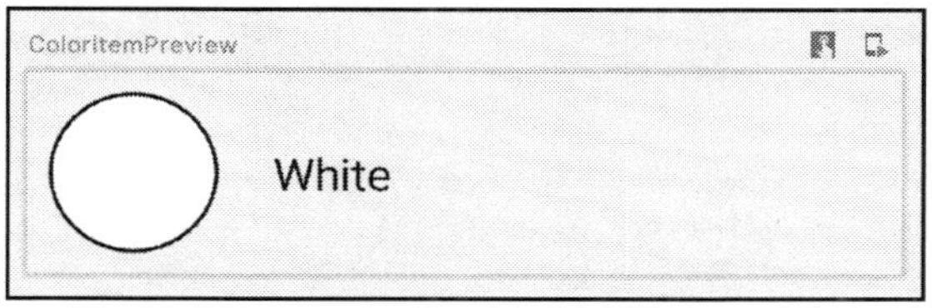

ColorItem — Preview

Great work! You've completed another composable! :]

Now, you can use this composable to complete the color picker.

Wrapping up the ColorPicker Composable

With `ColorItem` in place, it's a piece of cake to build `ColorPicker()`.

Add the following code to the top of **SaveNoteScreen.kt**, just above `ColorItem`:

```
@Composable
private fun ColorPicker(
  colors: List<ColorModel>,
  onColorSelect: (ColorModel) -> Unit
) {
  Column(modifier = Modifier.fillMaxWidth()) {
    Text(
      text = "Color picker",
      fontSize = 18.sp,
      fontWeight = FontWeight.Bold,
      modifier = Modifier.padding(8.dp)
    )
    LazyColumn(modifier = Modifier.fillMaxWidth()) {
      items(colors.size) { itemIndex ->
        val color = colors[itemIndex]
        ColorItem(
          color = color,
          onColorSelect = onColorSelect
        )
      }
    }
  }
}
```

As usual, there are a few imports that you need to add as well:

```
import androidx.compose.foundation.lazy.LazyColumn
import androidx.compose.foundation.layout.Column
import androidx.compose.ui.text.font.FontWeight
```

To create the `ColorPicker` in the code above, you used a `Column` to align its title and list of colors. You want the user to be able to scroll through the colors, so you used a `LazyColumn` to wrap them.

`ColorPicker` has two parameters: It takes the list of `ColorModels` and, like the `ColorItem`, it exposes the click event parameter.

To visualize what you've built so far, add the preview composable to the bottom of **SaveNoteScreen.kt**:

```
@Preview
@Composable
fun ColorPickerPreview() {
  ColorPicker(
    colors = listOf(
      ColorModel.DEFAULT,
      ColorModel.DEFAULT,
      ColorModel.DEFAULT
    )
  ) { }
}
```

Here, you invoked `ColorPicker()` and passed it a list of default colors. For `onColorSelect`, you passed an empty lambda, since you're not interested in interacting with the composable at this stage.

Build the project and check the preview panel to see this:

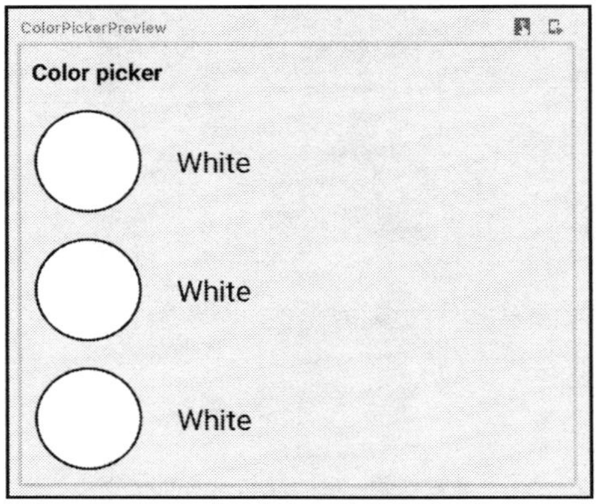

ColorPicker — Preview

Well done! Yet another composable under your belt. :]

You'll see the color picker in action in Chapter 7, "Managing State in Compose".

This is where this chapter ends. Hopefully, you now have a feeling for how powerful modifiers are. You can find the final code for this chapter by navigating to **06-using-compose-modifiers/projects/final**.

Key Points

- **Modifiers** tell a UI element how to lay out, display or behave within its parent layout. You can also say they **decorate** or **add behavior** to UI elements.
- You can **chain** several modifiers, one after the other, to **compose** them.
- The **order of modifiers** in the chain matters. Each modifier **prepares** the composable for the next modifier in the chain, but it also **modifies** the composable at the same time.
- Avoid **hard-coding** the values in your composables. Instead, **expose those values as properties** of the composable function.
- When creating custom composables, it's a good practice to **expose the modifier as a parameter** to allow the users of that composable to add other modifiers, as necessary.

Where to Go From Here?

Modifiers are a great tool to use when you style your composables. By this point, you should have a sense of what you can accomplish with them.

This chapter didn't cover all the modifiers that Compose offers since there are a lot of them. The good news is the principles are the same so you should feel safe using them with the knowledge you've gained.

When you play with composables, don't be afraid to dive deep and research which modifiers you can use on which components. You might be pleasantly surprised. :]

In the next chapter, you'll learn one of the **most important things** about Jetpack Compose: how to **manage states**. When you complete that chapter, **Jet Notes** will be one step closer to being a fully functional app.

Chapter 7: Managing State in Compose

By Denis Buketa

Great job on completing the first two chapters of this section. Now you know the basic principles of composing a UI and making it beautiful.

In this chapter, you'll change your focus from the UI of **JetNotes** to making it functional. To make any app functional, you need to know how to **manage state**, which is the topic of this chapter.

In this chapter, you'll learn:

- What **state** is.
- What **unidirectional data flow** is.
- How to think about **state** and **events** when creating **stateless** composables.
- How to use `ViewModel` and `LiveData` from **Android Architecture Components** to manage state in Compose.
- How to add functionality to the **Notes** screen.

Get ready to dive in by taking a deeper look at what state is and why it's critical for your app.

Understanding State

Before you can understand the **state management** theory, you need to define what **state** is.

At its core, every app works with specific values that can **change**. For example, **JetNotes** manages notes, and users can make changes to the list of notes. They can:

- Add new notes.
- Delete current notes.
- Change a note.
- Complete a note.

State is any **value** that **can change over time**. Those values can include anything from an entry in a database to a property of a class. And as the state changes, you need to **update the UI** to reflect those changes.

UI Update Loop

When you think about how users interact with Android apps, you can say that it's like having a conversation. Users communicate through events like clicking, dragging and speaking while the app responds by displaying the app's state.

Events are inputs generated outside the app, while the **state** is the result of the app's reaction to an event. In between, you have the **logic to update the state**.

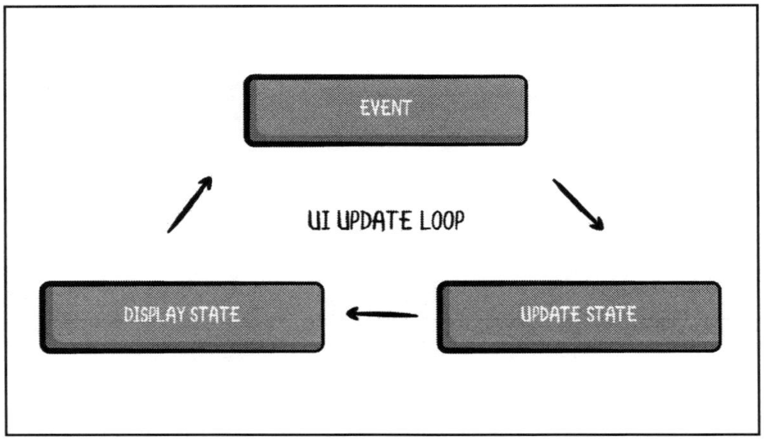

UI Update Loop

These three concepts form the **UI update loop**:

- **Event**: Input generated by the user or another part of the program.
- **Update state**: An event handler that reacts to the event and updates the state.
- **Display state**: The UI updates and displays the new state.

This is how all Android apps work. Understanding this concept is key to understanding how Compose manages state.

Handling State With Android UI Toolkit

Before going further, remind yourself how the current Android UI Toolkit manages state.

In Chapter 1, "Developing UI in Android", you had the chance to explore the data flow between the UI and the business logic for a basic Android component — a `Spinner`.

There, you saw that it's difficult to build a UI that represents the model — or a state, in this case — if the UI also owns and manages state.

That kind of design has some problems, including:

- **Testing**: It's difficult to test views like `Activity` or `Fragment` if the state of the UI is mixed in with them.
- **Partial state updates**: If the screen has a lot of events, it's easy to forget to update a part of the state, which can result in an incorrect UI.
- **Partial UI updates**: Whenever the state changes, you have to update the UI manually. The more things you have to update, the easier it is to forget something, once again resulting in an incorrect UI.
- **Code complexity**: When using this pattern, it's difficult to extract some of the logic. In the long run, the code tends to become difficult to read and understand.
- **No single source of truth**: Because both the UI and the model own the state, you have to make sure that they're in sync.
- **Update responsibility**: You don't always know if you're the one changing the `View` state, or if the event came from the user.

Keep this in mind as you learn about **unidirectional data flow** and how it can help.

Handling State With Unidirectional Data Flow

In the previous `Spinner` example, the data flow had multiple directions it could come from and multiple directions it could go to, depending on trigger events and UI updates it reflected. This means it's hard to keep everything in sync and its hard to know where the change is coming from at all times.

Unidirectional data flow on the other hand is a concept where both the state changes and UI updates have only one direction, as the name states. This means that state change events can only come from one source, usually from user interactions, and UI updates can come only from the state manager, the event handler or the model, however you want to refer to it.

Unidirectional data flow isn't a new concept in programming. It's well-established that it's a good idea to **decouple** components that **display state** in the UI from the parts of the app that **store and change state**.

Compose was built with unidirectional data flow in mind.

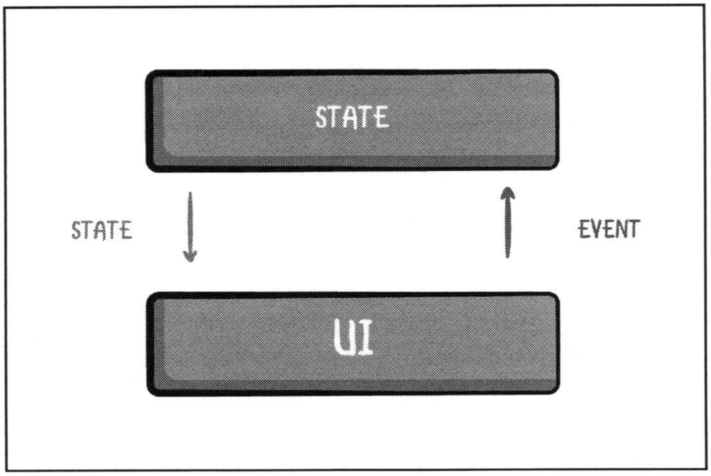

Unidirectional Data Flow

The key concept here is that **state flows down** and **events flow up**, as the image above shows.

Another key concept is that the UI **observes the state**. Every time there's new state, the UI displays it.

Here's how the UI update loop for an app that uses unidirectional data flow looks:

- **Event**: A **UI component** generates input and **passes it up**.
- **Update state**: An event handler **may or may not change** the state. For some UI components, the new state is already in the correct format, so it doesn't need to change.
- **Display state**: The UI **observes the state**. Upon creation, the new state is **passed down** to the UI that displays it.

Even though Compose didn't have a built-in `Spinner` at the time of this writing, you can reimagine how you used one in Chapter 1, "Developing UI in Android" with the unidirectional data flow in mind.

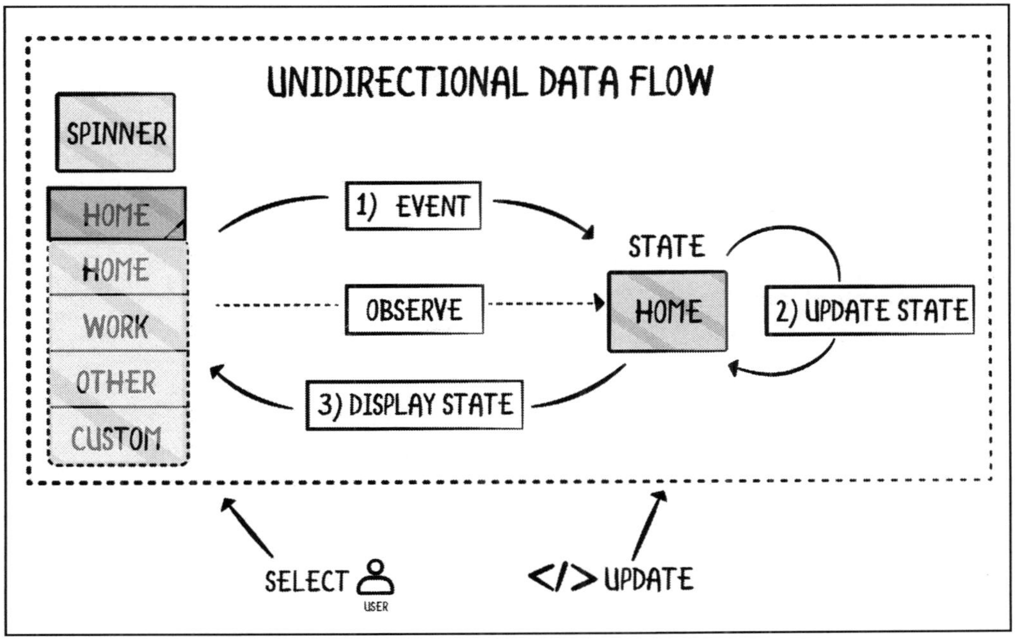

Unidirectional Data Flow

In the figure, you can see two distinct parts of the unidirectional data flow:

1. The **UI**, represented by the spinner.
2. The **state**, represented by `State` properties.

The `Spinner` observes the state and can generate events. An event handler may or may not update the state when the new event comes. When the state changes, the `Spinner` is aware of and displays that change.

Just as when you worked with it in the previous example, the user can interact with the `Spinner` — the main difference now is how you interact with it in the code. In code, you don't interact directly with the `Spinner`; you only update the state. Since the `Spinner` observes that state, the UI updates correctly when the state changes.

Following this pattern when using Jetpack Compose has several advantages:

- **Testability**: Since the UI is decoupled from the state, you can test each component in isolation.
- **State encapsulation**: Because state can only be updated in one place, you're less likely to create inconsistent states.
- **UI consistency**: Since your UI observes the state, the UI immediately reflects all state updates.
- **Single source of truth**: The UI and the model no longer share the state. State is only present in one place, which is now the single source of truth.
- **Clear responsibility for updates**: The UI component can only generate new events and only the user can interact with it. Within the code, you interact with the state itself, not the UI component.

Good! Now that you know the basic principles of state management that Jetpack Compose is built upon, you're ready to get your hands dirty, by adding your first feature to **JetNotes**. :]

Compose & ViewModel

As mentioned in the previous section, in unidirectional data flow, the UI observes the state. The Android framework offers some great **Android Architecture Components** that make it easy for you to follow that approach, including the `ViewModel` and `LiveData`.

A `ViewModel` lets you extract the **state** from the UI and define **events** that the UI can call to update that state. `LiveData` allows you to create **observable state holders** that provide a way for anyone to observe changes to the state.

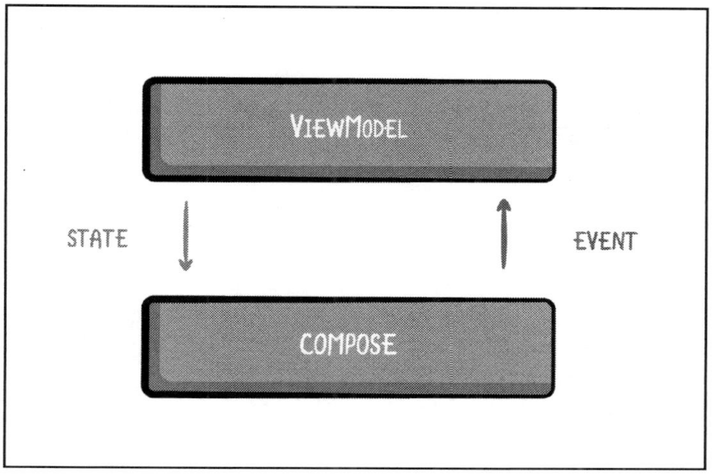

Unidirectional Data Flow With Architecture Components

You'll use the architecture shown in the figure above for your app.

The `ViewModel` will represent the **state**, while your composables will represent the **UI**. In your `ViewModels`, you'll use `LiveData` to hold state.

In your composables, you'll observe that state and propagate events from child composables to the `ViewModel`.

Enough theory, it's time to put this into practice! :]

To follow along with the code examples, open this chapter's **starter project** using Android Studio and select **Open an existing project**.

Next, navigate to **07-managing-state-in-compose/projects** and select the **starter** folder as the project root. Once the project opens, let it build and sync and you'll be ready to go!

Note if you skip ahead to the **final project**, you'll be able to see the **Notes** screen and the list of notes in it. :]

Creating the Notes Screen

So far, **JetNotes** has no screens. The only thing you can do with it at the moment is pull out the app drawer and inspect one note, which you use to track your progress. This is about to change. :]

Your next step is to create the **Notes** screen. To make it easier for you to work on this screen, the database already contains some notes and colors. If you're interested in the code behind them, check out `initDatabase()` in **RepositoryImpl.kt**.

Before you start implementing the `ViewModel`, you'll add the entry point for the **Notes** screen.

In the **screens** package, create a new Kotlin file named **NotesScreen.kt** and add the following code to it:

```
@Composable
fun NotesScreen(viewModel: MainViewModel) {

}
```

This creates your root composable function for **Notes**. Notice that `NotesScreen()` takes `MainViewModel` as a parameter. You need this because you'll observe states from the `MainViewModel` in `NotesScreen()`. You also need a reference to `MainViewModel` so you can pass events up to it from the UI.

For this to build successfully, you have to add these necessary imports:

```
import androidx.compose.runtime.Composable
import com.yourcompany.android.jetnotes.viewmodel.MainViewModel
```

Before adding any more code to **NotesScreen.kt**, you need to make this screen the default screen that appears when you open the app. To do this, first open **MainActivity.kt**. Add the following code just below the line where you defined `scaffoldState`:

```
val navController = rememberNavController()
```

With this you created `NavController`. `NavController` is the main API from the **Navigation component**, it allows you to easily manage navigation between your screen composables.

Next, replace the code inside **content** block with following:

```
NavHost(
```

```
    navController = navController,
    startDestination = Screen.Notes.route
  ) {
    composable(Screen.Notes.route) { NotesScreen(viewModel) }
  }
```

This ensures the **Notes** screen opens whenever you run the app.

`NavHost` is something you haven't yet encountered. Your screens define a navigation graph, with each screen implemented as a composable. `NavHost` allows you to connect your navigation graph with the `navController`. In `NavHost`, you define possible navigation routes and you associate each route with a specific screen composable. In the next chapter, you'll see how to use `navController` to navigate between screens.

Now, add the missing imports.

```
import androidx.navigation.compose.NavHost
import androidx.navigation.compose.composable
import androidx.navigation.compose.rememberNavController
import com.yourcompany.android.jetnotes.ui.screens.NotesScreen
```

Finally, build and run the app. You'll see an empty screen, like this:

Empty Notes Screens

OK, your canvas is ready!

In the next section, your next task is to connect `NotesScreen()` with `MainViewModel`.

Implementing Unidirectional Data Flow

Now you have an entry point to **Notes**, you need to implement `MainViewModel` so it supports unidirectional data flow.

Remember, there are two key concepts in play: **states** and **events**.

First, try your hand at breaking down which states are present here. The **Notes** screen displays a list of notes, which is the state of that screen. Each note contains a few states, which are all encapsulated in `NoteModel`.

Now, try to expose that state in your `MainViewModel`.

Open **MainViewModel.kt** and add the following code to the class:

```
val notesNotInTrash: LiveData<List<NoteModel>> by lazy {
  repository.getAllNotesNotInTrash().asLiveData()
}
```

`Repository`, which came pre-prepared in the starter project, exposes `getAllNotesNotInTrash()`, which returns the `Flow` of the list of `NoteModels`. Using `asLiveData()` on it, you can easily expose the `LiveData` state of the notes you want to display on the **Notes** screen.

Now, you need to add few imports:

```
import androidx.lifecycle.LiveData
import androidx.lifecycle.asLiveData
import com.yourcompany.android.jetnotes.domain.model.NoteModel
```

This was pretty simple. Next, you need to break down which events to pass from `NotesScreen` to `MainViewModel`. Looking at the design tells you that there are three events to handle. Users can:

- Click on a specific note.
- Click on a floating action button (FAB) to create a new note.
- Check off a note.

To handle these events, add the following to the bottom of `MainViewModel`:

```
fun onCreateNewNoteClick() {
  // TODO - Open SaveNoteScreen
}

fun onNoteClick(note: NoteModel) {
```

```
    // TODO - Open SaveNoteScreen in Edit mode
  }

  fun onNoteCheckedChange(note: NoteModel) {
    viewModelScope.launch(Dispatchers.Default) {
      repository.insertNote(note)
    }
  }
```

Here, you added three functions that represent three possible events that the view can pass.

- **onCreateNewNoteClick()**: You call this function when the user clicks on a FAB. Right now, its body is empty, but you'll complete it when you work on the **Save Note** screen.
- **onNoteClick()**: This reacts when the user clicks on any note. To know which note the user selected, it uses `NoteModel` as a parameter. Once again, its body will remain empty until after you complete the **Save Note** screen.
- **onNoteCheckedChange()**: You call this when the user clicks on a checkbox in any note. It tells the repository to update the specific note in the database.

Finally, to make Android Studio happy, add these imports as well:

```
import androidx.lifecycle.viewModelScope
import kotlinx.coroutines.Dispatchers
import kotlinx.coroutines.launch
```

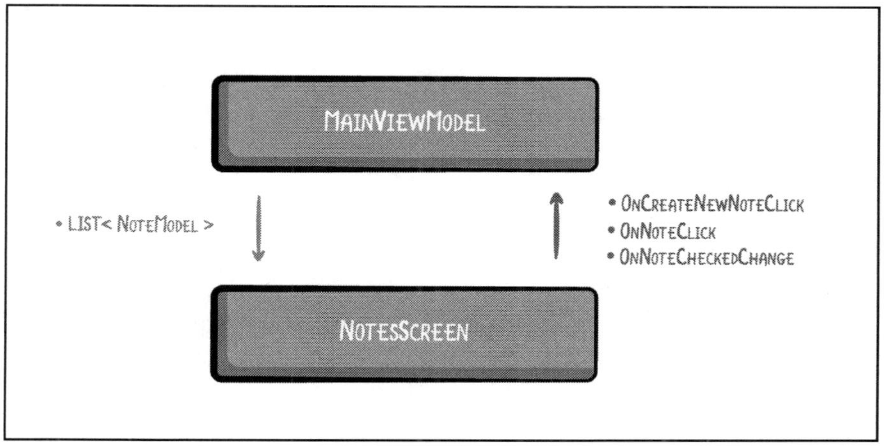

Unidirectional Data Flow — Notes Screen

Great job! You're now ready to use the `MainViewModel` in `NotesScreen`.

Creating the App Bar

Before connecting the `NotesScreen` to the `MainViewModel`, you need to implement the UI components that make up the **Notes** screen.

In your **Notes** screen, you'll need to add an app bar. But wait a second — check the design and you'll see that you need that app bar in *all* your screens. Therefore, it would be handy to implement it as a separate component and reuse it whenever you need it.

In **ui.components**, create a new Kotlin file named **TopAppBar.kt** and add the following code to it:

```
@Composable
fun TopAppBar(
  title: String,
  icon: ImageVector,
  onIconClick: () -> Unit,
) {
  Row(
    modifier = Modifier
      .fillMaxWidth()
      .height(56.dp)
      .background(color = MaterialTheme.colors.primarySurface)
  ) {
    Image(
      imageVector = icon,
      contentDescription = "Top App Bar Icon",
      colorFilter = ColorFilter
        .tint(MaterialTheme.colors.onPrimary),
      modifier = Modifier
        .clickable(onClick = onIconClick)
        .padding(16.dp)
        .align(Alignment.CenterVertically)
    )
    Text(
      text = title,
      color = MaterialTheme.colors.onPrimary,
      style = TextStyle(
        fontWeight = FontWeight.Medium,
        fontSize = 20.sp,
        letterSpacing = 0.15.sp
      ),
      modifier = Modifier
        .fillMaxWidth()
        .align(Alignment.CenterVertically)
        .padding(start = 16.dp, end = 16.dp)
    )
  }
}
```

This code creates an app bar composable you can reuse on multiple screens. It's a straightforward composable. You used a `Row` to align an icon and a text field next to each other. You should be familiar with all the modifiers and specific properties that you use here — you saw them in the previous chapter.

You also exposed a couple of parameters to let you customize the screen. `title` allows you to change the screen title, while `icon` lets you set any icon for the app bar. Finally, since the icon is clickable, you exposed `onIconClick` so the parent composable can react when the user clicks the icon.

The important concept here is `onIconClick`. You already saw this concept in Chapter 5, "Combining Composables". By exposing that specific parameter, you allow the **click event** to be **passed up** when the user interacts with this composable.

Pay attention to this concept going forward. You'll see it a lot in this chapter.

For the code above to work, you need to add some imports as well:

```
import androidx.compose.foundation.Image
import androidx.compose.foundation.background
import androidx.compose.foundation.clickable
import androidx.compose.foundation.layout.Row
import androidx.compose.foundation.layout.fillMaxWidth
import androidx.compose.foundation.layout.height
import androidx.compose.foundation.layout.padding
import androidx.compose.material.MaterialTheme
import androidx.compose.material.Text
import androidx.compose.material.primarySurface
import androidx.compose.runtime.Composable
import androidx.compose.ui.Alignment
import androidx.compose.ui.Modifier
import androidx.compose.ui.graphics.ColorFilter
import androidx.compose.ui.graphics.vector.ImageVector
import androidx.compose.ui.text.TextStyle
import androidx.compose.ui.text.font.FontWeight
import androidx.compose.ui.unit.dp
import androidx.compose.ui.unit.sp
```

Now, it's time to wrap up the `TopAppBar()`. Add the following code to the bottom of **TopAppBar.kt**:

```
@Preview
@Composable
private fun TopAppBarPreview() {
  JetNotesTheme {
    TopAppBar(
      title = "JetNotes",
      icon = Icons.Filled.List,
      onIconClick = {}
    )
  }
}
```

Here, you added the preview composable so you can check `TopAppBar()` in the preview panel. You also took an extra step and used `JetNotesTheme` as a wrapper to make `TopAppBar()` use the colors you defined in your theme. However, the preview would work without that, too.

Don't forget to include these imports as well:

```
import androidx.compose.material.icons.Icons
import androidx.compose.material.icons.filled.List
import androidx.compose.ui.tooling.preview.Preview
import com.yourcompany.android.jetnotes.theme.JetNotesTheme
```

Build the project and check the preview panel. You'll see something like this:

TopAppBar Composable — Preview

Great! You've built an app bar composable you can reuse in any screen you want. :]

The next thing you'll do is adapt `Note()` so you can use it for the **Notes** screen.

Stateless Composables

In `MainViewModel`, you exposed the list of `NoteModels` as a state, but your `Note()` still isn't ready to render a specific `NoteModel`.

If you check `Note()`, which you completed in the previous chapter, you see that its values are all hard-coded. You'll change that in this section.

Before writing any code, take a moment to think about which state you need to render a note and which events each note should expose.

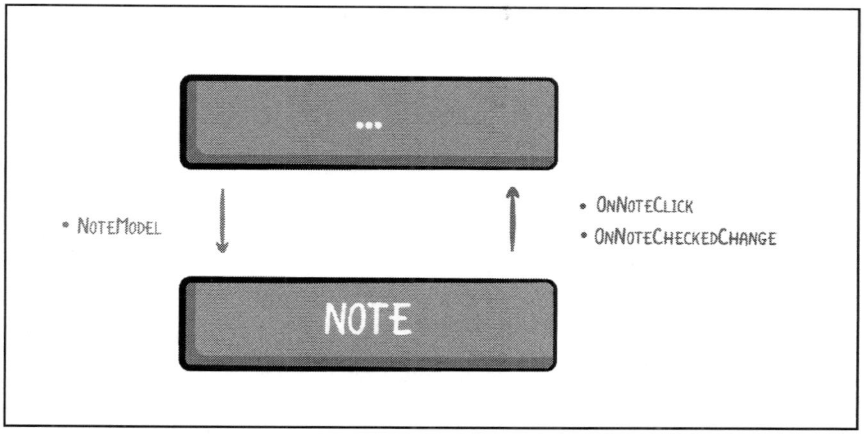

Unidirectional Data Flow — Note

As you saw before, `NotesScreen()` needs to be able to pass three events up to `MainViewModel` and two of those events are a note's responsibility.

Also, if you want to render the correct information in `Note()`, you need the data from a `NoteModel`. `NoteModel` is a state that a parent composable will pass down to `Note()`.

Now, you're ready to open **Note.kt** and add the following parameters to `Note()`:

```
@Composable
fun Note(
  note: NoteModel,
  onNoteClick: (NoteModel) -> Unit = {},
  onNoteCheckedChange: (NoteModel) -> Unit = {}
) {
    // ...
}
```

The parameters in the code above represent state and events that will be passed up and down between `Note()` and its parent composable.

An important principle is hidden in these parameters: **state hoisting**. If your composable has state, you can use state hoisting to make it **stateless**. State hoisting is a programming pattern where you **move state to the caller of a composable** by replacing internal state in a composable with **a parameter** and **events**.

For composables, this often means introducing two parameters to the composable:

- **value: T**: The current value to display.
- **onValueChange: (T) -> Unit**: An event that requests a change to a value, where T is the proposed new value.

The value T represents a generic type, that depends on the data and the UI you're showing. If you look at the parameters of `Note` again, you see you follow the same approach for your state and events. In that case, your T is actually a `NoteModel`.

By applying **state hoisting** to a composable, you make it stateless — which means it can't change any state itself. Stateless composables are easier to test, tend to have fewer bugs and offer more opportunities for reuse.

A **stateful** composable would be a composable that has a dependency on the final class, which can directly change a specific state. In this example, a **stateful** composable would be any parent composable that both has a dependency on `MainViewModel` and can call `MainViewModel.onNoteCheckedChange()`. Why that specific function? Because it changes the state in the `MainViewModel`.

Finally, import `NoteModel`:

```
import com.yourcompany.android.jetnotes.domain.model.NoteModel
```

Now that you understand stateless composables, your next step is to add the logic to render the `NoteModel` state.

Rendering NoteModel's State

To render the `NoteModel` in `Note()`, you need to replace your current, hard-coded values with the values from `NoteModel`.

Your first task is to update the code to use a color from `NoteModel` when you invoke a `NoteColor`. Still in `Note`, Modify `NoteColor` like this:

```
NoteColor(
  modifier = Modifier
    .align(Alignment.CenterVertically)
    .padding(start = 16.dp, end = 16.dp),
  color = Color.fromHex(note.color.hex),
  size = 40.dp,
  border = 1.dp
)
```

This is pretty straightforward. You use the utility function that parses the string color value from `NoteModel.color.hex` to `Color`. Before it will work, you need to add an import to a utility function:

```
import com.yourcompany.android.jetnotes.util.fromHex
```

Now, you're going to make sure that you show the correct title and content text. Edit `Column` like this:

```
Column(
  modifier = Modifier
    .weight(1f)
    .align(Alignment.CenterVertically)
) {
  Text(
    text = note.title, // edit code here
    ...
  )
  Text(
    text = note.content, // edit code here
    ...
  )
}
```

This is also easy to understand. All you did was replace the hard-coded values you used for the title and the content with `NoteModel.title` and `NoteModel.content`.

Now, the last thing to handle regarding state is the checkbox composable. Update the code that handles the checkbox, like this:

```
if (note.isCheckedOff != null) {
  Checkbox(
    checked = note.isCheckedOff,
    onCheckedChange = {},
    modifier = Modifier
      .padding(16.dp)
      .align(Alignment.CenterVertically)
  )
}
```

Here, you first check if `NoteModel.isCheckedOff` is null. If it is, that means the note isn't set up for the user to check it off, so it shouldn't show the checkbox.

If `NoteModel.isCheckedOff` *isn't null*, you invoke `Checkbox()` and pass that state as a parameter called `checked`. By doing that, you make sure the checkbox always has the right state.

Great job! `Note()` can successfully render the state that is **passed down** to it.
Your next step is to add the code that **passes events up**.

Passing up Note Events

Remember, the first of the two events that a note can pass up to a parent is when a user clicks the note. You'll handle that first, by updating the Row modifier in Note to allow that:

```
Row(
  modifier = Modifier
    .padding(8.dp)
    .shadow(1.dp, backgroundShape)
    .fillMaxWidth()
    .heightIn(min = 64.dp)
    .background(Color.White, backgroundShape)
    .clickable(onClick = { onNoteClick(note) }) // add code here
) {
  ...
}
```

Here, you made the Row clickable. As the user clicks on the Row, it triggers the internal onClick() handler from the modifier. That handler then notifies the parent, using onNoteClick(note). Doing so, it passes the NoteModel state of the clicked note up to the parent.

Finally, you need to add one import:

```
import androidx.compose.foundation.clickable
```

Well done! Now, you'll do the same thing for the second event. Update the Checkbox() by adding the following code to its onCheckedChange():

```
Checkbox(
  checked = note.isCheckedOff,
  onCheckedChange = { isChecked -> // add code here
    val newNote = note.copy(isCheckedOff = isChecked)
    onNoteCheckedChange(newNote)
  },
  modifier = Modifier
    .padding(16.dp)
    .align(Alignment.CenterVertically)
)
```

This a bit more complicated, but nothing you can't handle. :]

Whenever the user clicks the checkbox, it invokes `onCheckedChange()`, where `isChecked` contains the new value. You added the code creating a new `NoteModel` with the new `isCheckedOff` state.

After that, you call `onNoteCheckedChange(newNote)` and pass an event up to the parent with the new `NoteModel`.

Finally, you shouldn't forget to update the preview composable to use the new parameters you added to `Note`:

```
@Preview
@Composable
private fun NotePreview() {
  Note(note = NoteModel(1, "Note 1", "Content 1", null))
}
```

Build the project and you'll see something like this in the preview:

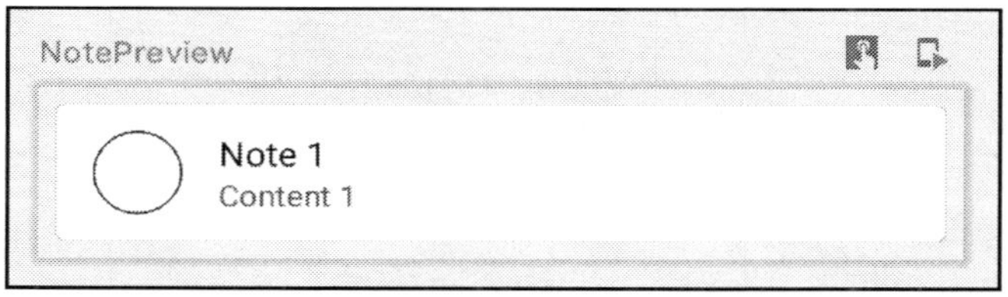

Notes Composable — Preview

Unidirectional Data Flow With Stateless Composables

Hoisting the state out of `Note()` has advantages: It's now easier to reason about the composable, reuse it in different situations and to test it. Plus, now you've decoupled `Note()` from how you store the state, if you modify or replace `MainViewModel`, you don't have to change how you implement `Note()`.

State hoisting allows you to extend **unidirectional data flow** to **stateless** composables. The unidirectional data flow diagram for these composables maintains state going down and events going up as more composables interact with the state.

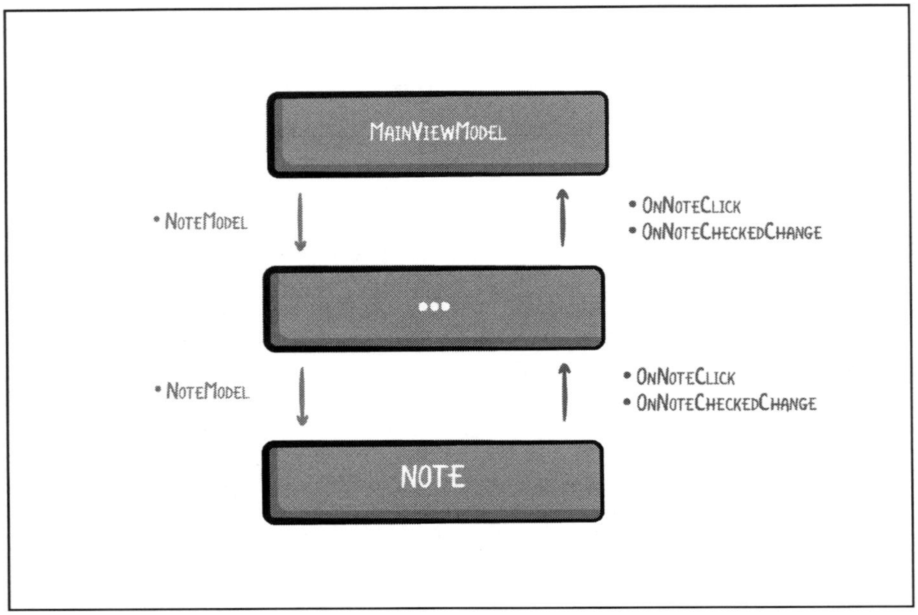

Unidirectional Data Flow — Note

It's important to understand a stateless composable can still interact with state that changes over time by using unidirectional data flow and state hoisting.

Check out the UI update loop for `Note()`:

- **Event**: You call `onNoteCheckedChange()` in response to the user clicking a checkbox in a note.
- **Update State**: `Note()` can't modify state directly. The caller may choose to modify state(s) in response to `onNoteCheckedChange()`. Up the `chain`, a parent composable will call `onNoteCheckedChange()` on `MainViewModel`. This, in turn, causes the `notesNotInTrash` to update and the event updating it will originate from where you called `onNoteCheckedChanged()`.
- **Display State**: When `notesNotInTrash` changes, you call `NotesScreen()` again with the updated state. That state will propagate down to a specific note. As you saw in previous chapters, calling composables in response to state changes is called **recomposition**.

You've now laid all the groundwork, and you're ready to let your users see their notes!

Displaying Notes in the Notes Screen

Now that `Note` is stateless, you're ready to display notes in the **Notes** screen.

Open **NotesScreen.kt** and update `NotesScreen()` by adding the following code to the body:

```
@Composable
fun NotesScreen(viewModel: MainViewModel) {

  val notes: List<NoteModel> by viewModel
    .notesNotInTrash
    .observeAsState(listOf())

  Column {
    TopAppBar(
      title = "JetNotes",
      icon = Icons.Filled.List,
      onIconClick = {}
    )
    LazyColumn {
      items(count = notes.size) { noteIndex ->
        val note = notes[noteIndex]
        Note(
          note = note,
          onNoteClick = {
            viewModel.onNoteClick(it)
          },
          onNoteCheckedChange = {
            viewModel.onNoteCheckedChange(it)
          }
        )
      }
    }
  }
}
```

OK, there are a couple of things to unpack here. The most interesting line is the first one, where you access the note's state from `MainViewModel`. You can break it apart like this:

- **val notes: List**: Declares a variable `notes` with the type `List<NoteModel>`.
- **viewModel.notesNotInTrash**: Returns an object with the type `LiveData<NoteModel>`.

- **.observeAsState(listOf())**: Converts LiveData<NoteModel> into a State<NoteModel> so Compose can react to value changes. You pass listOf() as an initial value to avoid possible null results before LiveData initializes. If you didn't pass the initial value, notes would be List<NoteModel>?, which is nullable.
- **by**: This keyword is the property delegate syntax in Kotlin. It automatically unwraps the State<List<NoteModel>> from observeAsState into a regular List<NoteModel>.

Composable functions get **subscribed** to a State any time you read the value property during its execution. Reading the notes' value when passing it to LazyColumn subscribed it to State<List<NoteModel>>. Any changes to that state will schedule a recomposition of NotesScreen().

The rest of the code handles emitting UI. You used a Column and put a TopAppBar and a LazyColumn into it.

Notice in LazyColumn(), you used Note(), which you adapted in the previous section. You pass NoteModel to pass down state. Finally, to allow each Note() to pass up events, you passed calls to viewModel.onNoteClick() and viewModel.onNoteCheckedChange().

Before building, you need to add these imports.

```
import androidx.compose.foundation.layout.Column
import androidx.compose.foundation.lazy.LazyColumn
import androidx.compose.material.icons.Icons
import androidx.compose.material.icons.filled.List
import androidx.compose.runtime.getValue
import androidx.compose.runtime.livedata.observeAsState
import com.yourcompany.android.jetnotes.domain.model.NoteModel
import com.yourcompany.android.jetnotes.ui.components.Note
import com.yourcompany.android.jetnotes.ui.components.TopAppBar
```

Now, build the project and run the app. You'll see something like this:

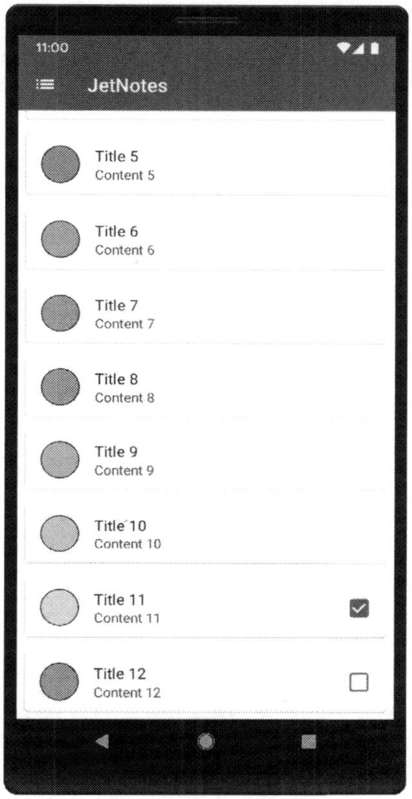

Notes Screen — List of notes

You can see the Notes created for you in the starter project. Scroll down to the last two notes and click a checkbox. You'll notice that state updates whenever you check off a note.

Extracting a Stateless Composable

Look at `NotesScreen()` code and you'll see it has a dependency on the final class, `MainViewModel`, which directly changes `notesNotInTrash`'s state. That makes it a stateful composable.

You can also see that the code that changes state is related to the list of notes. Both calls to `MainViewModel` are inside `LazyColumn()`.

Do you notice something? You could extract that code and make a stateless composable — which is what you'll do next.

Add the following code to the bottom of **NotesScreen.kt**:

```
@Composable
private fun NotesList(
  notes: List<NoteModel>,
  onNoteCheckedChange: (NoteModel) -> Unit,
  onNoteClick: (NoteModel) -> Unit
) {
  LazyColumn {
    items(count = notes.size) { noteIndex ->
      val note = notes[noteIndex]
      Note(
        note = note,
        onNoteClick = onNoteClick,
        onNoteCheckedChange = onNoteCheckedChange
      )
    }
  }
}

@Preview
@Composable
private fun NotesListPreview() {
  NotesList(
    notes = listOf(
      NoteModel(1, "Note 1", "Content 1", null),
      NoteModel(2, "Note 2", "Content 2", false),
      NoteModel(3, "Note 3", "Content 3", true)
    ),
    onNoteCheckedChange = {},
    onNoteClick = {}
  )
}
```

Don't forget to add the `Preview` import as well:

```
import androidx.compose.ui.tooling.preview.Preview
```

Whenever you extract a stateless composable, you should keep two things in mind:

- The **state** you're passing down.
- The **events** you're passing up.

`NotesList()` has a parameter of type `List<NoteModel>`, which represents state for `NotesList()`. You need a list of notes in order to **pass down** the `NoteModels` to each `Note()`.

As you learned above, every note needs to pass two events: a click on a note and a click on a checkbox. `NoteList` exposes the same events because it displays the list of notes. So, when you check the remaining parameters in `NotesList`, you see you added `onNoteCheckedChange: (NoteModel) -> Unit` and `onNoteClick: (NoteModel) -> Unit`, just as in `Note()`.

Once again, you applied the principle of state hoisting. Check the code inside `NotesList()` and you'll notice that this composable can't change any state. It can only pass state down or pass specific events up. It's decoupled from how its state, `List<NoteModel>`, is stored. By applying state hoisting, you made this composable stateless.

Finally, replace `LazyColumn` inside `NotesScreen` with `NotesList`:

```
Column {
  TopAppBar(
    title = "JetNotes",
    icon = Icons.Filled.List,
    onIconClick = {}
  )
  NotesList( // add code here
    notes = notes,
    onNoteCheckedChange = { viewModel.onNoteCheckedChange(it) },
    onNoteClick = { viewModel.onNoteClick(it) }
  )
}
```

This code is pretty straightforward, just be sure to notice you passed down the same arguments as before. For state, you passed `notes` and you also passed two calls to `MainViewModel`.

Now, build and run. In the app, you'll see the same screen as before, but you'll see your `NotesList` in the preview panel.

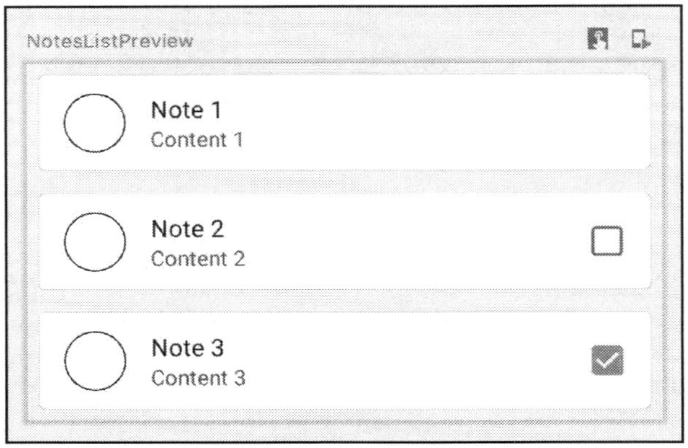

NotesList Composable — Preview

Well done! Before you wrap up this chapter, take a moment to review how you're passing state and events in the **Notes** screen.

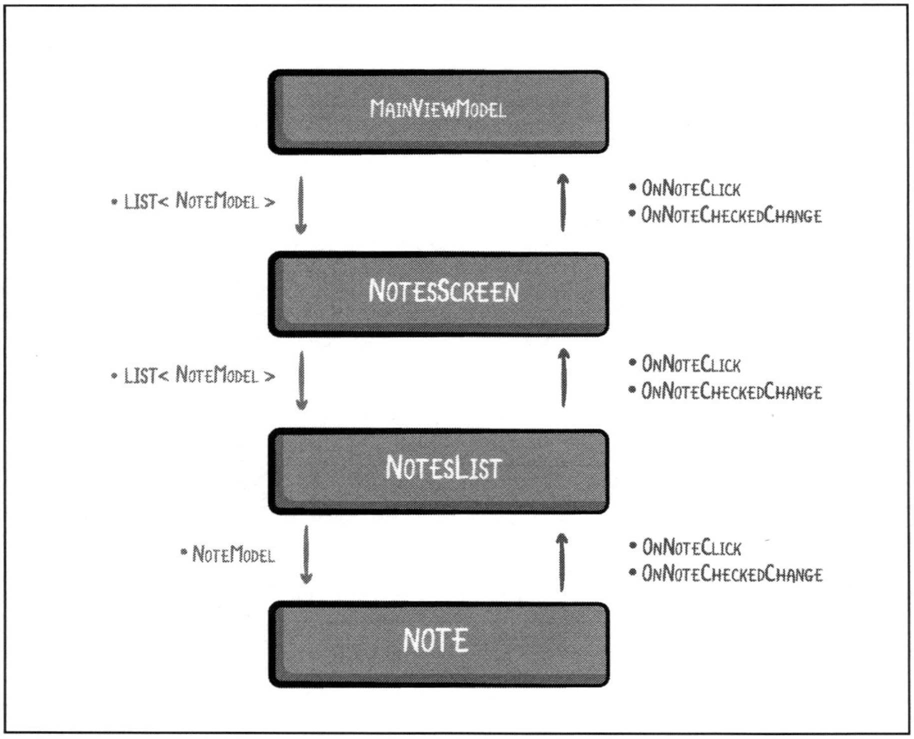

Unidirectional Data Flow — Notes Screen

This is the main concept behind **state management** in Compose. Always keep in mind that you **pass down** state and **pass up** events. Using **state hoisting** to create **stateless** composables makes that really easy.

Wow! You've made great progress on the **Notes** screen. :] You'll wrap it up in Chapter 8, "Applying Material Design to Compose".

Great job on completing this chapter! State management is a complex topic, and you'll see more of it in the following chapters as well.

You can find the final code for this chapter by navigating to **07-managing-state-in-compose/projects/final**.

Key Points

- **State** is any **value** that **can change over time**.
- The **UI update loop** is made of three key concepts: **event**, **update state** and **display state**.
- **Unidirectional data flow** is a design where **state flows down and events flow up**.
- You can use the Android Architecture Components, `ViewModel` and `LiveData`, to implement unidirectional data flow in Compose.
- A `ViewModel` lets you extract **state** from the UI and define **events** that the UI can call to update that state.
- `LiveData` allows you to create **observable state holders**.
- A **stateless** composable is a composable that cannot change any state itself.
- **State hoisting** is a programming pattern where you move state to the caller of a composable by replacing internal state in that composable with a parameter and events.

In the next chapter, you'll see how you can use **material components** to easily build UI. You'll replace some of the composables that use basic composables and you'll build the rest of the app. You'll also work more with state since there are two more screens to build!

Chapter 8: Applying Material Design to Compose

By Denis Buketa

Well done! You've arrived at the last chapter in this section. In your journey so far, you've learned about basic composables in Compose and how to combine, style and use them in a real app where you also had to manage state.

In this chapter, you'll:

- Learn how to use **Material Design composables**, which Jetpack Compose provides for you.
- Go over **state management** in more depth.
- Learn more about **Jetpack Compose navigation API**.
- Complete the **Save Note** screen.
- Learn about **Material theming**.
- Change **JetNotes** to support a **dark theme**.

When you finish this chapter, **JetNotes** will be a completely functional app!

Opening the Notes Screen

Before you can start working on the **Save Note** screen, you need a way to open it. By looking at the design, you can see that you've planned two ways to do that:

1. By clicking a floating action button (FAB), which will open the **Save Note** screen in **Create** mode, where the user can create a new note.
2. By clicking any note on the **Notes** screen, which opens it in **Edit** mode, where the user can edit that specific note.

You'll start with the first case. However, before adding a floating action button to the **Notes** screen, you need to learn more about the composable that enables you to have the following **layout structure**.

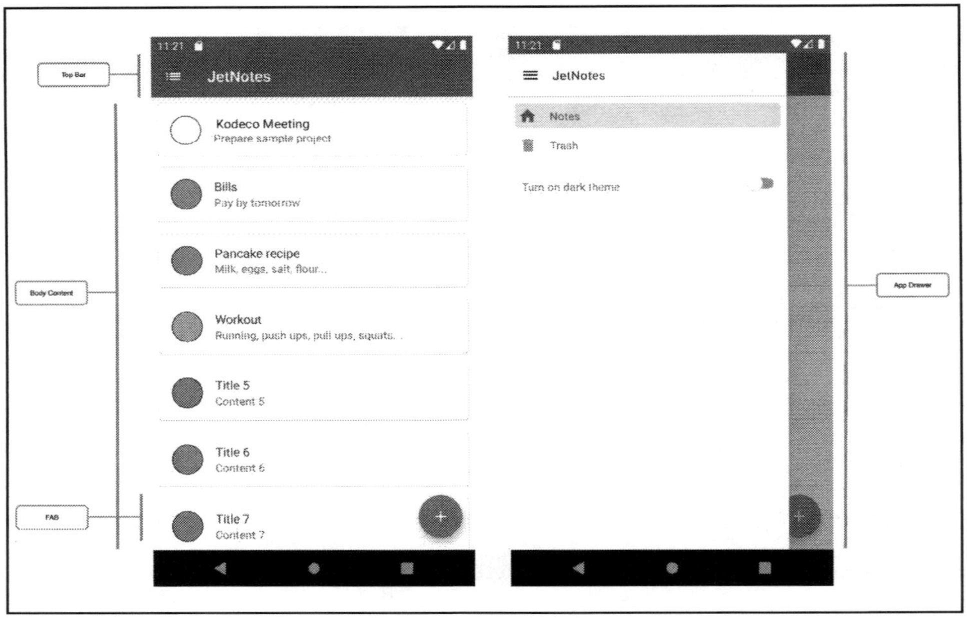

Notes Screen

Take a moment to look at the different parts of the screen. You have the:

- Top bar
- Body content
- Floating action button
- App drawer

This is a common layout structure for Android apps. Most apps today follow a similar design. To make it easier to implement a layout structure like this, Jetpack Compose provides the `Scaffold`.

Using Scaffold

To follow along with the code examples, open this chapter's **starter project** in Android Studio and select **Open an existing project**.

Next, navigate to **08-applying-material-design-to-compose/projects** and select the **starter** folder as the project root. Once the project opens, let it build and sync and you're ready to go!

Note that you can see the completed **JetNotes** app by skipping ahead to the **final project**.

For now, open **MainActivity.kt** and inspect the code inside `setContent()` block:

```
JetNotesTheme {
  val coroutineScope = rememberCoroutineScope()
  val scaffoldState: ScaffoldState = rememberScaffoldState()
  val navController = rememberNavController()

  Scaffold(
    scaffoldState = scaffoldState,
    drawerContent = {
      AppDrawer(
        currentScreen = Screen.Notes,
        onScreenSelected = { screen ->
          coroutineScope.launch {
            scaffoldState.drawerState.close()
          }
        }
      )
    },
    content = {
      NavHost(
        navController = navController,
        startDestination = Screen.Notes.route
      ) {
        composable(Screen.Notes.route) {
          NotesScreen(viewModel = viewModel)
        }
      }
    }
  )
}
```

The most important composable here is `Scaffold`. `Scaffold` implements the basic **Material Design** visual layout structure. It provides an API to combine several Material composables to construct your screen by ensuring they have a proper layout strategy and by collecting necessary data so the components will work together correctly. Here, it allowed you to construct your screen with the main content and app drawer.

The first parameter you passed to it is `scaffoldState`. `scaffoldState` is responsible for managing basic screen state, like drawer configuration for example. You initialized it with `rememberScaffoldState()`. This is a new concept for you, which you'll learn more about later. The knowledge from the previous chapter will help you understand it better.

Second, you pass an `AppDrawer()` for the `drawerContent` parameter. By passing `Screen.Notes` to `currentScreen`, you made sure the notes item is selected when the user opens the app drawer. For the second parameter, you passed an action that manages the `scaffoldState`.

Above `rememberScaffoldState()` call, you used `rememberCoroutineScope()` to retrieve a `CoroutineScope`. This function returns a `CoroutineScope` bound to this point in the composition using the optional `CoroutineContext` provided by `getContext()`. `getContext()` will only be called once and the same `CoroutineScope` instance will be returned across recompositions. This scope will be cancelled when this call leaves the composition.

You should use this scope to launch jobs in response to callback events such as clicks or other user interaction where the response to that event needs to unfold over time and be cancelled if the composable managing that process leaves the composition.

Notice you used a coroutine to call `scaffoldState.drawerState.close()`. If you check `DrawerState` documentation, you can see `open()` and `close()` are **suspendable** functions.

They open / close the drawer with an animation and **suspend** until the drawer is fully opened / closed or the animation has been canceled. Because of that, you have to call those methods within a coroutine.

The last parameter you added to the `scaffold` is `NavHost` responsible for displaying the Notes screen. For now at least. Later you'll expand its functionality. :]

Build and run your app.

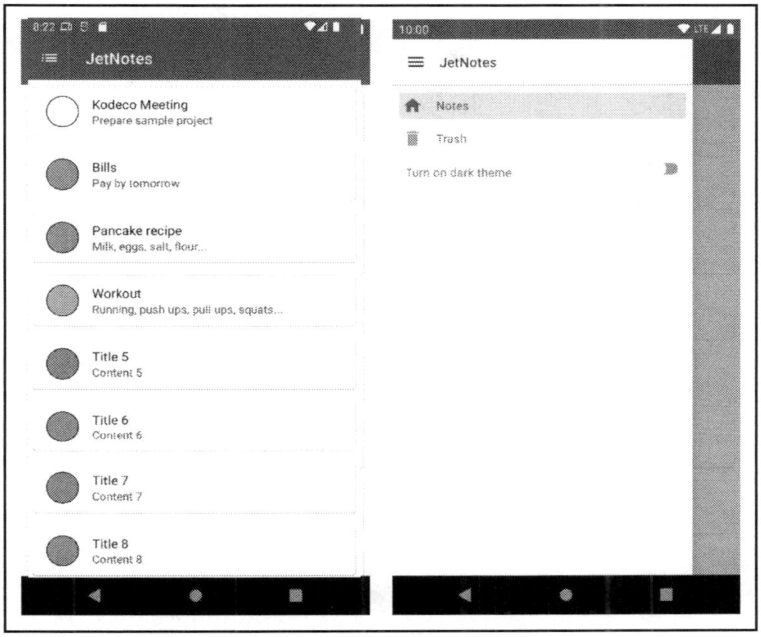

Notes Screen and App Drawer

For now, you can open the app drawer by dragging right from the left side of the screen.

Beside app drawer, `Scaffold()` allows you to add other structural composables for your screen. `This is theScaffold()`` signature from the Jetpack Compose documentation:

```
@Composable
fun Scaffold(
  modifier: Modifier = Modifier,
  scaffoldState: ScaffoldState = rememberScaffoldState(),
  topBar: @Composable () -> Unit = {},
  bottomBar: @Composable () -> Unit = {},
  snackbarHost: @Composable (SnackbarHostState) -> Unit =
{ SnackbarHost(it) },
  floatingActionButton: @Composable () -> Unit = {},
  floatingActionButtonPosition: FabPosition = FabPosition.End,
  isFloatingActionButtonDocked: Boolean = false,
  drawerContent: @Composable (ColumnScope.() -> Unit)? = null,
  drawerGesturesEnabled: Boolean = true,
  drawerShape: Shape = MaterialTheme.shapes.large,
  drawerElevation: Dp = DrawerDefaults.Elevation,
  drawerBackgroundColor: Color = MaterialTheme.colors.surface,
```

```
    drawerContentColor: Color =
contentColorFor(drawerBackgroundColor),
    drawerScrimColor: Color = DrawerDefaults.scrimColor,
    backgroundColor: Color = MaterialTheme.colors.background,
    contentColor: Color = contentColorFor(backgroundColor),
    content: @Composable (PaddingValues) -> Unit
)
```

Notice how it provides an API for the **top bar**, **bottom bar**, **floating action button**, **drawer** and **content**. You can pick and choose from these options, using only what you need.

In **MainActivity.kt**, you only used `drawerContent` and `content`. `Scaffold()` will make sure that the content you provided for the `drawerContent` is shown when you pull out the drawer and the content you provided for the `content` is below it.

Adding Scaffold to Notes Screen

As you just learned, `Scaffold()` allows you to add app drawer content. It also lets the user pull the drawer out by dragging it from the left side of the screen. Next, you are going to use it for top bar as well. Open **NotesScreen.kt** and replace `Column()` with `Scaffold()`. Also, notice that with the following code snippet you'll add one more parameter to the `NotesScreen()`:

```
@Composable
fun NotesScreen(
  viewModel: MainViewModel,
  onOpenNavigationDrawer: () -> Unit = {} // Add code here
) {

  // Observing notes state from MainViewModel
  ...

  // Add code below here

  val scaffoldState: ScaffoldState = rememberScaffoldState()

  Scaffold(
    scaffoldState = scaffoldState,
    topBar = {
      TopAppBar(
        title = "JetNotes",
        icon = Icons.Filled.List,
        onIconClick = { onOpenNavigationDrawer.invoke() }
      )
    },
```

```
      content = {
        if (notes.isNotEmpty()) {
          NotesList(
            notes = notes,
            onNoteCheckedChange = {
              viewModel.onNoteCheckedChange(it)
            },
            onNoteClick = { viewModel.onNoteClick(it) }
          )
        }
      }
    )
  }
```

Here's a breakdown of what you just did: You removed the `Column()` and its children, which you used to stack a `TopAppBar` and a `NotesList` on top of each other, and replaced it with `Scaffold()`. You also added a second parameter `onOpenNavigationDrawer` that allows you to notify the parent composable that the user clicked the navigation icon, informing the parent that the app drawer should be displayed.

Now, you need to add an import for `Scaffold`.

```
import androidx.compose.material.Scaffold
import androidx.compose.material.ScaffoldState
import androidx.compose.material.rememberScaffoldState
```

Before building and running the app, go to **MainActivity.kt** and pass a function that opens app drawer to the `onOpenNavigationDrawer` parameter.

```
JetNotesTheme {
  ...

  Scaffold(
    ...
    content = {
      NavHost(
        navController = navController,
        startDestination = Screen.Notes.route
      ) {
        composable(Screen.Notes.route) {
          NotesScreen(
            viewModel = viewModel,
            onOpenNavigationDrawer = {              // add code
here
              coroutineScope.launch {
                scaffoldState.drawerState.open()
              }
            }
```

```
                )
            }
        }
    }
)
}
```

With this, you defined a function that will modify `scaffoldState` and update `drawerState`. The result of that action will be the opened app drawer.

Build and run the app. You'll notice that the behavior is the same as before, but that you can now open the drawer by **clicking on the navigation icon** in the Notes screen:

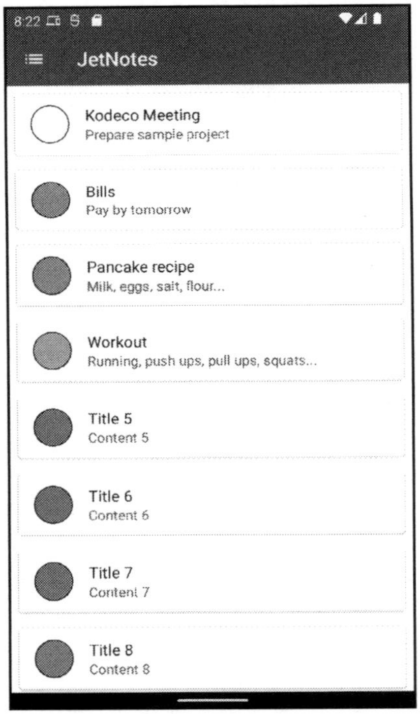

Notes Screen

Memory in Composable Functions

`Scaffold()` can manage two composables that have state: app drawer and snackbar. Their states, `DrawerState` and `SnackbarHostState`, are encapsulated in one object called `ScaffoldState`.

If you use one of these composables with `Scaffold`, you need to make sure their state updates accordingly and is preserved during recomposition.

Compose lets you **store values in the composition tree**. Another way of saying this is composable functions can access what happened the last time they were called. This is where `remember()` helps you.

Using remember

Here's how `remember()` looks in code:

```
@Composable
inline fun <T> remember(calculation: @DisallowComposableCalls ()
-> T): T
```

There are a couple of different variations of `remember()`. This one will remember the value that `calculation()` produces, which is evaluated during composition. During the recomposition, `remember()` will return the value produced by its `composition()`.

Also notice `@DisallowComposableCalls`, to avoid remembering composable functions within the remember call.

When you added `AppDrawer()` to `Scaffold()`, you used `rememberScaffoldState()` to create a `ScaffoldState`. This is its signature in the Jetpack Compose documentation:

```
@Composable
fun rememberScaffoldState(
  drawerState: DrawerState = rememberDrawerState(
    DrawerValue.Closed
  ),
  snackbarHostState: SnackbarHostState = remember {
    SnackbarHostState()
  }
): ScaffoldState
```

Notice how here, `remember()` creates and **remembers** a `SnackbarHostState`. For `DrawerState`, you use `rememberDrawerState()`, which will create and **remember** a `DrawerState`.

Look at that function's implementation:

```
@Composable
fun rememberDrawerState(
    initialValue: DrawerValue,
    confirmStateChange: (DrawerValue) -> Boolean = { true }
): DrawerState {
  return rememberSaveable(saver =
DrawerState.Saver(confirmStateChange)) {
      DrawerState(initialValue, confirmStateChange)
  }
}
```

Here, you can see `rememberSaveable()` is being used, which behaves similarly to `remember()` except the stored value will survive the activity or process recreation by using the saved instance state mechanism.

When it comes to the `DrawerState`, `rememberScaffoldState()` relies on `rememberSaveable()` to preserve the state during the recomposition and `Activity` recreation. In this example, there are two times the state will change: when the user opens the app drawer and when they close it.

You added two actions, and you made sure the `ScaffoldState` updates when the user clicks an icon or when `AppDrawer()` passes up the **close drawer** event.

For `SnackbarState`, `rememberScaffoldState()` relies on `remember()` to preserve the if the snackbar is visible or not during the recomposition. However, you won't worry about that for this app because it doesn't use a snackbar.

Finally, you passed `scaffoldState` to `Scaffold()`. That lets `Scaffold()` display the correct state when it changes. You're reading a lot about state and `Scaffold()` and how it preserves its state, but it's easier to just visualize what happens in the Jetpack Compose tree.

remember's Effect on the Composition Tree

Here's how the composition tree looks for `NotesScreen()`.

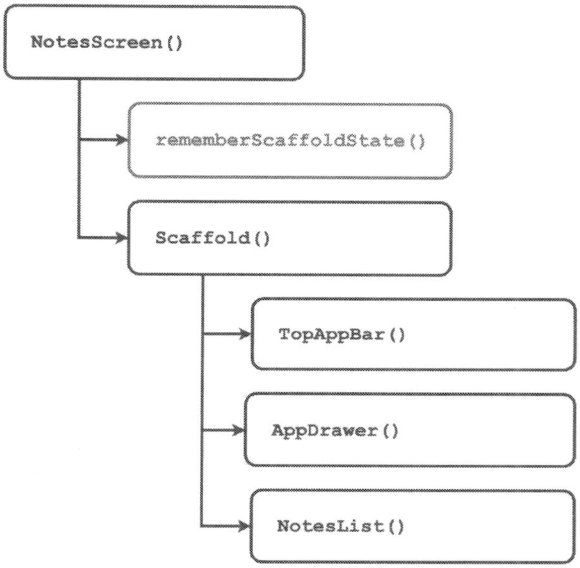

Notes Screen - Composition Tree

In Chapter 5, "Combining Composables", you learned there can be other types of nodes in the composition tree beside UI elements. This is one example. Calling `remember()` will result in an additional node in the tree that stores a specific value.

This also means values remembered in composition are forgotten as soon as their calling composable is removed from the tree. They will be re-initialized if the calling composable moves in the tree. For example, that could happen if you move items in a `LazyColumn` or a `LazyColumnFor`.

This was a nice digression to state management. But now it's time to come back to **Material Design composables**. :]

Continue to the next section, where you'll add a `FloatingActionButton` to the **Notes** screen.

Adding the FAB

A **floating action button** represents the primary action of a screen. In the **Notes** screen, the primary action is the action to create a new note.

In the previous section, you learned `Scaffold()` already provides an API to add the FAB to the layout. To implement it, update `Scaffold()` in **NotesScreen.kt**. Also, add a third parameter to the `NotesScreen()`:

```
@Composable
fun NotesScreen(
  viewModel: MainViewModel,
  onOpenNavigationDrawer: () -> Unit = {},
  onNavigateToSaveNote: () -> Unit = {}          // add code
here
) {

  // Observing notes state from MainViewModel
  ...

  val scaffoldState: ScaffoldState = rememberScaffoldState()

  Scaffold(
    ...,
    floatingActionButtonPosition = FabPosition.End,
    floatingActionButton = {
      FloatingActionButton(
        onClick = {
          viewModel.onCreateNewNoteClick()
          onNavigateToSaveNote.invoke()
        },
        contentColor = MaterialTheme.colors.background,
        content = {
          Icon(
            imageVector = Icons.Filled.Add,
            contentDescription = "Add Note Button"
          )
        }
      )
    },
    ...
  )
}
```

Here, you used `FloatingActionButton()` and passed it as the `floatingActionButton` parameter. You then pass `FabPosition.End` as the `floatingActionButtonPosition` parameter, which positions the FAB in the bottom-right corner.

`FloatingActionButton()` exposes a few more parameters, but you only used what you need. Clicking the button executes `onNavigateToSaveNote.invoke()` that should open a new screen and `viewModel.onCreateNewNoteClick()` that should prepare your state.

For the `content`, you passed an icon that renders as a plus sign. To make the content of the icon the same color as the background, you passed `MaterialTheme.colors.background` as the `contentColor`.

Android Studio will complain if you don't add these imports as well:

```
import androidx.compose.material.*
import androidx.compose.material.icons.filled.Add
```

Some of the imports might be condensed into the `import androidx.compose.material.*` statement, so make sure to clean up your imports and remove any redundant statements.

Build and run the app and you'll now see the FAB in the **Notes** screen.

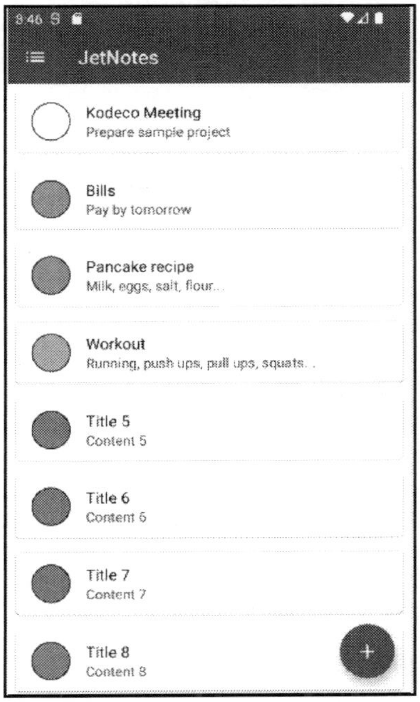

Notes Screen with Floating Action Button

Click it, but nothing will happen.

You'll change that once you implement an entry point to the **Save Note** screen.

Adding an Entry Point to Save Note Screen

In the previous section, you added the FAB that allows you to open the **Save Note** screen in the Create mode.

Before you can do that, however, you need to add an entry point composable for it. You'll do this in three steps:

1. You'll setup `MainActivityScreen()` to show different screens using Jetpack Compose navigation API.
2. You'll connect that composable to `MainActivity` as its content.
3. You'll call the `navController` to change the state, when the user taps on the `FloatingActionButton`.

Open **SaveNoteScreen.kt** and add the following composable at the top of the file:

```
@Composable
fun SaveNoteScreen(
  viewModel: MainViewModel,
  onNavigateBack: () -> Unit = {}
) {

}
```

Don't forget to include an import for `MainViewModel`:

```
import com.yourcompany.android.jetnotes.viewmodel.MainViewModel
```

With this, you created a composable function that represents the root of the **Save Note** screen. You defined two parameters. One that will allow you to pass the `MainViewModel` and one that you'll use to notify that the user performed an action to go back.

Using Jetpack Compose Navigation API to Change Screens

In the previous chapter, you added the code that opens the **Notes** screen whenever you start `MainActivity`. It's time to add logic to change screens based on `navController` state.

Open **MainActivity.kt** and add the following composable to the bottom of the file, outside `MainActivity`:

```
@OptIn(ExperimentalMaterialApi::class)
@Composable
private fun MainActivityScreen(
  navController: NavHostController,
  viewModel: MainViewModel,
  openNavigationDrawer: () -> Unit
) {
  NavHost(
    navController = navController,
    startDestination = Screen.Notes.route
  ) {
    composable(Screen.Notes.route) {
      NotesScreen(
        viewModel,
        openNavigationDrawer,
        { navController.navigate(Screen.SaveNote.route) }
      )
    }
    composable(Screen.SaveNote.route) {
      SaveNoteScreen(
        viewModel,
        { navController.popBackStack() }
      )
    }
    composable(Screen.Trash.route) {
      TrashScreen(viewModel, openNavigationDrawer)
    }
  }
}
```

With this code you added a composable that manages your screens. The main actors are `NavHost` and `NavHostController`. The `NavHostController` is responsible for managing the back stack of composables. If you want to access the state of the back stack you can use `currentBackStackEntryAsState()`.

Notice that to `NotesScreen()` you pass a function that uses `navController` to navigate to the Save Note screen. That function will open the Save Note screen and add that screen to the back stack. To the `SaveNoteScreen()` you pass a function that will pop that screen from the back stack.

For the code above to work, you need to add following imports as well:

```
import androidx.compose.material.ExperimentalMaterialApi
import androidx.compose.runtime.Composable
import
com.yourcompany.android.jetnotes.ui.screens.SaveNoteScreen
import com.yourcompany.android.jetnotes.ui.screens.TrashScreen
```

```
import androidx.navigation.NavHostController
```

You might ask yourself why did you have to add `@ExperimentalMaterialApi`. Some of the composables that you are going to build in this section will use an experimental API. To save you some time so that you don't have to go through each composable and add this annotation in the future, you'll add it now. Don't worry, you'll be aware of when you use something from the experimental material API.

Connecting MainActivityScreen to MainActivity

Next, you'll connect this composable to `MainActivity`, but also connect your app drawer with the navigation graph.

First, you'll connect you app drawer by updating the `setContent` block in the `MainActivity`:

```
...

val navBackStackEntry                                    // add
code here
  by navController.currentBackStackEntryAsState()

Scaffold(
  scaffoldState = scaffoldState,
  drawerContent = {
    AppDrawer(                                           // add
code here
      currentScreen = Screen.fromRoute(
        navBackStackEntry?.destination?.route
      ),
      onScreenSelected = { screen ->
        navController.navigate(screen.route) {
          // Pop up to start destination to avoid building the
          // stack for every screen selection
          popUpTo(
            navController.graph.findStartDestination().id
          ) {
            saveState = true
          }

          // Prevent copies of the same destination when screen
          // is reselected
          launchSingleTop = true

          // Restore state when selecting previously selected
          // screen
```

```
                restoreState = true
            }
            coroutineScope.launch {
                scaffoldState.drawerState.close()
            }
        }
    )
  },
  content = {
    ...
  }
)
```

You first initialized navBackStackEntry with navController.currentBackStackEntryAsState() so that you can observe changes in the back stack. In the AppDrawer(), you listen for that state and you pass a correct Screen to the currentScreen property when back stack changes.

For the onScreenSelected action, you use navController to navigate to the correct screen, but you also added a few modifications for that action. Whenever user selects a screen in the drawer, you pop up to start destination to avoid building the stack. You also used launchSingleTop = true to prevent copies of the same destination when screen is reselected. Lastly, you used restoreState = true to restore the state if previously selected screen is selected.

Now you have your app drawer connected with your navigation graph, update content block in the Scaffold in the MainActivity:

```
Scaffold(
  ...
  content = {
    MainActivityScreen(
      navController = navController,
      viewModel = viewModel,
      openNavigationDrawer = {
        coroutineScope.launch {
          scaffoldState.drawerState.open()
        }
      }
    )
  }
)
```

Add following imports:

```
import androidx.compose.runtime.getValue
import
androidx.navigation.NavGraph.Companion.findStartDestination
```

```
import androidx.navigation.compose.currentBackStackEntryAsState
```

You now have a way to change screens in the app! Build and run your app. Click the FAB in the **Notes** screen and see what happens.

You'll see that the **Save Note** screen opens... but it's empty. Don't worry, you'll add content to that screen in the following sections.

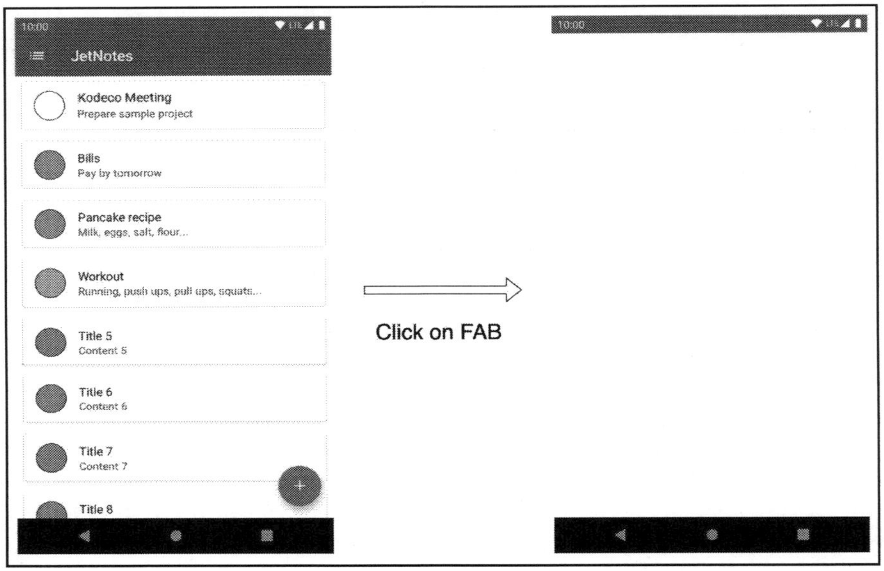

Opening Save Notes Screen

Clicking the **Back** button takes you back to Notes screen. By using the Jetpack Compose navigation API you get that functionality out of the box. When you click **back**, `navController` automatically pops the back stack.

You can also try opening the app drawer and selecting the **Trash** screen. You'll see that the **Trash** screen will open.

Adding the Top Bar

Until now, you've focused on adding code to open the **Save Note** screen. But now that you can open it, the **Save Note** screen is empty. In this section, you'll add composables to it. :]

You'll start with the top bar. Before diving straight into the code, look at the design. Again, you'll see that the screen has a familiar layout structure.

You can divide the **Save Note** screen into two parts: the top bar and the body content. Because of that, you can again use `Scaffold()` as your root composable.

Open **SaveNoteScreen.kt**, then update `SaveNoteScreen()`:

```
@Composable
fun SaveNoteScreen(
  viewModel: MainViewModel,
  onNavigateBack: () -> Unit = {}
) {
  Scaffold(
    topBar = {},
    content = {}
  )
}
```

With this, you added placeholders for your top bar and body content.

Don't forget to add the `Scaffold()` import, too:

```
import androidx.compose.material.Scaffold
```

Now, you can start working on the actual composables for the top bar.

Save Note Screen: Top Bar

Adding SaveNoteTopAppBar

In the **Save Note** screen, the top bar needs to support two different modes:

1. **Create mode**: This lets the user create a new note. There are two actions in the top bar that deal with this case: one to complete the note creation and one to open a color picker.
2. **Edit mode**: The user selects this to edit an existing note. This mode has three actions, one to save changes, one to open the color picker and one to delete the existing note.

Now that you've defined what you need, think about the top bar in terms of state and events. What state should be passed to the top bar and which events should you expose for the parent composable?

In total, there's one state that you should pass down to the top bar composable and four events that the top bar composable should expose. Next, you'll define `SaveNoteTopAppBar()` to allow that.

Add the following code below `SaveNoteScreen()`:

```
@Composable
private fun SaveNoteTopAppBar(
  isEditingMode: Boolean,
  onBackClick: () -> Unit,
  onSaveNoteClick: () -> Unit,
  onOpenColorPickerClick: () -> Unit,
  onDeleteNoteClick: () -> Unit
) {

}
```

Here are the important things to note in this code:

- **isEditingMode**: Represents whether the top bar is in Edit mode.
- **onBackClick**: Exposes an event when the user returns to the **Notes** screen.
- **onSaveNoteClick**: Exposes an event when the user saves a new or existing note.
- **onOpenColorPickerClick**: Exposes an event when the user opens the color picker.
- **onDeleteNoteClick**: Exposes an event when the user deletes the existing note.

Displaying the Top Bar

Now that you've prepared the root composable for the top bar, you'll add the composable that emits the top bar in the UI.

Add the following code to `SaveNoteTopAppBar()`:

```
TopAppBar(
  title = {
    Text(
      text = "Save Note",
      color = MaterialTheme.colors.onPrimary
    )
  }
)
```

Here, you used a Material Design composable: `TopAppBar`. This particular definition of `TopAppBar` has slots for the `title`, `navigationIcon` and `actions` — exactly what you need for the **Save Note** screen. You'll add each of these components, but for now, you added the `title`.

You represented the title with a simple `Text()`, where you defined the screen title and text color. Next you have to define the `navigationIcon` that will represent the back button. Do that by adding the `navigationIcon` parameter to `TopAppBar()`:

```
navigationIcon = {
  IconButton(onClick = onBackClick) {
    Icon(
      imageVector = Icons.Default.ArrowBack,
      contentDescription = "Save Note Button",
      tint = MaterialTheme.colors.onPrimary
    )
  }
}
```

For the `navigationIcon`, you passed `IconButton()` and defined the `onClick` action and the correct asset. This icon will display as a back arrow. This is pretty straightforward. Next add the `actions`:

```
actions = {
  // Save note action icon
  IconButton(onClick = onSaveNoteClick) {
    Icon(
      imageVector = Icons.Default.Check,
      tint = MaterialTheme.colors.onPrimary,
      contentDescription = "Save Note"
    )
  }

  // Open color picker action icon
  IconButton(onClick = onOpenColorPickerClick) {
    Icon(
      painter = painterResource(
        id = R.drawable.ic_baseline_color_lens_24
      ),
      contentDescription = "Open Color Picker Button",
      tint = MaterialTheme.colors.onPrimary
    )
  }
}
```

These two actions are represented by two `IconButtons`. The buttons will trigger `onSaveNoteClick` and `onOpenColorPickerClick` actions respectively. The final action you need to add is delete. Do that by adding the following code to `actions`:

```
// Delete action icon (show only in editing mode)
if (isEditingMode) {
  IconButton(onClick = onDeleteNoteClick) {
    Icon(
      imageVector = Icons.Default.Delete,
      contentDescription = "Delete Note Button",
      tint = MaterialTheme.colors.onPrimary
    )
  }
}
```

For the last action, you defined that the app should only add `IconButton()` if the top bar is in Edit mode.

Even though you didn't specify the layout structure for the `IconButtons`, they're still organized in a `Row`. That's because the `TopAppBar` defines `actions` like this: `actions: RowScope.() -> Unit = {}`. You define content that you passed for `actions` with a `RowScope`.

As usual, you need to add a couple of imports as well:

```
import androidx.compose.material.*
import androidx.compose.material.IconButton
import androidx.compose.material.MaterialTheme
import androidx.compose.material.TopAppBar
import androidx.compose.material.icons.Icons
import androidx.compose.material.icons.filled.ArrowBack
import androidx.compose.material.icons.filled.Check
import androidx.compose.material.icons.filled.Delete
import androidx.compose.ui.res.painterResource
import com.yourcompany.android.jetnotes.R
```

Now, add the preview composable for `SaveNoteTopAppBar`:

```
@Preview
@Composable
fun SaveNoteTopAppBarPreview() {
  SaveNoteTopAppBar(
    isEditingMode = true,
    onBackClick = {},
    onSaveNoteClick = {},
    onOpenColorPickerClick = {},
    onDeleteNoteClick = {}
  )
}
```

Build your project and, in the preview panel, you'll see something like this:

SaveNoteTopAppBar Composable (Editing Mode) — Preview

You can also play a little bit and pass `false` for `isEditingMode`. If you refresh your preview then, you'll see how your top bar looks when it's not in editing mode.

SaveNoteTopAppBar Composable (New Note Mode) — Preview

Awesome! Want to see your top bar in action? In the next section, you'll add `SaveNoteTopAppBar()` to the **Save Note** screen. :]

Displaying the SaveNoteTopAppBar Composable

Now that you've created the `SaveNoteTopAppBar()`, you can display it in the **Save Note** screen. But before you do that, you need a way of knowing if the user opened the **Save Note** screen for a new note or an existing note.

Open **MainViewModel.kt** and add the following code below `notesNotInTrash`:

```
private var _noteEntry =
MutableStateFlow<NoteModel>(NoteModel())
val noteEntry: LiveData<NoteModel> = _noteEntry.asLiveData()
```

With this, you added a state for a note entry that the user opened to edit in the **Save Note** screen. Both models will use this state, and you'll differentiate the two modes by using `NoteModel`'s ID.

Now, update `SaveNoteScreen()`:

```
@Composable
fun SaveNoteScreen(
  viewModel: MainViewModel,
  onNavigateBack: () -> Unit = {}
) {
  val noteEntry: NoteModel by viewModel.noteEntry
    .observeAsState(NoteModel())

  Scaffold(
    topBar = {
      val isEditingMode: Boolean = noteEntry.id != NEW_NOTE_ID
      SaveNoteTopAppBar(
        isEditingMode = isEditingMode,
        onBackClick = {
          onNavigateBack.invoke()
        },
        onSaveNoteClick = { },
        onOpenColorPickerClick = { },
        onDeleteNoteClick = { }
      ) },
    content = { }
  )
}
```

Here, you added the code to observe `viewModel.noteEntry`'s state. Whenever that state changes, `SaveNoteScreen()` will go through a recomposition.

In `Scaffold()`, you passed `SaveNoteTopAppBar()` for the `topBar` slot.

With `noteEntry.id`, you check if the screen is in Editing mode. If `NoteModel.id` equals `NEW_NOTE_ID`, the screen is in Create mode. Otherwise, it's in Editing mode.

For now, you just passed empty actions for the other events. You'll add them later.

Next, add the necessary imports:

```
import androidx.compose.runtime.getValue
import androidx.compose.runtime.livedata.observeAsState
import com.yourcompany.android.jetnotes.domain.model.NEW_NOTE_ID
import com.yourcompany.android.jetnotes.domain.model.NoteModel
```

Finally, build and run the app.

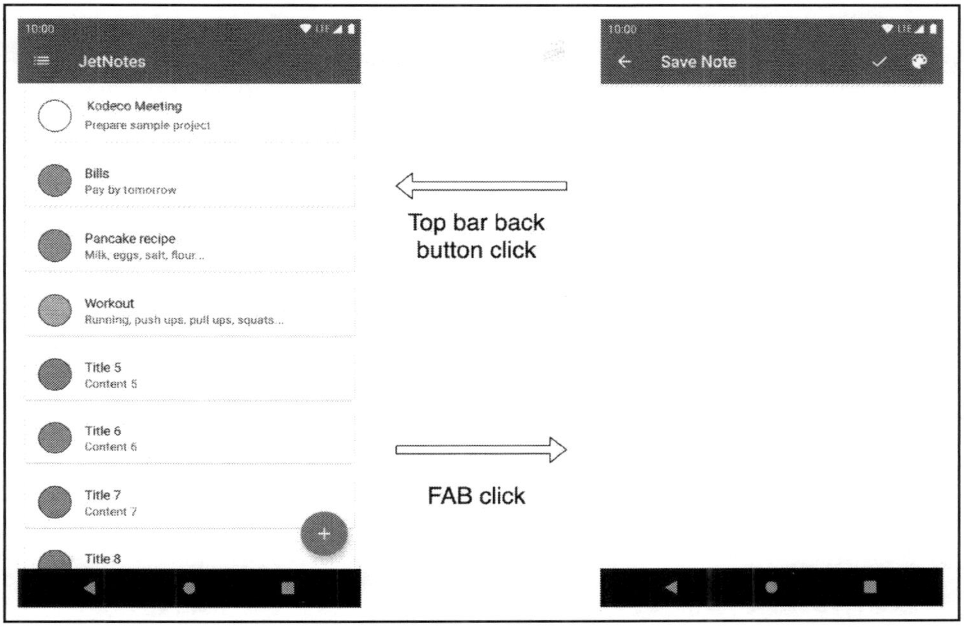

Adding the Top Bar to the Save Note Screen

Now, when you open the **Save Note** screen, you see the top bar. You can also go back to the **Notes** screen by clicking the **Back** button in the top bar.

Opening the Save Note Screen in Editing Mode

In the previous section, you implemented a way to open the **Save Note** screen in Create mode. Now, you'll add the logic that allows the user to edit an existing note.

Open **MainViewModel.kt** and update `onCreateNewNoteClick()` and `onNoteClick()` like this:

```
fun onCreateNewNoteClick() {
  _noteEntry.value = NoteModel()
}

fun onNoteClick(note: NoteModel) {
  _noteEntry.value = note
}
```

This is pretty simple. In the previous section, you defined `SaveNoteScreen()` will subscribe to `viewModel.noteEntry`'s state when it executes.

Here, you update that state with the correct `NoteModel`, depending on how the user opens the **Save Note** screen. If the user selected a note, you update the state with the selected note before opening the **Save Note** screen. If the user clicked the FAB, you update the state with an empty `NoteModel`.

Next, open **NotesScreen.kt** and update `NotesList()` with the function to open a Save Note screen:

```
@SuppressLint("UnusedMaterialScaffoldPaddingParameter")
@Composable
fun NotesScreen(
  viewModel: MainViewModel,
  onOpenNavigationDrawer: () -> Unit,
  onNavigateToSaveNote: () -> Unit = {}
) {

  ...

  Scaffold(
    ...
    content = {
      if (notes.isNotEmpty()) {
        NotesList(
          notes = notes,
          onNoteCheckedChange = {
            viewModel.onNoteCheckedChange(it)
          },
          onNoteClick = {
            viewModel.onNoteClick(it)
            onNavigateToSaveNote.invoke()           // add code
here
          }
        )
      }
    }
  )
}
```

Build and run, then click any note in the **Notes** screen.

Save Note Screen in Edit Mode

Note there are now three actions in the top bar, which means it's in Editing mode. That's because `isEditingMode` is set to `true` because `NoteModel.id` is not equal to `NEW_NOTE_ID`.

But there's still content missing, so let's implement that next.

Creating a Content Composable

You need to be able to edit notes in the **Save Note** screen, so your next step is to create a content composable to do that.

Refer to the design and you'll see that the user can use a color picker to select a color for the note. However, right now they can't see which color they picked. So your first task will be to implement the component that shows which color you picked from the color picker.

Displaying the Selected Color

To do this, go to **SaveNoteScreen.kt** and add the following composable below `SaveNoteTopAppBar()`:

```
@Composable
private fun PickedColor(color: ColorModel) {
  Row(
    Modifier
      .padding(8.dp)
      .padding(top = 16.dp)
  ) {
    Text(
      text = "Picked color",
      modifier = Modifier
        .weight(1f)
        .align(Alignment.CenterVertically)
    )
    NoteColor(
      color = Color.fromHex(color.hex),
      size = 40.dp,
      border = 1.dp,
      modifier = Modifier.padding(4.dp)
    )
  }
}
```

This is a pretty simple composable, and you're already familiar with its components. You've even built some of them yourself — like `NoteColor()`. :]

You used a `Row` to organize two elements, `Text()` and `NoteColor()`, next to each other. With modifiers, you added some padding and instructed `Text()` to use all the available width.

`PickedColor()` doesn't expose any events since its only job is to show which color the user picked, so it takes a `ColorModel` as the state to render.

Now, add the preview composable as well by adding the following code below `SaveNoteTopAppBarPreview()`:

```
@Preview
@Composable
fun PickedColorPreview() {
  PickedColor(ColorModel.DEFAULT)
}
```

Great! Now, build your project and check the preview panel. You'll see something like this:

PickedColorComponent Composable — Preview

Well done! You've completed one of your three tasks. Now, it's time to work on a component that allows you to make any note checkable.

Letting Users Check off a Note

In some cases, your users might want to check off a note — when they've completed a task, for example. By default, there's no option to indicate a note has been completed. Users need to mark notes as checkable if they want that feature. Your next step is to give them the possibility.

In **SaveNoteScreen.kt**, add the following composable below `SaveNoteTopAppBar()`:

```
@Composable
private fun NoteCheckOption(
  isChecked: Boolean,
  onCheckedChange: (Boolean) -> Unit
) {
  Row(
    Modifier
      .padding(8.dp)
      .padding(top = 16.dp)
  ) {
    Text(
      text = "Can note be checked off?",
      modifier = Modifier
        .weight(1f)
        .align(Alignment.CenterVertically)
    )
    Switch(
      checked = isChecked,
      onCheckedChange = onCheckedChange,
      modifier = Modifier.padding(start = 8.dp)
    )
  }
}
```

Just like `PickedColor()`, this composable's layout structure is pretty simple. You use a `Row()` to align a `Text()` with a `Switch()`.

`Switch()` is one of the **Material Design composables** in Jetpack Compose. It's familiar because it behaves the same as its counterpart in the current Android UI toolkit. You also used it earlier, when you implemented the app drawer.

When it comes to state and events, `NoteCheckOption()` takes a `Boolean` value for its state and exposes `onCheckedChange: (Boolean) -> Unit` as an event.

The parent passes down `isChecked`'s state so `Switch()` knows how to render itself. And whenever the user interacts with `Switch()`, an event with the new value will be sent up to the parent composable.

For this to work, you need to add one additional import:

```
import androidx.compose.material.Switch
```

Don't forget to give it a preview composable by adding the following code below `SaveNoteTopAppBarPreview()`:

```
@Preview
@Composable
fun NoteCheckOptionPreview() {
  NoteCheckOption(false) {}
}
```

Here, you pass `false` for the `isChecked` state and an empty action for `onCheckedChange`.

Build your project and you'll see your composable in the preview panel.

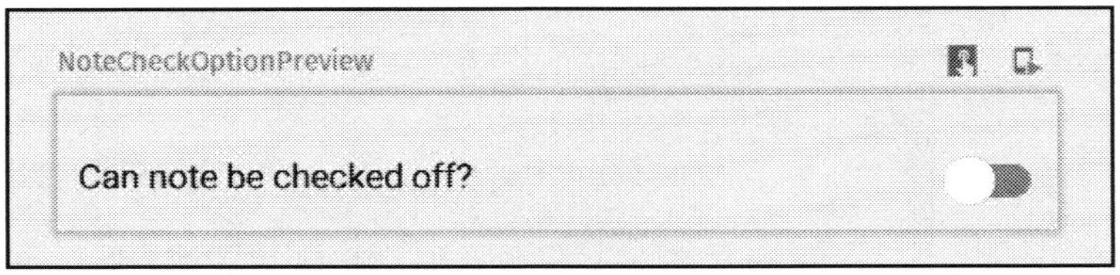

CanBeCheckedOffComponent Composable — Preview

Great job! There's just one more composable to add before assembling the content of the **Save Note** screen. :]

Adding a Title and Content

So far, you've added composables to represent the note's color and whether the user can check the note off when they complete a task. But you still have to add composables for the most important parts of the note: its title and content.

In **SaveNoteScreen.kt**, add the following code below `SaveNoteTopAppBar()`:

```
@Composable
private fun ContentTextField(
  modifier: Modifier = Modifier,
  label: String,
  text: String,
  onTextChange: (String) -> Unit
) {
  TextField(
    value = text,
    onValueChange = onTextChange,
    label = { Text(label) },
    modifier = modifier
      .fillMaxWidth()
      .padding(horizontal = 8.dp),
    colors = TextFieldDefaults.textFieldColors(
      backgroundColor = MaterialTheme.colors.surface
    )
  )
}
```

You'll use this composable for the text fields where the user enters the note's title and content. Here, you use the Material Design composable, `TextField()`.

`TextField()` lets you easily implement components to take the user's input. For state, the parent composable will pass `text` and `ContentTextField()` will pass up the change in the text as an event using `onTextChange: (String) -> Unit`. You also exposed a `label` to communicate what the text field is for. And you exposed a `modifier`, as good practice, allowing you to pass in custom modifiers at the call site.

Next, add a preview composable below `SaveNoteTopAppBarPreview()`:

```
@Preview
@Composable
fun ContentTextFieldPreview() {
  ContentTextField(
    label = "Title",
    text = "",
    onTextChange = {}
  )
}
```

Now, build your project and check the preview panel. There, you'll see `ContentTextFieldPreview()`:

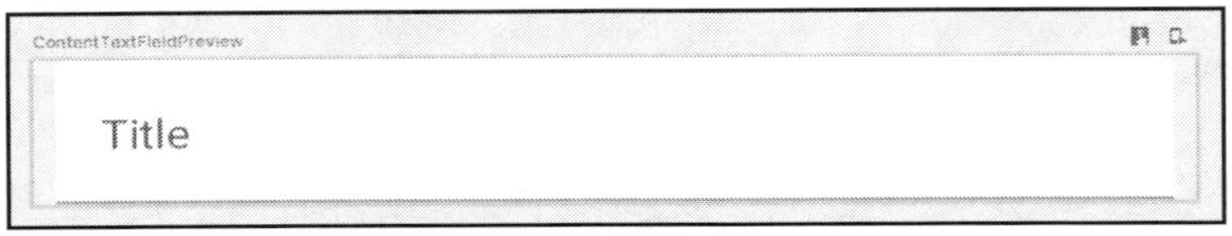

ContentTextField Composable — Preview

Excellent work! You now have all the pieces to create the content of the **Save Note** screen.

Building the Save Note Content

The next thing you'll do is put together all the composables that you created to make the **Save Note** screen content.

In **SaveNoteScreen.kt**, add `SaveNoteContent()` below `SaveNoteTopAppBar()`:

```
@Composable
private fun SaveNoteContent(
  note: NoteModel,
  onNoteChange: (NoteModel) -> Unit
) {
  Column(modifier = Modifier.fillMaxSize()) {

  }
}
```

This composable will represent the entire logic of creating and editing notes. You'll show the data from the `note` in input fields and other elements, and you'll use `onNoteChange()` to notify the parent when you want to save or update a note.

Now add the input fields to the `Column()`:

```
ContentTextField(
  label = "Title",
  text = note.title,
  onTextChange = { newTitle ->
    onNoteChange.invoke(note.copy(title = newTitle))
  }
)

ContentTextField(
  modifier = Modifier
    .heightIn(max = 240.dp)
    .padding(top = 16.dp),
```

```
    label = "Body",
    text = note.content,
    onTextChange = { newContent ->
      onNoteChange.invoke(note.copy(content = newContent))
    }
  )
```

These two `ContentTextFields` will represent the note title and body. You also added a bit of styling and respective `onTextChange` handlers to the input. Through them, you update the internal state of the `note` and let the parent know about the update.

Finally, add the `NoteCheckOption()` and the `PickedColor()` within `SaveNoteContent()`to represent more details of the `note`:

```
val canBeCheckedOff: Boolean = note.isCheckedOff != null

NoteCheckOption(
  isChecked = canBeCheckedOff,
  onCheckedChange = { canBeCheckedOffNewValue ->
    val isCheckedOff: Boolean? = if (canBeCheckedOffNewValue)
false else null

    onNoteChange.invoke(note.copy(isCheckedOff = isCheckedOff))
  }
)

PickedColor(color = note.color)
```

From the design, you see you want to organize the components in a column where the first two components are responsible for taking the user's input for a note's title and content. Below those two components is a `NoteCheckOption()` so the user can make the note checkable. The last composable in is `PickedColor()` that shows the color the user picked for the note.

Next, add the following import:

```
import androidx.compose.foundation.layout.fillMaxSize
import androidx.compose.foundation.layout.heightIn
```

It would be awesome to preview the `SaveNoteContent()` as well.

Add the following code below `SaveNoteTopAppBarPreview()`:

```
@Preview
@Composable
fun SaveNoteContentPreview() {
  SaveNoteContent(
    note = NoteModel(title = "Title", content = "content"),
```

```
        onNoteChange = {}
    )
}
```

Build the project and, in the preview panel, you'll see how `SaveNoteContent` looks:

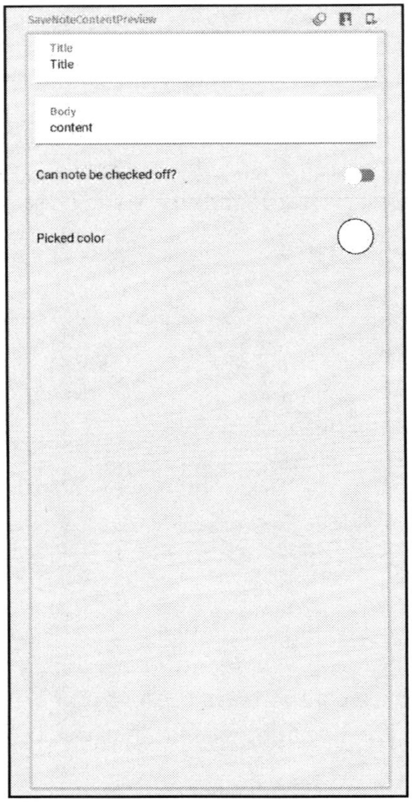

Content Composable — Preview

Wrapping up the Save Note Screen

Great job so far! You have just one more step before you're done with the UI for the **Save Note** screen. You'll now focus on `MainViewModel`, which you need to complete the **Save Note** screen.

Adding ViewModel Support

In `MainViewModel`, you already added the code to expose the `noteEntry` state, but you still need to add one more state. In the **Save Note** screen, the user can choose a color for a note. To display the list of colors the user can choose, you need to provide them to `SaveNoteScreen()`.

Open **MainViewModel.kt** and add the following code below `noteEntry`:

```
val colors: LiveData<List<ColorModel>> by lazy {
  repository.getAllColors().asLiveData()
}
```

The database already contains the colors you'll need. You simply exposed them here by adding the `LiveData`, which you can observe in `SaveNoteScreen()`.

Don't forget to add the following import:

```
import com.yourcompany.android.jetnotes.domain.model.ColorModel
```

Changing the noteEntry State

Next, you need to add support for changing the `noteEntry` state when the user interacts with the **Save Note** screen.

Add the following code to the `MainViewModel`:

```
fun onNoteEntryChange(note: NoteModel) {
  _noteEntry.value = note
}

fun saveNote(note: NoteModel) {
  viewModelScope.launch(Dispatchers.Default) {
    repository.insertNote(note)

    withContext(Dispatchers.Main) {
      _noteEntry.value = NoteModel()
    }
  }
}

fun moveNoteToTrash(note: NoteModel) {
  viewModelScope.launch(Dispatchers.Default) {
    repository.moveNoteToTrash(note.id)
  }
}
```

Time to break down each method:

With `onNoteEntryChange()`, you update the `noteEntry` state. You'll call this method each time the user makes a change in the **Save Note** screen.

`saveNote()` is responsible for updating the note in the database. If the user is creating a new note, you'll add a new entry in the database. If the user is editing an existing note, you'll update it instead. You use a coroutine to update the database in the background.

`moveNoteToTrash()` behaves similarly to `saveNote()`. It moves the note to the trash.

Connecting the SaveNoteScreen to the MainViewModel

Now that `MainViewModel` is ready, you can complete the UI part of the **Save Note** screen. Open **SaveNoteScreen.kt** and update `Scaffold()` in `SaveNoteScreen()`:

```
Scaffold(
  topBar = {
    val isEditingMode: Boolean = noteEntry.id != NEW_NOTE_ID
    SaveNoteTopAppBar(
      isEditingMode = isEditingMode,
      onBackClick = {
        onNavigateBack.invoke()
      },
      onSaveNoteClick = { // add code here
        viewModel.saveNote(noteEntry)
        onNavigateBack.invoke()
      },
      onOpenColorPickerClick = { },
      onDeleteNoteClick = { // add code here
        viewModel.moveNoteToTrash(noteEntry)
        onNavigateBack.invoke()
      }
    )
  },
  content = { // add code here
    SaveNoteContent(
      note = noteEntry,
      onNoteChange = { updateNoteEntry ->
        viewModel.onNoteEntryChange(updateNoteEntry)
      }
    )
  }
)
```

What you did here is you filled the `content` with `SaveNoteContent()`. That composable shows all the note's details and data, while letting you change it to update a note, or fill it in to create a new one. You also added the code that will close this screen when the user saves or deletes a note.

Great! Build and run your app.

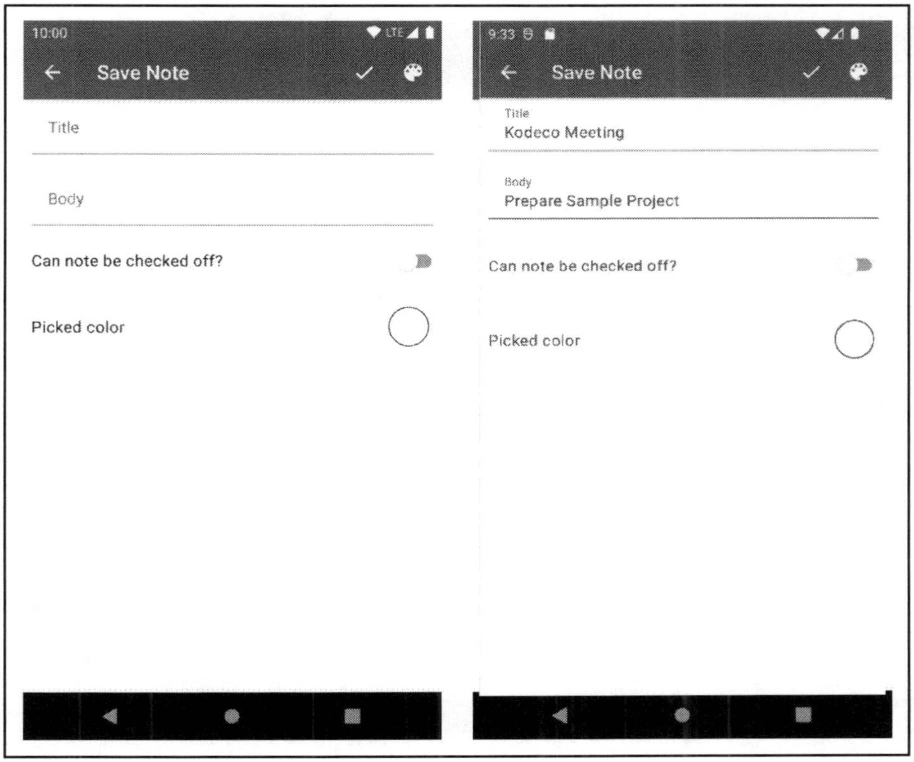

Save Note Screen

You can open the **Save Note** screen in Create mode to create a new note or you can click any note in the note list to open the screen in Editing mode.

Make a change in the title or body and click on the check icon in the top bar. You'll see that your change will save.

You can also move the note to the trash by clicking the trash icon.

Changing the Note's Color

There is still one thing missing: You still can't change the color of the notes. To fix that, update `SaveNoteScreen()` like this:

```
@Composable
@ExperimentalMaterialApi // add code here (BottomDrawer)
fun SaveNoteScreen(
  viewModel: MainViewModel,
  onNavigateBack: () -> Unit = {}
) {

  ...

  // add code here
  val colors: List<ColorModel> by viewModel.colors
    .observeAsState(listOf())

  // add code here
  val bottomDrawerState: BottomDrawerState =
    rememberBottomDrawerState(BottomDrawerValue.Closed)

  // add code here
  val coroutineScope = rememberCoroutineScope()

  Scaffold(
    topBar = {
      val isEditingMode: Boolean = noteEntry.id != NEW_NOTE_ID
      SaveNoteTopAppBar(
        ...,
        onOpenColorPickerClick = { // add code here
          coroutineScope.launch {
            bottomDrawerState.open()
          }
        },
        ...
      )
    },
    content = {
      BottomDrawer( // add code here
        drawerState = bottomDrawerState,
        drawerContent = {
          ColorPicker(
            colors = colors,
            onColorSelect = { color ->
              val newNoteEntry = noteEntry.copy(color = color)
              viewModel.onNoteEntryChange(newNoteEntry)
            }
          )
        },
        content = {
```

```
          SaveNoteContent(
            note = noteEntry,
            onNoteChange = { updateNoteEntry ->
              viewModel.onNoteEntryChange(updateNoteEntry)
            }
          )
        }
      )
    }
  )
}
```

First, check what you defined above `Scaffold()`: You subscribed `SaveNoteScreen()` to `viewModel.colors`'s state. That lets you pass that state to `ColorPicker()`.

Next, you created a `bottomDrawerState` of type `BottomDrawerState`. You need this for the new Material Design composable you used in `Scaffold()`. You also used it to open the bottom drawer when the user clicks on a color picker button in the top bar.

In `Scaffold()`, you wrapped `SaveNoteContent()` in a `BottomDrawer()`. `BottomDrawer()` is a Material Design composable that allows you to specify a modal drawer that's anchored to the bottom of the screen. In the time of writing, this was part of an experimental material API. Because of that you had to add `@ExperimentalMaterialApi` annotation to `SaveNoteScreen()`.

Notice that you passed `ColorPicker()` for the `drawerContent` and `SaveNoteContent()` for the `content`. The principle of state management for this drawer is similar to what you implemented for the `AppDrawer()` in `NotesScreen()`.

Before building the app, add following import:

```
import androidx.compose.runtime.rememberCoroutineScope
```

Build and run the app. Open **Save Note** and swipe up from the bottom of the screen or click on the color picker icon in the top bar.

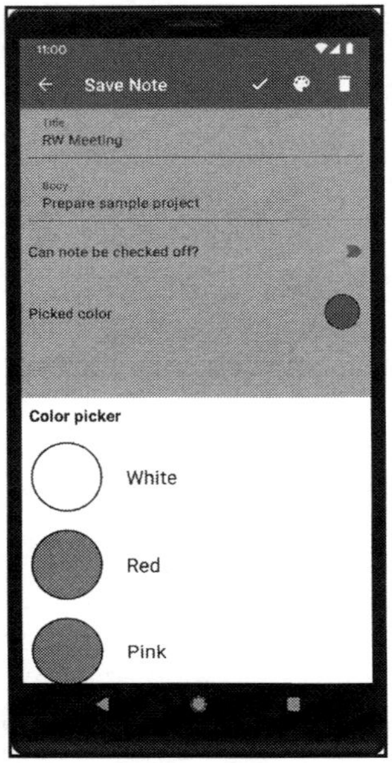

Color Picker on Save Note Screen

You can now change the color of any existing note or set a color for a new note. Next, you'll add a feature to confirm the user really wants to discard a note.

Confirming a Delete Action

While the **Save Note** screen is now functionally complete, it's always nice to pay attention to the details.

Right now, when the user clicks the trash icon in the top bar, the note will immediately move to the trash. However, it's a good practice to ask the user to confirm an action like that first.

In **SaveNoteScreen.kt**, add the following line before `Scaffold()`:

```
val moveNoteToTrashDialogShownState: MutableState<Boolean> =
rememberSaveable {
  mutableStateOf(false)
}
```

This state represents whether the dialog is visible.

Next, update the `SaveNoteTopAppBar()`, by changing the `onDeleteNoteClick` to the following:

```
SaveNoteTopAppBar(
  ...,
  onDeleteNoteClick = {
    moveNoteToTrashDialogShownState.value = true
  }
)
```

Now, when the user clicks the trash icon in the top bar, you'll update `moveNoteToTrashDialogShownState`'s value property to `true` to display the dialog. This piece of state will persist through configuration changes, using the `savedInstanceState`.

Finally, add the following code to the bottom of the content for `Scaffolds()`'s `bodyContent`:

```
Scaffold(
  topBar = { ... },
  content = {
    BottomDrawer(...)

    if (moveNoteToTrashDialogShownState.value) {
      AlertDialog(
        onDismissRequest = {
          moveNoteToTrashDialogShownState.value = false
        },
        title = {
          Text("Move note to the trash?")
        },
        text = {
          Text(
            "Are you sure you want to " +
                "move this note to the trash?"
          )
        },
        confirmButton = {
          TextButton(onClick = {
            viewModel.moveNoteToTrash(noteEntry)
            onNavigateBack.invoke()
          }) {
            Text("Confirm")
          }
        },
        dismissButton = {
          TextButton(onClick = {
            moveNoteToTrashDialogShownState.value = false
          }) {
            Text("Dismiss")
```

```
          }
        }
      )
    }
  }
)
```

Here, you used the Material Design's `AlertDialog()`. It exposes parameters like `onDismissRequest`, `confirmButton` and `dismissButton`, which you can use to customize buttons and actions. It behaves like the standard `AlertDialog`, where you give the user an option to do agree to your request, or cancel or dismiss the request

Before running the app, add following imports:

```
import androidx.compose.runtime.MutableState
import androidx.compose.runtime.mutableStateOf
import androidx.compose.runtime.saveable.rememberSaveable
```

Build and run the app. Open any note and move it to the trash to see your alert dialog.

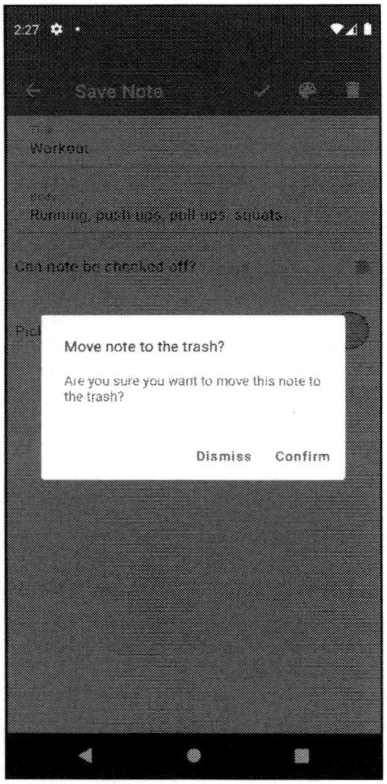

Alert Dialog in Save Note Screen

You can even change the device's orientation and the dialog will still display. This is a much better user experience.

Using Material Design Composables in the Notes Screen

The Material Design composables that Jetpack Compose provide are all built with basic composables. When you built the **Notes** screen, you implemented the top app bar and note cards in the same way. But since Material Design composables offer additional support for theming, it's useful to replace the composables you built with Material Design's.

Open **NotesScreen.kt** and replace `TopAppBar()` in `Scaffold()` with Material Design's `TopAppBar`:

```
Scaffold(
  topBar = {
    TopAppBar(
      title = {
        Text(
          text = "JetNotes",
          color = MaterialTheme.colors.onPrimary
        )
      },
      navigationIcon = {
        IconButton(onClick = {
          onOpenNavigationDrawer.invoke()
        }) {
          Icon(
            imageVector = Icons.Filled.List,
            contentDescription = "Drawer Button"
          )
        }
      }
    )
  },
...
)
```

This is the same as the Material `TopAppBar` you used above.

Don't forget to replace the import for the old `TopAppBar` with the Material one:

```
import androidx.compose.material.TopAppBar
```

Using a Material Composable for Note

There's one more thing you can replace with Material Design composables: your `Note()`.

Open **Note.kt** and replace its entire contents with:

```
val background = if (isSelected)
  Color.LightGray
else
  MaterialTheme.colors.surface

Card(
  shape = RoundedCornerShape(4.dp),
  modifier = modifier
    .padding(8.dp)
    .fillMaxWidth(),
  backgroundColor = background
) {
  ListItem(
    text = { Text(text = note.title, maxLines = 1) },
    secondaryText = {
      Text(text = note.content, maxLines = 1)
    },
    icon = {
      NoteColor(
        color = Color.fromHex(note.color.hex),
        size = 40.dp,
        border = 1.dp
      )
    },
    trailing = {
      if (note.isCheckedOff != null) {
        Checkbox(
          checked = note.isCheckedOff,
          onCheckedChange = { isChecked ->
            val newNote = note.copy(isCheckedOff = isChecked)
            onNoteCheckedChange.invoke(newNote)
          },
          modifier = Modifier.padding(start = 8.dp)
        )
      }
    },
    modifier = Modifier.clickable {
      onNoteClick.invoke(note)
    }
  )
}
```

Here, you used a `Card()` and a `ListItem()` to implement `Note()`. The `Card()` is a simple composable, `Cards` are **surfaces** that display content and actions on a single topic. You can customize their `shape`, `backgroundColor`, `contentColor`, `border` and `elevation`.

The `ListItem()` is a Material Design implementation of list items. They represent items in a list, that have the distinct Material Design look and feel. You used its `text` for the title, `secondaryText` for content, `icon` for the `NoteColor()` and `trailing` for the `Checkbox`.

At the time of writing, `ListItem()` was a part of an experimental material API so add `@ExperimentalMaterialApi` annotation to `Note()`, as well as the `modifier` parameter:

```
@Composable
@ExperimentalMaterialApi // here
fun Note(
  modifier: Modifier = Modifier, // here
  note: NoteModel,
  onNoteClick: (NoteModel) -> Unit = {},
  onNoteCheckedChange: (NoteModel) -> Unit = {},
  isSelected: Boolean = false
) {
...
}
```

You are going to have to do that for all composables that explicitly or implicitly use `Note()`. Those are: `NotePreview()`, `NotesList()`, `NotesScreen` and `NotesListPreview()`.

You also need to add imports for the new composables that you used:

```
import androidx.compose.material.Card
import androidx.compose.material.ListItem
import androidx.compose.material.*
```

Build and run the app. You'll see that the **Notes** screen looks the same as before, but most of your composables are now Material Design composables. Nicely done!

Before wrapping up the chapter, there's one more thing to explore: **adding a theme**. You'll briefly learn about Material Design themes and how to support a dark theme for your app.

Theming in Compose

Every Android app has a specific color palette, typography and shapes. Jetpack Compose offers an implementation of the Material Design system that makes it easy to specify your app's thematic choices.

In JetNotes, you don't play much with typography and shapes, but the app uses a certain color palette throughout all its screens. **Theme.kt** contains the definitions of all JetNotes' colors:

```
private val LightThemeColors = lightColors(
  primary = green,
  primaryVariant = greenDark,
  secondary = red
)

private val DarkThemeColors = lightColors(
  primary = green,
  primaryVariant = greenDark,
  secondary = red
)

@Composable
fun JetNotesTheme(content: @Composable () -> Unit) {
  val isDarkThemeEnabled =
    isSystemInDarkTheme() ||
JetNotesThemeSettings.isDarkThemeEnabled

  val colors = if (isDarkThemeEnabled) DarkThemeColors else
LightThemeColors

  MaterialTheme(colors = colors, content = content)
}
```

There are two color definitions: `LightThemeColors` and `DarkThemeColors`. Currently, they share the same definition because the app doesn't support a dark theme — yet! :]

The core element to implement theming in Jetpack Compose is `MaterialTheme()`. `JetNotesTheme()` observes the state when the app should change to a dark theme. When you configure specific colors, you call `MaterialTheme()` and pass those colors to it, but you also pass the content that these colors apply to. Typography and shapes work the same way.

Then, you retrieve the parameters passed into this composable using `MaterialTheme()`. You've done this a few times when you were implement the app. This object exposes the properties of `colors`, `typography` and `shapes`.

Every Material component you used throughout the app has defined which properties to use by default. Since you used Material components and colors from `MaterialTheme()` when you built JetNotes, adding support for a dark theme is as easy as defining a dark color palette. :]

Open **Theme.kt** and replace `DarkThemeColors()` with this:

```
private val DarkThemeColors = darkColors(
  primary = Color(0xFF00A055),
  primaryVariant = Color(0xFF00F884),
  secondary = red,
  onPrimary = Color.White,
)
```

Add the following imports:

```
import androidx.compose.material.darkColors
import androidx.compose.ui.graphics.Color
```

Build and run the app. Open the navigation drawer and turn on the dark theme.

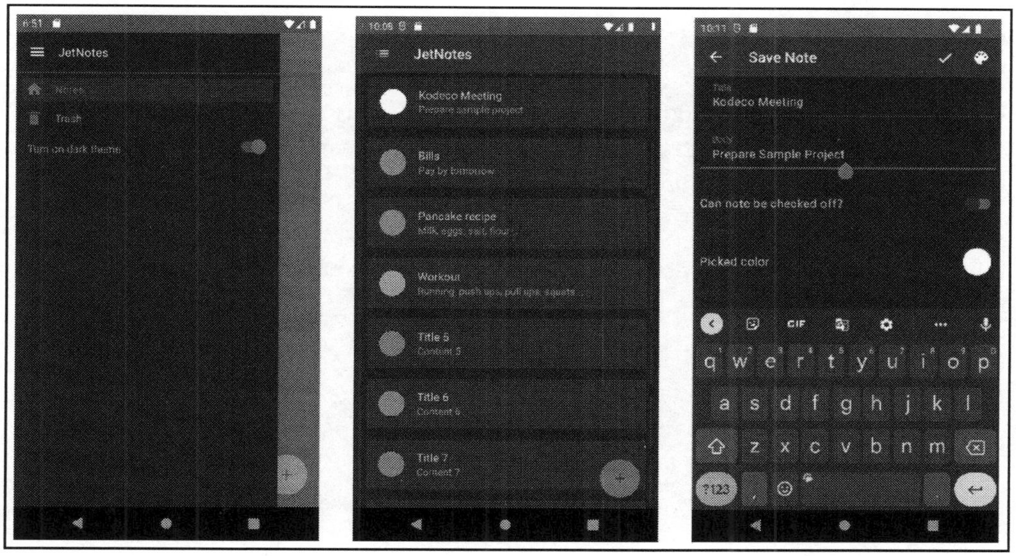

Dark Theme

Congratulations! You made it to the end of the second section! **JetNotes** is now a fully functional app. :]

Key Points

- Jetpack Compose provides **composables** that make it easy to follow **Material Design**.
- With `remember()`, Compose lets you **store values in the composition tree**.
- Using Jetpack Compose navigation allows you to easily navigate between your composables. Navigation is structured around back stack.
- Jetpack Compose offers a Material Design implementation that allows you to theme your app by specifying the **color palette**, **typography** and **shapes**.
- Using `MaterialTheme()`, you define a theme for your app, that customizes colors, typography and shapes.
- To define light and dark colors for different themes, you use `lightColors()` and `darkColors()`, respectively.

Where to Go From Here?

Hopefully, this was a fun ride for you. You've come a long way, from using just basic composables to managing states with Material Design composables. In the next section, you'll work on a more complex app, **JetReddit**! There, you'll learn more about how to build complex UI, how animations work and more.

But don't worry, with the knowledge you've gained so far, you won't have any problems taking on that challenge. :]

Section III: Building Complex Apps With Jetpack Compose

Now that you've built your app's basic UI, it's time to take it to another level. In this section, you'll apply custom, complex designs that help you stand out from thousands of similar apps! This usually involves building **complex custom components** and applying **animations** to represent state changes when your users interact with the UI.

Over the next five chapters, you'll dive deeper into the Jetpack Compose API to learn how to:

- Connect Compose UI to legacy Android code.
- React to Compose UI lifecycles.
- Animate different state changes and user interactions.
- How to use Jetpack Compose in conjunction with the old View UI Toolkit

In the process, you'll build an awesome app that represents a real-world project and you'll apply some best practices to improve the **user experience**.

Chapter 9: Using ConstraintSets in Composables

By Prateek Prasad

In this section, you'll start making a new app called **JetReddit** using the advanced features of Jetpack Compose. JetReddit is a composable version of the Reddit app in Kodeco style. :]

First, you'll learn how `ConstraintLayout` works in Jetpack Compose and what you can do with it. Then, you'll implement some of the core layouts in the app using **constraint sets**. Let's get on it!

To follow this chapter, you need to know how `ConstraintLayout` works.

`ConstraintLayout` is, as its name says, a layout. Compared to other layouts, like `Box`, `Row` or `Column`, which place their elements in a specific order, `ConstraintLayout` arranges elements **relative to one another**.

Understanding ConstraintLayout

While the layout or container composables you have worked with so far are simple to understand, they have inherent limitations when positioning children. They are constrained(pun intended) by their **directionality**. They can only position elements in the x, y, or z coordinate at a time. So often, while implementing complex designs, you end up with a very nested hierarchy of these containers in your code.

`ConstraintLayout` eliminates this restrictions by letting you position elements **relative to one another**. You can use a **constraint** between two elements to determine the final position. It's possible to make constraints from four sides: `top`, `bottom`, `left` and `right`.

> **Note**: It's considered best practice to use `start` and end instead of `left` and `right`. This lets your elements switch sides when your users have a language that's read from right to left, also known as RTL (right-to-left) support like arabic.

ConstraintLayout Example

To make constraints easier to understand, look at the image below:

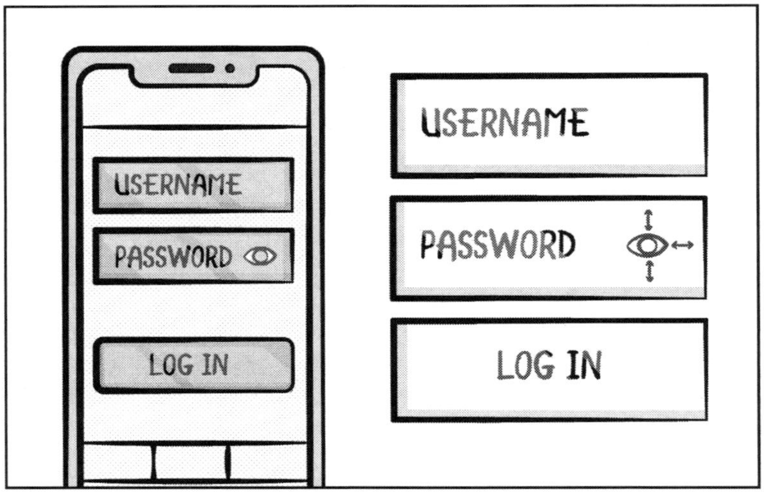

Constraint Layout Example

On the left side of the image, you see a basic login form with two inputs and a button. Inside the password input, you see a small eye icon that toggles whether or not the password displays in plain text, or if it's hidden.

On the right side of the image, you see the zoomed-in buttons corresponding to the login form. Around the eye icon, arrows show the constraint directions. When you position your element on the screen, you have to think from the perspective of that element relative to the other elements.

In simple words, you can say that the eye icon is in the vertical center of the password element. It's also constrained to the end of the password element, with a small space between the icon and the end of the box. When you set constraints, you follow this approach to model the positional information of the different elements.

Now, to implement that positioning. First, you make the constraint between the top of the icon and the top of the password element. Next, you make a constraint between the bottom of the icon and the bottom of the password element. Since one constraint pulls the icon to the top and the other one pulls to the bottom, the icon ends up in the vertical center.

Finally, you add a constraint between the end of the eye icon and the end of the password element. This positions the eye icon at the far-right side of the password element. To get the desired result, all you need to do is add a margin on the right side.

Now that you understand the theory behind `ConstraintLayout`, you're ready to learn how to work with it in compose.

ConstraintLayout in Jetpack Compose

In Jetpack Compose, there's a composable with the same name called `ConstraintLayout`. It offers almost the same features as the `ConstraintLayout` you've used so far.

```
@Composable
fun ConstraintLayout(
    modifier: Modifier = Modifier,
    optimizationLevel: Int = Optimizer.OPTIMIZATION_STANDARD,
    crossinline content: @Composable ConstraintLayoutScope.() ->
Unit
)
```

This composable takes only three parameters:

- The `modifier` to expose styling options, which is pretty standard.
- `optimizationLevel` that sets the optimization level when managing constraints. The default option is `OPTIMIZATION_STANDARD` which optimizes direct constraints and barriers.
- `content`, which represents any number of composables that'll be its children.

Now, imagine that you have a scenario like in the image above, where you want to position the eye icon inside the password input element. Here's how you'd do that in Compose:

```
val (passwordInput, eyeIcon) = createRefs()

Icon(
    imageVector = ImageVector.vectorResource(id =
R.drawable.ic_eye),
    contentDescription = stringResource(id = R.string.eye),
    modifier = Modifier.constrainAs(eyeIcon) {
      top.linkTo(passwordInput.top)
      bottom.linkTo(passwordInput.bottom)
      end.linkTo(passwordInput.end)
    }.padding(end = 16.dp)
)
```

First, you create references for the elements inside the `ConstraintLayout` using `createRefs()`.

> **Note**: Since there is no concept of layout IDs in compose, you need to tie each composable with a reference which you later use for defining the constraints.

Next, you set the vector resource and call `constrainAs()`. `constrainAs()` sets the reference for the current element, then defines the constraints between it and other elements within a lambda function.

For this situation, you set the `eyeIcon` reference and make three constraints, as shown in the image. You make each of those constraints by calling `linkTo()`. You link the top of the eye icon to the top of the password input, the bottom of the eye icon to the bottom of the password input and the end of the eye icon to the end of the password input.

Finally, you set the padding at the end of the eye icon to get that small space shown in the image.

Keep in mind that this example works on the assumption that you've already constrained other elements, like the password input.

Now that you have some essential knowledge about working with the `ConstraintLayout()`, you're ready to start building your new app.

Implementing the App Drawer Layout

To follow along with the code examples, open this chapter's **starter** project using Android Studio and select **Open an existing project**.

Next, navigate to **09-using-constraint-layout-in-composables/projects** and select the starter folder as the project root. Once the project opens, let it build and sync and you'll be ready to go!

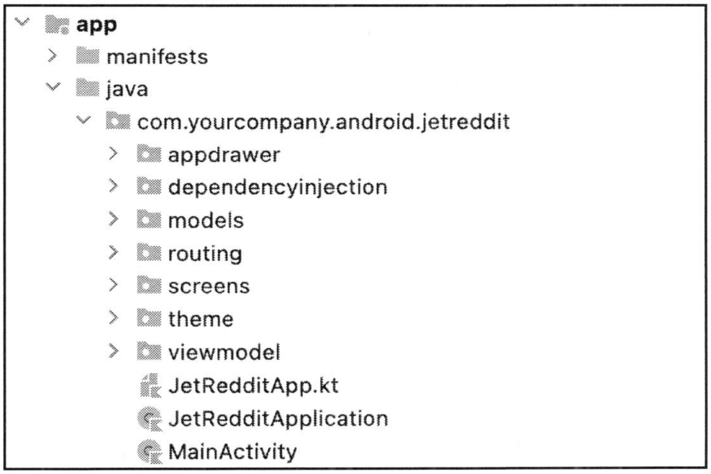

Project Hierarchy

There are several packages and classes already prepared for you, so you don't have to worry about handling navigation, dependency injection and theme switching. If this looks a bit overwhelming, don't worry, you only need to make changes to the **appdrawer** and **screens** packages.

To work with the `ConstraintLayout`, you need to add the following dependency in your module level **build.gradle** file:

```
implementation "androidx.constraintlayout:constraintlayout-
compose:$current-version"
```

This dependency is already added for you in your starter project, but keep it in mind when you are making new projects as it has a different version as compared to other Jetpack Compose dependencies.

Once you're familiar with the file organization, build and run the app. You'll see this screen:

Starting Screen

Here, you see a top bar and a bottom bar with three different icons. Clicking on any of them will display an empty screen and the title in the top bar will change. Clicking on the **Account** icon in the top bar displays an empty app drawer.

Your first step in creating JetReddit is to build the **app drawer**. Your goal is to make a screen similar to the one in the official Reddit app, which looks like this:

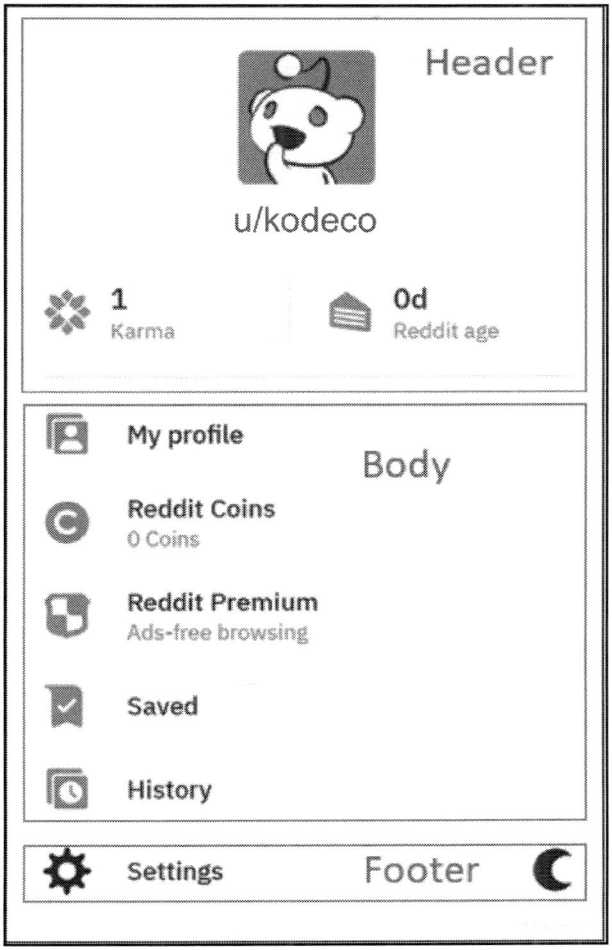

Reddit App Drawer

The screen is split into three different sections: header, body and footer. You'll implement each of them individually in the coming sections.

Before starting, check the root layout implementation for the app drawer by opening **appdrawer/AppDrawer.kt** and taking a look at `AppDrawer()`:

```
@Composable
fun AppDrawer(
  modifier: Modifier = Modifier,
  onScreenSelected: (Screen) -> Unit
) {
  Column(
    modifier = modifier
      .fillMaxSize()
      .background(color = MaterialTheme.colors.surface)
  ) {
    AppDrawerHeader()

    AppDrawerBody(onScreenSelected)

    AppDrawerFooter(modifier)
  }
}
```

The composable has a `Column` as the root element with three custom composables as children that correspond to the header, the body and the footer in the previous screenshot. Your first step is to implement the header.

Examining the header section of the Reddit screenshot shows that you can break it down into smaller parts. First, you'll need to add a profile icon with the user name below it. Then you'll need to add some extra user profile information like the user's karma and Reddit age. Finally, there's a divider that separates the header from the body.

Implementing the User Icon and Name

You'll implement the user icon and user name first. You'll add them in a `Column`, because they need to be ordered vertically. Add the following code to the `AppDrawerHeader` method stub:

```
@Composable
private fun AppDrawerHeader() {
  Column(
     modifier = Modifier.fillMaxWidth(),
     horizontalAlignment = Alignment.CenterHorizontally
  ) {
    Image(
       imageVector = Icons.Filled.AccountCircle,
       colorFilter = ColorFilter.tint(Color.LightGray),
       modifier = Modifier
           .padding(16.dp)
```

```
          .size(50.dp),
      contentScale = ContentScale.Fit,
      alignment = Alignment.Center,
      contentDescription = stringResource(id =
R.string.account)
    )
  }
}
```

In this code, you add a `Column` that centers everything horizontally. You put the provided account image at the top, below which you'll add a `Text` with the default user name and a `Divider` to separate the header from the body. Update `AppDrawerHeader` to do that now:

```
@Composable
private fun AppDrawerHeader() {
  Column(
     modifier = Modifier.fillMaxWidth(),
     horizontalAlignment = Alignment.CenterHorizontally
  ) {
    ... Image Composable here ...
    Text(
      text = stringResource(R.string.default_username),
      color = MaterialTheme.colors.primaryVariant
    )
  } // end of Column

  Divider(
    color = MaterialTheme.colors.onSurface.copy(alpha = .2f),
    modifier = Modifier.padding(
      start = 16.dp,
      end = 16.dp,
      top = 16.dp
    )
  )
}
```

The `Text` is using the `default_username` resource and you added an `onSurface` color to the `Divider`, with a custom alpha value. The divider also has some extra padding to make it look nicer while it separates the header from the body of the drawer.

Build and run the app, then open the drawer.

App Drawer Header Without Profile Info

At this point you can see the whole header section, except for the profile info, which you'll implement next.

Adding the Profile Info

To get a better understanding of what you need to implement, look at the following image:

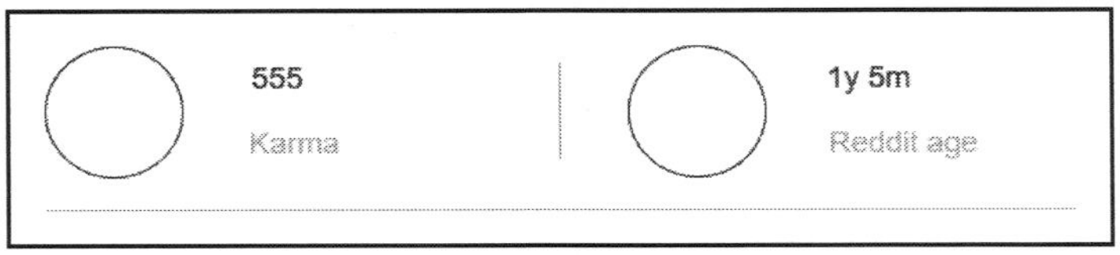

Profile Info

As you see, this image includes repeated elements. This is good because it means you can extract components and reuse them multiple times.

That's exactly what you'll do within the code. You'll extract those components into a composable called `ProfileInfoItem`, containing an `Icon` and two `Text` composables.

Extracting Reusable Components

Because these components require relative constraints, you'll use a `ConstraintLayout`. Add the following code to `ProfileInfoItem()`:

```
@Composable
private fun ProfileInfoItem(
...
) {
  val colors = MaterialTheme.colors

  ConstraintLayout(modifier = modifier) {
    val (iconRef, amountRef, titleRef) = createRefs() //
references
    val itemModifier = Modifier

    Icon(
      contentDescription = stringResource(id = textResourceId),
      imageVector = iconAsset,
      tint = Color.Blue,
      modifier = itemModifier
        .constrainAs(iconRef) {
          centerVerticallyTo(parent)
          start.linkTo(parent.start)
        }.padding(start = 16.dp)
    )
  }
}
```

To begin building the reusable item, you need to create a `ConstraintLayout`, children references and an `Icon` as its child. Again, using `createRefs()` you can create up to 16 component references and constrain them accordingly.

You then create a variable called `itemModifier`. It's good practice to differentiate between parent and item modifiers.

Finally, using `constrainAs(iconRef)`, `centerVertically(parent)` and `linkTo(parent.start)`, you tell the `Icon` where you want to position it. Specifically, you want it to be centered vertically within the parent and at the very start of the parent, with a small amount of padding.

Now, below the `Icon`, add the `Text` that'll represent the amount of karma points or the Reddit age:

```
@Composable
private fun ProfileInfoItem(
...
) {
  val colors = MaterialTheme.colors

  ConstraintLayout(modifier = modifier) {
    ...
    Text(
      text = stringResource(amountResourceId),
      color = colors.primaryVariant,
      fontSize = 10.sp,
      modifier = itemModifier
        .padding(start = 8.dp)
        .constrainAs(amountRef) {
          top.linkTo(iconRef.top)
          start.linkTo(iconRef.end)
          bottom.linkTo(titleRef.top)
        }
    )
  }
}
```

This should be familiar now, as you want this element to be relative to the `iconRef` and the `titleRef`. You constrain it as `amountRef`, linking it to the `top` and the `end` of the `iconRef`. You also link the `bottom` of the amount `Text` to the `top` of the title `Text`, which you'll add next.

Underneath the amount text composable, add the following Text composable:

```
@Composable
private fun ProfileInfoItem(
...
) {
  val colors = MaterialTheme.colors

  ConstraintLayout(modifier = modifier) {
    ...
    Text(
      text = stringResource(textResourceId),
      color = Color.Gray,
      fontSize = 10.sp,
      modifier = itemModifier
        .padding(start = 8.dp)
        .constrainAs(titleRef) {
          top.linkTo(amountRef.bottom)
          start.linkTo(iconRef.end)
          bottom.linkTo(iconRef.bottom)
```

```
        }
      )
    }
  }
```

You add the text composable and constrain it to the `iconRef`, but this time at the `bottom` instead of the `top`. You also linked the `top` of the `titleRef` to the `bottom` of the `amountRef`.

It's important to know that you'll use `ProfileInfoItem()` inside `ProfileInfo()`, which has its own `ConstraintLayout` as a root. To avoid **constraint conflicts** between the parent and child composables, you have to pass the `modifier` from the parent as a parameter and set it to the child's `ConstraintLayout`.

Also, creating new references within this `ConstraintLayout` lets you avoid the previously mentioned conflicts when using multiple `ConstraintLayout` instances.

Build the app and take a look at the preview section to see the result.

Profile Info Item Preview

Don't worry if the colors are a bit off, they'll change to match the theme once you run the app.

Completing ProfileInfo

Now, you'll use your freshly made composable to complete `ProfileInfo()`. Replace the code of `ProfileInfo()` with the following implementation:

```
@Composable
fun ProfileInfo(modifier: Modifier = Modifier) {
  ConstraintLayout(
      modifier = modifier
          .fillMaxWidth()
          .padding(top = 16.dp)
  ) {
    val (karmaItem, divider, ageItem) = createRefs()
    val colors = MaterialTheme.colors

    ProfileInfoItem(
```

```
          Icons.Filled.Star,
          R.string.default_karma_amount,
          R.string.karma,
          modifier = modifier.constrainAs(karmaItem) {
            centerVerticallyTo(parent)
            start.linkTo(parent.start)
          }
        )

        Divider(
          modifier = modifier
            .width(1.dp)
            .constrainAs(divider) {
              centerVerticallyTo(karmaItem)
              centerHorizontallyTo(parent)
              height = Dimension.fillToConstraints
            },
          color = colors.onSurface.copy(alpha = .2f)
        )

        ProfileInfoItem(
          Icons.Filled.ShoppingCart,
          R.string.default_reddit_age_amount,
          R.string.reddit_age,
          modifier = modifier.constrainAs(ageItem) {
            start.linkTo(divider.end)
            centerVerticallyTo(parent)
          }
        )
      }
    }
```

Here, you add a `ConstraintLayout` as the root and create references for the three elements that it contains: karma, divider and age. You constrained the karma item at the start of the parent, centered vertically.

Next, you add a divider in the vertical center of the parent and the horizontal center of the first `ProfileInfoItem`.

Finally, you added another `ProfileInfoItem` containing the age information to the right of the divider and centered it vertically.

Using constraints like this should be more and more familiar to you because constraints work just like they did in the XML version of the `ConstraintLayout`. The main difference is that you have to write them in code, but with the amazing Compose syntax, that's a piece of cake! :]

Now, add `ProfileInfo()` to `AppDrawerHeader()`:

```
@Composable
private fun AppDrawerHeader() {
  Column(
     modifier = Modifier.fillMaxWidth(),
     horizontalAlignment = Alignment.CenterHorizontally
  ) {
    Image(
       ...
    )

    Text(
       ...
    )
    ProfileInfo() // Add here
  }

  Divider(
     ...
  )
}
```

This shows the missing profile information in the header.

Build and run the app to see the result.

App Drawer Header With Profile Info

You can now see the profile info section, split into two parts by a divider.

With this, you've completed the header section and had the chance to familiarize yourself with working with `ConstraintLayout`.

All right, it's time to move on to the body!

Implementing the App Drawer's Body

The body of the app drawer is the easier part to implement, since you don't need to use a `ConstraintLayout`.

The body section in the Reddit screenshot is your reference, but you'll implement a simplified version of it. You only need to add two buttons here, one to open the profile and the other to view the saved screens.

The button composable, `ScreenNavigationButton`, has already been prepared for you in the starter code. This composable has an `icon`, a `label` and an `onClickAction`.

Next, add the following code to `AppDrawerBody()`:

```
@Composable
private fun AppDrawerBody(onScreenSelected: (Screen) -> Unit) {
  Column {
    ScreenNavigationButton(
      icon = Icons.Filled.AccountBox,
      label = stringResource(R.string.my_profile),
      onClickAction = {
        onScreenSelected.invoke(Screen.MyProfile)
      }
    )

    ScreenNavigationButton(
      icon = Icons.Filled.Home,
      label = stringResource(R.string.saved),
      onClickAction = {
        onScreenSelected.invoke(Screen.Subscriptions)
      }
    )
  }
}
```

Here, you add two `ScreenNavigationButtons` for the drawer's body. Currently, the action you pass to the buttons only closes the drawer and shows an empty screen because you haven't implemented those screens yet. You'll take care of that in the coming chapters.

Note that both buttons are set inside the `Column`. You did this so you can preview this composable, but it's not necessary since the root composable `AppDrawer` already uses a `Column`.

Remember that you passed `onScreenSelected` as an argument in `AppDrawer()`:

```
fun AppDrawer(
  onScreenSelected: (Screen) -> Unit,
  modifier: Modifier = Modifier) {
    ...
    AppDrawerBody(onScreenSelected)
    ...
}
```

Build and run the app, then open the app drawer once again.

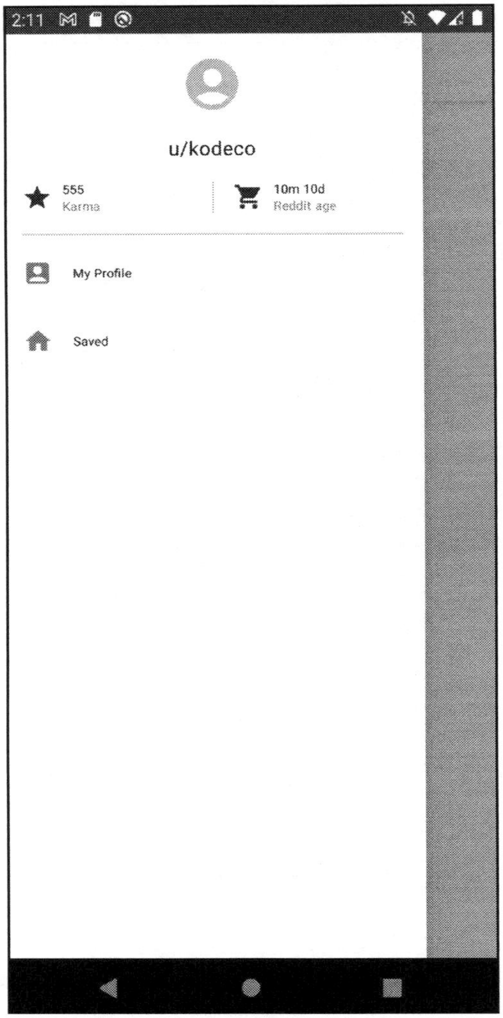

App Drawer Body

You can now see the two buttons below the header section. When you click on either of them, the drawer closes.

Implementing the App Drawer Footer

Once again, check the Reddit screenshot, but this time, pay closer attention to the bottom of the screen. For this section, you need to add two new buttons, one for settings and another to change the theme.

Start by adding the initial `ConstraintLayout` setup to the `AppDrawerFooter()`:

```
@Composable
private fun AppDrawerFooter(modifier: Modifier = Modifier) {
  ConstraintLayout(
    modifier = modifier
      .fillMaxSize()
      .padding(
        start = 16.dp,
        bottom = 16.dp,
        end = 16.dp
      )
  ) {

    val colors = MaterialTheme.colors
    val (settingsImage, settingsText, darkModeButton) =
createRefs()
  }
}
```

Here you add the `ConstraintLayout`, styled it with modifiers and prepared all the references you'll need to position its children. Next, add the settings `Icon` and its label within the `ConstraintLayout`:

```
@Composable
private fun AppDrawerFooter(modifier: Modifier = Modifier) {
  ConstraintLayout(
    ...
  ) {
    ...
    Icon(
      modifier = modifier.constrainAs(settingsImage) {
        start.linkTo(parent.start)
        bottom.linkTo(parent.bottom)
      },
      imageVector = Icons.Default.Settings,
      contentDescription = stringResource(id =
R.string.settings),
      tint = colors.primaryVariant
    )
```

```
      Text(
        fontSize = 10.sp,
        text = stringResource(R.string.settings),
        style = MaterialTheme.typography.body2,
        color = colors.primaryVariant,
        modifier = modifier
          .padding(start = 16.dp)
          .constrainAs(settingsText) {
            start.linkTo(settingsImage.end)
            centerVerticallyTo(settingsImage)
          }
      )
    }
  }
```

These two elements are positioned at the bottom of the parent. The `Icon` sits at the start of the parent, while the label is linked to the end of the `settingsImage`. The rest of the code should be self-explanatory, as its mostly styling the `Text` and the `Icon`.

Now add the last element to the footer—the theme `Icon`:

```
@Composable
private fun AppDrawerFooter(modifier: Modifier = Modifier) {
  ConstraintLayout(
    ...
  ) {
    ...
    Icon(
      imageVector = ImageVector.vectorResource(id =
R.drawable.ic_moon),
      contentDescription = stringResource(id =
R.string.change_theme),
      modifier = modifier
        .clickable(onClick = { changeTheme() })
        .constrainAs(darkModeButton) {
          end.linkTo(parent.end)
          bottom.linkTo(settingsImage.bottom)
        },
      tint = colors.primaryVariant
    )
  }
}
```

The theme `Icon` follows the same principles, except that it's constrained to the `bottom` and `end` of the parent. Also, for the theme icon, you added an `onClick` action to change the theme by calling `changeTheme()`. This function is pre-built for you in the starter project.

Build and run the app, then open the drawer.

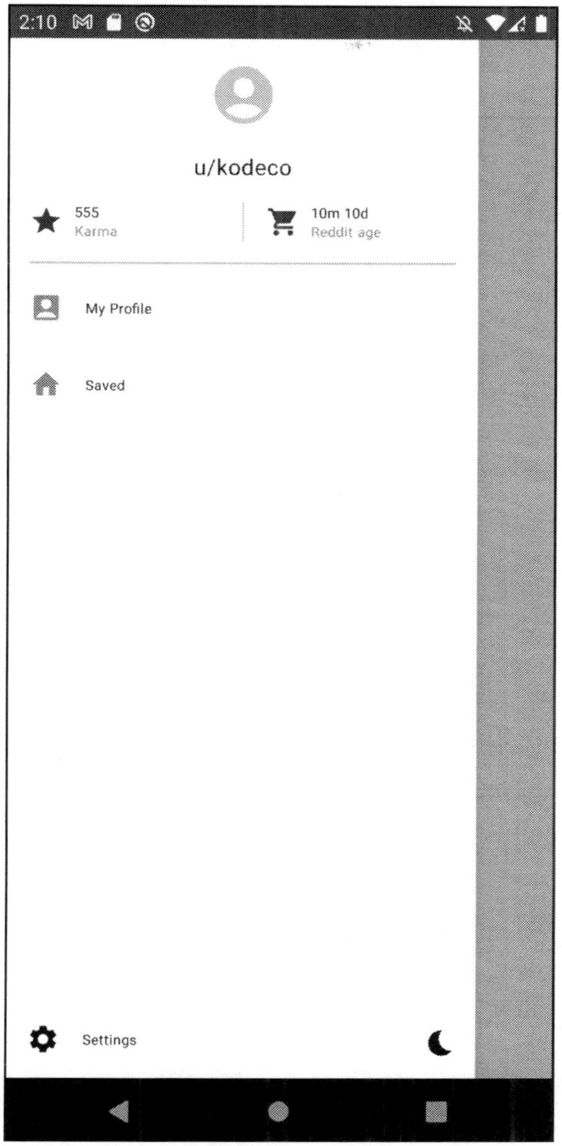

App Drawer Footer

There's now a footer inside the drawer with the settings and the theme icons. If you click on the theme icon, the app will change to the dark theme, which has all the colors already defined.

Advanced Features of ConstraintLayout

`ConstraintLayout` makes building UI much easier than before. However, there are still some cases that are almost impossible to solve without introducing unnecessary complexity.

For example, consider the case from earlier in the chapter, when you made the profile info composable in the drawer. That setup had some elements at the left side of the screen and others close to the vertical line in the center.

Now, imagine that there was no vertical line. How would you position your elements to start from the center of the screen? One idea is to place an element in the center that's invisible and position your other elements relative to that object. The solution is a lot like that, only more optimized. These are known as **Guidelines8

Guidelines

A **guideline** is an invisible object you use as a helper tool when you work with `ConstraintLayout`. You can create a guideline from any side of the screen and use one of two different ways to give it an offset:

- You can specify the fixed amount of `dp` you want the offset to be.
- You can give the **screen percentage** if you want the guideline to display in the same place, regardless of the screen size.

You use different functions to create guidelines, depending on where you want to place them. In your previous example, where you needed a guideline in the vertical center, you could use either of the following options:

```
createGuidelineFromStart(0.5f)
createGuidelineFromEnd(0.5f)
```

This creates a **vertical anchor** that's half a screen away from the start or half a screen away from the end. The anchor is a virtual helper that isn't displayed on the screen, but which allows you to make constraints to it. Here's an example of how to use one:

```
val verticalGuideline = createGuidelineFromStart(0.5f)
Icon(
  imageVector = iconAsset,
  contentDescription = stringResource(id =
R.string.some_string),
  modifier = Modifier
```

```
        .constrainAs(iconReference) {
            start.linkTo(verticalGuideline)
            top.linkTo(parent.top)
            bottom.linkTo(parent.bottom)
        }
)
```

Here, you create a vertical guideline at the center of the screen. Next, you add an icon that's centered vertically and starts from your guideline's position, the vertical center.

You can also use any of the following functions to create an anchor, depending on your need. For **vertical anchors** you can choose from:

- `createGuidelineFromStart()`
- `createGuidelineFromAbsoluteLeft()`
- `createGuidelineFromEnd()`
- `createGuidelineFromAbsoluteRight()`

For **horizontal anchors**, you have the following functions:

- `createGuidelineFromTop()`
- `createGuidelineFromBottom()`

You then use the vertical anchor to make vertical constraints and the horizontal anchor to make horizontal constraints.

Vertical constraints are:

- Start
- AbsoluteLeft
- End
- AbsoluteRight

Horizontal constraints are:

- Top
- Bottom

Note that all constraints and anchors with the **absolute** prefix represent the absolute left or right of the screen, regardless of the different layout directions, such as right-to-left.

If you want to learn more about guidelines, check out the official documentation: https://developer.android.com/jetpack/compose/layouts/constraintlayout#guidelines.

Barriers

Now that you know how to position objects at specific places on the screen, it's time to think about some other problems you can solve.

Take a look at the image below to better understand the next problem:

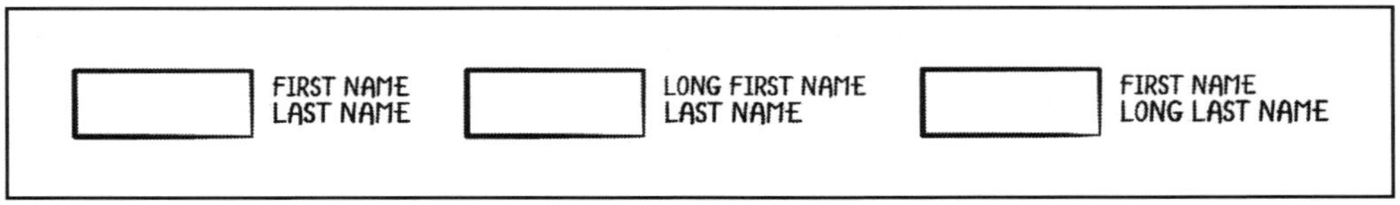

Barrier

On the left side of the image, you see a button and two text fields: first and last name. In this scenario, you want to place the button to the left of the two text fields. In the first example, these texts have almost the same width, so the button will always be on the left, no matter which text you constrain to it.

In the second example, you have a long first name and a short last name. To have the button on the left side of both texts, you need to constrain it to the start of the first name, because that's the longer one.

In the last example, you have the opposite situation. To have the button on the left side of the two texts, you need to constrain it to the start of the last name.

From these examples, you can see that for this to work, the button should sometimes be constrained to the first name and sometimes to the last name, depending on which one is bigger.

To solve this problem, you add a **barrier** within the `ConstraintLayout`. A barrier is an element that can contain multiple constraint references.

Here's how you can use barriers to solve the problem from the previous example:

```
ConstraintLayout(modifier = Modifier.fillMaxSize()) {
  val (button, firstName, lastName) = createRefs()
  val startBarrier = createStartBarrier(firstName, lastName)

  Text(
    text = "long first name",
    modifier = Modifier.constrainAs(firstName) {
```

```
        end.linkTo(parent.end)
        top.linkTo(parent.top)
      }
    )

    Text(
      text = "last name",
      modifier = Modifier.constrainAs(lastName) {
        end.linkTo(parent.end)
        top.linkTo(firstName.bottom)
      }
    )

    Button(
      content = {},
      onClick = {},
      modifier = Modifier.constrainAs(button) {
        end.linkTo(startBarrier)
      }
    )
}
```

First, you create constraint references for all three elements. Next, you create a **start barrier** by passing the references for the first and last name. You use the start barrier when you want to set a constraint to multiple elements from their left side.

Finally, you make a constraint from the end of the button to the start barrier. This will ensure that the button is always constrained to the element with the larger width, resolving the problem.

As with guidelines, you can create a barrier from any side by calling one of the following functions:

- `createStartBarrier()`
- `createAbsoluteLeftBarrier()`
- `createEndBarrier()`
- `createAbsoluteRightBarrier()`
- `createTopBarrier()`
- `createBottomBarrier()`

Chains

The final problem that you might face when using `ConstraintLayout` is when you have multiple elements that are constrained to each other. Here are the possible scenarios:

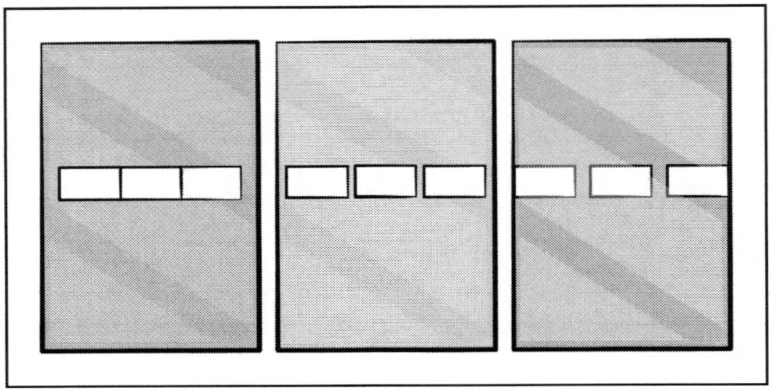

Chains

You can see three different screens, each containing three elements. In the first case, the elements are placed together in the middle, one next to the other. In the second case, they're spaced evenly from each other and the screen edges. In the last case, the elements are still evenly spaced, but they start at the edge of the screen.

With your current knowledge of constraints, if you had these three elements, you could constrain the elements to each other from both sides and to the parent at the edges. By doing this, you could achieve the first result, but not the other two.

Cases like these are solved with **chains**. A chain allows you to reference multiple elements that are constrained to each other, forming a chain as in the image above. Once you have a chain, you can specify the `ChainStyle` you want. There are three types of `ChainStyles`, which correspond to the scenarios described earlier:

- **Packed**: All the elements are packed in a group, as in the first example.
- **Spread**: All the elements are spread evenly from each other and the edges, as in the second example.
- **SpreadInside**: All the elements are spread evenly from each other but start at the edges, as in the third example.

Here is an example that uses `ChainStyle.SpreadInside`:

```
val (firstElement, secondElement, thirdElement) = createRefs()

Button(
  modifier = Modifier
  .constrainAs(firstElement) {
    start.linkTo(parent.start)
    end.linkTo(secondElement.start)
    top.linkTo(parent.top)
    bottom.linkTo(parent.bottom)
  }
)

Button(
  modifier = Modifier
  .constrainAs(secondElement) {
    start.linkTo(firstElement.end)
    end.linkTo(thirdElement.start)
    top.linkTo(parent.top)
    bottom.linkTo(parent.bottom)
  }
)

Button(
  modifier = Modifier
  .constrainAs(thirdElement) {
    start.linkTo(secondElement.end)
    end.linkTo(parent.end)
    top.linkTo(parent.top)
    bottom.linkTo(parent.bottom)
  }
)

createHorizontalChain(
    firstElement,
    secondElement,
    thirdElement,
    chainStyle = ChainStyle.SpreadInside
)
```

Note that applying a specific `ChainStyle` will only work if you create a chain between the elements. In the previous code, you do this by setting the constraint references between the three buttons. Also, keep in mind that you can create both vertical and horizontal chains.

Check out the official `ChainStyle` documentation for more information: https://developer.android.com/jetpack/compose/layouts/constraintlayout#chains.

That was an overview of the most complex layout you can currently use in Android. By now, you should be able to make a screen of any complexity using what you've learned.

Keep this in mind because, in the next chapter, that's exactly what you'll be doing: making a complex UI to further implement the features in your JetReddit app.

You'll combine everything you learned so far and you'll use the component-based approach reuse as much code as possible. See you in the next chapter!

Key Points

- `ConstraintLayout` positions its children **relative** to each other.
- Add `implementation androidx.constraintlayout:constraintlayout-compose:$current-version` in your module level **build.gradle** file to use `ConstraintLayout`.
- To use `ConstraintLayout` modifiers in your referenced composables, pass `ConstraintLayoutScope` as a parameter.
- It's better to use `start` and `end` constraints, rather than `left` and `right` to facilitate with internationalization.
- Use `createRefs()` to create constraint references for your composables.
- Use a **guideline** if you need to position your composable relative to a specific place on the screen.
- Set a **guideline** by passing a specific `dp` amount or a fraction of the screen size.
- Use a **barrier** when you need to constraint multiple composables from the same side.
- Use a **chain** when you need multiple elements constrained to each other.
- Use `ChainStyle` to specify the kind of chain to use.

Chapter 10: Building Complex UI in Jetpack Compose

By Prateek Prasad

Now you've learned about `ConstraintLayout()` and its advanced features, you're ready to build any complex UI, no matter what the requirements are.

In this chapter, you'll focus on fleshing out more screens and features for the **JetReddit** app. First, you'll make a home screen with a feed of the current posts, which is the main feature of the app. Then, you'll build a screen where you can see a feed of your favorite and recently visited **subreddits**.

Building the Home Screen

To understand your task, take a look at the following example from the original Reddit app:

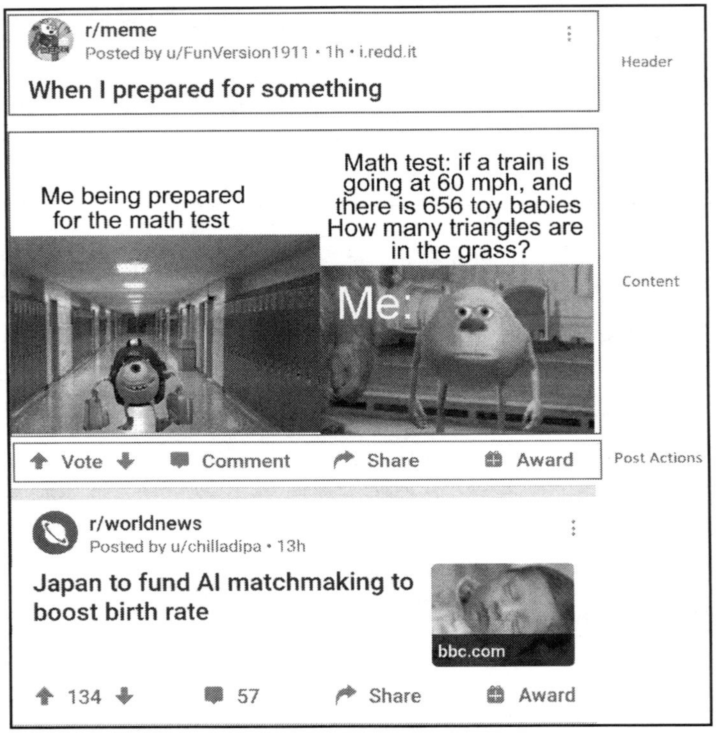

Reddit Home Screen

Here, you see a home screen with two posts. The screen consists of a header, content and post actions. There are two types of content, a text and an image. Keep in mind that the user will most certainly have more than two posts, so the whole screen is scrollable. As in previous chapters, you'll implement this screen step-by-step.

Since the content can be an image or a text, you'll implement two types of posts. The best way to do this is to have these post type variants as separate composables, so the only thing you need to do in code is change between the two types based on the data.

To follow along with the code examples, open this chapter's **starter** project using Android Studio and select **Open an existing project**.

Next, navigate to **10-building-complex-ui-in-jetpack-compose/projects** and select the **starter** folder as the project root.

Once the project opens, let it build and sync and you're ready to go!

You might already be familiar with the project hierarchy from the previous chapter, but in case you aren't, check out this image:

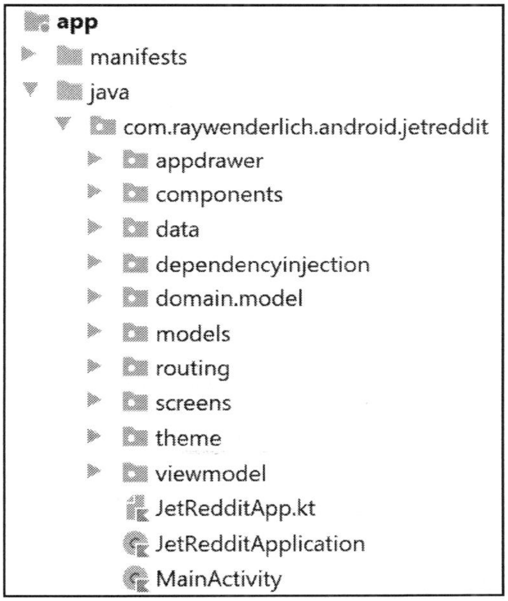

Project Hierarchy

There are several packages here, but you'll only change the code within **screens**, to implement new features of the app, and **components** for custom composables — for example, `Post()`, which those screens need.

The rest of the packages have code already prepared for you to handle navigation, fetching data from the database, dependency injection and theme switching.

Once you're familiar with the file organization, build and run the app. You'll see a screen like this:

Starting Screen

It's an empty home screen. It only contains the app drawer from the previous chapter.

You're ready to go now. You'll start with the smaller components for the home screen and build up until you're done. Your first task is to implement the post's header.

Adding a Post Header

Each post on the home screen has a header that contains the following information: the subreddit it belongs to, the name of the user who posted it, how old the post is and its title.

For your first step, open **Post.kt** inside **components** and replace `Header()` with the following code:

```
@Composable
fun Header(post: PostModel) {
    Row(modifier = Modifier.padding(start = 16.dp)) {
      Image(
```

```
          ImageBitmap.imageResource(id =
R.drawable.subreddit_placeholder),
          contentDescription = stringResource(id =
R.string.subreddits),
          Modifier
              .size(40.dp)
              .clip(CircleShape)
      )
      Spacer(modifier = Modifier.width(8.dp))
      Column(modifier = Modifier.weight(1f)) {
        Text(
            text = stringResource(R.string.subreddit_header,
post.subreddit),
            fontWeight = FontWeight.Medium,
            color = MaterialTheme.colors.primaryVariant
        )
        Text(
            text = stringResource(R.string.post_header,
post.username, post.postedTime),
            color = Color.Gray
        )
      }
      MoreActionsMenu()
    }

    Title(text = post.title)
}
```

Here's what you did with this code:

- First, you added a `Row()` where you placed the icon.
- Next, you added a `Column()` to position the two texts one below the other.
- At the end of the `Row()`, you added a **MoreActionsMenu** button, which was already prepared for you.
- Finally, you placed `Title()` outside the `Row()`. `Title()` is a `Text()` with custom styling already done for you.

To see your new header, build the project and open the split view to see the previews. Once the build finishes, look at the preview called `HeaderPreview`:

Header Preview

The header now has all the the elements it needs to have. Don't worry that the colors don't match your design, they'll change to fit the theme when you run the app.

The next component you'll write is the voting action button.

Building the Voting Action Button

The voting action button has two images and a text, which makes it slightly different from other action buttons. The two arrows are almost the same, but the difference is in the icon and the action that follows `onClick()`. Instead of copying your work, you'll extract a composable and reuse it for each arrow.

Replace `ArrowButton()` code with the following:

```
@Composable
fun ArrowButton(onClickAction: () -> Unit, arrowResourceId: Int)
{
  IconButton(onClick = onClickAction, modifier =
Modifier.size(30.dp)) {
      Icon(
        imageVector = ImageVector.vectorResource(arrowResourceId),
        contentDescription = stringResource(id = R.string.upvote),
        modifier = Modifier.size(20.dp),
        tint = Color.Gray
      )
  }
}
```

Here, you added `IconButton()` with a custom `tint` value and size. You pass `onClick()` lambda and the vector resource as parameters because you want to reuse this composable for both the up and down arrows.

To see your arrow button, build the project and look at the preview screen under `ArrowButtonPreview()`:

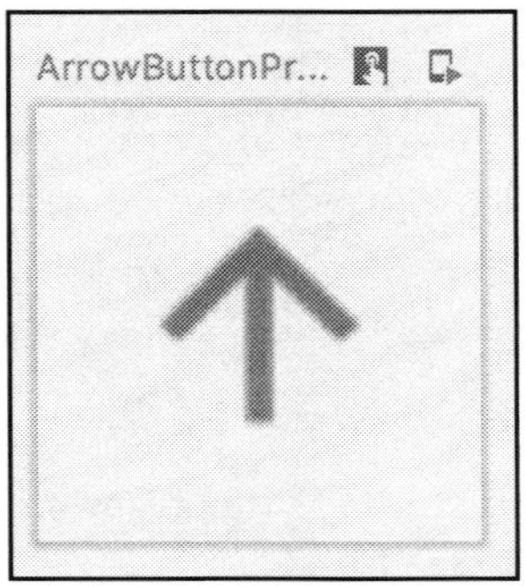

Arrow Button Preview

You see a simple up arrow. Now, you'll use this composable to complete the voting action button.

Replace `VotingAction()` code with:

```
@Composable
fun VotingAction(
  text: String,
  onUpVoteAction: () -> Unit,
  onDownVoteAction: () -> Unit
) {
  Row(verticalAlignment = Alignment.CenterVertically) {
    ArrowButton(onUpVoteAction,
R.drawable.ic_baseline_arrow_upward_24)
    Text(
      text = text,
      color = Color.Gray,
      fontWeight = FontWeight.Medium,
      fontSize = 12.sp
    )
    ArrowButton(onDownVoteAction,
R.drawable.ic_baseline_arrow_downward_24)
  }
}
```

You added a `Row()` with two `ArrowButtons` and a `Text()` in between. For each `ArrowButton()` you passed a different `onClick()` lambdas and vector drawable. That lets you set a different arrow image and the handler that defines what happens after clicking the button.

Build the project and look at the preview section under `VotingActionPreview()`:

Voting Action Button Preview

You now see the two arrows, one for up-voting and one for down-voting. In the middle, you see the total number of votes.

The actions for commenting, sharing and awarding are very similar so they're pre-made for you. If you're interested in how they work, look at `PostAction()` in the starter project.

The last thing that's missing to complete `Post()` are its two content types. This time, you'll use a different approach: building the `Post()` before you finish the content.

Building the Post

You might wonder how you'll build `Post()` without first implementing the content. To find out how — and why — make the following changes to `Post()`:

```
@Composable
fun Post(post: PostModel, content: @Composable () -> Unit = {})
{
  Card(shape = MaterialTheme.shapes.large) {
    Column(modifier = Modifier.padding(
      top = 8.dp,
      bottom = 8.dp)
    ) {
      Header(post)
      Spacer(modifier = Modifier.height(4.dp))
      content.invoke()
      Spacer(modifier = Modifier.height(8.dp))
      PostActions(post)
    }
  }
}
```

First, you add a `Card()` and a `Column()` to lay out the composable. Then, you add a `Header()`, `content` and `PostActions()`.

It looks like you call `content` here even though you haven't implemented it yet. That's because, this time, you're using a composable as a function parameter, which you invoke precisely where you need it.

`content` is present, but it's empty by default unless you provide it. You achieve this by providing `{}`, which returns empty content for the composable function.

Build the app and look at `PostPreview()` under the preview section:

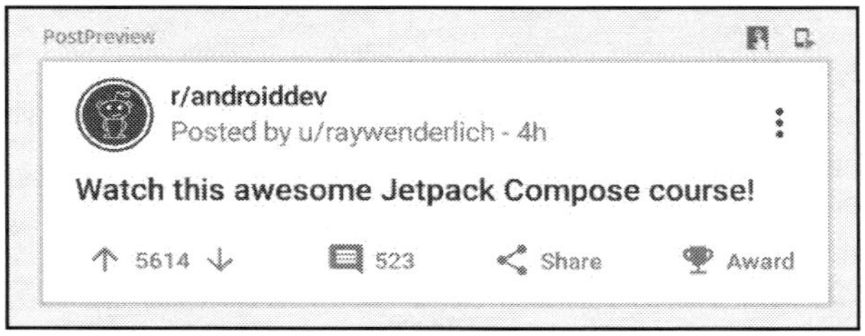

Post Preview

As you see, the post already contains the header and the actions. The only thing missing is the content. You'll address that part now.

Adding the Content

Look at `TextPost()` and `ImagePost()`:

```
@Composable
fun TextPost(post: PostModel) {
  Post(post) {
    TextContent(post.text)
  }
}

@Composable
fun ImagePost(post: PostModel) {
  Post(post) {
    ImageContent(post.image ?: R.drawable.compose_course)
  }
}
```

The functions are already built for you because they only call `Post()` and pass one parameter: either `TextContent()` or `ImageContent()`, depending on what type of content you need to display. Feel free to check them out if you're curious about their implementation. :]

Next, find the following preview code at the end of the file:

```
@Preview
@Composable
fun ImagePostPreview() {
  Post(DEFAULT_POST) {
    ImageContent(DEFAULT_POST.image ?:
R.drawable.compose_course)
  }
}
```

The preview code is using a `Post()` with `ImageContent()` passed in as a composable parameter.

To see it in action, build the app and take a look at the preview section under `ImagePostPreview()`:

Image Post Preview

Nice looking post! The post shows an image and you can see how a post will look if using `ImageContent()`.

Your `Post()` is now complete with all its content and you're ready to finish the home screen.

Adding Multiple Posts

To complete the home screen implementation, you need to add the ability to display multiple posts using `Post()`, which you just created. The posts should vary by type and content.

In this project, the **database**, **repository** and **viewmodel** layers are already prepared for you because you already covered them in Chapter 7, "Managing State in Compose".

Your task is to fetch the post data using the predefined classes and then render the content inside `HomeScreen()`.

To start, open the **HomeScreen.kt** file and replace `HomeScreen()` code with the following:

```
@Composable
fun HomeScreen(viewModel: MainViewModel) {
  val posts: List<PostModel> by
viewModel.allPosts.observeAsState(listOf())

  LazyColumn(modifier = Modifier.background(color =
MaterialTheme.colors.secondary)) {
    items(posts) {
      if (it.type == PostType.TEXT) {
        TextPost(it)
      } else {
        ImagePost(it)
      }
      Spacer(modifier = Modifier.height(6.dp))
    }
  }
}
```

To complete this screen, you did the following:

- First, you fetched all the posts from the database, which are observed as a state to handle recomposition.
- Next, you added a `LazyColumn()` to make a scrollable list of the fetched posts.
- Finally, you rendered the post depending on its type and put a `Spacer()` at the bottom to separate the items, using `items()` from the `LazyColumn`.

Build and run the app, then take a look at the main screen when the app opens:

Home Screen

You now see a list of multiple posts with different content, which you can scroll through. Excellent work!

Now you've finished the home screen, your next task is to make the Subreddits screen.

Building the Subreddits Screen

First, take a look at the image below to understand what you'll build:

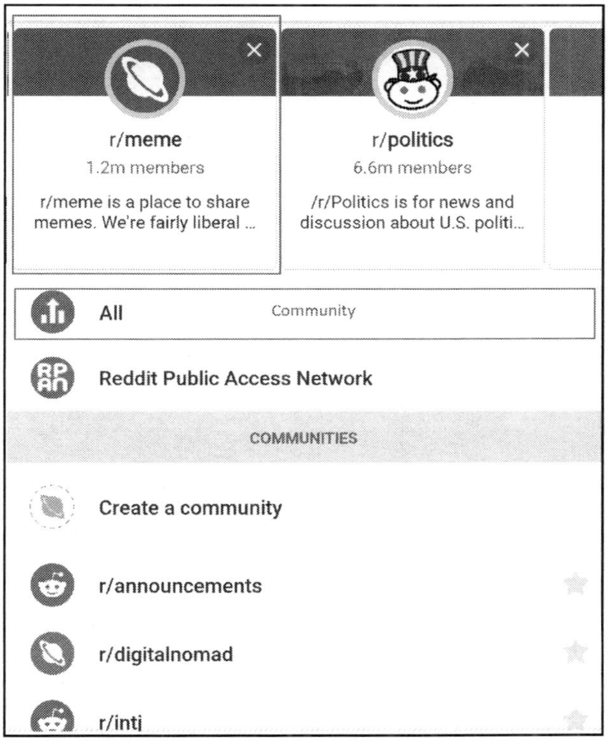

Subreddit Screen Example

The screen consists of two main parts: a horizontally scrollable list of subreddit items and a vertically scrollable `Column()` that contains both the subreddit list and a list of communities.

The two items you'll build are outlined in red. At the top, you see the **subreddit body**, which hold a subreddit item. Below it, you find the **community item**, which builds the list of communities.

Building the Subreddit Body

Look at the **subreddit body** from the example image once more. It consists of a background image, an icon and three texts. Since some elements overlap, you'll use `ConstraintLayout()` for flexibility.

Open **screens/SubredditsScreen.kt** and replace the code inside `SubredditBody` with the following:

```
@Composable
fun SubredditBody(subredditModel: SubredditModel, modifier:
Modifier = Modifier) {
  ConstraintLayout(
    modifier = modifier
      .fillMaxSize()
      .background(color = MaterialTheme.colors.surface)
  ) {
    val (backgroundImage, icon, name, members, description) =
createRefs() // 1

    SubredditImage( // 2
      modifier = modifier.constrainAs(backgroundImage) {
        centerHorizontallyTo(parent)
        top.linkTo(parent.top)
      }
    )

    SubredditIcon( // 3
      modifier = modifier.constrainAs(icon) {
        top.linkTo(backgroundImage.bottom)
        bottom.linkTo(backgroundImage.bottom)
        centerHorizontallyTo(parent)
      }.zIndex(1f)
    )

    SubredditName( // 4
      nameStringRes = subredditModel.nameStringRes,
      modifier = modifier.constrainAs(name) {
        top.linkTo(icon.bottom)
        centerHorizontallyTo(parent)
      }
    )

    SubredditMembers( // 5
      membersStringRes = subredditModel.membersStringRes,
      modifier = modifier.constrainAs(members) {
        top.linkTo(name.bottom)
        centerHorizontallyTo(parent)
      }
    )
```

```
      SubredditDescription( // 6
        descriptionStringRes =
subredditModel.descriptionStringRes,
        modifier = modifier.constrainAs(description) {
          top.linkTo(members.bottom)
          centerHorizontallyTo(parent)
        }
      )
    }
  }
```

There is a lot happening here, so here's a breakdown:

1. You first create necessary constraint references using `createRefs()`. They represent the five elements you'll show in a subreddit.
2. The first element is the image, which is centered horizontally and linked to the top of the parent. `SubredditImage()` is already built for you. Check out its definition if you wish to learn more.
3. Centered horizontally within the parent and vertically within the `backgroundImage` lies the `SubredditIcon()`. You also used `zIndex()` to raise the icon above the `backgroundImage`. In Jetpack Compose, the composables' order doesn't determine their order on the z-axis like in XML. The order is determined by which composable renders first. This may mean that `SubredditImage()` might sometimes appear above `SubredditIcon()`

   To avoid that, you use `zIndex()`, which changes the z-axis stacking of composables that share the same parent. The greater the `zIndex()` value is, the later the app will draw the composable. The default value for `zIndex()` is **0**. By setting it to **1**, you ensured the app will always draw `SubredditIcon()` on top.
4. You put the `SubredditName()` at the bottom of the `SubredditIcon()`, centered horizontally within the parent.
5. The `SubredditMembers()` follows the `SubredditName()`.
6. And finally, the `SubredditDescription()` follows `SubredditMembers()`.

To see the changes, build the app and look at the preview section under `SubredditBodyPreview`:

Subreddit Body Preview

Adjusting the Elements' Height and Shadowing

The elements' positions are correct, but their height is wrong and there are no visible shadows at the edge.

To fix the height and shadow problem. Replace the `Subreddit()` code with the following:

```
@Composable
fun Subreddit(subredditModel: SubredditModel, modifier: Modifier
= Modifier) {
  Card(
    backgroundColor = MaterialTheme.colors.surface,
    shape = RoundedCornerShape(4.dp),
    modifier = modifier
      .size(120.dp)
      .padding(
        start = 2.dp,
        end = 2.dp,
        top = 4.dp,
        bottom = 4.dp
      )
  ) {
    SubredditBody(subredditModel)
  }
}
```

This code wraps the `SubredditBody()` inside a `Card()` and sets that card's size, colors and padding.

Build the app and look at the preview section under `SubredditPreview()`:

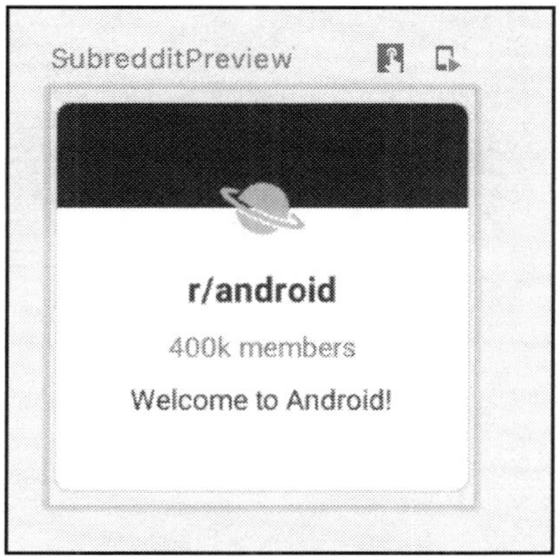

Subreddit Preview

The size of the composable is now correct and you can see the shadows at the border. Nice job! You've just finished another piece of the puzzle.

Next, you'll build the **community item**.

Building the Community Item

The community item is fairly simple; it only has an icon and a text. To build it, change `Community()` code to:

```
@Composable
fun Community(text: String, modifier: Modifier = Modifier,
onCommunityClicked: () -> Unit = {}) {
  Row(modifier = modifier
    .padding(start = 16.dp, top = 16.dp)
    .fillMaxWidth()
    .clickable { onCommunityClicked.invoke() }
  ) {
    Image(
        bitmap = ImageBitmap.imageResource(id =
R.drawable.subreddit_placeholder),
        contentDescription = stringResource(id =
R.string.community_icon),
        modifier = modifier
            .size(24.dp)
            .clip(CircleShape)
    )
    Text(
        fontSize = 10.sp,
        color = MaterialTheme.colors.primaryVariant,
        text = text,
        fontWeight = FontWeight.Bold,
        modifier = modifier
            .padding(start = 16.dp)
            .align(Alignment.CenterVertically)
    )
  }
}
```

The implementation here is straightforward, so requires little explanation. It consists of a clickable `Row()` with an `Image()` and a `Text()` after it.

Build the app and look at the preview section under `CommunityPreview()`:

Community Preview

You see an icon and a community text, as you expect.

Next, you'll build the list that contains all the main and added communities.

Adding a Community List

In this section, you'll add the a list to show the communities available. Add the following code inside `Communities()`:

```
@Composable
fun Communities(modifier: Modifier = Modifier) {
  mainCommunities.forEach {
    Community(text = stringResource(it))
  }

  Spacer(modifier = modifier.height(4.dp))

  BackgroundText(stringResource(R.string.communities))

  communities.forEach {
    Community(text = stringResource(it))
  }
}
```

There are two lists of `String` resources prepared for you already. `mainComunities` and `communities`. In the first part of the screen, you added the main communities and in the second part, you added the communities.

Both lists are separated with a `Spacer()` and a `BackgroundText()`, which are pre-constructed for you. `BackgroundText()` is a `Text()` that contains a background color and fills the whole width of the screen.

Build the app and look at the preview section under `CommunitiesPreview()`:

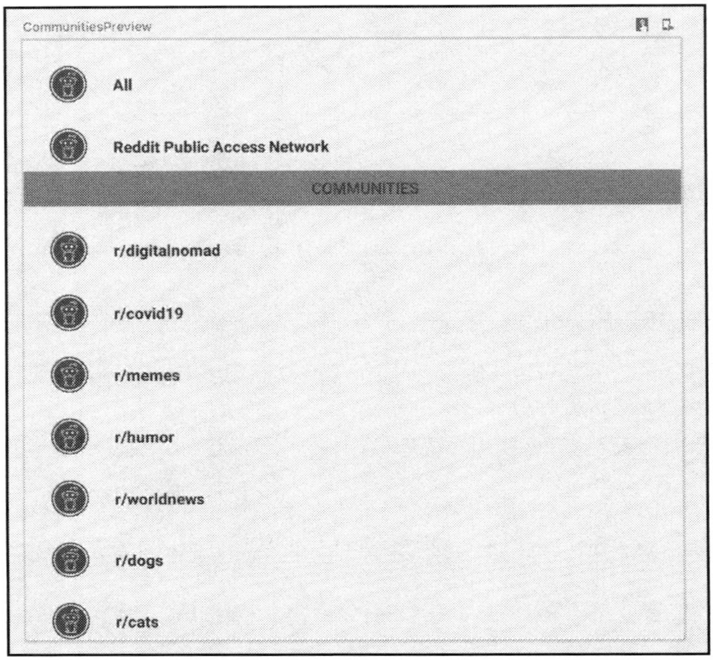

Communities Preview

You see both lists of communities separated by the content generated by `BackgroundText()`. The colors will update when you run the app on a device.

Now that you have all the necessary components, you're ready to finish `SubredditsScreen()`.

Finishing the Screen

The last part of the puzzle to build `SubredditsScreen()` is to combine everything you've built so far into a list that the user can scroll horizontally and vertically.

Start by replacing `SubredditsScreen` with the following:

```
@Composable
fun SubredditsScreen(modifier: Modifier = Modifier) {
  Column(modifier =
modifier.verticalScroll(rememberScrollState())) {
    Text(
      modifier = modifier.padding(16.dp),
      text =
```

```
stringResource(R.string.recently_visited_subreddits),
   fontSize = 12.sp,
   style = MaterialTheme.typography.subtitle1
  )

  LazyRow(
   modifier = modifier.padding(end = 16.dp)
  ) {
   items(subreddits) { Subreddit(it) }
  }
  Communities(modifier)
 }
}
```

With the previous code, you added a scrollable `Column()` as the root so the user can scroll vertically.

Next, you add a `Column()` with a subtitle at the top. To create the list of horizontally scrolled subreddits, you use `LazyRow()` and pass an already-prepared list of `SubredditModels` to `items()`.

Finally, you add `Communities()` to display all the communities.

Build the app and run it on your device this time. Once you install the app, click the middle icon in the bottom bar.

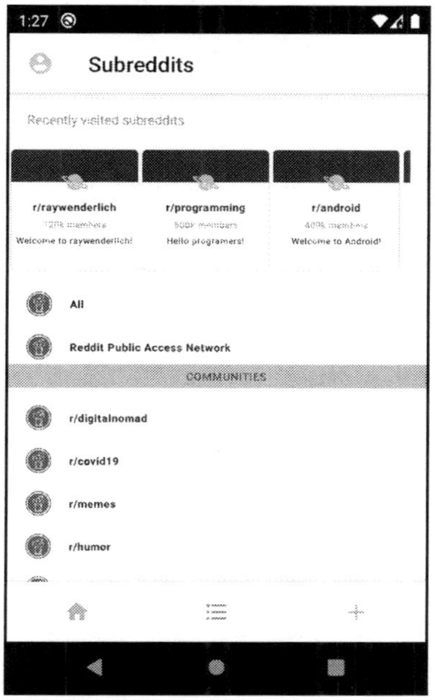

Subreddits Screen

You see the list of subreddits at the top, which the user can scroll horizontally. Below that is the list of communities. The whole screen scrolls vertically — try it out!

Congratulations! You've built the main part of the JetReddit app and learned how to build complex elements. You can find the completed code for this chapter in **10-building-complex-ui-in-jetpack-compose/projects/final**.

Key Points

- If you see parts of a screen that repeat, use a component-based approach to extract them into separate composables.
- Use `Preview` for iterating on the implementation of the components until you've built your whole screen.
- Use `emptyContent()` to display empty content inside the composable.
- Use `zIndex()` if multiple composables overlap and you want to change their order of display in the z-axis.

In this chapter, you learned how to make complex UI elements as well as the importance of following the component-based approach to break complex UI into simpler parts. You're now ready to build any complex UI in your own apps.

In the next chapter, you'll learn how to react to Compose's lifecycle and continue building your `JetReddit` app.

See you there!

Chapter 11: Reacting to Compose Lifecycle

By Prateek Prasad

In previous chapters, you focused on building the **JetReddit** app by adding advanced layouts and complex UI.

In this chapter, you'll learn how to react to the lifecycle of composable functions. This approach will allow you to execute your code at specific moments while your composable is active.

Jetpack Compose offers a list of events that can trigger at specific points in the the lifecycle, called **effects**. Throughout this chapter, you'll learn about the different kinds of effects and how to use them to implement your logic.

Events in Compose

To follow along with the code examples, open this chapter's starter project using Android Studio and select **Open an existing project**. Navigate to **11-reacting-to-compose-lifecycle/projects** and select the **starter** folder as the project root. Once the project opens, let it build and sync and you're ready to go!

You might already be familiar with the project hierarchy from the previous chapters, but in case you aren't, look at the following image:

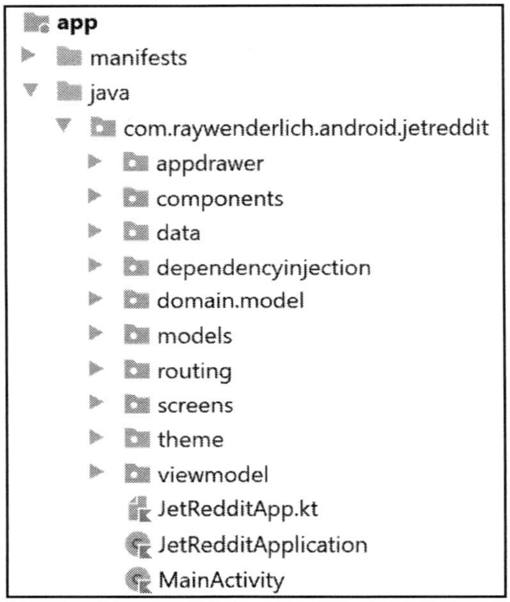

Project Hierarchy

In this chapter, you'll only work with two of these packages:

- **screens**, to implement a new screen
- **routing**, to add a new routing option.

The rest of the packages are already prepared to handle navigation, fetching data from the database, dependency injection and theme switching for you.

Once you're familiar with the file organization, build and run the app. You'll see:

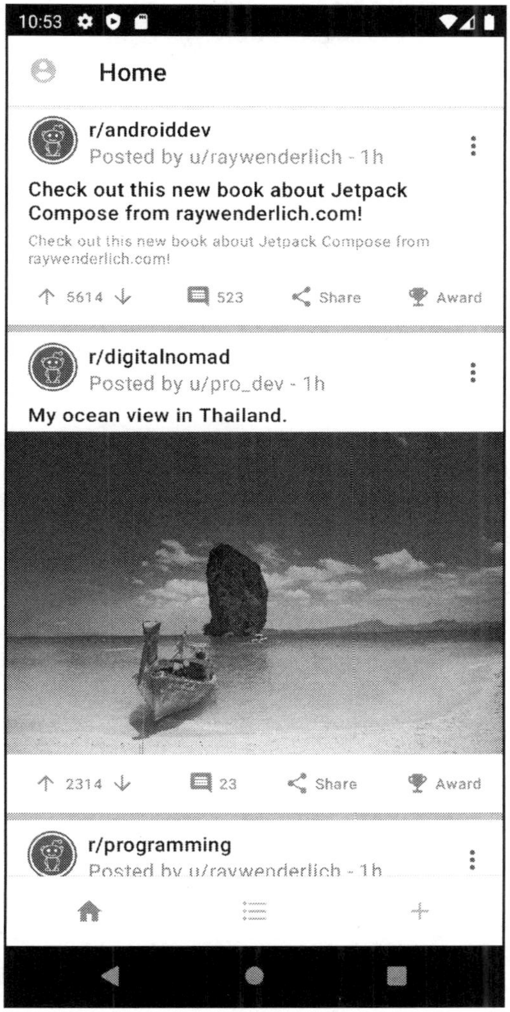

Home Screen

This is a fully implemented home screen. When you browse the app, you'll notice that two screens are pre-built and implemented for you: **My Profile**, in the app drawer, and **New Post**, the third option in the bottom navigation.

In this chapter, you'll implement the option to choose a community inside the **New Post** screen:

New Post Screen

Implementing the Community Chooser

You'll implement a community chooser like the one the original Reddit app uses. Look at the following image for reference:

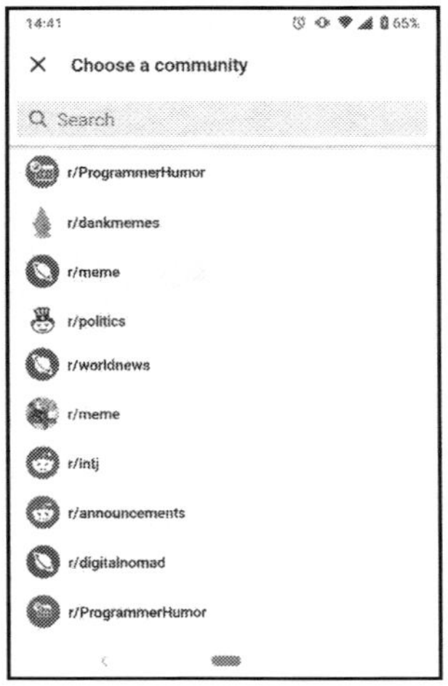

Reddit Community Chooser

The community chooser contains a toolbar, a search input field and a list of communities. To fetch the community list, you'll use a `ViewModel` that contains pre-defined methods.

Open the **ChooseCommunityScreen.kt** file and look at the code. There are three composables: `ChooseCommunityScreen()` for the whole screen, `SearchedCommunities()` for the community list and `ChooseCommunityTopBar()`, for the pre-built top navigation bar.

Creating a List of Communities

Just like in the previous chapters, you'll build the smaller components first, starting with `SearchedCommunities()`. Start by changing `SearchedCommunities()` code to the following:

```
@Composable
fun SearchedCommunities(
  communities: List<String>,
  viewModel: MainViewModel?,
  modifier: Modifier = Modifier
) {
  communities.forEach {
    Community(
      text = it,
      modifier = modifier,
      onCommunityClicked = {
        viewModel?.selectedCommunity?.postValue(it)
        JetRedditRouter.goBack()
      }
    )
  }
}
```

In the composable parameters, you see a list of strings that represent community names, the `MainViewModel` to update the data and a default `Modifier`.

First, you iterate over the `communities` list and create a `Community()` for each element. You already made `Community()` in the previous chapter, so this is a perfect opportunity to reuse it.

Next, for each of the community elements, you pass its name and a `modifier`, then set the `onCommunityClicked` action. When the user clicks any of the communities, you notify the other composables about the selected value using `selectedCommunity`, which is stored inside the `viewModel`.

Finally, you close the screen after the user selects the community by calling `goBack()` on the `JetRedditRouter`.

To see the changes, add the preview code at the bottom of **ChooseCommunityScreen.kt**:

```
@Preview
@Composable
fun SearchedCommunitiesPreview() {
  Column {
    SearchedCommunities(defaultCommunities, null, Modifier)
  }
}
```

Build the app and look at the preview section. You see a list of communities with three elements:

Searched Communities Preview

Making the Community List Searchable

The next step is to add a `TextField()` to search the communities according to user input. Replace `ChooseCommunityScreen()` with the code below:

```
@Composable
fun ChooseCommunityScreen(
  viewModel: MainViewModel,
  modifier: Modifier = Modifier,
  onBackSelected: () -> Unit
) {
  val scope = rememberCoroutineScope()
  val communities: List<String> by
viewModel.subreddits.observeAsState(emptyList())
  var searchedText by remember { mutableStateOf("") }
  var currentJob by remember { mutableStateOf<Job?>(null) }
  val activeColor = MaterialTheme.colors.onSurface

  LaunchedEffect(Unit) {
      viewModel.searchCommunities(searchedText)
  }

  Column {
      ChooseCommunityTopBar(onBackSelected = onBackSelected)
      TextField(
```

```
            value = searchedText,
            onValueChange = {
                searchedText = it
                currentJob?.cancel()
                currentJob = scope.async {
                    delay(SEARCH_DELAY_MILLIS)
                    viewModel.searchCommunities(searchedText)
                }
            },
            leadingIcon = {
                Icon(
                    Icons.Default.Search,
                    contentDescription = stringResource(id =
R.string.search)
                )
            },
            label = { Text(stringResource(R.string.search)) },
            modifier = modifier
                .fillMaxWidth()
                .padding(horizontal = 8.dp),
            colors = TextFieldDefaults.outlinedTextFieldColors(
                focusedBorderColor = activeColor,
                focusedLabelColor = activeColor,
                cursorColor = activeColor,
                backgroundColor = MaterialTheme.colors.surface
            )
        )
        SearchedCommunities(communities, viewModel, modifier)
    }
}
```

Here, you first created a `coroutineScope` by calling `rememberCoroutineScope()`.

> **Note**: `rememberCoroutineScope()` is a `SuspendingEffect`, which is a type of an effect in Compose. It creates a `CoroutineScope`, which is bound to the composition. `CoroutineScope` is only created once, and it stays the same even after recomposition. Any `Job` belonging to this scope will be canceled when the scope leaves the composition.

Then, you create three states: one for the list of communities, which is observed from the database. The second for `searchedText`, which updates based on user input. The third stores your search `Job`.

Next, you called `LaunchedEffect(Unit)` to search the communities when the composition is first composed. Searching for an empty string will return all communities from the database.

`LaunchedEffect(key)` runs the block of code whenever the composable enters recomposition, as long as the `key` you passed in changes between recompositions. Because you passed in `Unit`, which is a constant, it's only going to run once — the first time the element is shown.

Finally, you added a `Column()` with three composables: the pre-built `ChooseCommunityTopBar()`, `TextField()` to capture the user input and `SearchedCommunities()` to display the list of communities.

With each value change inside `TextField()`, this code cancels the previous `Job` and starts a new one inside the scope you already created.

Inside the code block of the coroutine, you added `delay()` with a 300-millisecond delay. This prevents a new community search from starting each time the user types a new character, unless more than 300 milliseconds pass between keystrokes. Updating `searchedText` cancels the previous `Job` and a new one launches with a new delay.

Build and run, then open the **New Post** screen by selecting the third option in the bottom navigation.

Click the **Choose a community** button to open the screen you just implemented:

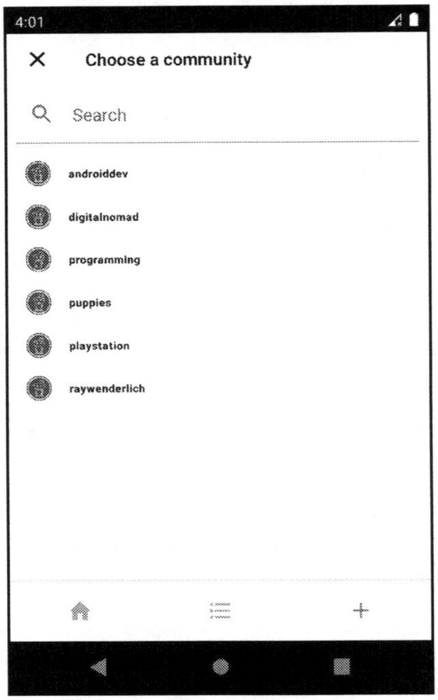

Community Chooser

You see a list of communities and a search input field that you can use to filter the current list. If you type fast, the list won't update until you wait for more than 300 milliseconds.

Currently, you're fetching data from a local database, but when searches use a remote API, this implementation saves your network data and reduces the number of requests a server might receive.

If you want to go back without selecting a community, you can click the **Close** icon from the top app bar. But what happens when you click the built-in back button on your device? The app closes instead of navigating to the previous screen.

Next, you'll learn about effects in Jetpack Compose.

Effects in Compose

To understand the topic of effects more clearly, you first need to learn how side effects work in Compose.

Side effects in programming are defined as operations that trigger a change in the value of anything outside the scope of a function.

An example of this is when a mutable object is passed to a function and changes some of that function's properties resulting in an undesired result.

Such changes can affect other parts of the code that use the same object, so you need to be careful when applying them.

The biggest problem with side effects is that you don't have control over when they actually occur. This is problematic in composables because the code inside them executes every time a recomposition takes place. Effects can help you by giving you control over when the code executes.

Here are more details about specific effects.

SideEffect

`SideEffect()` ensures that your event only executes when a composition is successful. If the composition fails, the event is discarded. In addition, only use it when you don't need to dispose the event, but want it to run with every recomposition.

Take a look at the snippet below:

```
@Composable
fun MainScreen(router: Router) {
  val drawerState = rememberDrawerState(DrawerValue.Closed)

  SideEffect {
    router.isRoutingEnabled = drawerState.Closed
  }
}
```

In this snippet, `SideEffect()` changes the state of the router. You disable the routing in the app when the drawer is closed: otherwise, you enable it. In this case, `router` is a `singleton` and you don't want to dispose it because other screens are using it for navigation.

The next effect, `LaunchedEffect()`, is similar to `rememberCoroutineScope()`, which you used earlier.

LaunchedEffect

`LaunchedEffect` launches a coroutine into the composition's `CoroutineScope`. You can perform any async operation within its scope. Just like `rememberCoroutineScope()`, its coroutine is canceled when `LaunchedEffect` leaves the composition and will relaunch on recomposition.

See the example below to get a deeper insight:

```
@Composable
fun SpeakerList(searchText: String) {
  var communities by remember
{ mutableStateOf(emptyList<String>()) }
  LaunchedEffect(searchText) {
    communities = viewModel.searchCommunities(searchText)
  }

  Communities(communities)
}
```

This snippet is similar to what you did when you implemented the search feature in `ChooseCommunityScreen()`.

When you implemented `ChooseCommunityScreen`, `searchText` was a mutable state depending on the user input. This time, `searchText` is a function parameter and isn't saved as a mutable state. According to the Google guidelines, you should follow this approach to prevent performance issues.

`LaunchedEffect` initiates the first time it enters the composition and every time the parameter changes. It cancels all running `Jobs` during the parameter change or upon leaving the composition.

You now learned all effect types, but there are functions that might help you use those effects for more specific situations. These functions create different kinds of states that should be used inside effect composables. The first function on the list is `rememberUpdatedState()`.

RememberUpdatedState

When using `LaunchedEffect`, it is initiated every time the passed parameter changes. If you want to use a constant parameter that never changes, your effect will never restart which is a problem if you have values that need to be updated.

In this case, you can use `rememberUpdatedState` on your value that needs to be updated. This creates a reference to that value and allows it to update when the composable is recomposed. The example when you would need this approach is a splash screen:

```
@Composable
fun LandingScreen(onSplashFinished: () -> NetworkData) {

  val currentOnSplashFinished by
rememberUpdatedState(onSplashFinished)

  LaunchedEffect(Unit) {
    delay(SplashWaitTimeMillis)
    currentOnSplashFinished()
  }
}
```

When the splash screen starts, you want to set a timeout for how long it should last and do some background work if you app requires it. When some of your background work is done, you might want to update the values in your composable which triggers the recomposition.

To update the value of your `onSplashFinished` lambda, you wrap it with `rememberUpdatedState` and then used inside the `LaunchedEffect` with `Unit` as a parameter. Since `Unit` is a constant value, the effect will never restart to ensure that your splash screen always has the same wait time, but your lambda will still be invoked with the latest value after the timeout is finished.

The next function that will help you when using effects is `produceState`.

ProduceState

Sometimes you want to do some work in the background and pass the result down to the presentation layer. Remember that composable functions have `States` and any data used in composables needs to be converted into compose `State` in order to be used and survive the recomposition.

You can use `produceState` to write a function that fetches data and converts it directly into compose `State`. In the following code, you can see an example of loading books by author.

```
@Composable
fun loadBooks(author: String, booksRepository: BooksRepository):
State<Result<List<Book>>> {
  return produceState(initialValue = Result.Loading, author,
booksRepository) {

    val books = booksRepository.load(author)

    value = if (books == null) {
      Result.Error
    } else {
      Result.Success(books)
    }
  }
}
```

The function has two parameters, an `author` and `booksRepository`. `ProduceState` is called to create a coroutine and fetch the books and directly convert them to a composable `State`. If either of the two passed parameters change, the job will be canceled and relaunched with the new values.

This allows you to create a composable with the return type and call it from other composables like you would usually do in your `presenters` or `viewmodels`. Note that the name convention for composables with return type is to start with lowercase letter like other non-composable functions.

Migrate Effects

If you used older versions of Jetpack Compose, you might have have a few different effects that were not mentioned in this chapter. Those effects are now removed, but you can still achieve the same implementation using `LaunchedEffect`, `DisposableEffect` and `SideEffect`.

To migrate to the newer version, you can use this cookbook prepared for you:

```
// onActive without subject parameter
onActive {
  someFunction()
}
```

Replace with:

```
LaunchedEffect(Unit) {
  someFunction()
}
```

You can replace `onActive()` without subject parameter by using `LaunchedEffect` with a constant value like `Unit` or `true`. This will ensure that the effect is used once, on the first composition.

Next, if you're using it like so:

```
// onActive with subject parameter
onActive(parameter) {
  someFunction()
}
```

Replace it with:

```
LaunchedEffect(parameter) {
  someFunction()
}
```

If you use subject parameter with your `onActive()`, you can just replace it with `LaunchedEffect`.

Then if you're using something like:

```
// onActive with onDispose
onActive {
  val disposable = getData()

  onDispose {
    disposable.dispose()
  }
}
```

Replace it with:

```
DisposableEffect(Unit) {
  val disposable = getData()

  onDispose {
    disposable.dispose()
  }
}
```

Like in the example without the subject parameter, you can replace `onActive()` with `onDispose()` inside by using `DisposableEffect` with a constant value like `Unit` or `true`.

Finally, if you're using:

```
// onCommit without subject parameter
onCommit {
  someFunction()
}
```

Replace it with:

```
SideEffect {
  someFunction()
}
```

You can replace `onCommit()` without a subject parameter by using `SideEffect` with a constant value like `Unit` or `true`. This will ensure that the effect is used on the first composition, and again for every recomposition. To use `onCommit()` with the subject parameter or `onDispose()` inside, use the same code as for `onActive()`.

Key Points

- Use `rememberCoroutineScope()` when you are using coroutines and need to cancel and relaunch the coroutine after an event.
- Use `LaunchedEffect()` when you are using coroutines and need to cancel and relaunch the coroutine every time your parameter changes and it isn't stored in a mutable state.
- `DisposableEffect()` is useful when you aren't using coroutines and need to dispose and relaunch the event every time your parameter changes.
- `SideEffect()` triggers an event only when the composition is successful and you don't need to dispose the `subject`.
- Use `rememberUpdatedState()` when you want to launch your effect only once but still be able to update the values.
- Use `produceState()` to directly convert non-composable states into composable states.
- Names of the composables with a return type should start with the lowercase letter.

Where to Go From Here?

Congratulations! Now, you know how to react to Compose lifecycle, which is one of the most complex parts of Jetpack Compose. At this point, you've seen an overview of how to solve some of the most complex and important problems you encounter while working with Compose.

In the next chapter, you'll learn how to use animations to make your UI more beautiful. Animations are fun — and finally easy to do — so read on and enjoy!

Chapter 12: Animating Properties Using Compose

By Denis Buketa

Great job on completing the previous chapter. So far, in the third section of this book, you've learned how to use `ConstraintLayout`, build complex UI and react to Compose lifecycles. Those things are certainly fun, but what's even more fun? Playing with animations! And that's what you'll do now. :]

In this chapter, you'll learn how to:

- **Animate composable properties** using `animate*AsState()`.
- Use `updateTransition()` to **animate multiple properties** of your composables.
- **Animate composable content**.
- **Implement an animated button** to join a subreddit.
- **Implement an animated toast** that displays when the user joins a subreddit.

Before diving straight into the animation world, you'll create a composable representing a button that lets users join an imaginary subreddit.

You'll start by implementing a simple button, like the one shown below:

Simple Join Button

If a user hasn't joined the subreddit yet, they can do so by clicking the blue button with the **plus** icon. If the user is a member already, a white button with a blue check represents that state. Clicking the button again returns it to its previous state.

To follow along with the code examples, open this chapter's **starter project** in Android Studio and select **Open an existing project**.

Next, navigate to **12-animating-properties-using-compose/projects** and select the **starter** folder as the project root. Once the project opens, let it build and sync and you're ready to go!

Note that if you skip ahead to the final project, you'll find the completed button with all the animation logic implemented.

Now that you're all set, it's time to start coding.

Building JoinButton

In the **components** package, add a new file named **JoinButton.kt**, then open it and add the following code:

```
@Composable
fun JoinButton(onClick: (Boolean) -> Unit = {}) {

}

enum class JoinButtonState {
```

```
    IDLE,
    PRESSED
}

@Preview
@Composable
fun JoinButtonPreview() {
  JoinButton(onClick = {})
}
```

Not much to see here. You just created a root composable for your button and added a preview. Right now, there's nothing to preview because you haven't added any content yet.

You also added `JoinButtonState`, which represents the state of the button, The two options for the state are `IDLE` or `PRESSED`.

Next, add the following code to `JoinButton()`:

```
var buttonState: JoinButtonState
  by remember { mutableStateOf(JoinButtonState.IDLE) }

// Button shape
val shape = RoundedCornerShape(corner = CornerSize(12.dp))

// Button background
val buttonBackgroundColor: Color =
  if (buttonState == JoinButtonState.PRESSED)
    Color.White
  else
    Color.Blue

// Button icon
val iconAsset: ImageVector =
  if (buttonState == JoinButtonState.PRESSED)
    Icons.Default.Check
  else
    Icons.Default.Add
val iconTintColor: Color =
  if (buttonState == JoinButtonState.PRESSED)
    Color.Blue
  else
    Color.White

Box(
  modifier = Modifier
    .clip(shape)
    .border(width = 1.dp, color = Color.Blue, shape = shape)
    .background(color = buttonBackgroundColor)
    .size(width = 40.dp, height = 24.dp)
    .clickable(onClick = {
```

```
        buttonState =
          if (buttonState == JoinButtonState.IDLE) {
            onClick.invoke(true)
            JoinButtonState.PRESSED
          } else {
            onClick.invoke(false)
            JoinButtonState.IDLE
          }
      }),
    contentAlignment = Alignment.Center
  ) {
    Icon(
      imageVector = iconAsset,
      contentDescription = "Plus Icon",
      tint = iconTintColor,
      modifier = Modifier.size(16.dp)
    )
  }
```

This might look like a lot of code, but you'll see that it's pretty simple. Here's a breakdown, starting from the top.

You first declared a `buttonState` with `remember()`. Ideally, you'd represent your state with `PostModel`, but this simplified approach is enough to demonstrate how animations work.

Next, you used `RoundedCornerShape()` to define the `shape` of the button.

You also defined the button's background color, which will change depending on the `buttonState`. When the button has `JoinButtonState.PRESSED`, it will be white. When it's `JoinButtonState.IDLE`, it will be blue.

Next, you defined the button's icon and icon color. When the button's state is `JoinButtonState.PRESSED`, you'll represent the icon with a white plus sign. If it's `JoinButtonState.IDLE`, you'll represent it with a blue check mark.

The last thing you added is the code that emits the button's UI. You used `Box()` to define the button shape and background and `Icon()` to define how the button's icon will look.

For that code to work, you need to add a few imports as well:

```
import androidx.compose.foundation.shape.CornerSize
import androidx.compose.foundation.shape.RoundedCornerShape
import androidx.compose.foundation.background
import androidx.compose.foundation.border
import androidx.compose.foundation.clickable
import androidx.compose.foundation.layout.Box
import androidx.compose.foundation.layout.size
```

```
import androidx.compose.material.Icon
import androidx.compose.material.icons.Icons
import androidx.compose.material.icons.filled.Add
import androidx.compose.material.icons.filled.Check
import androidx.compose.runtime.*
import androidx.compose.ui.Alignment
import androidx.compose.ui.Modifier
import androidx.compose.ui.draw.clip
import androidx.compose.ui.graphics.Color
import androidx.compose.ui.graphics.vector.ImageVector
import androidx.compose.ui.tooling.preview.Preview
import androidx.compose.ui.unit.dp
```

Great! Now, build the project and check the preview panel.

JoinButton — Idle State

Note that you can change `buttonState`'s initial state to `PRESSED`, to preview the different settings for your button.

JoinButton — Pressed State

Awesome! Next, you'll add this button to `Post()`.

Adding JoinButton to Post

Before animating `JoinButton()`, you'll add it to `Post()` so you can see it in the app.

Open **Post.kt** and edit `Header()` to look like this:

```
@Composable
fun Header(
  post: PostModel,
  onJoinButtonClick: (Boolean) -> Unit = {} // here
) {
  Row(
    modifier = Modifier.padding(start = 16.dp),
```

```
    verticalAlignment = Alignment.CenterVertically // here
  ) {
    Image(
      ImageBitmap.imageResource(id =
R.drawable.subreddit_placeholder),
      contentDescription = stringResource(id =
R.string.subreddits),
      Modifier
        .size(40.dp)
        .clip(CircleShape)
    )
    Spacer(modifier = Modifier.width(8.dp))
    Column(modifier = Modifier.weight(1f)) {
      Text(
        text = stringResource(
          R.string.subreddit_header,
          post.subreddit
        ),
        fontWeight = FontWeight.Medium,
        color = MaterialTheme.colors.primaryVariant
      )
      Text(
        text = stringResource(
          R.string.post_header,
          post.username,
          post.postedTime
        ),
        color = Color.Gray
      )
    }
    Spacer(modifier = Modifier.width(4.dp)) // here
    JoinButton(onJoinButtonClick) // here
    MoreActionsMenu()
  }

  Title(text = post.title)
}
```

In the code above, you added:

1. `verticalAlignment` to `Row()` to center the header content vertically.
2. `JoinButton()` and `Spacer()` to `Header()`.
3. `onJoinButtonClick` to `Header()`.

Excellent! Now, build and run the app. Check how your posts look:

Posts With the Join Button

Click one of the `JoinButtons` and you'll see how the icon and the background change instantly.

Animating the JoinButton Background

So far, you've made the button background change from one color to another when the state changes. In this section, you'll animate that transition.

In **JoinButton.kt**, replace the current definition of `buttonBackgroundColor` with the following code:

```
// Button background
val buttonBackgroundColor: Color by animateColorAsState(
  if (buttonState == JoinButtonState.PRESSED)
    Color.White
  else
```

```
    Color.Blue
)
```

Add one more import as well:

```
import androidx.compose.animation.animateColorAsState
```

Here, you wrapped the `if` clause that defined two different background colors with `animateColorAsState()`. By doing that, you implemented the animation between the two colors when the state changes.

With this simple change, you added your first animation. Can you even believe how easy that was? :]

Now, take a closer look at `animateColorAsState()`. It is just one of the `animate*AsState()` functions. In the Jetpack Compose documentation, you'll find a dozen different `animate*AsState()` signatures that allow you to animate a dozen different properties out of the box, including `Float`, `Color`, `Dp`, `Position`, `Size` and other. You can even define your own properties.

All those definitions have something in common: You use them for **fire-and-forget** animations. Once you create a fire-and-forget animation, the app will memorize its position, like other composables. To trigger the animation, or alter the course of the animation, you simply supply a different target to the composable.

The `animate*AsState()` functions are the simplest animation APIs in Compose for animating a single value. You only provide the end value (or target value), and the API starts animation from the current value to the specified value.

Now build and run the app. Click on any `JoinButton` in the app and notice how the background color changes.

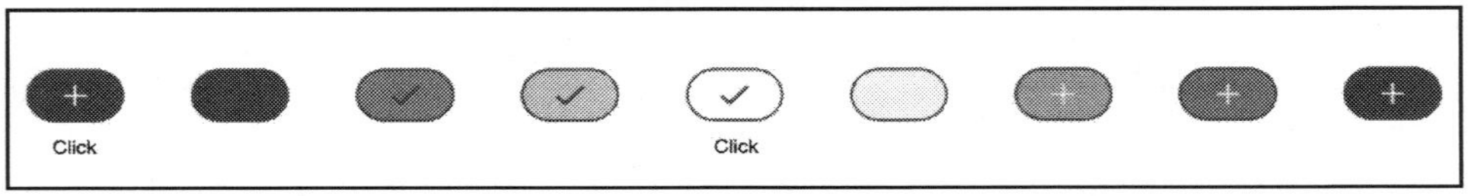

Join Button's Background Animation

The figure shows how the button looks across several frames of the animation. Notice how the icon changes immediately after the click, while the background slowly transitions from one color to another. What's really impressive here is how easy it was to implement this animation, which makes your app even nicer!

Using Transitions to Animate JoinButton

In the previous section, you saw how to animate one property of your composables. Now, you'll add more content to `JoinButton()`. This will give you the opportunity to animate several properties at once.

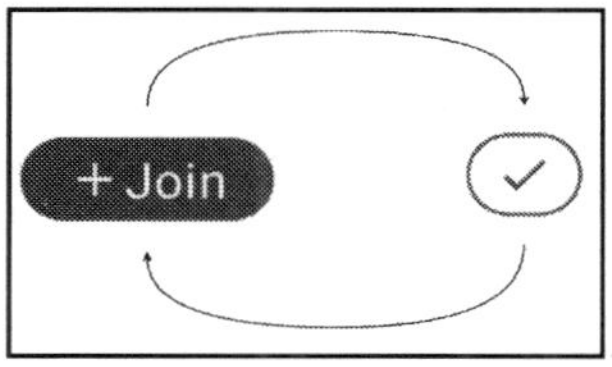

Join Button With More Content

The figure shows how you'll change `JoinButton`'s appearance in the `JoinButtonState.IDLE` state.

Before adding any code, analyze how you'll accomplish this animation. Which properties do you have to animate? To give the button its new look, you need to:

1. Animate the **background**, as you did in the previous example.
2. Change the icon. You'll change the asset the same way as before, but you'll improve that change by animating the **icon color**.
3. **Hide** and **show** the text depending on the state.
4. Animate the button's **width**.

So you need to animate **four** different properties. Keep that in mind when adding the following code.

Defining the Transition

To animate these properties, you'll use `Transition`. `Transition` manages one or more animations as its children and runs them simultaneously between multiple states.

In **JoinButton.kt**, add the following code to `JoinButton()`, just below `shape`:

```
val transition = updateTransition(
  targetState = buttonState,
  label = "JoinButtonTransition"
)
```

Add this import as well:

```
import androidx.compose.animation.core.updateTransition
```

updateTransition creates and remembers an instance of Transition and updates its state. When targetState changes, Transition will run all of its child animations towards their target values specified for the new targetState. You'll add those target values next. You also passed in the label property, which lets you inspect and debug those animations in Android Studio.

Next, you'll define child animations. Replace buttonBackgroundColor definition with the following code:

```
val duration = 600
val buttonBackgroundColor: Color
  by transition.animateColor(
    transitionSpec = { tween(duration) },
    label = "Button Background Color"
  ) { state ->
    when (state) {
      JoinButtonState.IDLE -> Color.Blue
      JoinButtonState.PRESSED -> Color.White
    }
  }
```

Add these imports as well:

```
import androidx.compose.animation.animateColor
import androidx.compose.animation.core.tween
```

Here, you defined the transition duration and first child animation in your transition. You used animateColor which is one of animate* extension functions that allows you to define a child animation in your transition. You specified the target values for each of the states. These animate* functions return an animation value that is updated every frame during the animation when the transition state is updated with updateTransition.

You also used tween(). With tween(), you created a TweenSpec configured with the given duration, delay and easing curve. Since you only specified a duration, the code uses 0 for delayMillis and FastOutSlowInEasing() for easing.

Easing is a way to adjust an animation's fraction. The fraction represents how far along the animation you are and its values are within the [0, 1] range, or [0, 100], representing the percent of the animation you finished.

Easing allows transitioning elements to speed up and slow down, rather than moving at a constant, linear, rate.

Next, add the remaining child animations. Below `buttonBackgroundColor`, add the following code:

```
val buttonWidth: Dp
  by transition.animateDp(
    transitionSpec = { tween(duration) },
    label = "Button Width"
  ) { state ->
    when (state) {
      JoinButtonState.IDLE -> 70.dp
      JoinButtonState.PRESSED -> 32.dp
    }
  }
val textMaxWidth: Dp
  by transition.animateDp(
    transitionSpec = { tween(duration) },
    label = "Text Max Width"
  ) { state ->
    when (state) {
      JoinButtonState.IDLE -> 40.dp
      JoinButtonState.PRESSED -> 0.dp
    }
  }
```

Don't forget to add these imports:

```
import androidx.compose.ui.unit.Dp
import androidx.compose.animation.core.animateDp
```

Finally, replace the current `iconTintColor` definition with this:

```
val iconTintColor: Color
  by transition.animateColor(
    transitionSpec = { tween(duration) },
    label = "Icon Tint Color"
  ) { state ->
    when (state) {
      JoinButtonState.IDLE -> Color.White
      JoinButtonState.PRESSED -> Color.Blue
    }
  }
```

Great! You've now prepared everything you need for your transition, but you still have to **connect** this code with the composables you want to animate.

Connecting the Transition to the Composables

Properties `buttonBackgroundColor` and `iconTintColor` are already in place so you don't have to change that.

Next, replace the `Box()` definition with the following:

```
Box(
  modifier = Modifier
    .clip(shape)
    .border(width = 1.dp, color = Color.Blue, shape = shape)
    .background(color = buttonBackgroundColor)
    .size(
      width = buttonWidth, // here
      height = 24.dp
    )
    .clickable(onClick = {
      buttonState =
        if (buttonState == JoinButtonState.IDLE) {
          onClick.invoke(true)
          JoinButtonState.PRESSED
        } else {
          onClick.invoke(false)
          JoinButtonState.IDLE
        }
    }),
  contentAlignment = Alignment.Center
) {
  Row(    // here
    verticalAlignment = Alignment.CenterVertically
  ) {
    Icon(
      imageVector = iconAsset,
      contentDescription = "Plus Icon",
      tint = iconTintColor,
      modifier = Modifier.size(16.dp)
    )
    Text(   // here
      text = "Join",
      color = Color.White,
      fontSize = 14.sp,
      maxLines = 1,
      modifier = Modifier.widthIn(
        min = 0.dp,
        max = textMaxWidth // here
      )
    )
  }
}
```

First, notice how you changed `Box()`'s content. You used a `Row()` to align an `Icon()` and a `Text()` beside one another. Second, notice how you didn't have to change how you access specific transition properties in `Box()`'s modifier and how you're using it for `Icon()` and `Text()`. Just like before, you used `buttonBackgroundColor` to access the button background or `iconTintColor` to access the icon tint color.

Add the following imports as well.

```
import androidx.compose.foundation.layout.Row
import androidx.compose.foundation.layout.widthIn
import androidx.compose.material.Text
import androidx.compose.ui.unit.sp
```

And that's it! This is now a complete button that will animate from one state to another. Build and run the app. You'll now see the new `JoinButton` in the posts.

Posts With the Completed Join Button

Click the button in any of the posts and see how it animates from one state to the other.

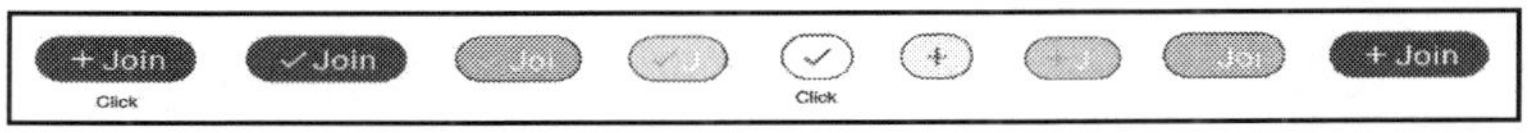

Join Button Animation

You see how the button's width and text change as well as the color animations in the button's background and icon.

Animating Composable Content

So far, you've seen how to animate the properties of your composables. In this section, you'll explore a different approach to creating animations by learning how to animate composable content.

In this section, you'll implement a toast composable that appears when the user joins a subreddit. It will look like this:

Joined Toast

This toast will appear any time you join a new subreddit, by tapping the `JoinButton`. There are a few things you need to do, to implement such behavior, so let's start by creating the initial toast composable.

Adding JoinedToast

In **components**, create a new file named **JoinedToast.kt**. Then, add the following code to it:

```
@Composable
```

```
fun JoinedToast(visible: Boolean) {
  ToastContent()
}

@Composable
private fun ToastContent() {
  val shape = RoundedCornerShape(4.dp)
  Box(
    modifier = Modifier
      .clip(shape)
      .background(Color.White)
      .border(1.dp, Color.Black, shape)
      .height(40.dp)
      .padding(horizontal = 8.dp),
    contentAlignment = Alignment.Center
  ) {
    Row(verticalAlignment = Alignment.CenterVertically) {
      Icon(
        painter = painterResource(
          id = R.drawable.ic_planet
        ),
        contentDescription = "Subreddit Icon"
      )
      Spacer(modifier = Modifier.width(8.dp))
      Text(text = "You have joined this community!")
    }
  }
}

@Preview
@Composable
fun JoinedToastPreview() {
  JoinedToast(visible = true)
}
```

Here's what the code above does. You used a `Box()` to give your toast a specific background, shape, size and padding. In the `Box()`, you added a `Row()` to align an `Icon()`, `Spacer()` and `Text()`.

For this to work, add the following imports as well:

```
import androidx.compose.foundation.background
import androidx.compose.foundation.border
import androidx.compose.foundation.layout.*
import androidx.compose.foundation.shape.RoundedCornerShape
import androidx.compose.material.Icon
import androidx.compose.material.Text
import androidx.compose.runtime.Composable
import androidx.compose.ui.Alignment
import androidx.compose.ui.Modifier
import androidx.compose.ui.draw.clip
```

```
import androidx.compose.ui.graphics.Color
import androidx.compose.ui.res.painterResource
import androidx.compose.ui.tooling.preview.Preview
import androidx.compose.ui.unit.dp
import com.yourcompany.android.jetreddit.R
```

Build the project and check the preview panel to see your composable.

JoinedToast Composable — Preview

Awesome! Next, you'll animate the toast. :]

Animating JoinedToast

In **JoinedToast.kt**, replace the `JoinedToast()` code with the following:

```
@Composable
fun JoinedToast(visible: Boolean) {
  AnimatedVisibility(
      visible = visible,
      enter = slideInVertically(initialOffsetY = { +40 }) +
          fadeIn(),
      exit = slideOutVertically() + fadeOut()
  ) {
    ToastContent()
  }
}
```

Android Studio will complain if you don't add these imports as well.

```
import androidx.compose.animation.AnimatedVisibility
import androidx.compose.animation.fadeIn
import androidx.compose.animation.slideInVertically
import androidx.compose.animation.slideOutVertically
import androidx.compose.animation.fadeOut
```

Here, you wrapped `ToastContent()` with `AnimatedVisibility()`, which animates the appearance and disappearance of its content as the visible value changes.

This is `AnimatedVisibility()`'s signature, taken from the Jetpack Compose documentation:

```
@Composable
fun AnimatedVisibility(
```

```
    visible: Boolean,
    modifier: Modifier = Modifier,
    enter: EnterTransition = fadeIn() + expandIn(),
    exit: ExitTransition = shrinkOut() + fadeOut(),
    label: String = "AnimatedVisibility",
    content: @Composable() AnimatedVisibilityScope.() -> Unit
)
```

You can define different `EnterTransition` and `ExitTransition` in `enter` and `exit` for the appearance and disappearance animations. There are three types of `EnterTransition` and `ExitTransition`: **fade**, **expand/shrink** and **slide**. By using the + sign, you combine the enter and exit transitions. The combination's order doesn't matter since the transition animations start simultaneously.

Now, back to your code. You passed `visible` from `JoinedToast()` to `AnimatedVisibility()`. With that, you'll control when the animation triggers. When `visible` changes to `true`, it triggers the enter animation. Otherwise, it triggers the exit animation.

For the enter transition, you combined two transitions: `slideInVertically()` and `fadeIn()`. `slideInVertically()` slides the content vertically from a starting offset defined in `initialOffsetY` to `0`. You control the direction of the slide by configuring `initialOffsetY`. A positive initial offset means the animation will slide up, whereas a negative value will slide the content down.

For the exit transition, you used `slideOutVertically()` and `fadeOut()`.

Bringing the JoinedToast Home

Before you can see this animation in action, you need to add `JoinedToast()` to `HomeScreen()`.

Start by opening **HomeScreen.kt** and update `HomeScreen()` like this:

```
@Composable
fun HomeScreen(viewModel: MainViewModel) {
  val posts: List<PostModel>
      by viewModel.allPosts.observeAsState(listOf())

  var isToastVisible by remember { mutableStateOf(false) }

  val onJoinClickAction: (Boolean) -> Unit = { joined ->
    isToastVisible = joined
    if (isToastVisible) {
      Timer().schedule(3000) {
        isToastVisible = false
      }
```

```
      }
    }

    Box(modifier = Modifier.fillMaxSize()) {
      LazyColumn(modifier = Modifier.background(color =
  MaterialTheme.colors.secondary)) {
        items(posts) {
          if (it.type == PostType.TEXT) {
            TextPost(it, onJoinButtonClick = onJoinClickAction)
          } else {
            ImagePost(it, onJoinButtonClick = onJoinClickAction)
          }
          Spacer(modifier = Modifier.height(6.dp))
        }
      }

      Box(
        modifier = Modifier
          .align(Alignment.BottomCenter)
          .padding(bottom = 16.dp)
      ) {
        JoinedToast(visible = isToastVisible)
      }
    }
  }
```

Add the following imports as well:

```
import androidx.compose.foundation.layout.Box
import androidx.compose.foundation.layout.fillMaxSize
import androidx.compose.foundation.layout.padding
import androidx.compose.ui.Alignment
import com.yourcompany.android.jetreddit.components.JoinedToast
import java.util.Timer
import kotlin.concurrent.schedule
```

You did a couple of things in the code above. You wrapped a `LazyColumn()` with a `Box()`, which allows you to fill the max size of the screen. You also added a second `Box()` and added `JoinedToast()` to its content. This second `Box()` lets you position `JoinedToast()` at the bottom. Then, you used `remember()` to define the visibility state of the toast.

Next, you defined the `onJoinClickAction`. Tapping any `JoinButton` triggers `onJoinClickAction()` and displays a toast. After three seconds, you hide the toast by changing `isToastVisible` to false.

Finally, you used `onJoinClickAction` as a parameter for the different posts. However, right now, the `TextPost()` and `ImagePost()` don't have an `onJoinButtonClick` parameter, so you'll see an error. You're going to fix that next.

Adding onJoinButtonClick to the Posts

Open **Post.kt** and replace `TextPost()`, `ImagePost()` and `Post()` with the following code:

```
@Composable
fun TextPost(
  post: PostModel,
  onJoinButtonClick: (Boolean) -> Unit = {}
) {
  Post(post, onJoinButtonClick) {
    TextContent(post.text)
  }
}

@Composable
fun ImagePost(
  post: PostModel,
  onJoinButtonClick: (Boolean) -> Unit = {}
) {
  Post(post, onJoinButtonClick) {
    ImageContent(post.image!!)
  }
}

@Composable
fun Post(
  post: PostModel,
  onJoinButtonClick: (Boolean) -> Unit = {},
  content: @Composable () -> Unit = {}
) {
  Card(shape = MaterialTheme.shapes.large) {
    Column(
      modifier = Modifier.padding(
        top = 8.dp,
        bottom = 8.dp
      )
    ) {
      Header(post, onJoinButtonClick)
      Spacer(modifier = Modifier.height(4.dp))
      content.invoke()
      Spacer(modifier = Modifier.height(8.dp))
      PostActions(post)
    }
  }
}
```

What's most important here is that you added `onJoinButtonClick` to the `TextPost`, `ImagePost` and `Post` signatures and passed it down to the `Header()`. Excellent work! The header already passes `onJoinButtonClick` to `JoinButton()` and handles everything, so you don't have to update those composables.

Whew! Now, build and run the app. Click any `JoinButton` and observe the toast's enter and exit animations.

Joined Toast

With that, you used three different APIs to animate your composables. Well done!

Key Points

- You use `animate*AsState()` for **fire-and-forget** animations targeting **single properties** of your composables. This is very useful for animating size, color, alpha and similar simple properties.
- You use `Transition` and `updateTransition()` for **state-based** transitions.
- Use `Transitions` when you have to animate **multiple properties** of your composables, or when you have multiple states between which you can animate.
- Transitions are very good when showing content for the first time or leaving the screen, menu, option pickers and similar. They are also great when animating between multiple states when filling in forms, selecting options and pressing buttons!
- You use `AnimatedVisibility()` when you want to animate the appearance and disappearance of composable content.
- `AnimatedVisibility()` lets you combine different types of visibility animations and lets you define directions if you use predefined transition animations.

Hopefully, this was a fun ride for you. You had the chance to play with three different APIs to create some simple, yet beautiful animations. What follows is the last chapter of this book. You've come a long way indeed!

In the next chapter, you'll see how to combine the old `View` framework with Jetpack Compose and how both can coexist in the same codebase.

See you there! :]

Chapter 13: Adding View Compatibility

By Denis Buketa

Congratulations on reaching the **last chapter** of this section!

So far, you've learned a lot about **Jetpack Compose**. In the book's first section, you learned about basic composables. In the second, you saw how to use Compose when building a real app. In the third section, you learned how to build a more complex UI and how to make simple but beautiful animations.

In this chapter, you'll finish your journey by learning the basic principles of **combining** Jetpack Compose and the old `View` framework, which can coexist in the same codebase. That knowledge will make it easier for you to gradually migrate your apps to Jetpack Compose.

Introducing the Chat Screen and the Trending View

To follow along with the code examples, open this chapter's **starter project** in Android Studio and select **Open an existing project**.

Then, navigate to **13-adding-view-compatibility/projects** and select the **starter** folder as the project root. Once the project opens, let it build and sync and you're ready to go! You can see the completed project by skipping ahead to the **final project**.

Also make sure to clean the app's storage, before running the project.

For this chapter, we've added a few things to the **starter** project.

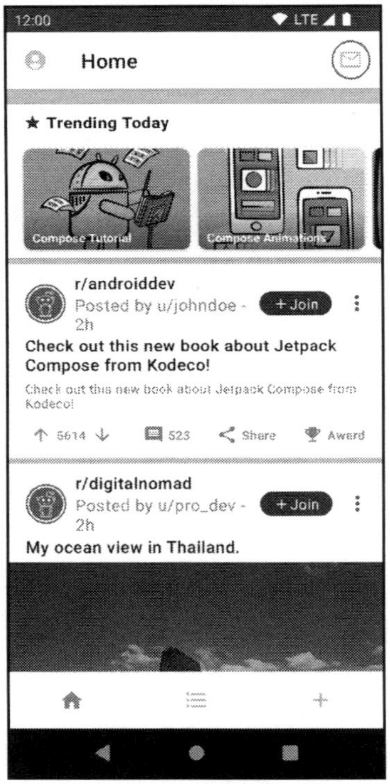

Home Screen Chat Button

These additions include a new **Chat** screen, which uses the old `View` framework. Access it by clicking the new **Chat icon** in the top bar of the **Home** screen, as you can see in the previous image.

If you tap that button, you'll open the following screen:

Chat Screen

In this chapter, you'll replace the **Start Chatting** button with a button made up of composable functions. To see the final implementation, check out **screens/ChatActivity.kt** and **res/layout/activity_chat.xml**. You'll also build a **Trending Today** component that will be the first item on the **Home** screen's list.

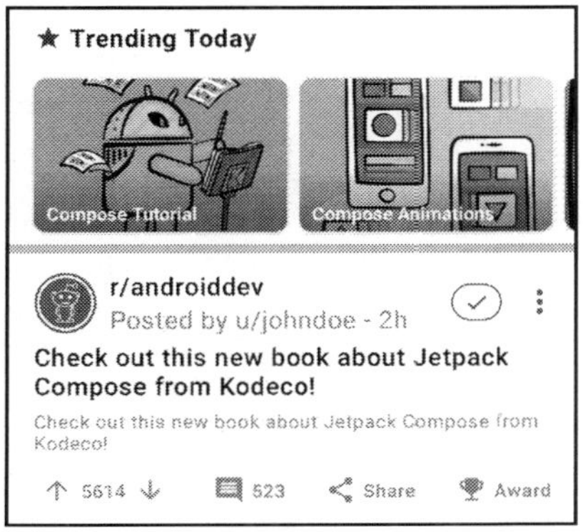

Trending View

You'll build the entire component using composables, except for one piece of functionality: **Trending topic**. This will use the `View` framework in **views/TrendingTopicView.kt** and **res/layout/view_trending_topic.xml**.

Next, you'll see how Jetpack Compose and the `View` framework work together.

Using Composables With the View Framework

Learning how to use composables with the old `View` framework will make it easier to migrate existing screens to Jetpack Compose. You'll start with small components and gradually migrate the whole screen.

Furthermore, some components are easier to make using Jetpack Compose. There's no reason *not* to use those components when the framework allows it. :]

You'll start by implementing the **Start Chatting** button using Jetpack Compose.

Implementing the Start Chatting Button

Open **ChatActivity.kt** and add the following code below `ChatActivity`:

```
@Composable
private fun ComposeButton(onButtonClick: () -> Unit) {
  val buttonColors = buttonColors(
    backgroundColor = Color(0xFF006837),
    contentColor = Color.White
  )

  Button(
    onClick = onButtonClick,
    elevation = null,
    shape = RoundedCornerShape(corner = CornerSize(24.dp)),
    contentPadding = PaddingValues(
      start = 32.dp,
      end = 32.dp
    ),
    colors = buttonColors,
    modifier = Modifier.height(48.dp)
  ) {
    Text(
      text = "Start chatting".toUpperCase(Locale.US),
      fontSize = 16.sp,
      fontWeight = FontWeight.Medium
    )
  }
}

@Preview
@Composable
private fun ComposeButtonPreview() {
  ComposeButton { }
}
```

To break down the code, you added a root composable, `ComposeButton()`, for the button. You then exposed `onButtonClick` so it can react to clicks.

To emit the button UI, you used `Button()` from the `material` composables. You specified the background and content color with `buttonColors()` and passed in the `backgroundColor` and the `contentColor`. You also set the shape and styled the text to match the current implementation.

You also added `@Preview` to visualize how your button looks in Android Studio.

For this to work, you have to add the following imports as well:

```
import androidx.compose.foundation.layout.PaddingValues
import androidx.compose.foundation.layout.height
import androidx.compose.foundation.shape.CornerSize
import androidx.compose.foundation.shape.RoundedCornerShape
import androidx.compose.material.Button
import androidx.compose.material.ButtonDefaults.buttonColors
import androidx.compose.material.Text
import androidx.compose.runtime.Composable
import androidx.compose.ui.Modifier
import androidx.compose.ui.graphics.Color
import androidx.compose.ui.text.font.FontWeight
import androidx.compose.ui.tooling.preview.Preview
import androidx.compose.ui.unit.dp
import androidx.compose.ui.unit.sp
import java.util.*
```

Build the project and check the preview panel. You'll see something like this:

ComposeButton Preview

Adding ComposeButton to ChatActivity

Next, you have to replace the old implementation with the composable button. Open **activity_chat.xml** in the **layout** resource folder and replace the old `AppCompatButton` with the following:

```
<androidx.compose.ui.platform.ComposeView
    android:id="@+id/composeButton"
    android:layout_width="wrap_content"
    android:layout_height="48dp"
    android:layout_marginTop="16dp"
```

```
    app:layout_constraintEnd_toEndOf="parent"
    app:layout_constraintStart_toStartOf="parent"
    app:layout_constraintTop_toBottomOf="@+id/subtitle" />
```

You also have to update `ChatActivity`. In **ChatActivity.kt**, replace `onCreate()` with the following code:

```
override fun onCreate(savedInstanceState: Bundle?) {
  // Switch to AppTheme for displaying the activity
  setTheme(R.style.Theme_JetReddit)

  super.onCreate(savedInstanceState)
  binding = ActivityChatBinding.inflate(layoutInflater)
  val view = binding.root
  setContentView(view)

  binding.backButton.setOnClickListener {
    finish()
  }

  binding.composeButton.setContent {
    MaterialTheme {
      ComposeButton { showToast() }
    }
  }
}
```

Don't forget to add the following import for `MaterialTheme`:

```
import androidx.compose.material.MaterialTheme
```

The old button's implementation used `AppCompatButton` in **activity_chat.xml**. Here, you replaced that with `ComposeView`, which is a `View` that can **host** Jetpack Compose UI content. Compose needs a host `Activity` or `Fragment` to render UI.

`setContent()` supplies the **content composable function** for the view in `ChatActivity`'s `onCreate()`.

`ComposeView` requires that the window it's attached to contains a `ViewTreeLifecycleOwner`. This `LifecycleOwner` disposes the underlying composition when the host lifecycle is destroyed. That allows you to attach and detach the view repeatedly while preserving the composition.

Build and run the app. Open the Chat screen and check out your new button. The button looks and acts the same as the old one did.

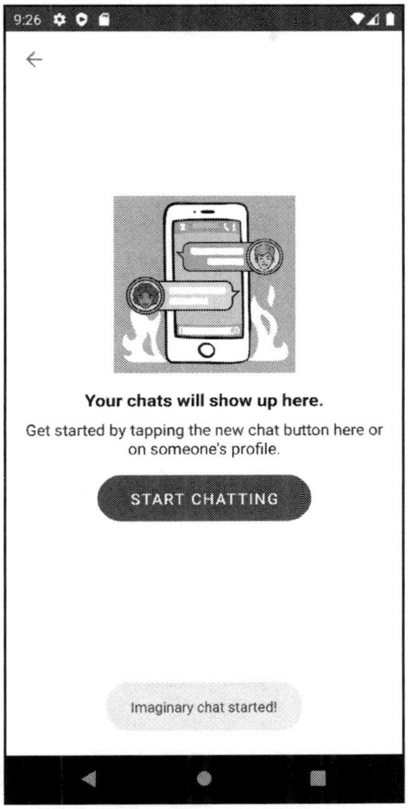

ComposeButton in Chat Screen

Great job! That was easy, wasn't it? With `ComposeView`, you can gradually migrate any screen that uses the old `View` framework. Once you migrate the layout, you can even remove the hosting `Activity` or `Fragment` and implement the whole screen using just Jetpack Compose.

But the great thing is that you can mix and match the two frameworks however you like it.

Using View With Jetpack Compose

Now, reverse the situation. Imagine that you decided to implement a screen or a component using Jetpack Compose, but for some reason — time restrictions, framework support, etc. — it would be easier to reuse a custom `View` you already implemented in that new screen. Well, Jetpack Compose allows you to do that! :]

In this section, you'll implement the component for **Trending Topics**.

Trending Topics

For this component, `TrendingTopicView` has been prepared for you. It represents one item in the scrollable list of topics. To see the implementation, check **TrendingTopicView.kt** and **view_trending_topic.xml**.

Before you implement that component, you need to make a few modifications to **HomeScreen.kt**.

Preparing the Home Screen

Before you can add **Trending Topics** as part of the scrollable list in the Home screen, you need to prepare the code to support different types of items in the list.

Open **HomeScreen.kt** and add the following code at the bottom:

```
private data class HomeScreenItem(
  val type: HomeScreenItemType,
  val post: PostModel? = null
)

private enum class HomeScreenItemType {
  TRENDING,
  POST
}

private data class TrendingTopicModel(
```

```
    val text: String,
    @DrawableRes val imageRes: Int = 0
)
```

You added `HomeScreenItem`, which represents one item in the list, then defined its type with `HomeScreenItemType`. If the item's type is `POST`, the `post` parameter will contain data for the post. Otherwise, it will be `null`.

You also added `TrendingTopicModel`, which contains the data for one topic item that will be visible in the **Trending Topics** component.

To finish, add one additional import:

```
import androidx.annotation.DrawableRes
```

Adding TrendingTopic

Next, you'll create a composable to represent one topic item. Add the following code below `HomeScreen()`:

```
@Composable
private fun TrendingTopic(trendingTopic: TrendingTopicModel) {
  AndroidView({ context ->
    TrendingTopicView(context).apply {
      text = trendingTopic.text
      image = trendingTopic.imageRes
    }
  })
}

@Preview
@Composable
private fun TrendingTopicPreview() {
  TrendingTopic(trendingTopic = TrendingTopicModel(
    "Compose Animations",
    R.drawable.jetpack_compose_animations)
  )
}
```

To make Android Studio happy, add the following imports as well:

```
import androidx.compose.ui.tooling.preview.Preview
import androidx.compose.ui.viewinterop.AndroidView
import com.yourcompany.android.jetreddit.R
import com.yourcompany.android.jetreddit.views.TrendingTopicView
```

Here, you added a root composable called `TrendingTopic` for one topic item. It takes `TrendingTopicModel` as an argument.

The star of the show is `AndroidView()`.

```
@Composable fun <T : View> AndroidView(
    factory: (Context) -> T,
    modifier: Modifier = Modifier,
    update: (T) -> Unit = NoOpUpdate
): Unit
```

`AndroidView()` composes an Android `View` obtained from `factory()`. The `factory` block will be called **exactly once** to obtain the `View` you need to compose. It's also **guaranteed to be invoked on the UI thread**. Therefore, in addition to creating the `factory`, the block can also perform one-off initializations and set `View`'s properties.

The app might run `update()` **multiple times** on the UI thread, as well, due to recomposition. It's the right place to set `View` properties that depend on the state. When the state changes, the block will re-execute to set the new properties. The block will also run **once**, right after `viewBlock()` completes.

In your code, you passed `trendingView` as `viewBlock()`. In `update()`, you left it as a `NoOpUpdate`, which is an empty lambda function, that doesn't update the IO.

You also added the preview composable so you can preview `TrendingTopic()` in the preview panel.

Build the project and check the preview panel and you'll see:

TrendingTopic Preview

Building a List of Trending Topics

Now that you have a composable that represents one trending topic, you'll work on a composable to represent the whole component with multiple trending topics.

Add the following code below `HomeScreen()`:

```
@Composable
private fun TrendingTopics(
  trendingTopics: List<TrendingTopicModel>,
  modifier: Modifier = Modifier
) {
  Card(
    shape = MaterialTheme.shapes.large,
    modifier = modifier
  ) {
    Column(modifier = Modifier.padding(vertical = 8.dp)) {
      // "Trending Today" heading
      Row(
        modifier = Modifier.padding(horizontal = 16.dp),
        verticalAlignment = Alignment.CenterVertically
      ) {
        Icon(
          modifier = Modifier.size(18.dp),
          imageVector = Icons.Filled.Star,
          tint = Color.Blue,
          contentDescription = "Star Icon"
        )
        Spacer(modifier = Modifier.width(4.dp))
        Text(
          text = "Trending Today",
          fontWeight = FontWeight.Bold,
          color = Color.Black
        )
      }

      Spacer(modifier = Modifier.height(8.dp))
    }
  }
}
```

This is a larger piece of code, but the structure of the components is very simple. You add a card that will hold the entire trending topic section. You add `Column()` as the root of `Card()`, as you'll have two elements ordered vertically. The first is `Row()` that holds the title and the star icon. Then second will be all the trending topic items.

Now add the last piece of code right after the last `Spacer()`, that represents the trending topic items:

```
LazyRow(
  contentPadding = PaddingValues(
    start = 16.dp,
    top = 8.dp,
    end = 16.dp
  ),
  content = {
    itemsIndexed(
      items = trendingTopics,
      itemContent = { index, trendingModel ->
        TrendingTopic(trendingModel)
        if (index != trendingTopics.lastIndex) {
          Spacer(modifier = Modifier.width(8.dp))
        }
      }
    )
  }
)
```

This code is pretty straightforward. For the trending topics content, you added `LazyRow()`. Within it, you built `TrendingTopic()` for each item in the list. You also added some padding to each item using `contentPadding`.

For this to work, you also have to add the following imports:

```
import androidx.compose.material.Card
import androidx.compose.material.Icon
import androidx.compose.material.Text
import androidx.compose.material.icons.Icons
import androidx.compose.foundation.layout.Column
import androidx.compose.foundation.layout.Row
import androidx.compose.foundation.layout.size
import androidx.compose.foundation.layout.width
import androidx.compose.foundation.layout.PaddingValues
import androidx.compose.foundation.lazy.LazyRow
import androidx.compose.foundation.lazy.itemsIndexed
import androidx.compose.material.icons.filled.Star
import androidx.compose.ui.graphics.Color
import androidx.compose.ui.text.font.FontWeight
```

Before adding the preview composable, first add the dummy data you'll use as an argument. Add the following above `HomeScreen()`:

```
private val trendingItems = listOf(
  TrendingTopicModel(
    "Compose Tutorial",
    R.drawable.jetpack_composer
  ),
  TrendingTopicModel(
    "Compose Animations",
    R.drawable.jetpack_compose_animations
  ),
  TrendingTopicModel(
    "Compose Migration",
    R.drawable.compose_migration_crop
  ),
  TrendingTopicModel(
    "DataStore Tutorial",
    R.drawable.data_storage
  ),
  TrendingTopicModel(
    "Android Animations",
    R.drawable.android_animations
  ),
  TrendingTopicModel(
    "Deep Links in Android",
    R.drawable.deeplinking
  )
)
```

This is just dummy data that represents fake trending topics. The images you used here were already prepared for you.

Now that you have the dummy data, add the preview composable above `TrendingTopicPreview()`:

```
@Preview
@Composable
private fun TrendingTopicsPreview() {
  TrendingTopics(trendingTopics = trendingItems)
}
```

Build the project and check the preview panel. You'll see this:

TrendingTopics Preview

Adding TrendingTopics to the Home Screen

`TrendingTopics()` is now ready to use in the **Home** screen. Before integrating it into `HomeScreen()`, however, you have to add logic to map the trending items to `HomeScreenItems`.

In **HomeScreen.kt**, add the following code below `HomeScreen()`:

```
private fun mapHomeScreenItems(
    posts: List<PostModel>
): List<HomeScreenItem> {
  val homeScreenItems = mutableListOf<HomeScreenItem>()

  // Add Trending item
  homeScreenItems.add(
      HomeScreenItem(HomeScreenItemType.TRENDING)
  )

  // Add Post items
  posts.forEach { post ->
    homeScreenItems.add(
        HomeScreenItem(HomeScreenItemType.POST, post)
    )
  }

  return homeScreenItems
}
```

This function takes a list of `PostModels` and returns a list of `HomeScreenItems`, where the first item is of type `HomeScreenItemType.TRENDING`.

Now, add the code to invoke this method just above the `Box()` that defines `HomeScreen()`'s content:

```
fun HomeScreen(viewModel: MainViewModel) {
    ...

    // Add this line
    val homeScreenItems = mapHomeScreenItems(posts)

    Box(modifier = Modifier.fillMaxSize()) {
        LazyColumn(...)
        ...
    }
}
```

With this, you mapped the list of `PostModels` to a list of `HomeScreenItems`.

Finally, update the `LazyColumn()` in `HomeScreen()`, like this:

```
LazyColumn(
  modifier = Modifier
    .background(color = MaterialTheme.colors.secondary),
  content = {
    items(
      items = homeScreenItems,
      itemContent = { item ->
        if (item.type == HomeScreenItemType.TRENDING) {
          TrendingTopics(
            trendingTopics = trendingItems,
            modifier = Modifier.padding(
              top = 16.dp,
              bottom = 6.dp
            )
          )
        } else if (item.post != null) {
          val post = item.post
          if (post.type == PostType.TEXT) {
            TextPost(
              post = post,
              onJoinButtonClick = onJoinClickAction
            )
          } else {
            ImagePost(
              post = post,
              onJoinButtonClick = onJoinClickAction
            )
          }
          Spacer(modifier = Modifier.height(6.dp))
        }
      })
  }
)
```

Here, you added the logic that emits either `TrendingTopics()`, `TextPost()` or `ImagePost()`, depending on the `item.type` and `item.post` content.

Good job! :]

Build and run the app and check out your fancy trending topics component at the top of the Home screen.

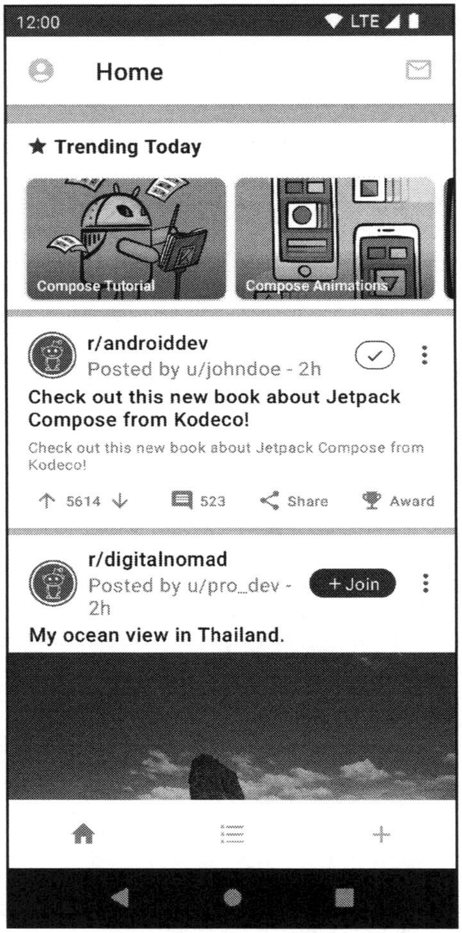

Trending Topics on the Home Screen

Excellent work! You just learned the basic principles of combining Jetpack Compose and the old `View` framework. This will allow you to migrate any app to Jetpack Compose with no trouble! :]

Key Points

- Use `ComposeView` when you want to use a composable within the `View` framework. `ComposeView` is a `View` that can **host Jetpack Compose UI content**.
- Use `setContent()` to **supply the content composable function for the view**.
- `AndroidView()` lets you create a composable from the Android `View`.
- `AndroidView()` composes an Android `View` obtained from `factory()`. `factory()` will be called **exactly once** to obtain the `View` to compose. It's also **guaranteed** to be invoked on the UI thread.
- The `update()` block of the `AndroidView` can be run **multiple times (on the UI thread) due to recomposition**. It's the right place to set `View` properties that depend on state.

Where to Go From Here?

Congratulations, you just completed the **Adding View Compatibility** chapter!

You are definitely ready to adopt Jetpack Compose even if you already have an app built with the old View framework. Just start bit by bit and in no time you'll only write Compose! :]

In the next section, you will learn about how to write UI tests for your Compose code and how to handle accessibility. See you there!

Section IV: UI Testing & Accessibility

So far, you've focused on building up knowledge of how Jetpack Compose works. You now know how to builda fairly complex app using Compose, well done on achieving this! Apps that are of high quality are built this way and also incorporate two new concepts you'll learn about, **UI Testing** and **Accessibility**

In the next two chapters, you'll dive into each of these topics and learn how to:

- Build a suite of UI tests to verify your Jetpack Compose UI works as expected
- Support Accessibility features in your app through Compose

These are two chapters you are going to want to read to take your Compose skills and **user experience** to the next level.

Chapter 14: UI Tests in Jetpack Compose

By Prateek Prasad

Congratulations on wrapping up the JetReddit app. Throughout the last thirteen chapters, you learned about the fundamentals of Jetpack Compose and built the JetReddit app from the ground up.

It's time to verify the app's functionality and learn how UI testing works in Jetpack Compose. In this chapter, you'll learn how to write UI tests for your screens and components in Jetpack Compose and how assertions work. Let's jump straight in!

Loading the Starter Project

To follow along with the code examples, open this chapter's starter project in Android Studio and select **Open an existing project**.

Next, navigate to **14-ui-tests-in-compose/projects** and select the **starter** folder as the project root. Once the project opens, let it build and sync, and you're ready to go!

It's the same app you've worked on, with a few structural changes to the code.

Open the **JetRedditApp.kt** file. Here, the ViewModel is no longer passed as a parameter to `JetRedditApp` composable. Instead, you now have separate state objects and event handlers to render the UI and pass events to the parent activity hosting the composable:

```
@Composable
fun JetRedditApp(
    allPosts: List<PostModel>,
```

```
    myPosts: List<PostModel>,
    communities: List<String>,
    selectedCommunity: String,
    savePost: (post: PostModel) -> Unit,
    searchCommunities: (searchedText: String) -> Unit,
    communitySelected: (community: String) -> Unit,
) {
    JetRedditTheme {
        AppContent(
            allPosts,
            myPosts,
            communities,
            selectedCommunity,
            savePost,
            searchCommunities,
            communitySelected
        )
    }
}
```

This slight change in structure will go a long way in helping you set up the test environment in the absence of a proper dependency injection setup.

The dependencies required for testing your composables have been added to the app's build.gradle file as shown below:

```
  // Compose testing dependencies
  androidTestImplementation "androidx.compose.ui:ui-test:
$compose_version"
  androidTestImplementation "androidx.compose.
  ui:ui-test-junit4:$compose_version"
  debugImplementation "androidx.compose.ui:ui-test-manifest:
$compose_version"
```

Before writing your first UI test, it's good to understand how tests work in Jetpack Compose.

> **Note**: Please ensure you use an emulator or device running a modern version of Android before running the tests in this chapter. Some older versions of Android may report failing tests.

Behind the Scenes of UI Tests in Jetpack Compose

UI tests for composables fall into the instrumentation test category, just like espresso tests, as you need a physical device or an emulator to run them.

There are a few essential aspects to note, however, in how testing works. In Jetpack Compose, your UI is represented as a **tree of nodes**. The parent is at the root node, and all children are further down the tree hierarchy. This tree contains all the visual information required to render the UI of your app.

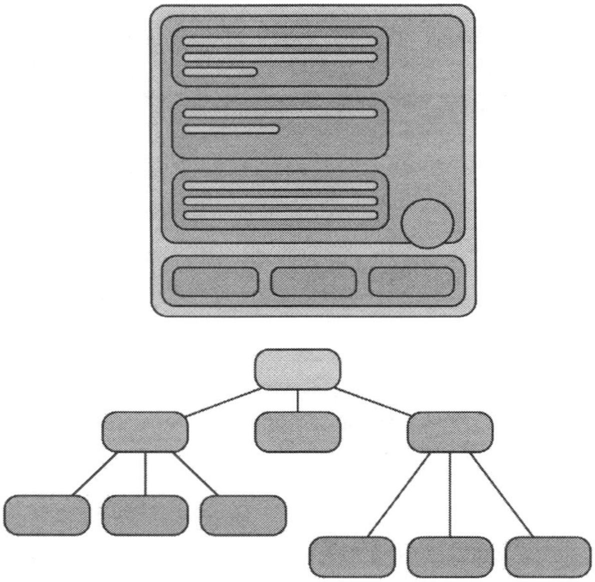

The framework maintains an additional tree in addition to the UI tree that contains further information about each node. It's called the **Semantics tree**, and as the name suggests, it describes each element's *'semantic meaning.'*

Semantic properties include content description, text, actions assigned to the node and reference to the node's parent and children (if any). It's an alternate representation of a UI node used by the accessibility services and for finding and matching components in UI tests using matchers.

Now that you understand the theory behind tests in Jetpack Compose, it's time to write your first one.

Testing UI Components in Jetpack Compose

Just like previewing and deploying individual components in Jetpack Compose, you can also write UI tests for them in isolation. Testing components in isolation allows you the ease and flexibility to set up a contained environment to test individual UI variations quickly.

You will first write tests for your **Post** composable.

Open the **PostTest.kt** file in the **androidTest** source directory and replace the first TODO comment with the following:

```
@get:Rule(order = 0)
val composeTestRule = createComposeRule()
```

Add following imports as well:

```
import androidx.compose.ui.test.junit4.createComposeRule
import org.junit.Rule
```

The `createComposeRule()` creates a test rule you will use to host your composable for testing and for performing assertions.

When writing tests for composables, there are three key ways of interacting with elements:

- **Finders** let you select one or multiple nodes in the Semantics tree to make assertions or perform actions on them.
- **Assertions** are used to verify that the elements exist or have the required attributes.
- **Actions** inject simulated user events into the elements, such as clicks or other gestures.

Update the `title_is_displayed()` method like below:

```
@Test
fun title_is_displayed() {
  val post = PostModel.DEFAULT_POST
  composeTestRule.setContent {
      Post(post = post)
  }
```

```
  composeTestRule.onNodeWithText(post.title).assertIsDisplayed()
}
```

Add following imports as well:

```
import com.yourcompany.android.jetreddit.components.Post
import com.yourcompany.android.jetreddit.domain.model.PostModel
import androidx.compose.ui.test.assertIsDisplayed
import androidx.compose.ui.test.onNodeWithText
```

In the snippet above, you created a post object. You then used the rule created earlier to call `setContent()` and invoke the **Post** composable.

Finally, you used the rule to assert that a node with text containing the post title is displayed.

Run the test to see if it passes.

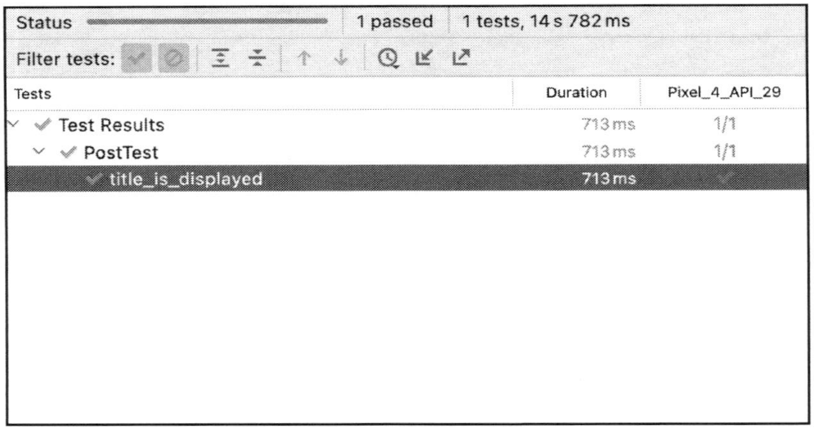

Next, you will write a test to assert that the like count of the post object is displayed.

Update the `like_count_is_displayed()` as shown below:

```
@Test
fun like_count_is_displayed() {
  val post = PostModel.DEFAULT_POST
  composeTestRule.setContent {
      Post(post = post)
  }
  composeTestRule.onNodeWithText(post.likes).assertIsDisplayed()
}
```

The steps here are similar to the previous test, except you assert that the post's like count is displayed in a node.

For your next test, you will assert that the image is shown for a post containing a valid image. But before writing the test, there's an additional step required.

Open **Post.kt** file and add the `testTag()` modifier to the `ImageContent` composable as shown below:

```
modifier = Modifier
  .fillMaxWidth()
  .aspectRatio(painter.intrinsicSize.width /
painter.intrinsicSize.height)
  .testTag(Tags.POST_IMAGE)
```

Add the following imports as well:

```
import androidx.compose.ui.platform.testTag
import com.yourcompany.android.jetreddit.util.Tags
```

A test tag adds a helpful tag to a composable for it to be found from within tests. In this case, you are assigning a **POST_IMAGE** tag predefined in the `Tags` object in the **util** package of the project.

Now update the `image_is_displayed_for_post_with_image()` in the `PostTest` class as follows:

```
@Test
fun image_is_displayed_for_post_with_image() {
  val post = PostModel.DEFAULT_POST
  composeTestRule.setContent {
      ImagePost(post = post)
  }

  composeTestRule.onNodeWithTag(Tags.POST_IMAGE,
true).assertIsDisplayed()
}
```

Add the following imports:

```
import androidx.compose.ui.test.onNodeWithTag
import com.yourcompany.android.jetreddit.components.ImagePost
import com.yourcompany.android.jetreddit.util.Tags
```

In this test, you use the `onNodeWithTag()` finder method to find a node with the tag **POST_IMAGE** and then assert that it is being displayed.

Now that you have the basics of writing UI tests covered, try writing the test for `text_is_displayed_for_post_with_text()` yourself to practice. If you get stuck, you can find the solution in the **final** project.

Writing Tests for Screens

Having covered component-level tests, it's now time to look at how UI testing works for screens.

Since screens are built by composing smaller components, the tests will look similar to what you have written.

Open the **JetRedditAppTest.kt** file and replace the first `TODO` comment with the following:

```
@get:Rule(order = 0)
val composeTestRule =
createAndroidComposeRule(MainActivity::class.java)
```

Add the following imports:

```
import androidx.compose.ui.test.junit4.createAndroidComposeRule
import org.junit.Rule
```

Here, instead of using `createComposeRule()` you are using `createAndroidComposeRule` in order to access the MainActivity.

> **Note**: Access to the activity is required in this test file since you will be using string resources in the matchers, which need access to the **context**.

Next, update the `app_shows_home_screen()` with the following:

```
@Test
fun app_shows_home_screen() {
  composeTestRule.activity.setContent { //1
      JetRedditApp(
          allPosts = PostDataFactory.createPosts(), //2
          myPosts = PostDataFactory.createPosts(),
          communities = PostDataFactory.createCommunities(),
          selectedCommunity = PostDataFactory.randomString(),
          savePost = {},
          searchCommunities = {},
          communitySelected ={}
      )
  }

  //3
  composeTestRule.onNodeWithText(
    composeTestRule.activity.getString(R.string.home)
```

```
    ).assertIsDisplayed()
  }
```

Before you proceed, import the necessary files:

```
import androidx.activity.compose.setContent
import androidx.compose.ui.test.assertIsDisplayed
import androidx.compose.ui.test.onNodeWithText
import com.yourcompany.android.jetreddit.factory.PostDataFactory
```

A lot is going on in the code above, so here's a breakdown:

1. You are using the activity property of the rule to set the content to the `JetRedditApp()` composable.
2. The `JetRedditApp()` composable receives dummy data from the **PostDataFactory.kt** file with a few utility functions for testing.
3. The `onNodeWithText()` matcher uses the String received from the `getString()` function to assert that the home screen is displayed.

For the next test, you will verify that the **subreddits** screen is displayed when you click on the communities tab in the bottom app bar. But first, you need to add test tags to the bottom navigation items so you can find them in the test.

Open the **JetRedditApp.kt** file and in the `BottomNavigationComponent()` composable, add the modifier as shown below:

```
BottomNavigation(modifier = modifier) {
  items.forEach {
    BottomNavigationItem(
      modifier = Modifier.testTag(it.screen.route),

                ....

    )
  }
}
```

Add the following imports as well:

```
import androidx.compose.ui.platform.testTag
```

You are using the route property of the screen as the test tag for each navigation item. Now update the `app_shows_subreddits_screen()` with the following:

```
@Test
```

```
fun app_shows_subreddits_screen() {
    composeTestRule.activity.setContent { //1
        JetRedditApp(
            allPosts = PostDataFactory.createPosts(),
            myPosts = PostDataFactory.createPosts(),
            communities = PostDataFactory.createCommunities(),
            selectedCommunity = PostDataFactory.randomString(),
            savePost = {},
            searchCommunities = {},
            communitySelected ={}
        )
    }

    composeTestRule.onNodeWithTag(
        Screen.Subscriptions.route
    ).performClick() //2

    composeTestRule.onNodeWithText(
     composeTestRule.activity.getString(R.string.subreddits)
   ).assertIsDisplayed() //3
}
```

Add the following imports to clear off the red lines:

```
import androidx.compose.ui.test.onNodeWithTag
import androidx.compose.ui.test.performClick
import com.yourcompany.android.jetreddit.routing.Screen
```

Here's a breakdown of what's going on:

1. You set the `JetRedditApp` as the composable for the rule's activity.
2. You use the `onNodeWithTag()` finder to find the node with route label for the communities tab and use the `performClick()` action to click it.
3. You then assert that the communities tab is displayed.

Run the test to see if it passes.

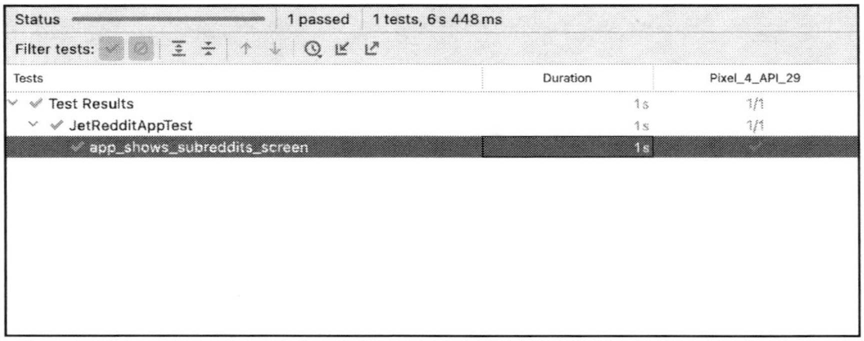

Next, you will write a test to assert that the drawer is displayed when you click on the icon in the app bar.

First you need to add a tag to the app bar icon. Open the **JetRedditApp.kt** file and in the `TopAppBar` composable add the following test tag to the navigation icon as shown below:

```
navigationIcon = {
 IconButton(
  modifier = Modifier.testTag(Tags.ACCOUNT_BUTTON),
  onClick = {
  coroutineScope.launch { scaffoldState.drawerState.open() }
 }) {
                    ...
 }
}
```

Add the following import statement:

```
import com.yourcompany.android.jetreddit.util.Tags
```

Next, update `app_shows_drawer()` in **JetRedditAppTest.kt** file as follows:

```
@Test
fun app_shows_drawer() {

  composeTestRule.activity.setContent {
      JetRedditApp(
          allPosts = PostDataFactory.createPosts(),
          myPosts = PostDataFactory.createPosts(),
          communities = PostDataFactory.createCommunities(),
          selectedCommunity = PostDataFactory.randomString(),
          savePost = {},
          searchCommunities = {},
          communitySelected ={}
      )
  }

  composeTestRule.onNodeWithTag(
      Tags.ACCOUNT_BUTTON
  ).performClick()

  composeTestRule.onNodeWithText(

composeTestRule.activity.getString(R.string.default_username)
  ).assertIsDisplayed()

}
```

Add the following import as well:

```
import com.yourcompany.android.jetreddit.util.Tags
```

Like the previous test, you find the node with the tag **ACCOUNT_BUTTON**, click it and then assert if the drawer is displayed. Run the test to confirm it passes.

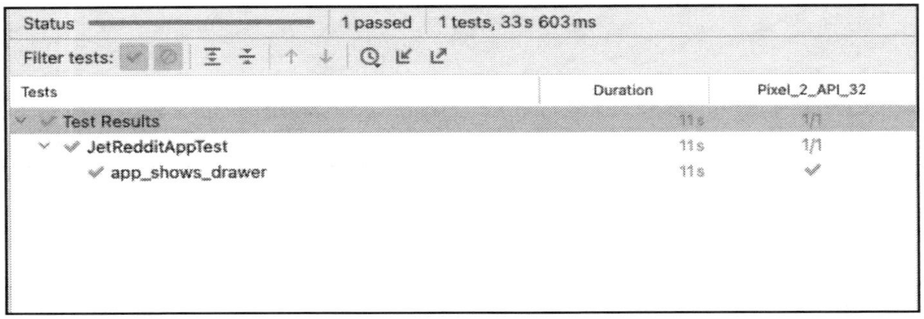

For your next test, you will verify if a the message is displayed when you click on the join button in the post composable.

First, add the tags to the join button and the toast composable.

Open the **JoinButton.kt** file and add `testTag(Tags.JOIN_BUTTON)` to the end of the modifier chain of the enclosing Box:

```
@Composable
fun JoinButton(onClick: (Boolean) -> Unit = {}) {
  ...
  ...
  Box(
      modifier = Modifier
        .clip(shape)
        ...
        ...
        .testTag(Tags.JOIN_BUTTON) // add here
  ) {
    ...
    ...
  }
}
```

Add the necessary import statement as well:

```
import androidx.compose.ui.platform.testTag
import com.yourcompany.android.jetreddit.util.Tags
```

Next, open the **HomeScreen.kt** file and add the test tag to the `Box`, wrapping the `JoinedToast` composable as shown below:

```
Box(
 modifier = Modifier
   .align(Alignment.BottomCenter)
   .padding(bottom = 16.dp)
   .testTag(Tags.JOINED_TOAST)
) {
 JoinedToast(visible = isToastVisible)
}
```

Add the following imports before proceeding:

```
import androidx.compose.ui.platform.testTag
import com.yourcompany.android.jetreddit.util.Tags
```

Now, update the `app_shows_toast_when_joining_community()` in **JetRedditAppTest.kt** file as follows:

```
@Test
fun app_shows_toast_when_joining_community() {
  composeTestRule.activity.setContent {
      JetRedditApp(
          allPosts = PostDataFactory.createPosts(),
          myPosts = PostDataFactory.createPosts(),
          communities = PostDataFactory.createCommunities(),
          selectedCommunity = PostDataFactory.randomString(),
          savePost = {},
          searchCommunities = {},
          communitySelected ={}
      )
  }

  composeTestRule.onAllNodes(
      hasTestTag(Tags.JOIN_BUTTON)
  ).onFirst().performClick()


composeTestRule.onNodeWithTag(Tags.JOINED_TOAST).assertIsDisplay
ed()
}
```

The test above is similar to previous ones except for one key difference. The home screens shows a list of posts, all of which have a join button.

In this test, you used the `onAllNodes()` finder and performed the click action on the first one using the `onFirst()` helper function.

Run the test to make sure it passes.

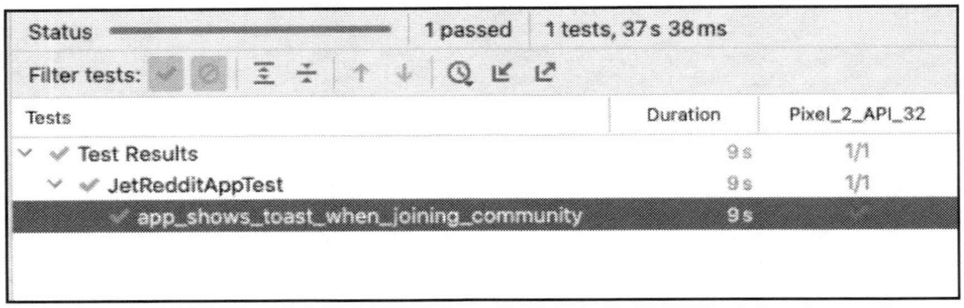

Before closing off the chapter you will take a look at how to write UI tests for hybrid screens that are built using a combination of **Android Views** and **composables**.

Writing Tests for Hybrid Screens

In a hybrid setup you will often find composables inside an XML view hierarchy and views inside composable trees.

This is going to be what most Android projects will look like for a few years until Compose becomes mainstream and the de-facto option for building user interfaces.

Good thing about writing tests for such situations is that you do not require any special setup. You will use **Espresso** for finding and matching Android Views and the **ComposeTestRule** for finding and matching your compose components.

In the **JetReddit** app you have a hybrid setup in two places:

- The `TrendingItem` in the Home screen which is an Android View inside a composable tree.
- The `ComposeButton` inside `ChatActivity` which is a composable inside an android view based tree hierarchy.

You will write a few basic tests for both of these components.

First up, the `ComposeButton`.

Open the **JetRedditApp.kt** file and in the `TopAppBar()` composable, add the modifier as shown below in the `IconButton`:

```
if (screen == Screen.Home) {
  IconButton(
    modifier = Modifier.testTag(Tags.CHAT_BUTTON), // add here
    onClick = {
```

```
        context.startActivity(
          Intent(context, ChatActivity::class.java)
        )
      }) {

          ...

     }
}
```

Next, open the **JetRedditAppTest.kt** file and update the `chat_button_is_displayed()` as follows:

```
@Test
fun chat_button_is_displayed() {

  //1
  composeTestRule.onNodeWithTag(
    Tags.CHAT_BUTTON
  ).performClick()

  //2
  Espresso.onView(withId(R.id.composeButton))
    .check(matches(isDisplayed()))
}
```

Add the following imports as well:

```
import androidx.test.espresso.Espresso
import androidx.test.espresso.assertion.ViewAssertions.matches
import androidx.test.espresso.matcher.ViewMatchers.isDisplayed
import androidx.test.espresso.matcher.ViewMatchers.withId
```

Here's a breakdown of what's going on in the snippet above:

1. You used the `composeTestRule` to find the node with the tag `CHAT_BUTTON` and used the `performClick()` action to click it
2. You then used the regular Espresso `withId()` matcher to find the button with id `R.id.composeButton` and assert that it was displayed.

As you can see, there's nothing special about this test aside from the fact that you use both `Espresso` and the `ComposeTestRule` to perform the assertion.

Run the test to confirm it passes.

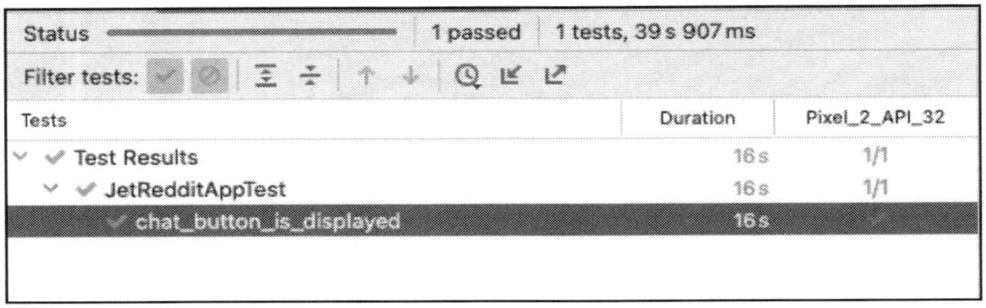

For your final test, you will assert that the `TrendingItem` is displayed correctly on the screen.

Open the **TrendingItemTest.kt** file and create the test rule as follows:

```
@get:Rule
val composeTestRule = createComposeRule()
```

Next, update the `trending_item_is_displayed()` method as follows:

```
@Test
fun trending_item_is_displayed() {
    val topic = TrendingTopicModel(
        "Compose Tutorial",
        R.drawable.jetpack_composer
    )

    composeTestRule.setContent {
        TrendingTopic(topic)
    }

    composeTestRule.onNodeWithTag(Tags.TRENDING_ITEM)
      .assertIsDisplayed()
}
```

Add the following imports before proceeding:

```
import androidx.compose.ui.test.assertIsDisplayed
import androidx.compose.ui.test.junit4.createComposeRule
import androidx.compose.ui.test.onNodeWithTag
import com.yourcompany.android.jetreddit.util.Tags
import org.junit.Rule
import com.yourcompany.android.jetreddit.screens.TrendingTopic
import
com.yourcompany.android.jetreddit.screens.TrendingTopicModel
```

Finally, open **HomeScreen.kt** and update the `TrendingTopic` composable like so:

```
  AndroidView(modifier = Modifier.testTag(Tags.TRENDING_ITEM),
factory = { context ->
    TrendingTopicView(context).apply {
      text = trendingTopic.text
      image = trendingTopic.imageRes
    }
  })
```

Here, you add a test tag to the `AndroidView` so it can found in the UI tests.

With the setup done, you can see the process is similar to previous tests that you wrote in this chapter. You created an instance of the `TrendingTopicModel` and set it as the content of the test rule. You then used the `onNodeWithTag()` finder, to find the item and assert it was displayed.

Finally, run the test to confirm it passes.

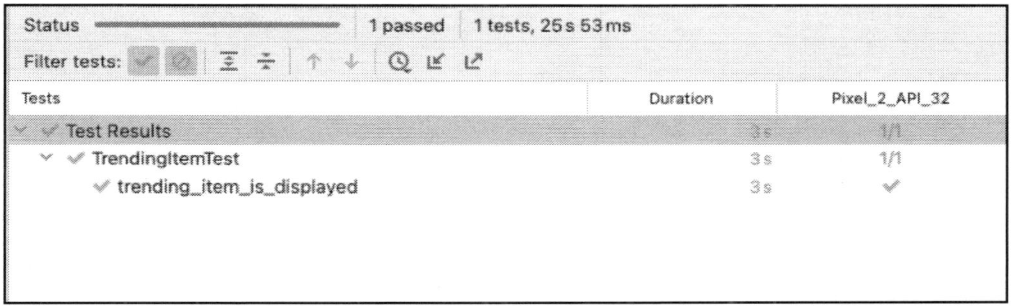

With this final test wrapped up, you now have all the skills needed to write tests for most scenarios and UI variants you can think of. Use the learnings from the previous tests to finish things off with the `app_shows_new_post_screen()` on your own.

If you need help, refer to the solution in the **final** project.

For a list of all available finders and actions, visit the compose testing cheatsheet (https://developer.android.com/jetpack/compose/testing-cheatsheet).

Key Points

- UI tests for composables fall under the instrumentation test category.
- The compose runtime maintains an alternate representation of the UI tree called **Semantics tree**.
- You can use **Finder** functions to find specific nodes of the tree based on criteria like text, tags or actions
- You can use **Action** functions to interact with specific UI elements in your tests.

Chapter 15: Accessibility in Jetpack Compose

By Denis Buketa

Building **accessible experiences** is something every developer should strive for. Not only because you'll make your app available to people with **disabilities**, but because you'll also help people who might find them in **short-term disability** situations where those features might be useful.

Unfortunately, accessibility features are often skipped over when implementing mobile apps. In this chapter, you'll learn how **easy** and **simple** it is to build accessibility features in **Jetpack Compose**.

Accessibility covers many things: impaired vision, color blindness, impaired hearing, cognitive disabilities, and temporary situations people find themselves in. It's impossible to cover all those cases in this chapter, but you'll have a chance to implement the most common use cases step by step.

You'll learn how to:

- Correctly implement **touch target size**.
- Add **visual element descriptions**.
- Add **click labels**.
- Create **custom actions**.
- Make it easier to navigate by using **headings**.
- **Merge** multiple elements in one semantic unit.
- **Lift toggle behavior** from switches and checkboxes.
- Define **state descriptions**.

For testing the code, you'll use **TalkBack** — accessibility tools used by people with visual impairments.

> **Note:** If you are not familiar with TalkBack, please refer to the official documentation: https://support.google.com/accessibility/android/answer/6283677?hl=en.

It is important to emphasize that TalkBack might behave differently depending on the device and TalkBack version you have installed. You can check the version in the TalkBack settings and you can also check controls for your version if you go to **TalkBack settings** and check **Customize gestures** or **Customize menu** options. There is also an option that allows you to practice the gestures to get used to them.

If you open **Customize gestures** screen, you'll be able to see all the gestures you can do: **1 finger** gestures, **1 finger angle**, **2 fingers**, etc. In this chapter, we use **multi-finger gestures** for some actions.

If your TalkBack version doesn't support multi-finger gestures, you should be able to find an alternative within your available options. For example, 1 finger angle **Swipe up then right** gesture and **Tap with 3 fingers** have the same result: **Open TalkBack menu**. We'll remind you of that for examples where this is important.

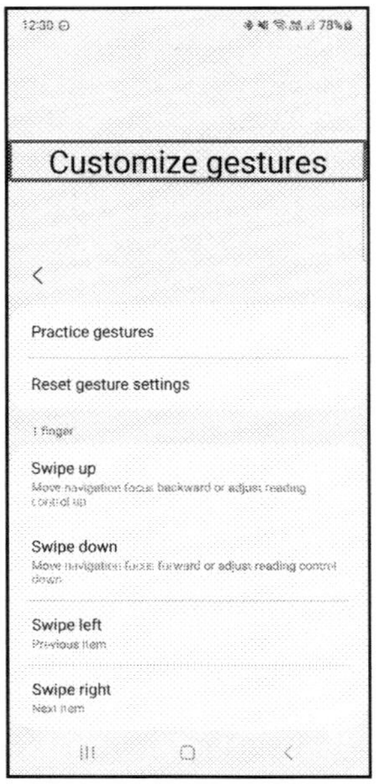

Customize gestures

Semantic Properties

Before you jump straight into coding, you should understand the basic principles of how accessibility services interpret UI elements. **Accessibility services** need information about UI elements to understand the UI. Jetpack Compose defines that information using **semantic properties**.

Some composables can define that information by interpreting their children composables. Other composables might use some modifiers that fill that information. And in some cases, there isn't enough information, so developers need to fill it using semantic properties.

In this chapter, you won't go into more details about Compose semantics, but you'll learn how to use them to manually fill accessibility information.

> **Note**: If you want to learn more about Compose semantics, check out the official documentation: https://developer.android.com/jetpack/compose/semantics.

Implementing Accessible Touch Target Size

To follow along with the code examples, open this chapter's **starter project** in Android Studio and select **Open an existing project**.

Then, navigate to **15-accessibility-in-jetpack-compose/projects** and select the **starter** folder as the project root. Once the project opens, let it build and sync and you're ready to go! You can see the completed project by skipping ahead to the **final project**.

Also make sure to clean the app's storage, before running the project.

For this chapter, we've purposely made some components less accessibility friendly. Don't worry, you'll make sure that by the end of this chapter, all those components follow accessibility best practices. :]

We've also added a new **Post** screen that you can open by clicking on the **first post** in the list. This is for learning purposes and by clicking on other posts **Post** screen won't be opened.

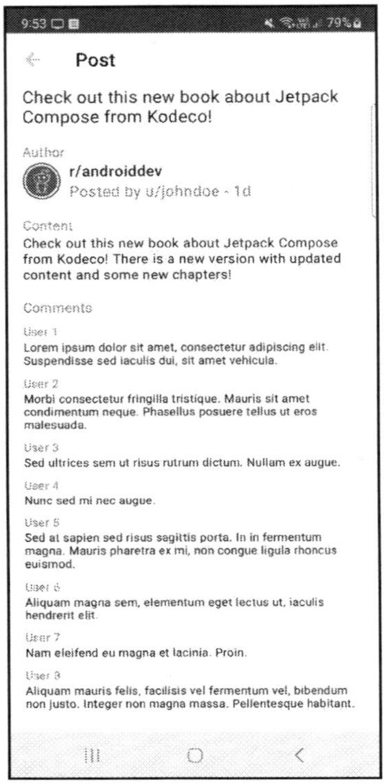

Post Screen

Before you continue, go to device **Settings** and turn on the **TalkBack** service.

> **Note**: If you are not familiar with how to turn on TalkBack service, please refer to official documentation: https://support.google.com/accessibility/android/answer/6007100.

Once you've done that, open JetReddit app. You'll probably see something like this:

JetReddit with TalkBack

TalkBack has focused on the first focusable element on the screen. Swipe right two times and navigate to the **Chat icon**. Notice how its touch area doesn't meet the minimal requirements specified by **Material Design**. Screen elements that the user can interact with should have a width and height of at least **48dp**.

Open **JetRedditApp.kt** and find `Icon()` in `TopAppBar()`. Note that its size is set to **24dp**. One way to fix its touch area is the following:

```
Icon(
  modifier = Modifier
    .clickable {
      context.startActivity(
        Intent(context, ChatActivity::class.java))
    }
    .padding(12.dp)     // HERE
    .size(24.dp),
  imageVector = Icons.Filled.MailOutline,
  tint = Color.LightGray,
  contentDescription = null
)
```

Here, you added a padding to the icon. With that padding you increased the touch area to **48dp**.

Another way you can solve this problem is by replacing the `Icon()` with `IconButton()`:

```
IconButton(onClick = {
  context.startActivity(
    Intent(context, ChatActivity::class.java)
  )
}) {
  Icon(
    Icons.Filled.MailOutline,
    tint = Color.LightGray,
    contentDescription = null
  )
}
```

Build and run your app. You should see that your Chat icon now meets the minimum requirements for touch area.

Chat icon with good touch area

By using the **Material components**, you'll make sure that your app follows best accessibility practices.

Adding Visual Element Descriptions

In this section, you'll further improve the **Chat icon**. Visual elements like `Image()` and `Icon()` have `contentDescription` parameters for which you can pass the text used by accessibility services to describe what that element represents.

Some users might not be able to see or interpret visual elements in your app, and in those cases, you can use the `contentDescription` to add more information.

When TalkBack focuses on the Chat icon, it communicates to the user the following message: *Button. Double tap to activate*. If your users couldn't see this icon, they would not know why the button is there.

In **JetRedditApp.kt** for the Chat icon, replace the `null` in `contentDescription` with a meaningful message;

```
IconButton(onClick = {
  context.startActivity(
    Intent(context, ChatActivity::class.java)
  )
}) {
  Icon(
    Icons.Filled.MailOutline,
    tint = Color.LightGray,
    contentDescription = "Navigate to chat"
  )
}
```

Build and run the app and focus on the Chat icon. TalkBack will now communicate the following: *Navigate to chat. Button. Double tap to activate*. This is much better and your user will be aware of what will happen if they press that button.

Adding a Click Label

In the previous section, you added a description to the Chat icon that explains what it represents. In this section, you'll add a description of what happens when the user clicks on it.

You are still working on the same `IconButton()`, so find it and add a specific modifier to it:

```
IconButton(
  modifier = Modifier.semantics { // HERE
    onClick(label = "open Chat", action = null)
```

```
    },
    onClick = {
      context.startActivity(
        Intent(context, ChatActivity::class.java)
      )
    }
  ) {
    Icon(
      Icons.Filled.MailOutline,
      tint = Color.LightGray,
      contentDescription = "Navigate to chat"
    )
  }
```

Add following imports as well:

```
import androidx.compose.ui.semantics.onClick
import androidx.compose.ui.semantics.semantics
```

You added `Modifier.semantics()`, which allows you to define **semantic properties**. With it, you specified an action to be performed when the user clicks on an `IconButton()`.

Build and run the app and select the Chat icon.

Accessible Chat Icon

You should hear TalkBack communicating a following message: *Navigate to chat. Button. Double tap to open chat.*

You don't have to always use `Modifier.semantics()` to set click labels. You can set them when using `Modifier.clickable()`. The following code snippet shows how you could've done it if you haven't used `IconButton()`:

```
Icon(
  modifier = Modifier
    .clickable(
      onClickLabel = "open Chat"   // HERE
    ) {
      context.startActivity(
        Intent(context, ChatActivity::class.java)
      )
    }
    .padding(12.dp)
    .size(24.dp),
  imageVector = Icons.Filled.MailOutline,
  tint = Color.LightGray,
  contentDescription = "Navigate to Chat"
)
```

This would've produced the same result.

Now your users will know what this icon represents and what will happen when they click on it.

Implementing Custom Actions

Next, you'll focus on making your posts accessibility friendly. If you try swiping right to navigate through posts, you'll notice many actions you must go through before TalkBack focuses on the next post.

Focusable elements in Post

In the image above, you can see the many focusable elements on each post.

Now, if you imagine your users trying to navigate through posts quickly, you can guess that it will be a challenging experience. To make that navigation more pleasant, you can group actions your user can perform on each post.

Before grouping those actions, you'll first make those elements unfocusable by TalkBack.

Open **Post.kt** and modify two composables, `MoreActionsMenu()` and `PostActions()`:

```
@Composable
fun MoreActionsMenu() {
  var expanded by remember { mutableStateOf(false) }

  Box(modifier = Modifier
    .wrapContentSize(Alignment.TopStart)
    .clearAndSetSemantics { }              // HERE
  ) {
    ...
  }
}

// Rest of Post.kt content
...

@Composable
fun PostActions(post: PostModel) {
  Row(
    modifier = Modifier
      .fillMaxWidth()
      .padding(start = 16.dp, end = 16.dp)
      .clearAndSetSemantics { },          // HERE
    horizontalArrangement = Arrangement.SpaceBetween,
    verticalAlignment = Alignment.CenterVertically
  ) {
    ...
  }
}
```

Next, open **JoinButton.kt** and modify `Text()` composable in it:

```
@Composable
fun JoinButton(onClick: (Boolean) -> Unit = {}) {

  ...

  Box(
    ...
  ) {
    Row(verticalAlignment = Alignment.CenterVertically) {
```

```
        Icon(
          imageVector = iconAsset,
          contentDescription = null,
          tint = iconTintColor,
          modifier = Modifier
            .size(16.dp)
        )
        Text(
          text = "Join",
          color = Color.White,
          fontSize = 14.sp,
          maxLines = 1,
          modifier = Modifier
            .widthIn(
              min = 0.dp,
              max = textMaxWidth
            )
            .clearAndSetSemantics { }            // HERE
        )
      }
    }
  }
```

Add the following imports as well:

```
import androidx.compose.ui.semantics.clearAndSetSemantics
```

You used `Modifier.clearAndSetSemantics()` which **clears the semantic of all descendants elements (nodes)** and allows you to set new semantics. After clearing those semantics, TalkBack won't focus those elements if you try navigating through posts the same way you did previously.

If you build and run your app, you'll notice that now only the post element itself is focusable by TalkBack and that by swiping to the right, you can quickly go through posts.

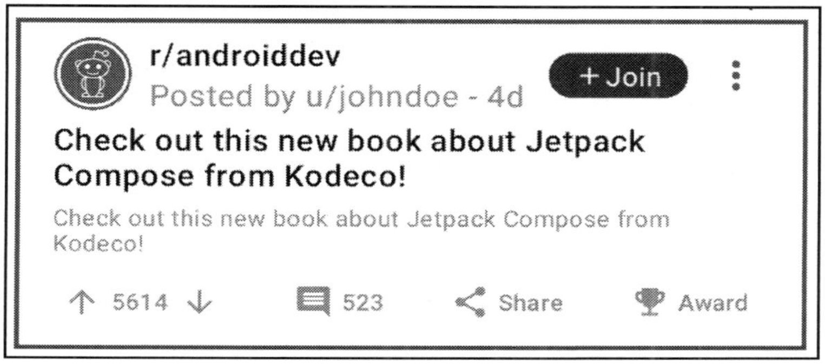

Post without focusable elements

After these changes, your users can navigate more easily, but they no longer have the ability to perform any post actions.

Open **Post.kt** and modify `Card()` in `Post()` accordingly :

```
@Composable
fun Post(
  post: PostModel,
  onJoinButtonClick: (Boolean) -> Unit = {},
  onPostClicked: () -> Unit = {},
  content: @Composable () -> Unit = {}
) {
  Card(
    shape = MaterialTheme.shapes.large,
    onClick = { onPostClicked.invoke() },
    modifier = Modifier.semantics { // HERE
      customActions = listOf(
        CustomAccessibilityAction(
          label = "Join",
          action = { /* Join / Leave */ true }
        ),
        CustomAccessibilityAction(
          label = "Save post",
          action = { /* Save post */ true }
        ),
        CustomAccessibilityAction(
          label = "Upvote",
          action = { /* Upvote */ true }
        ),
        CustomAccessibilityAction(
          label = "Downvote",
          action = { /* Downvote */ true }
        ),
        CustomAccessibilityAction(
          label = "Navigate to comments",
          action = { /* Navigate to comments */ true }
        ),
        CustomAccessibilityAction(
          label = "Share",
          action = { /* Share */ true }
        ),
        CustomAccessibilityAction(
          label = "Award",
          action = { /* Award */ true }
        )
      )
    }
  ) {
    ...
  }
}
```

Add these imports as well:

```
import androidx.compose.ui.semantics.customActions
import androidx.compose.ui.semantics.CustomAccessibilityAction
```

Here you again used `Modifier.semantic()` to define **custom actions**. Custom actions are defined with `CustomAccessibilityAction()`, which allows you to specify the **label** and result of the **action**.

Build and run your app. When you focus the post, notice the last part of TalkBack message. In our version of TalkBack, after describing the content, it will communicate: *Actions available. Use tap with three fingers to view.*

It's suggesting to the user that they can open a TalkBack menu for more actions. Depending on your TalkBack version, you should be able to do that with one of the following gestures: **tapping with three fingers** on the post, **swiping up then right** or **swiping down then right**. One of those gestures should open a dialog as in image below. If this doesn't work, go to TalkBack settings and find a gesture for opening TalkBack menu.

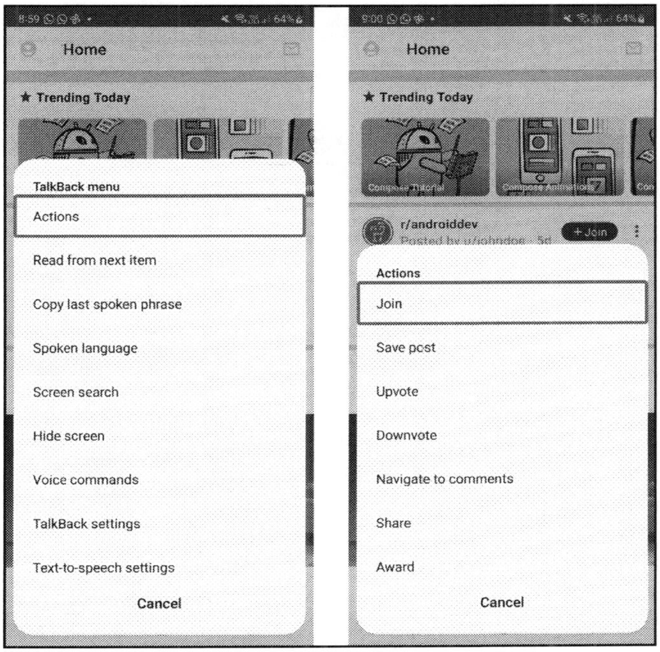

Post Custom Actions

Now your users can easily navigate through posts while being able to perform all post actions.

Navigating Through Headings

In this section you'll again work on improving a specific navigation experience in the app. Open the app, focus the first post by tapping on it, and double tap on the screen to open a **Post screen**. As mentioned at the beginning of this chapter, this was added for learning purposes and it only works for the first post in the list.

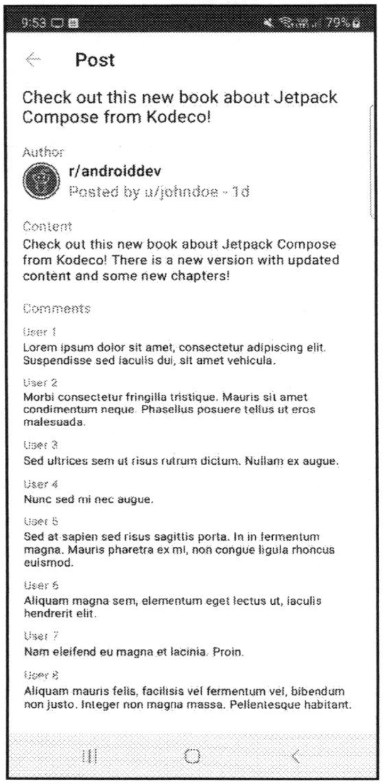

Post Screen

This screen contains a lot of text and users with visual impairments could have difficulty navigating through it. If you take a better look at the screen, you can see that it is organized in a couple of sections: title, author, content and comments.

It would be great if there was a way to allow your users to quickly navigate through those sections. :]

Configuring TalkBack Reading Control

TalkBack allows you to navigate by headings. Before you continue updating the code, make sure that you configure the TalkBack to navigate by headings.

In **Customize gesture** screen in TalkBack options you can find how to change **reading control**. By default, reading controls include:

- Characters
- Words
- Lines
- Paragraphs
- Headings
- Controls
- Links
- Speech rate
- Language

In the version of TalkBack used here, to change between previous or next reading control you use the following gestures:

- Swipe up then down / Swipe down then up,
- Swipe up with 3 fingers / Swipe down with 3 fingers,
- Swipe left with 3 fingers / Swipe right with 3 fingers.

Navigate between different reading controls until you see Headings:

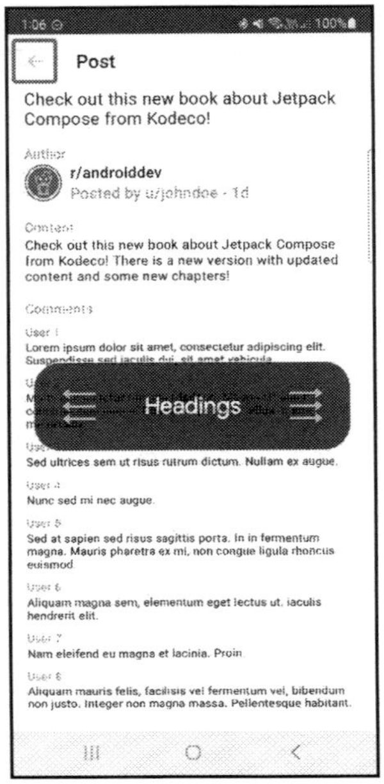

Selecting Heading Reading Controls

> **Note**: If you are still having problems configuring reading controls, please refer to official documentation: https://support.google.com/accessibility/android/answer/6006598.

Adding Headings

After you've done that, try to swipe down with one finger and notice the TalkBack response: *No next heading*. That means that there are no headings configured on that screen.

Open **PostScreen.kt** and modify `TitleSection()` and `SectionDescriptor()`:

```
@Composable
private fun TitleSection() {
  Text(
    text = "Check out this new book about Jetpack Compose from
Kodeco!",
    color = colors.primaryVariant,
    fontSize = 18.sp,
    modifier = Modifier
```

```
        .padding(horizontal = 16.dp)
        .semantics { heading() }                // HERE
    )
}

@Composable
private fun SectionDescriptor(text: String) {
  Text(
    text = text,
    color = Color.Gray,
    fontSize = 14.sp,
    modifier = Modifier
      .padding(horizontal = 16.dp)
      .semantics { heading() }                  // HERE
  )
}
```

Don't forget to also add following imports:

```
import androidx.compose.ui.semantics.heading
import androidx.compose.ui.semantics.semantics
```

With this, you marked specific screen sections as accessibility headings.

Build and run your app and try again navigating by **swiping down or up with one finger**.

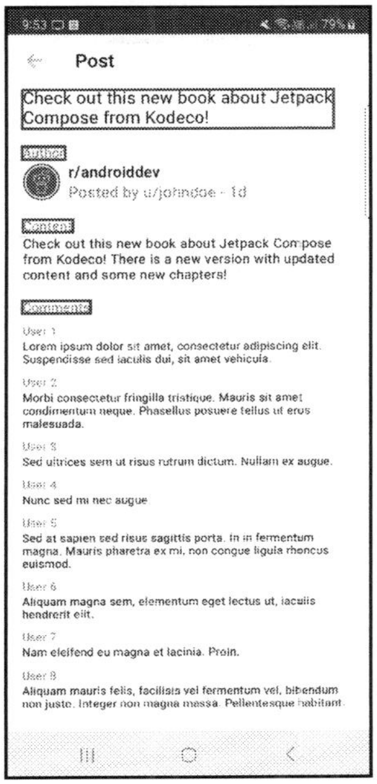

Post Screen Headings

You'll notice that now your users can quickly find section of interest and then continue from there.

Custom Merging

You've probably noticed that when it comes to accessibility, you try to minimize the number of focus changes while keeping the same context. In this section, you'll learn how to **merge composables** in one semantic unit so that your users don't have to go through each element.

In **Post screen**, you can notice that when navigating in author section, TalkBack will focus subreddit name element and then author element. Those two elements could be merged to one semantic element.

In `AuthorSection()`, update the modifier like this:

```
@Composable
private fun AuthorSection() {
  SectionDescriptor(text = "Author")
  Row(
    modifier = Modifier
      .padding(start = 16.dp)
      .semantics(mergeDescendants = true) { }           // HERE
    ,
    verticalAlignment = Alignment.CenterVertically
  ) {
    ...
  }
}
```

With this, you merged all `Row()` descendants as one logical unit.

If you build and run your app, you'll notice that TalkBack will read both the subreddit name and author element together.

Lifting Toggle Behavior

In this section, you'll learn how to **lift toggleable state up** from the toggle composable itself to its containing composable.

Open **Subreddits screen** and take a look at it.

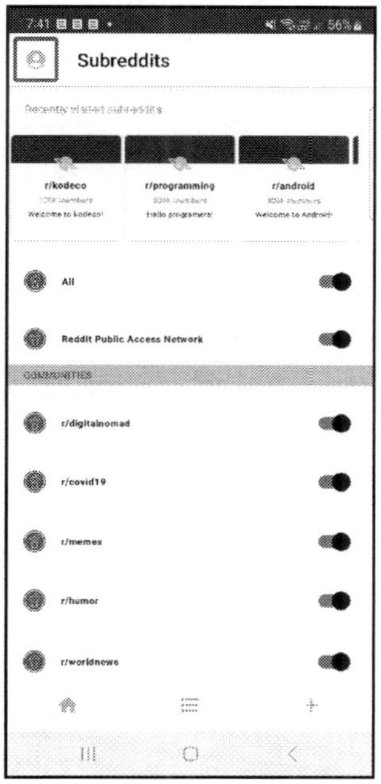

Subreddits Screen

Each subreddit element currently has two focusable elements: **name** and **switch**. When TalkBack focuses on the switch, it communicates to the user the switch state. The users need to remember the context of how they got to this switch to understand what might happen.

To make it easier for your users to understand that context, you can lift up the toggleable state from the switch.

Open **SubredditsScreen.kt** and modify `Community()` composable:

```
@Composable
fun Community(
  text: String,
  modifier: Modifier = Modifier,
  showToggle: Boolean = false,
  onCommunityClicked: () -> Unit = {}
) {
  var checked by remember { mutableStateOf(true) }

  val defaultRowModifier = modifier
    .padding(start = 16.dp, end = 16.dp, top = 16.dp)
    .fillMaxWidth()

  val rowModifier = if (showToggle) {       // HERE
    defaultRowModifier
      .toggleable(
        value = checked,
        onValueChange = { checked = it },
        role = Role.Switch
      )
  } else {
    defaultRowModifier.clickable { onCommunityClicked.invoke() }
  }

  Row(
    modifier = rowModifier,                 // HERE
    verticalAlignment = Alignment.CenterVertically
  ) {
    ...

    if (showToggle) {
      Switch(
        checked = checked,
        onCheckedChange = null              // HERE
      )
    }
  }
}
```

With `Modifier.toggleable()`, you can configure component to be toggleable via input and accessibility events. This now allows your user to double tap the whole element to toggle it.

For this to work, please add the following imports as well:

```
import androidx.compose.foundation.selection.toggleable
import androidx.compose.ui.semantics.Role
```

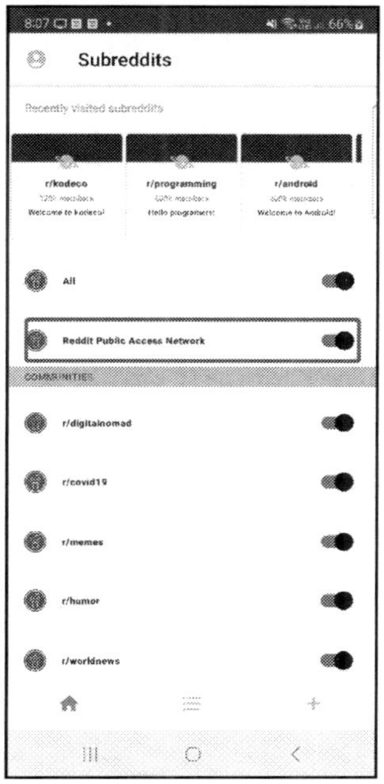

Toggleable Subreddit

If you build and run your app, you'll notice that the whole subreddit element gets focusable by TalkBack and you can toggle it by double tapping.

Adding State Descriptions

In the previous section you lifted the toggleable state. You can further improve the user experience by adding a better state description.

Again, expand the modifier you created in the previous section:

```
@Composable
fun Community(
  text: String,
  modifier: Modifier = Modifier,
  showToggle: Boolean = false,
  onCommunityClicked: () -> Unit = {}
) {
```

```
  var checked by remember { mutableStateOf(true) }

  val defaultRowModifier = modifier
    .padding(start = 16.dp, end = 16.dp, top = 16.dp)
    .fillMaxWidth()

  val rowModifier = if (showToggle) {
    defaultRowModifier
      .toggleable(
        value = checked,
        onValueChange = { checked = it },
        role = Role.Switch
      )
      .semantics {
        stateDescription = if (checked) {        // HERE
          "Subscribed"
        } else {
          "Not subscribed"
        }
      }
  } else {
    defaultRowModifier.clickable { onCommunityClicked.invoke() }
  }

  ...
}
```

Add following imports as well:

```
import androidx.compose.ui.semantics.semantics
import androidx.compose.ui.semantics.stateDescription
```

With this, you've overridden the default TalkBack's interpretation of switch state (on/off). When you now focus the subreddit element, TalkBack will first communicate *Subscribed* or *Not subscribed* for that subreddit.

Excellent work! You just learned the basic principles of accessibility in Jetpack Compose. Your app can now definitely be used by more users! :]

Key Points

- When implementing screen elements that the user can interact with, think about its size. Their width and height should be **at least 48dp**.
- You should use the **contentDescription** to add more information to visual elements for users who might not be able to see or interpret them.
- Adding a **click label** adds more context about what will happen when the user interacts with the screen elements.
- **Custom actions** make your app easier to navigate using a screen reader and group common actions for specific screen elements.
- Defining **semantic headings** allows users to quickly jump between sections on your screens.
- You can use **custom merging** when screen elements can be grouped into one logical unit.
- By **lifting the toggle behavior** from some screen elements, you add more context to the toggleable element.
- **State descriptions** can further add more context to toggleable elements.

Where to Go From Here?

Congratulations, you just completed the Accessibility in Jetpack Compose chapter!

As mentioned at the beginning, in this chapter you covered most common use cases and there is always room to improve the accessibility of your app.

Don't be afraid to learn more about the subject. Check out the Jetpack Compose course (https://www.kodeco.com/30117730-jetpack-compose-accessibility-getting-started) if you want to get a second example of implementing accessibility features using Compose from the ground up.

Wishing you all the best in your continued Jetpack Compose adventures!

Section V: Glances & Keeping Upto Date With Jetpack Compose

Well done on reaching section V of the book. You now know how to build a high quality app using **Jetpack Compose**, making sure it is tested appropriately via **UI Testing**, and finally levaging **Accessibility** features so your app can be used by a large audience.

In this section you'll look at a new area of Compose being created called **Jetpack Glance**, a new way to build Widgets using Compose. You'll also look at how to keep your Jetpack Compose knowledge upto date with the latest releases.

By the end of the section you'll learn:

- What Jetpack Glance is and build a Widget using it
- How significant Jetpack Compose is to the Developer community.

Chapter 16: Creating Widgets Using Jetpack Glance

By Denis Buketa

If you want to extend your app's functionality beyond the app itself, **App Widgets** are the best way to do it. They allow you to provide some features of your app as **at-a-glance** views that live in your user's home screen.

According to Google's blog announcement for Jetpack Glance, **84%** of users use at least one widget. That gives you a sense of how important it is to at least be familiar with the basics of building app widgets.

In this chapter, you'll learn how **simple** it is to build app widgets using **Jetpack Glance**.

You'll learn:

- What is **Jetpack Glance**.
- How to **define essential characteristics** of your app widget using `AppWidgetProvider`.
- How to use `GlanceAppWidgetReceiver` to **instantiate** your app widget and **update** it.
- How to **create UI** layouts using `GlanceAppWidget`.
- How to handle **actions** in the widget.

> **Note**: If you want to check Google's announcement of Jetpack Glance, please refer to the official Google blog: https://android-developers.googleblog.com/2021/12/announcing-jetpack-glance-alpha-for-app.html.

Introducing Jetpack Glance

Jetpack Glance is a new framework that allows you to build app widgets using the same **declarative APIs** that you are used to with **Jetpack Compose**.

Beside using the similar APIs, it uses Jetpack Compose **Runtime** to translate a `Composable` into a `RemoteView`, which it then displays in an app widget. It also depends on Jetpack Compose **Graphics** and **UI** layers that you covered in the very first chapter of this book.

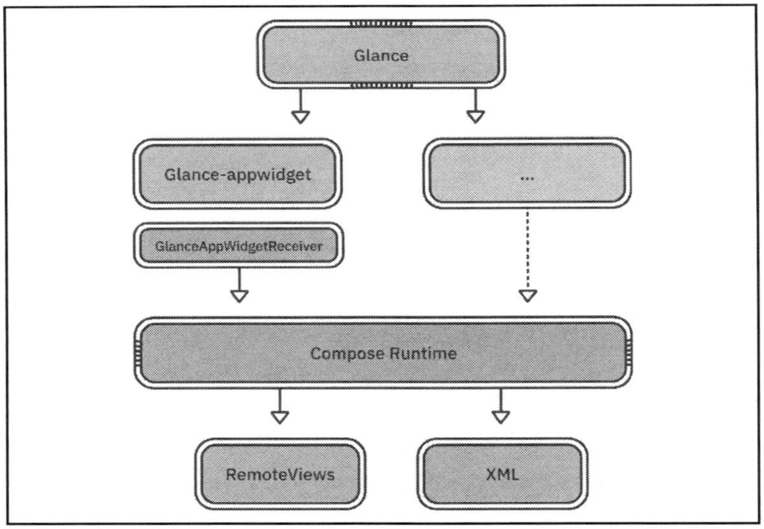

Glance Structure

Keep in mind that these dependencies mean that **Glance** requires for you to **enable Compose** in your project, but it's **not directly interoperable** with other Jetpack Compose UI elements. Because of that, you'll notice that in this chapter you'll use `GlanceModifier` instead of `Modifier` and some other composables will be imported from `androidx.glance` package instead of `androidx.compose` package.

Defining Essential Characteristics of Your App Widget

To follow along with the code examples, open this chapter's **starter project** in Android Studio and select **Open an existing project**.

Then, navigate to **16-creating-widgets-using-jetpack-compose-glance/projects** and select the **starter** folder as the project root. Once the project opens, let it build and sync and you're ready to go! You can see the completed project by skipping ahead to the **final project**.

In this chapter you're going to build a widget that displays the list of subreddits which you can find in the **Subreddits** screen. For learning purposes, imagine that the depicted switches allow you to toggle on or off notifications for a specific subreddit:

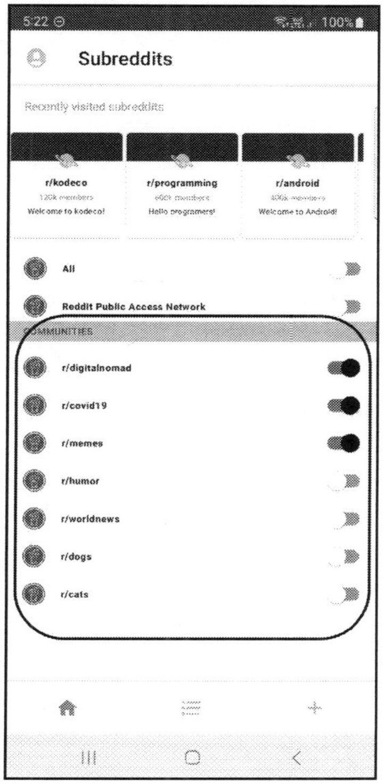

Subreddits Screen

To enable you to focus only on building your widget, we made some improvements in the app:

- In `MainViewModel`, we added `toggleSubreddit()` which triggers the logic for storing the switch information to preferences.
- In `SubredditsScreen()`, we added the logic that calls that method when you toggle a specific switch.
- We added **app_widget_loading.xml** and **app_widget_subreddits_preview.xml**, which you'll use when building the widget.

If you want to verify this functionality, you can toggle some switches, kill the app, and relaunch it. You'll notice that all switches are as you left them.

OK, now when you know what you are building, you're ready to begin your **Jetpack Glance** journey. :]

In **res/xml** folder, create a new file named **app_widget_subreddits.xml** and add the following code to it:

```
<?xml version="1.0" encoding="utf-8"?>
<appwidget-provider xmlns:android="http://schemas.android.com/
apk/res/android"
  android:description="@string/app_widget_description"
  android:minWidth="100dp"
  android:minHeight="100dp"
  android:minResizeHeight="100dp"
  android:minResizeWidth="100dp"
  android:initialLayout="@layout/app_widget_loading"
  android:previewLayout="@layout/app_widget_subreddits_preview"
  android:resizeMode="horizontal|vertical"
  android:targetCellWidth="3"
  android:targetCellHeight="3"
  android:widgetCategory="home_screen">
</appwidget-provider>
```

This file contains the information that defines **essential characteristics** of your widget.

- You specified the **description** for the widget picker.
- You defined a couple of **width and height attributes** with `min*`, `minResize*` and `targetCell*`. With this, you defined default size in terms of grid cells. Cell attributes are ignored in Android 11 and lower. You also defined min height and width, and widget's absolute minimum size when the user tries to resize the widget.

- With `resizeMode` you specified the rules for **widget resizing**.
- For the `initialLayout` you used the already available file `layout/app_widget_loading` that will be shown **before the content** you'll build with **Jetpack Glance** is configured.
- With `previewLayout` you defined how the widget will look like **after it's configured**. For that attribute you also used prepared `layout/app_widget_subreddits_preview` layout.
- With `widgetCategory` you can specify if your widget can be displayed on **home screen** (`home_screen`) and/or l**ock screen** (`keyguard`).

> **Note**: For more information about all widget attributes, please refer to the official documentation: https://developer.android.com/develop/ui/views/appwidgets#AppWidgetProviderInfo.

Creating the Hello Glance Widget

In this section you'll create a *Hello Glance* widget so that you get one step closer to displaying your widget on screen.

Create **jetreddit/appwidget** package and create **SubredditsWidget.kt** file in it. Then add the following content to it:

```
import androidx.compose.runtime.Composable
import androidx.compose.ui.graphics.Color
import androidx.glance.GlanceModifier
import androidx.glance.appwidget.GlanceAppWidget
import androidx.glance.background
import androidx.glance.layout.Alignment
import androidx.glance.layout.Box
import androidx.glance.layout.fillMaxSize
import androidx.glance.text.Text

class SubredditsWidget : GlanceAppWidget() {
  @Composable
  override fun Content() {
    Box(
      modifier = GlanceModifier
        .fillMaxSize()
        .background(Color.White),
      contentAlignment = Alignment.Center
    ) {
```

```
            Text(text = "Hello Glance")
        }
    }
}
```

With this you created a simple widget that will display a text when configured. You extended `GlanceAppWidget` that handles the **composition** and also **communicates** with the `AppWidgetManager`. The `AppWidgetManager` is responsible for updating **widget states**, keeping the information about installed widgets and related state.

> **Note**: For more information about `AppWidgetManager`, please refer to the official documentation: https://developer.android.com/develop/ui/views/appwidgets.

Notice that in your `SubredditsWidget()` you overrode composable function `Content()`. That function allows you to **define the UI** for your widget. Whenever you update your widget, the system will start a composition and translate its content to `RemoteViews`. Finally, the system will send it to the `AppWidgetManager`.

Displaying the Widget on the Home Screen

The final step before you can see your widget on the home screen is to create `AppWidgetProvider`.

In **SubredditsWidget.kt**, add the following code at the bottom:

```
class SubredditsWidgetReceiver : GlanceAppWidgetReceiver() {

  override val glanceAppWidget: GlanceAppWidget =
    SubredditsWidget()
}
```

GlanceAppWidgetReceiver is the implementation of AppWidgetProvider. It uses GlanceAppWidget to generate the remote views. Because of that, you were required to define SubredditsWidget() for the glanceAppWidget property.

For this to compile, you have to add the following import:

```
import androidx.glance.appwidget.GlanceAppWidgetReceiver
```

Next, open **AndroidManifest.xml** and at the end of the application tag add the following:

```
<receiver
  android:name=".appwidget.SubredditsWidgetReceiver"
  android:enabled="@bool/glance_appwidget_available"
  android:exported="false">
  <intent-filter>
    <action
android:name="android.appwidget.action.APPWIDGET_UPDATE" />
  </intent-filter>

  <meta-data
    android:name="android.appwidget.provider"
    android:resource="@xml/app_widget_subreddits" />
</receiver>
```

For android:name you have to provide the **name** of the AppWidgetProvider used by the widget. In your case, that is SubredditsWidgetReceiver.

With the intent-filter, you defined that the provider can react to the ACTION_APPWIDGET_UPDATE broadcast. This broadcast you have to explicitly declare. For other widget broadcasts, AppWidgetManager will automatically send them when needed.

With meta-data you defined the **essential characteristic** for this widget. You defined those in the **Defining Essential Characteristics of Your App Widget** section of this chapter.

Now is the time to check your widget in action! :]

Build and run your app. Once your app opens, close it and find the app launcher. If you long press the app launcher, you'll see that you can now add a widget for it:

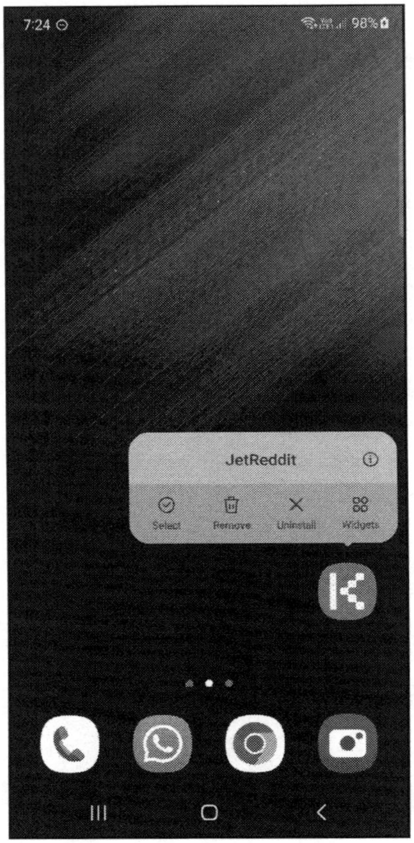

Widget Option in Launcher

If you select **Widgets**, you should see the preview of your widget:

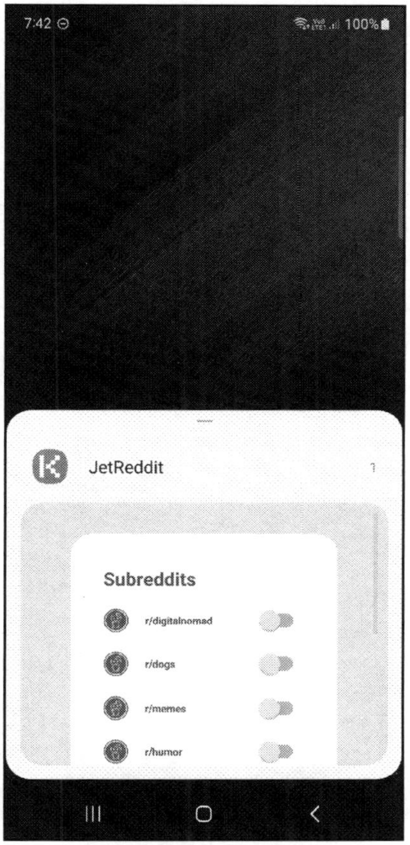

Widget Preview

On that step, you'll be able to **drag** your widget to the screen. When dragging, you should see the preview of your widget and once you drop it, you'll see the content you defined in `SubredditsWidget`:

Widget on Home Screen

These are all the steps that you need to do for displaying your widget on the home screen. Next, you'll add some more content to the widget! :]

Adding Subreddits to the Widget

Before you start implementing the rest of the UI, it is important to mention that `@Preview` still doesn't work for Jetpack Glance. You'll be coding the UI for the widget and then building the project later to see it.

First, add the `Subreddit()` composable to **SubredditsWidget.kt**:

```
@Composable
fun Subreddit(@StringRes id: Int) {
```

```
  val checked: Boolean = false

  Row(
    modifier = GlanceModifier
      .padding(top = 16.dp)
      .fillMaxWidth(),
    verticalAlignment = Alignment.CenterVertically
  ) {

    Image(
      provider = ImageProvider(
        R.drawable.subreddit_placeholder
      ),
      contentDescription = null,
      modifier = GlanceModifier.size(24.dp)
    )

    Text(
      text = LocalContext.current.getString(id),
      modifier = GlanceModifier
        .padding(start = 16.dp)
        .defaultWeight(),
      style = TextStyle(
        color = FixedColorProvider(
          color = MaterialTheme.colors.primaryVariant
        ),
        fontSize = 10.sp,
        fontWeight = FontWeight.Bold
      )
    )

    Switch(
      checked = checked,
      onCheckedChange = null
    )
  }
}
```

This is pretty much the same composable you use in `SubredditsScreen()`, but with **Glance composables**. Add the following imports:

```
import androidx.annotation.StringRes
import androidx.compose.material.MaterialTheme
import androidx.compose.ui.unit.dp
import androidx.compose.ui.unit.sp
import androidx.glance.LocalContext
import androidx.glance.Image
import androidx.glance.ImageProvider
import androidx.glance.appwidget.Switch
import androidx.glance.layout.Row
import androidx.glance.layout.padding
import androidx.glance.layout.size
```

```
import androidx.glance.layout.fillMaxWidth
import androidx.glance.text.FontWeight
import androidx.glance.text.TextStyle
import androidx.glance.unit.FixedColorProvider
import com.yourcompany.android.jetreddit.R
```

Notice that all composables are from the `androidx.glance` package.

Next, you'll create the title composable and you'll use `Subreddit()` to create a list of subreddits:

```
@Composable
fun WidgetTitle() {
  Text(
    text = "Subreddits",
    modifier = GlanceModifier.fillMaxWidth(),
    style = TextStyle(
      fontWeight = FontWeight.Bold,
      fontSize = 18.sp,
      color = FixedColorProvider(Color.Black)
    ),
  )
}

@Composable
fun ScrollableSubredditsList() {
  LazyColumn {
    items(communities) { communityId ->
      Subreddit(id = communityId)
    }
  }
}
```

Add the following imports as well:

```
import androidx.glance.appwidget.lazy.LazyColumn
import androidx.glance.appwidget.lazy.items
import com.yourcompany.android.jetreddit.screens.communities
```

These composables represent your title and list of subreddits.

Finally, replace the **Hello Glance** definition in the `Content()` composable with:

```
@Composable
override fun Content() {
  Column(
    modifier = GlanceModifier
      .fillMaxSize()
      .padding(16.dp)
      .appWidgetBackground()
```

```
        .background(Color.White)
        .cornerRadius(16.dp)
    ) {
      WidgetTitle()
      ScrollableSubredditsList()
    }
  }
```

Add the following imports as well:

```
import androidx.glance.layout.Column
import androidx.glance.appwidget.appWidgetBackground
import androidx.glance.appwidget.cornerRadius
```

If you now remove the old widget, build and run the app, and try again adding the widget to the Home screen. You should see something like this:

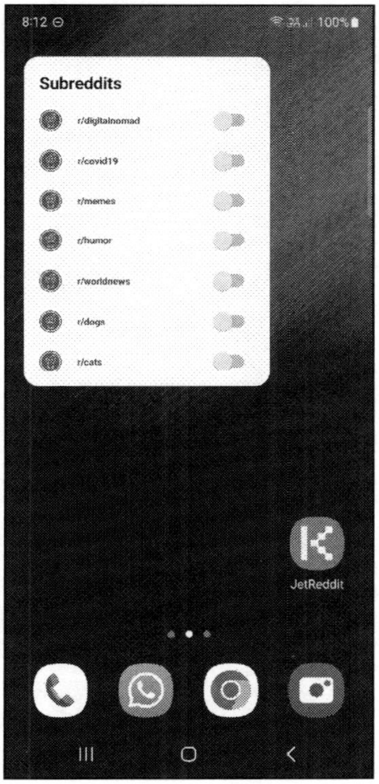

Subreddits Widget

If you now try to interact with the widget, you'll notice that you can switch on/off subreddits, but that change is not visible in your app. This is also true vice versa. You'll work on that next! :]

Handling Widget Actions

First, let's handle the `onCheckedChange()` action in `Switch()`. When working with widgets, you handle user actions using the `ActionCallback` interface.

Add the following code to **SubredditsWidget.kt**:

```
private val toggledSubredditIdKey =
ActionParameters.Key<String>("ToggledSubredditIdKey")

class SwitchToggleAction : ActionCallback {
  override suspend fun onAction(
    context: Context,
    glanceId: GlanceId,
    parameters: ActionParameters
  ) {
    val toggledSubredditId: String =
      requireNotNull(parameters[toggledSubredditIdKey])
    val checked: Boolean =
      requireNotNull(parameters[ToggleableStateKey])

    updateAppWidgetState(context, glanceId) { glancePrefs ->
      glancePrefs[booleanPreferencesKey(toggledSubredditId)] =
checked
    }

    SubredditsWidget().update(context, glanceId)
  }
}
```

For this to work, you need the following imports:

```
import androidx.glance.action.ActionParameters
import androidx.glance.appwidget.action.ActionCallback
import androidx.glance.appwidget.action.ToggleableStateKey
import androidx.glance.appwidget.state.updateAppWidgetState
import androidx.glance.GlanceId
import androidx.datastore.preferences.core.booleanPreferencesKey
import android.content.Context
```

Here, you defined the `ActionCallback` that will be executed **in response to the user action**. The important thing to notice is that it will be executed **before the widget content is updated**.

You've overriden `onAction()` with three parameters: `Context`, `GlanceId` and `ActionParameters`.

- `Context` gives you **access to the app context** and you'll use it later to communicate with the JetReddit app.

- `GlanceId` tells you **what widget** triggered the action so that you can update its content in response to the action.
- With `ActionParameters` you can **pass data** between the widget and `ActionCallback`.

Notice that you also defined `ActionParameters.Key`. That is the key for `ActionParameters` and in this case you use it for passing the subreddit ID for which a switch has been toggled on or off. Right now you don't have the code that passes that information using that key, but you added the code to read that ID from `ActionParameters`.

After reading the value, you call `updateAppWidgetState()` which updates the state of an app widget using the global `PreferencesGlanceStateDefinition`. Here, it is important to use the **correct** `glanceId`.

Finally, you call `SubredditsWidget().update()` which **triggers the composition** of `Content()` and sends the result to the `AppWidgetManager`.

Now, edit the `Subreddit()` like this:

```
@Composable
fun Subreddit(@StringRes id: Int) {

  // HERE
  val preferences: Preferences = currentState()
  val checked: Boolean =
preferences[booleanPreferencesKey(id.toString())] ?: false

  Row(...) {

    ...

    Switch(
      checked = checked,
      // HERE
      onCheckedChange = actionRunCallback<SwitchToggleAction>(
        actionParametersOf(
          toggledSubredditIdKey to id.toString()
        )
      )
    )
  }
}
```

Here you used `actionRunCallback()`, which creates an `Action` that executes `SwitchToggleAction`. With `actionParametersOf()` you passed the subreddit ID that you'll read in `SwitchToggleAction`.

You also added the code that will initialize the `checked` property with the value from the app widget state. For this to work, add the following imports:

```
import androidx.glance.appwidget.action.actionRunCallback
import androidx.glance.action.actionParametersOf
import androidx.glance.currentState
import androidx.datastore.preferences.core.Preferences
```

If you now build the app and create a new widget, you won't notice anything changed. However, with this code you made your widget **stateful**. It now manages its own state. That can be used to connect it to the app so that the widget is synced with switches in the app.

Connecting the Widget With the JetReddit App

At the beginning of the chapter, it was mentioned that the JetReddit app now stores states of the switches in preferences.

You can leverage that to sync the widget with the app. In **SubredditsWidget.kt**, edit the `onAction()` in `SwitchToggleAction` like this:

```
override suspend fun onAction(
  context: Context,
  glanceId: GlanceId,
  parameters: ActionParameters
) {
  val toggledSubredditId: String =
requireNotNull(parameters[toggledSubredditIdKey])
  val checked: Boolean =
requireNotNull(parameters[ToggleableStateKey])

  updateAppWidgetState(context, glanceId) { glancePreferences ->
    glancePreferences[booleanPreferencesKey(toggledSubredditId)]
= checked
  }

  // HERE
  context.dataStore.edit { appPreferences ->
    appPreferences[booleanPreferencesKey(toggledSubredditId)] =
checked
  }

  SubredditsWidget().update(context, glanceId)
}
```

Add the following imports as well:

```
import
com.yourcompany.android.jetreddit.dependencyinjection.dataStore
import androidx.datastore.preferences.core.edit
```

With this change, you added the logic that modifies JetReddit's preferences when you toggle a switch in the widget. That means that the state from the widget will be propagated to the app.

Remove the widget if you have it on the home screen, run the app and create a new widget. Try toggling off and on some switches in the widget and then check the Subreddits screen in the app.

You'll notice that changes in the widget are propagated to the app. However, it still doesn't work the other way around. You'll tackle that next!

What you need to do next is to update the widget state when **it's created** and also update its state when the user toggles switches **in the app**.

To do that, add the following code to `SubredditsWidgetReceiver`:

```
private suspend fun updateAppWidgetPreferences(
  subredditIdToCheckedMap: Map<Int, Boolean>,
  context: Context,
  glanceId: GlanceId
) {
  subredditIdToCheckedMap.forEach { (subredditId, checked) ->
    updateAppWidgetState(context, glanceId) { state ->
      state[booleanPreferencesKey(subredditId.toString())] =
checked
    }
  }
}

private fun Preferences.toSubredditIdToCheckedMap(): Map<Int,
Boolean> {
  return communities.associateWith { communityId ->
    this[booleanPreferencesKey(communityId.toString())] ?: false
  }
}
```

You added an `updateAppWidgetPreferences()` method that you'll use to **instantiate the widget state** with the information about the switches stored in the JetReddit's preferences.

You also added a helper method `toSubredditIdToCheckedMap()`. This method maps the information from JetReddit's preferences to a `Map` where the key is the subreddit ID and the value represents if it is toggled on or off.

Now, complete `SubredditsWidgetReceiver` by adding the following:

```
private val coroutineScope = MainScope()

override fun onUpdate(
  context: Context,
  appWidgetManager: AppWidgetManager,
  appWidgetIds: IntArray
) {
  super.onUpdate(context, appWidgetManager, appWidgetIds)

  coroutineScope.launch {

    // Step 1: Get GlanceId for your widget
    val glanceId: GlanceId? = GlanceAppWidgetManager(context)
      .getGlanceIds(SubredditsWidget::class.java)
      .firstOrNull()

    if (glanceId != null) {
      // Step 2: Collect JetReddit's preferences
      withContext(Dispatchers.IO) {
        context.dataStore.data
          .map { preferences ->
preferences.toSubredditIdToCheckedMap() }
          .collect { subredditIdToCheckedMap ->

            // Step 3: Update app widget state
            updateAppWidgetPreferences(subredditIdToCheckedMap,
context, glanceId)

            // Step 4: Update app widget content
            glanceAppWidget.update(context, glanceId)
          }
      }
    }
  }
}

override fun onDeleted(context: Context, appWidgetIds: IntArray)
{
  super.onDeleted(context, appWidgetIds)
  coroutineScope.cancel()
}
```

Finish by adding the following imports:

```
import android.appwidget.AppWidgetManager
import kotlinx.coroutines.*
import kotlinx.coroutines.flow.map
import androidx.glance.appwidget.GlanceAppWidgetManager
```

Let's unpack what you did here. You've overridden the `onUpdate()` method. The OS calls this method in response to the `AppWidgetManager#ACTION_APPWIDGET_UPDATE` broadcast. That's the moment when the app widget provider needs to provide `RemoteViews` for its app widgets.

In this case, that happens when you create this widget on the screen. In other words, this allows you to prepare your widget's state before it renders it first content.

The first step you did in that method was to **get an app widget ID** because that is what you need to call the `update()` method on it. Second, you **fetched the JetReddit's state** from preferences. You then **updated the app widget's state**. And lastly, you **updated the widget**.

It is also important to notice that the coroutine you created will be alive until the widget is **deleted**, so whenever the user changes something in the JetReddit's state, the widget will be updated with that data as well. You cancel the `coroutineScope` in `onDeleted()` method to clear up the resources.

If you now delete the previous widget, run the app and create a new widget, you'll notice that your widget's state is completely synced with your JetReddit's state. You can even try toggling the switches in the widget or the app. You'll see that they stay in sync.

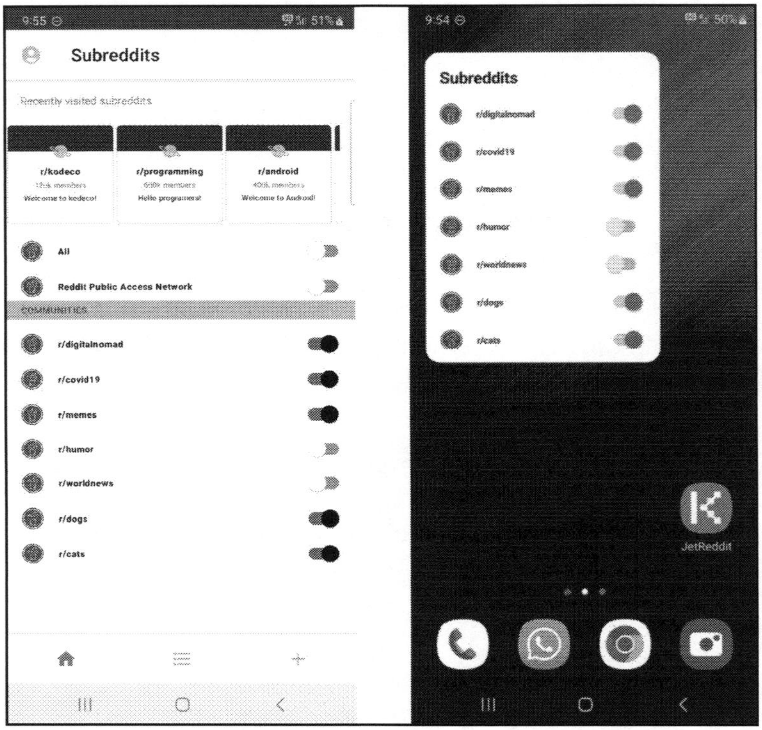

Widget connected with JetReddit

Excellent work! With this you've completed this chapter! You just learned the basics of working with **Jetpack Glance**. Your users can now have **JetReddit widget** on their home screen! :]

Key Points

- **Jetpack Glance** is a new framework that allows you to build app widgets using **declarative APIs** that you are used to with Jetpack Compose.
- To define widget's essential characteristic, you need to create a `appwidget-provider` in **res/xml** folder.
- You use `GlanceAppWidget` to define the widget UI and to communicate with the `AppWidgetManager`.
- You need to create `GlanceAppWidgetReceiver` and define in the **AndroidManifest.xml** for your app to be able to create widgets.
- If you want to **handle widget actions**, you'll use `ActionCallback`.
- `ActionParameters` enables you to pass data between app widget and `ActionCallback`.
- To make your app widget **stateful**, you can update its state with `updateAppWidgetState()`.
- The `onUpdate()` method in `GlanceAppWidgetReceiver()` allows you to update the widget state once the user creates it.

Where to Go From here?

Congratulations, you just completed the **Creating Widgets Using Jetpack Glance** chapter!

With these new skills, we don't doubt you'll implement some exciting new widgets for your apps.

Wishing you all the best in your continued Jetpack Compose adventures!

Chapter 17: Keeping up to Date With Jetpack Compose

By Prateek Prasad

Jetpack Compose is still a relatively new technology, so developers must stay up to date with the latest development, new feature announcements and best practices.

So far in this book, you learned how to build apps using Jetpack Compose. In this chapter, you will learn about some strategies and resources you can use to stay on top of the latest and greatest in the Jetpack Compose ecosystem.

Official Sources

Jetpack Compose Documentation

The best and most reliable resource to learn about Jetpack Compose and to get all the new updates are the channels from Google.

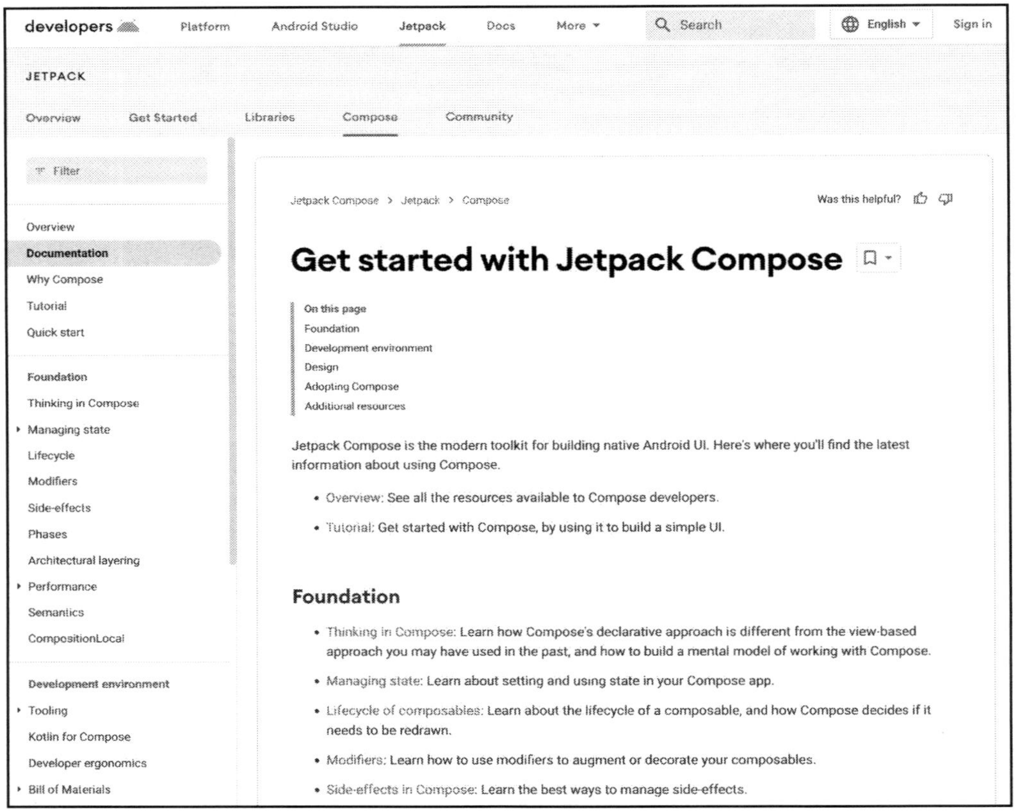

The first one is the Jetpack Compose documentation. Google has done an excellent job curating the resources into helpful paths, which they update promptly. You can check it out at https://developer.android.com/jetpack/compose/documentation.

Accompanist

Google also provides a public repository on GitHub called Accompanist. Accompanist provides supplementary APIs for Compose that are considered experimental. Experimental means the API isn't regarded as final and is being changed depending on feedback from the developer community.

This repository is worth keeping an eye on as it gives a glimpse into what Google may introduce into Compose. You can check the repository out at https://github.com/google/accompanist.

Android Developers Blog

Another great resource to keep on your reading list is the Android Developers blog on Medium (https://medium.com/androiddevelopers).

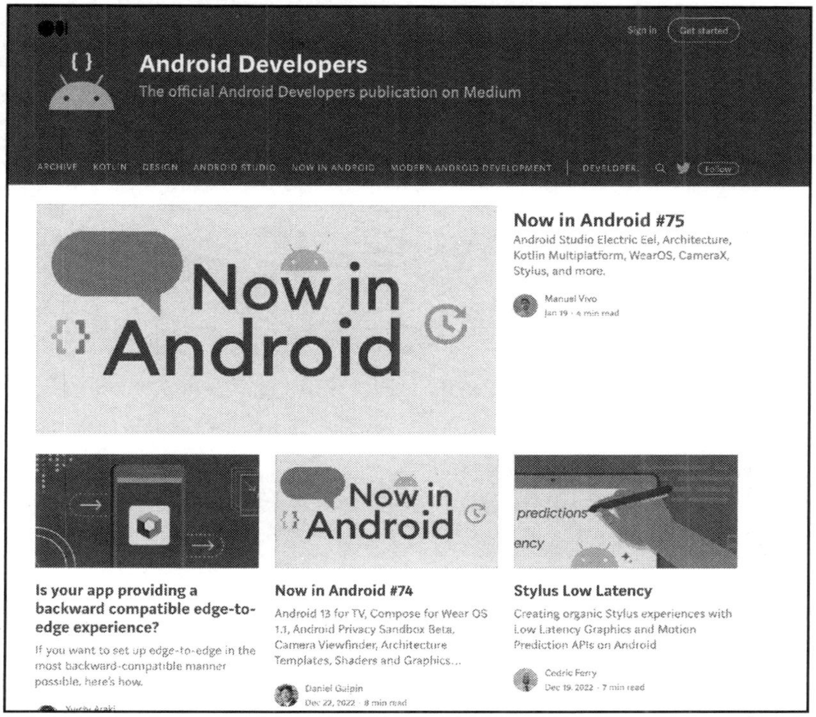

The blog has articles on Jetpack Compose and covers news and tutorials related to other Android libraries.

Android Developers YouTube Channel

The Android Developers YouTube channel (https://www.youtube.com/@AndroidDevelopers) should be on your YouTube subscriptions if you like consuming video content over blog posts.

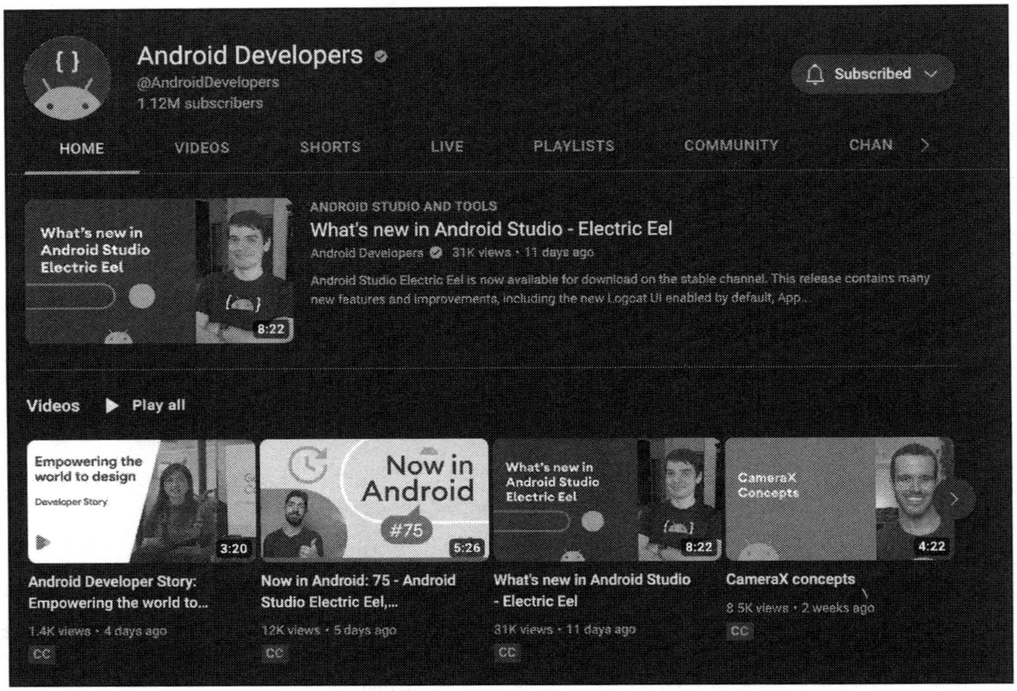

They cover regular news around Android Development and have curated playlists around topics like Jetpack Compose.

Android Developers Backstage Podcast

If you have been writing Android apps for a while, you are no stranger to the Android Developers Backstage podcast (https://adbackstage.libsyn.com/).

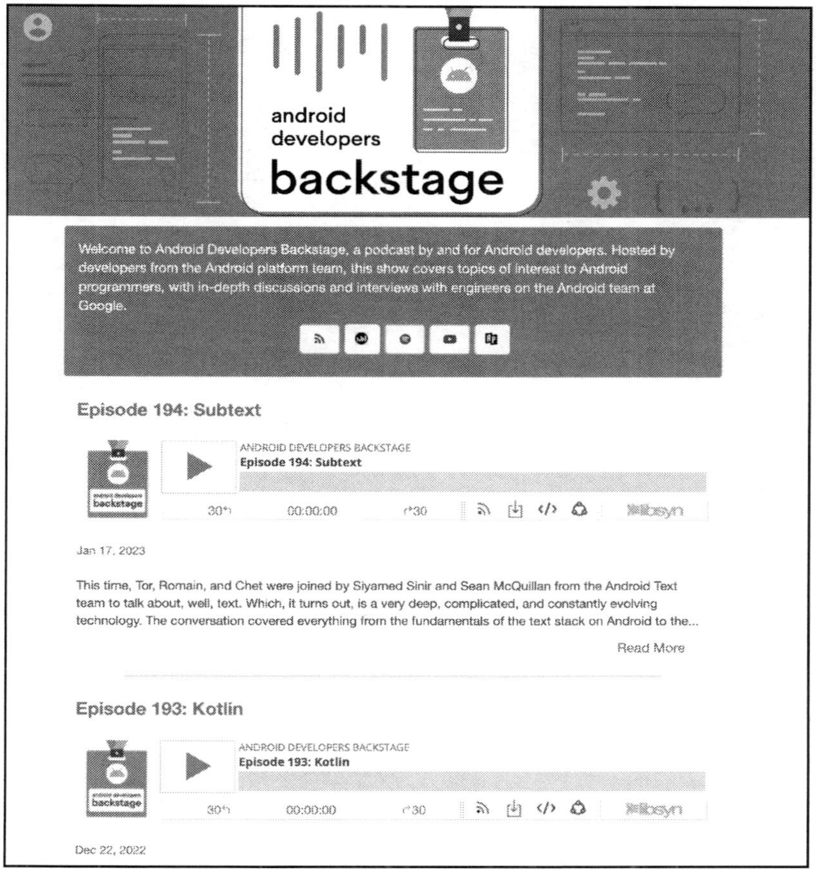

Chet, Roman, and Tor from Google regularly host Googlers working on the libraries and features you enjoy and have had several hosts who wrote the compose framework. These episodes offer many behind-the-scenes insights how design decisions were made.

Jetpack Compose Sample Apps

If you like jumping straight into code and getting your hands dirty with the latest and most cutting-edge stuff, then the official sample apps repository (https://github.com/android/compose-samples) is the place to go.

These projects are the quickest to adopt the new features announced in the alpha releases, and they also show the best practices around working with compose in different situations within your existing project.

Community Resources

Jetpack Compose has a large thriving community behind it. So aside from resources offered by Google, several resources within the community are worth keeping track of.

Conferences and Meetups

Considering how new Jetpack Compose is, there is an ocean of content available online by experts for you to consume. Most flagship android conferences have been dominated by Jetpack Compose-related content.

Droidcon (https://www.droidcon.com/) is one example of such a conference. It runs several chapters worldwide and also publishes session recordings.

Twitter

The last resource on this list is, of course, Twitter. Developers worldwide are building cool things with Jetpack Compose and sharing them publicly.

A quick and easy way to filter things is to check out the #jetpackcompose (https://twitter.com/hashtag/jetpackcompose?src=hashtag_click) hashtag.

While you are at it, you should also follow the @AndroidDev (https://twitter.com/AndroidDev) profile, where they share news about new launches, upcoming events, and highlight community contributions,

With this handy list of resources you will not miss out any important announcement around Jetpack Compose.

Platforms of the Future

Jetpack Compose has gained a lot of traction in the android community and with JetBrains working on their fork of Compose i.e. JetBrains Compose, it is expected that Compose will be supported on a variety of platforms, including desktop and web, as well as other new emerging platforms.

While things are still very new in this area, here are some resources to help you stay on top of the news.

Jetpack Compose on WearOS

The APIs to use Compose on WearOS are very similar to their mobile counterparts. There are however some key differences to be aware of.

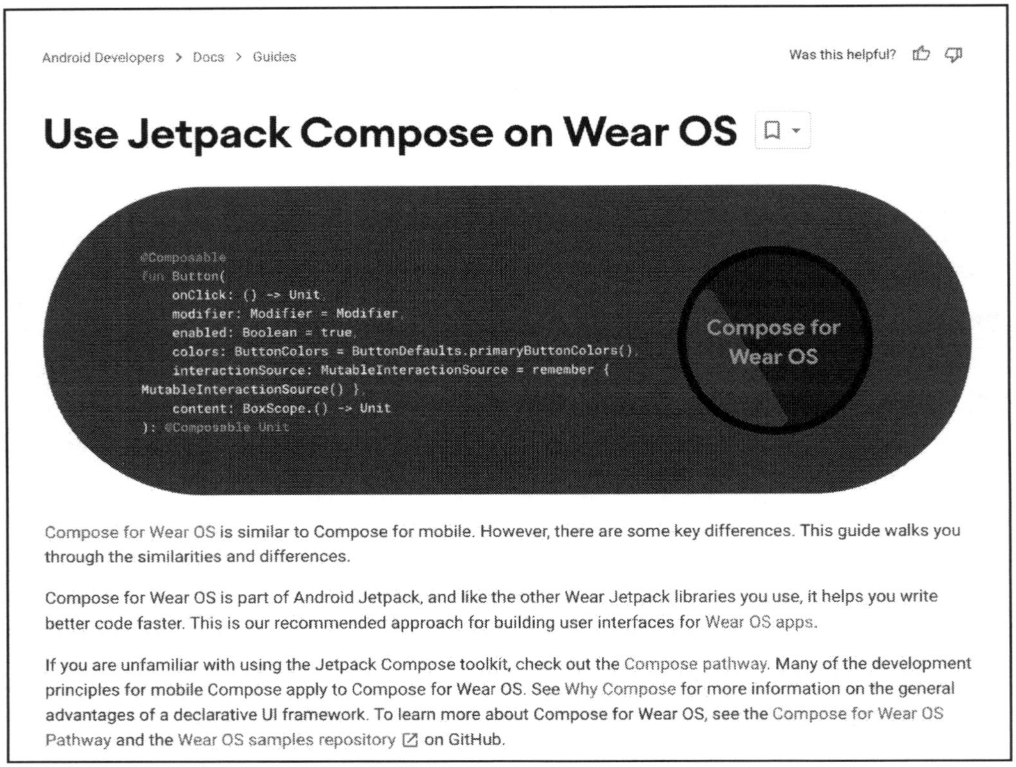

To learn all about how to use Compose on WearOS check out the documentation (https://developer.android.com/training/wearables/compose).

Compose for Desktop

JetBrains has published their artifacts to use Compose APIs to build desktop applications. A lot of the knowledge from Jetpack Compose will carry over to the desktop platform.

To stay on top of all developments in this area, visit the Compose for Desktop (https://www.jetbrains.com/lp/compose-desktop/) web page.

Compose Multiplatform

Compose is also gaining traction on Web, Linux, Windows and other emerging platforms with the artifacts being available for the same.

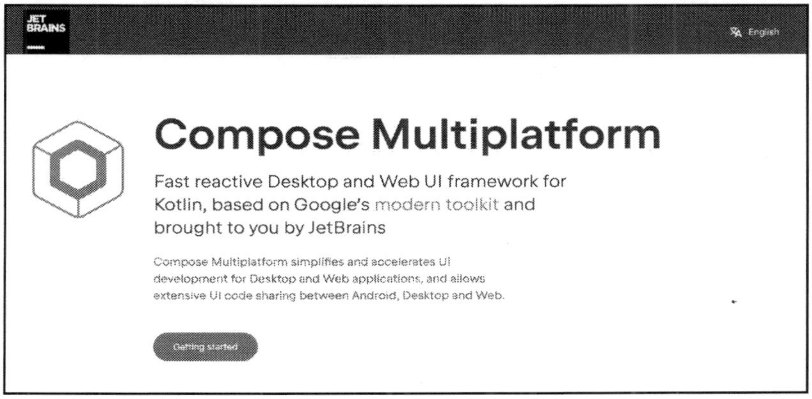

This is still an evolving space with things changing rapidly. If you are keen on jumping in however, visit the Compose Multiplatform (https://www.jetbrains.com/lp/compose-mpp) web page.

Key Points

- Jetpack Compose is rapidly evolving so its important to stay up to date.
- Google offers several helpful resources in various formats for you to consume.
- There is an active community behind Jetpack Compose.
- You can also learn more about new developments in Jetpack Compose through community initiatives like events, meet-ups, and social media.
- Compose is actively being ported to other platforms like WearOS, Desktop, Web etc.

18 Conclusion

Wow, we've taken a heck of a journey together! Throughout this book, you've jumped into a completely new framework and came out as an expert on Jetpack Compose. Jetpack Compose is a powerful new UI toolkit, and after reading the book you know how to use a wide variety of tools that Compose exposes.

You learned about Compose's fundamental components and how they compare to the legacy UI toolkit in Android. Furthermore, you saw how easy it is to remember and handle the state in Compose, and how you can directly connect it to the rest of your app's architecture. You explored many options when it comes to styling your app including dark and light themes, modifiers and even Material Design and animations.

You moved onto adding UI Testing and Accessibility support, adding Compose to Apps that use the old UI toolkit and even looking at how to build Widgets using Jetpack Glance.

Using this knowledge will let you build beautiful apps with ease, as well as reuse your code across different projects. But it's not just that — writing UI code is *so much fun* in Jetpack Compose that you'll constantly be looking for nice new things to build, or new components to style.

The best part is Jetpack Compose is still constantly being updated. There are always new versions to explore and new features to master on the horizon. It's impossible to teach everything there is to know about such an awesome framework, so we hope you'll practice it on your own projects.

If you want to explore more content about Jetpack Compose, we recommend watching our Jetpack Compose course (https://www.kodeco.com/17332237-jetpack-compose), which builds another cool app and explores all of these concepts using different components. Also, be sure to check out Jetpack Compose Animations Tutorial: Getting Started (https://www.kodeco.com/13282144-jetpack-compose-animations-tutorial-getting-started) to play around with more animations that you can build easily with Compose!

If you have any questions or comments as you work through this book, please visit our forums at https://forums.kodeco.com and look for the Jetpack Compose forum category.

Thank you again for purchasing this book. Your continued support is what makes the books, tutorials, videos and other things we do at Kodeco possible. We truly appreciate it!

– The *Jetpack Compose by Tutorials* team

Section VI: Appendices

This supplementary section is for appendices to accompany the book. In this section there's a handy set of comparisions of UI components between the old UI Toolkit and Jetpack Compose. Use this if you want to have an idea what like for like components exist.

Appendix A: ViewGroups / Widgets to Jetpack Compose Cheatsheet

By Prateek Prasad

Since Jetpack Compose is still relatively new, you will find yourself working in hybrid codebases for a while, comprising older features built-in XML and newer ones adopting compose.

This is a reasonably standard adoption pattern for any new technology. With this in mind, before concluding the book, here's a handy cheatsheet you can use to find the Jetpack Compose equivalent for the most common Android Views on Android.

This guide should be a quick reference whenever you build a new UI in composing or converting an existing screen to Compose.

ViewGroup and Their Equivalents

- `LinearLayout` - To stack items linearly in compose, you can use a `Row` for laying out items horizontally or a `Column` for laying out items vertically.
- `FrameLayout` - To stack items on top of one another, use a `Box` composable.
- `RelativeLayout` - Relative layout lets you lay items out relative to one another. While there is no direct equivalent for a RelativeLayout in compose, you can use a combination of `Row`, `Column` and `Box` with the `align` modifiers to achieve the same result.
- `ConstraintLayout` - To lay out items relative to one another based on constraints, Jetpack Compose offers a similarly named composable, `ConstraintLayout`.

Composables for Building Lists

An everyday use case in any app is to present data as a list. In the XML world, you would use a RecyclerView for the job but compose offers a few variations based on the orientation and arrangement.

- Vertical List - `LazyColumn()`
- Horizontal List - `LazyRow()`
- Vertical Grid - `LazyVerticalGrid()`
- Horizontal Grid - `LazyHorizontalGrid()`

Each of the above composables offers parameters and modifiers for content padding, item placement etc.

Common View Use Cases and Their Compose Equivalents

Here's a quick rundown of the most common views, their most common use cases in XML, and their Jetpack Compose equivalents.

- `TextView` - `Text()`.
- `TextView` with Span-based styling - Use a `Text()` composable with an `AnnotatedString` as the text parameter.
- `TextView`, which is clickable - Use the `clickable()` modifier but if you require sub-sections of the text to be clickable, use the `ClickableText()` composable instead.
- `EditText` - `TextField()`.
- `TextInputLayout` - `OutlinedTextField()`.
- `ImageView` - `Image()` composable. Based on the kind of asset you need to show _(bitmap, animated vector drawable etc.)_, you need to use the respective `painterResource` as the parameter.
- `ImageView`, where the image needs to be loaded from the internet - Use the composables offered by third-party libraries like `Coil` or `Glide`.
- `Button` - `Button()` composable.

- Text only Button - `TextButton()` composable.
- `ScrollView` - Based on the orientation, use the `Row()` or `Column()` composable with the `scrollable()` modifier.
- Button with Material Theming - `MaterialButton()` composable.
- App bar (bottom) - `BottomAppBar()`.
- App bar (top) - `TopAppBar()`.
- Bottom navigation - `BottomNavigation()`.
- `FloatingActionButton` - `FloatingActionButton()`.
- FloatingActionButton (extended style) - `ExtendedFloatingActionButton()`.
- `CardView` - `Card()`.
- `CheckBox` - `Checkbox()`.
- `Dialog` - `AlertDialog()`.
- Navigation Drawer - `ModalDrawer()`.
- Progress indicator (circular) - `CircularProgressIndicator()`.
- Progress indicator (linear) - `LinearProgressIndicator()`.
- BottomSheet - `BottomSheetScaffold()`.

While this list is not exhaustive, it covers 90% of the views you would use daily and their composed equivalents. You can keep this list handy when converting your views to Jetpack Compose or when you need to find the available alternative for a view.

Made in the USA
Monee, IL
13 September 2026

62980071R10254